COMMODITY

TRADER'S

A L M A N A C

2 0 1 3

For Active Traders of Futures, Forex, Stocks, Options, and ETFs

Jeffrey A. Hirsch and John L. Person

WILEY

John Wiley & Sons, Inc.

Published by John Wiley & Sons, Inc., Hoboken, New Jersey
Published simultaneously in Canada

Editor	Jeffrey A. Hirsch, stocktradersalmanac.com
Contributing Editor	John L. Person, nationalfutures.com
Director of Research	Christopher Mistal
Production Editor	Melissa Lopez
Charts, Data & Research	TradeNavigator.com
Additional Data	Pinnacledata.com

Additionally, the risk of loss in trading futures and options can be substantial; therefore, only genuine risk funds should be used. Futures and options may not be suitable investments for all individuals, and individuals should carefully consider their financial condition in deciding whether to trade. *For information on the CFTC Disclosure of Risk or the CFTC Consumer Advisory on Seasonality visit http://www.CFTC.gov and/or http://www.cftc.gov/enf/enfseasonaladvisory.htm.*

For general information about our other products and services, please contact our Customer Care Department within the United States at 800-762-2974, outside the United States at 317-572-3993 or fax 317-572-4002.

Wiley also publishes its books in a variety of electronic formats. Some content that appears in print may not be available in electronic books.

For more information about Wiley products, visit our Web site at www.wiley.com. Also visit www.stocktradersalmanac.com for information about the *Commodity Trader's Almanac* and other market data.

ISBN: 978-1-118-15986-6 (cloth)
ISBN: 978-1-118-28228-1 (ebk)
ISBN: 978-1-118-28392-9 (ebk)
ISBN: 978-1-118-28634-0 (ebk)
10 9 8 7 6 5 4 3 2 1

Printed in China

THE 2013 COMMODITY TRADER'S ALMANAC

CONTENTS

INTRODUCTION TO THE SEVENTH EDITION

It is impossible to predict the future. That is why we rely on seasonal and historical analysis to help understand, or better yet, to remind us what price trends have occurred in the past and how often these trends perform. These patterns typically occur as a direct result of perennial supply and demand changes year after year. Every year has differences, from changes in monetary and fiscal policies to global macroeconomic situations to presidential election year cycles to extreme weather and other exogenous events.

2013 promises to be a dynamic year for commodity markets. No matter which party is elected, energy reform will likely be on the slate. Currently, we lack a national policy on "fracking" procedures, the process by which water and chemicals are injected into the earth to extract oil and natural gas. As of June 2012, policy decisions are in individual states' legislative hands. If we do see a shift toward more cleaner burning fuels, then natural gas may see ramped-up production, creating a shift in fossil fuel demand.

The first half of 2012 left the U.S. in a serious weather situation, wreaking havoc on farmers and ranchers. Earlier than normal hot and dry conditions reduced yields in corn and soybeans as well as creating massive wildfires throughout Colorado. The global economy, hurt by a European debt crisis and economic contraction in China, was partially to blame for decelerated U.S. economic growth. As a result, in June 2012, Ben Bernanke lowered the Federal Reserve's estimated gross domestic production (GDP) at 1.9 % to 2.4% from a previous estimate of 2.4% to 2.9%. The decelerating pace of job growth in the U.S. led the Federal Reserve to reaffirm and commit to keeping a near-zero interest rate policy through 2014. They even expanded their bond buying program, called "Operation Twist," which was designed to add liquidity to the faltering financial system.

We believe we will have the perfect storm for continued volatility for stocks, bonds, safe haven instruments like gold and silver, agricultural markets, as well as foreign currencies in 2013 as a result of this ongoing global economic situation and the severe drought that has devastated the U.S. corn and soybean crops. The seasonal analysis provided in the *Commodity Traders Almanac 2013* will likely prove to be a very valuable resource for active traders in these markets.

The new 2013 edition has several new additions and changes. We have added heating oil, including two new trades on pages 14 and 92 that replace the January short S&P trade and the October long corn trade; and advanced options strategies and trading tactics on pages 6–9. We have also added more exchange traded funds (ETFs) and exchange traded notes (ETNs). ETNs are similar to exchange traded funds, but differ in structure. ETNs are products that are issued as senior debt notes, while ETFs represent a stake in an underlying market.

The complete listing of all the Futures First Notice and Last Trading and Option Expiration Dates for all 20 markets covered on pages 118 and 119 also appears on the weekly planner pages and in the 2013 Strategy Calendar on pages 10 and 11. For the third Friday of the month, when equity, stock index, ETF, and ETN standard options expire, we have encircled the dates in the 2013 Strategy Calendar and added a "witch" to those dates in the weekly calendar pages. Three witches appear on Triple Witching day, the third Friday at the end of each quarter in March, June, September, and December when equity index futures expire. There are new case studies on pages 120–123, including the "crack" spread, the "NOB" spread, and a new millennium "sell in May" trade using a vertical call spread, and the COT report is updated on pages 128–130.

Many of the trades in 2012 were outstanding and there were the typical busts where trades did not fare so well, but the trader who was armed with the information packed in these pages had much better odds for overall success. Part of the path to better trading results lies in risk as well as trade management. Several tools may help traders uncover trades that are worthy of resources and consideration. Each featured trade shows the statistics of each year, allowing you to review past performance as a guide to what the average typical profit and loss has been for each specific trade.

This year's edition will prepare you for the most active and pertinent trading opportunities on a monthly and seasonal basis by showing you the following:

✔ Seasonal tendencies and the respective potential risks and rewards
✔ Detailed statistical data on past market price action
✔ Insights on options and spread strategies to help manage your risks
✔ The nuances of trading the various aspects of related markets
✔ Annual highs and lows for the top commodity markets
✔ Reminder alerts on trades on the calendar pages
✔ First Notice, Last Trade, and Options Expiration on the calendar pages
✔ Contract specifications with highly correlated ETFs, ETNs, and stocks

It is important to remember to use this *Almanac* as a reference guide and to compare current events against history. We have included the data that allows the reader to distinguish which years had predominantly bigger price moves and to compare where current prices and trends stand against past historic data.

Here is wishing you a healthy and prosperous 2013!

Jeffrey A. Hirsch and John L. Person

ADVANCED OPTIONS TRADING STRATEGIES AND TACTICS

Last year we introduced several ways to take advantage of seasonal trade ideas as presented throughout these pages. We started with basic options strategies: what goes into theoretical options pricing, including the Greeks and Volatility. We also went into spread trading methods. This year we want to follow up with these two trading methodologies and expand on the ever-evolving options product choices.

WEEKLY OPTIONS

First, for traders wanting to take advantage of the S&P 500 stock index (and individual stocks) seasonal moves there are weekly options provided by the Chicago Board Options Exchange (CBOE). Simply stated, weekly options are listed to provide trading opportunities on a week-to-week basis. This eliminates buying excessive time value (Theta).

Typically, weekly options are listed on Thursday and expire the following Friday. This gives traders an opportunity to take a directional trade into a weekend with the advantage of potentially profiting from increased leverage and reduced costs associated with purchasing option premium without undue time value decay risks.

More importantly, weekly options allow traders to take advantage of a directional move that they might normally hesitate on due to a news-driven market event, such as a major economic report, a Federal Reserve announcement, or a pending foreign central bank meeting, and even a major earnings report.

On the last trading day or expiration in the S&P 500 (SPX) weekly option the close is at 3:00 PM (CT). The non-expiring weekly options close at 3:15 PM (CT). Weekly options offer traders the ability to use simple as well as advanced options strategies from outright long calls or puts to complex Iron Condors and Butterflies or simply hedging with a collar strategy to get through a weekend within the options expiration week time horizon.

OPTIONS STRATEGIES

Vertical Bull and Bear (debit) spreads are the most common options strategies traders employ. The term "vertical" is used to reference the fact that as you look at the options chain or ladder of strike prices it is straight up or down as you are using the same expiration month. A bull call spread simply buys a closer-to-the-money call option and sells a further out or higher (generally one or two strike prices) call option. The bear spread is the exact opposite, which entails buying a close-to-the-money put option and selling a further away strike price put option.

The reason for the "spread" is to reduce costs associated with buying option premiums while being able to enjoy a profit if the market moves in the desired direction by the expiration date. Times to implement vertical spreads are during periods of increased volatility and when an expected move is less than 30 days. This helps to reduce costs as higher volatility increases premiums paid, and the more time an option has until expiration the more premium or cost is associated with the options value.

A different version of a Bull or Bear Spread is the Calendar Spread. These can also be used for a directional play with call or put options. For a bull calendar spread one would sell the near-term expiration slightly out-of-the-money call option and simultaneously buy the longer dated expiration call option. Ideally, one would be looking to match the Deltas (correlation to the change in the underlying) on both call options. In addition you would not want to sell an option with less than 30 days until expiration and buy the call with more than 90 days until expiration.

This strategy is done to capture time decay. It gives limited risk as well as limited profit potential. Again the general rule is to sell the nearby expiring option that is near or slightly out of the money. To exit the trade as the nearby option expires, simply offset the position. The option with no time value that is still slightly out of the money will have lost almost all of its value while the long option that has a longer dated maturity will have retained a majority of its value. You profit from the time decay (Theta) of the closer expiration option that you sold. This is a great strategy for those who believe the market may not move in the 30-days-or-less time frame and then see a market move after expiration. Seasonal traders who are looking a month before a seasonal low is due in a commodity may wish to employ this type of options strategy.

There are strategies for all occasions, especially when looking at seasonal trends. Just remember in the options markets to employ buying strategies when volatility is low relative to the historic norm or as compared to past or prior months. The purpose of the *Commodity Traders Almanac* is to bring you a statistical edge by examining seasonal price moves in the underlying markets while introducing to you ways to capture a trading opportunity. The two options strategies mentioned above will give traders an idea and a better advantage of capturing a market move without having to time the entry on the exact hour of the exact day of a seasonal directional price move.

BINARY OPTIONS

The newest way to trade seasonal short-term trades from the *Commodity Traders Almanac* may be through the use of Binary Options offered on NADEX, a Chicago-based derivatives exchange (http://www.nadex.com/). Binary Options are classified as a limited-risk derivative product. These instruments are simply based on an idea that the price of a market will be above or below a specific price at the prescribed time, either end of day or end of week. Products traded are offered for these U.S. markets: Stock Indexes, Foreign Currencies, Crude Oil, Natural Gas, Gold, Silver, Copper, Corn, Soybeans, and events or special economic reports. The concept is based on a simple yes-or-no proposition.

The Binary Options markets through NADEX offer an intuitive way to trade the financial markets with relatively low collateral using a regulated and transparent trading environment. The benefits of Binary Options are suitable for the retail trader looking for high leverage and hedging opportunities with limited defined risks. One specific benefit is the cost of each trade. The transaction costs are 90 cents per lot to initiate a trade, and to offset a trade. However, if an option settles out of the money, there is no commission fee charged. If you trade more volume, the commission rate declines as well; in fact NADEX is the only exchange in the U.S. that enables individuals to become direct members. Membership is free and there are no charges in setting up accounts for U.S. residents.

Pricing on Binary Options depends on two factors; the amount of time until expiration and the intrinsic value, which is the value assigned from the current market price to the distance of the option strike price. The value of the option at expiration is either going to be

(continued on next page)

worth $0 or $100. Let's examine this scenario. On the open of the U.S. session at 8:30 AM (CT) with the current price in the S&P 500 futures at 1305 you believe at the end of the day the market will rally and move to close up on the day above or greater than 1312. A daily expiration Binary Option with an S&P futures strike price of 1312 might cost $30.00. The most you can lose is the 30.00 plus a 90-cent fee. If the market closes at 1312.25 on the close, then the option closed greater than 1312. Your option would be worth $100. Your profit would be $68.20: $100 minus the two commissions of 90 cents minus $30.00 for a net profit of $68.20. On the other hand, if the market did rally and closed at 1312 or lower, then you would lose your $30.00 per option investment as the market did not close above 1312.

The concept is the same for the weekly Binary Options. You can place a trade on Monday morning, expecting a rally by Friday's close. This just may be a great new way for traders to incorporate seasonal trades with limited-risk short-term trades. Just like American-style option expiration, traders can offset the position prior to the expiration time or day. You are not required to hold the option for a "do-or-die" trade.

Using the scenario above, let's say if the market rallied early in the morning, trading above 1318, the 1312 strike price option may be worth close to $86.00. A trader can offset the trade with less profit and exit the trade at that time rather than hold the trade until the day's close. The same concept applies to the weekly Binary Options. This allows more flexibility to the trader to close out a position with a profit rather than to hold onto the trade with time risk in case the market sold back down under the 1312 strike level. On the other side of the coin, say the market traded sideways without any price appreciation for the first two hours of the day and the trader feels the market may in fact head lower into the close. The option may now be worth $20.00; it is at that point one could close out the position and assume the loss of only $10.00 rather than the entire $30.00 premium paid.

SPREAD TRADES

Last year we covered several top commodity spreads such as an Intra-market Live Cattle trade involving buying an October contract and selling the deferred April of the following year. We also covered Cattle versus Hogs, Wheat versus Corn, and the energy complex's "crack" spread. This year you will find a more in-depth case study on the crack spread on page 120. This year we want to share how to use a spread chart to identify strength or weakness relative to a similar or like market or product.

You might be familiar with the term "Sell in May and Go Away" or the "Best Six Months Switching Strategy," created by Jeff's father, Yale Hirsch, who founded the *Stock Traders Almanac* (now edited by Jeff). Here is another way to take advantage of a seasonal strategy in the S&P 500, at least indirectly. Besides comparing one commodity to another to determine relative strength, we can also use a spread chart to examine other indexes or sector groups to one another. The CTA examines the S&P 500, but there are other stock indexes to analyze and trade, specifically the NASDAQ 100 futures (NQ), the Russell 2000 futures (TF), and the Mini-Dow Futures (YM). As for stock traders we can use a host of ETFs and even inverse leveraged ETFs that are specific to each one of these stock index groups.

In Figure 1, the upper section is a spread or relative strength chart comparing the Russell 2000 as represented by the ETF iShares Russell 2000 (IWM) against the S&P 500 or the

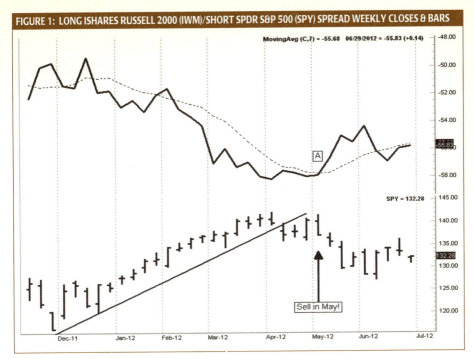

FIGURE 1: LONG ISHARES RUSSELL 2000 (IWM)/SHORT SPDR S&P 500 (SPY) SPREAD WEEKLY CLOSES & BARS

MovingAvg (C,7) = -55.68   06/29/2012 = -55.83 (+0.14)

[A]

SPY = 132.28

Sell in May!

Dec-11   Jan-12   Feb-12   Mar-12   Apr-12   May-12   Jun-12   Jul-12

Chart courtesy TradeNavigator.com

ETF SPDR S&P 500 (SPY). When using a spread chart always select a line chart feature. Overlaid is a seven-period simple moving average based on closing prices, which is the dotted line. In the lower quadrant is the bar chart on the (SPY) in order for you to compare the spread versus the S&P 500.

In theory, as the stock market rises led by blue chips we see the small-cap sector lag or underperform. Since the start of 2012, that was exactly what occurred as the spread chart was in a decline while the (SPY) was in a solid up trend. However, when we entered into the seasonally weak period in May, the small-cap sector started to outperform the overall market. This is evident as shown at point A on the chart. The spread chart (Long IWM–Short SPY) moved up, crossing above the moving average. This helped confirm a change in market condition and the potential weakness for the overall stock market.

There are several ways to confirm a change in trend. One can use indicators such as Stochastics, MACD, hybrid indicators like an advanced CCI indicator, or even Persons Pivots. By using the relative strength comparative analysis, or spread charts, one can get another layer of confirmation or a truer sense of market direction from a noncorrelated yet confirming indicator. This analysis methodology is applicable for all types of traders who use seasonal analysis.

In fact, we have a case study of what might seem to be a fairly sophisticated trade using this exact methodology applying one of the options strategies covered in this section and how it was applied using an inverse ETF. This case study can be found on page 122. With the creation of ETFs and options the world of spread opportunities is endless. Once again the main focus is the seasonal trend of markets. How we trade these opportunities is up to each individual. What we want to do is to shed light on the various ways to take advantage of these trades using low risk and state-of-the-art products.

2013 STRATEGY CALENDAR

(Equity, Equity Index, ETF, and ETN Option expiration dates circled)

MONDAY	TUESDAY	WEDNESDAY	THURSDAY	FRIDAY	SATURDAY	SUNDAY
31 FN: HG, GC, SI, S / LT: HO	**1** JANUARY New Year's Day	**2**	**3**	**4** FN: HO / OE: CC, LC, BP, EC, SF, JY	**5**	**6**
7	**8**	**9**	**10**	**11** OE: KC	**12**	**13**
14 LT: S	**15** OE: SB	**16** OE: CL	**17**	**(18)** OE: SP	**19**	**20**
21 Martin Luther King Day	**22** LT: CL	**23**	**24** FN: CL	**25** OE: US, C, S, W	**26**	**27**
28 OE: HO, NG, HG, GC, SI	**29** LT: NG, HG, GC, SI	**30** FN: NG	**31** FN: HG, GC, SI / LT: HO	**1** FEBRUARY OE: CC, LC	**2**	**3**
4 FN: HO, LC	**5**	**6**	**7**	**8** OE: KC, BP, EC, SF, JY	**9**	**10**
11	**12**	**13** Ash Wednesday	**14** ♥ FN: CC / LT: LH / OE: CL, LH	**(15)** OE: SP, SB	**16**	**17**
18 Presidents' Day	**19**	**20** FN: KC / LT: CL	**21**	**22** FN: CL / OE: US, C, S, W	**23**	**24**
25 OE: HO, NG, HG, GC, SI	**26** LT: NG, HG, GC, SI	**27** FN: NG	**28** FN: US, HG, GC, SI, C, S, W / LT: HO, SB, LC	**1** MARCH FN: SB / OE: CC, LC	**2**	**3**
4 FN: HO	**5**	**6**	**7**	**8** OE: KC, BP, EC, SF, JY	**9**	**10** Daylight Saving Time Begins
11	**12**	**13**	**14** LT: SP, C, S, W / OE: SP	**(15)** OE: CL, SB	**16**	**17** ☘ St. Patrick's Day
18 LT: KC, BP, EC, SF, JY	**19** LT: US	**20** LT: CL	**21**	**22** FN: CL / OE: US, C, S, W	**23**	**24**
25 OE: HO, NG, HG, GC, SI	**26** Passover LT: NG, HG, GC, SI	**27** FN: NG	**28** FN: HG, GC, SI / LT: HO	**29** Good Friday	**30**	**31** Easter
1 APRIL	**2** FN: HO	**3**	**4**	**5** OE: CC, LC, BP, EC, SF, JY	**6**	**7**
8 FN: LC	**9**	**10**	**11**	**12** LT: LH / OE: KC, LH	**13**	**14**
15 Tax Deadline OE: SB	**16**	**17** FN: CC / OE: CL	**18**	**(19)** OE: SP	**20**	**21**
22 FN: KC / LT: CL	**23**	**24**	**25** FN: CL / OE: HO, NG, HG, GC, SI	**26** LT: NG, HG, GC, SI / OE: US, C, S, W	**27**	**28**
29 FN: NG	**30** FN: HG, GC, SI, C, S, W / LT: HO, SB, LC	**1** MAY FN: SB	**2**	**3** FN: HO / OE: CC, LC, BP, EC, SF, JY	**4**	**5**
6	**7**	**8**	**9**	**10** OE: KC	**11**	**12** Mother's Day
13	**14** LT: C, S, W, LH / OE: LH	**15** LT: CC / OE: SB	**16** OE: CL	**(17)** OE: SP	**18**	**19**
20 LT: KC	**21** LT: CL	**22**	**23**	**24** OE: US, C, S, W	**25**	**26**
27 Memorial Day	**28** OE: HO, NG, HG, GC, SI	**29** LT: NG, HG, GC, SI	**30** FN: NG	**31** FN: US, HG, GC, SI / LT: HO / OE: CC, LC	**1** JUNE	**2**
3	**4** FN: HO	**5**	**6**	**7** OE: CC, LC, BP, EC, SF, JY	**8**	**9**
10 FN: LC	**11**	**12**	**13** OE: KC	**14** LT: LH / OE: LH	**15**	**16** Father's Day
17 FN: CC / LT: BP, EC, SF, JY / OE: CL, SB	**18**	**19**	**20** FN: KC / LT: SP, CL / OE: SP / LT: US	**(21)** OE: US, C, S, W	**22**	**23**
24 FN: CL	**25** OE: HO, NG, HG, GC, SI	**26** LT: NG, HG, GC, SI	**27**	**28** FN: HG, GC, SI, / LT: HO, SB, LC / FN: NG	**29**	**30**

Market closed on shaded weekdays; closes early when half-shaded.

2013 STRATEGY CALENDAR

(Equity, Equity Index, ETF, and ETN Option expiration dates circled)

MONDAY	TUESDAY	WEDNESDAY	THURSDAY	FRIDAY	SATURDAY	SUNDAY
1 JULY — FN: SB	2 — FN: HO	3	4 Independence Day	5 — OE: CC, LC, BP, EC, SF, JY	6	7
8	9	10	11	12 — LT: C, S, W / OE: KC	13	14
15 — LT: LH / OE: SB, LH	16 — LT: CC	17	18 — OE: CL	(19) — LT: KC / OE: SP	20	21
22 — LT: CL	23	24 — FN: CL	25 — OE: HG, GC, SI	26 — OE: US, HO, NG, C, S, W	27	28
29 — LT: NG, HG, GC, SI	30 — FN: NG	31 — FN: HG, GC, SI, S / LT: HO	1 AUGUST	2 — FN: HO / OE: CC, LC	3	4
5 — FN: LC	6	7	8	9 — OE: KC, BP, EC, SF, JY	10	11
12	13	14 — LT: S, LH / OE: LH	15 — OE: CL, SB	(16) — OE: SP	17	18
19 — FN: CC	20 — LT: CL	21	22	23 — FN: CL, KC / OE: US, C, S, W	24	25
26	27 — OE: HO, NG, HG, GC, SI	28 — LT: NG, HG, GC, SI	29 — FN: NG	30 — FN: US, HG, GC, SI, C, S, W / LT: HO, LC	31	1 SEPTEMBER
2 Labor Day	3	4	5 — FN: HO — Rosh Hashanah	6 — OE: CC, LC, BP, EC, SF, JY	7	8
9	10	11	12	13 — LT: C, S, W, CC / OE: KC	14 Yom Kippur	15
16 — LT: BP, EC, SF, JY / OE: SB	17	18 — OE: CL	19 — LT: SP, US / OE: SP	(20) — LT: CL / OE: US, C, S, W	21	22
23	24 — FN: CL	25 — OE: HO NG, HG, GC, SI	26 — LT: NG, HG, GC, SI	27 — FN: NG	28	29
30 — FN: HG, GC, SI / LT: HO, SB	1 OCTOBER — FN: SB	2 — FN: HO	3	4 — OE: CC, LC, BP, EC, SF, JY	5	6
7 — FN: LC	8	9	10	11 — OE: KC	12	13
14 Columbus Day — LT: LH / OE: LH	15 — OE: SB	16	17 — OE: CL	(18) — OE: SP	19	20
21	22 — LT: CL	23	24	25 — FN: CL / OE: US, C, S, W	26	27
28 — OE: HO, NG, HG, GC, SI	29 — LT: NG, HG, GC, SI	30 — FN: NG	31 🎃 — FN: HG, GC, SI, S / LT: HO, LC	1 NOVEMBER — OE: CC, LC	2	3 Daylight Saving Time Ends
4 — FN: HO	5 Election Day	6	7	8 — OE: KC, BP, EC, SF, JY	9	10
11 Veterans' Day	12	13	14 — LT: S	(15) — FN: CC / OE: SP, CL, SB	16	17
18	19	20 — FN: KC / LT: CL	21	22 — FN: CL / OE: US, C, S, W	23	24
25 — OE: HO, NG, HG, GC, SI	26 — LT: NG, HG, GC, SI	27 — FN: NG	28 Thanksgiving / Chanukah	29 — FN: US, HG, GC, SI, C, W / LT: HO	30	1 DECEMBER
2	3 — FN: HO	4	5	6 — OE: CC, LC, BP, EC, SF, JY	7	8
9 — FN: LC	10	11	12	13 — LT: C, W, CC, LH / OE: KC, LH	14	15
16 — LT: BP, EC, SF, JY / OE: CL, SB	17	18	19 — LT: KC	(20) — LT: SP, US, CL / OE: SP	21	22
23 — FN: CL	24	25 Christmas	26 — OE: HO, NG, HG, GC, SI	27 — LT: NG, HG, GC, SI / OE: US, C, S, W	28	29
30 — FN: NG	31 — FN: HG, GC, SI, S / LT: HO, LC	1 JANUARY New Year's Day	2	3 — FN: HO	4	5

Right margin month labels: JULY · AUGUST · SEPTEMBER · OCTOBER · NOVEMBER · DECEMBER

JANUARY ALMANAC

JANUARY						
S	M	T	W	T	F	S
		1	2	3	4	5
6	7	8	9	10	11	12
13	14	15	16	17	18	19
20	21	22	23	24	25	26
27	28	29	30	31		

◆ STOCKS AND BONDS

S&P 500 has shown a tendency to see mild declines after the New Year (page 138), as investors sell positions to defer capital gain taxes on profits, but the overall strength from October can last into April. Traders can look to take advantage of the January break (page 22). This trade has a reliable trend registering a 73.3% success rate. 30-year Treasury bond prices have a tendency to continue their decline (page 106), as investors are reallocating money into stocks.

FEBRUARY						
S	M	T	W	T	F	S
					1	2
3	4	5	6	7	8	9
10	11	12	13	14	15	16
17	18	19	20	21	22	23
24	25	26	27	28		

◆ ENERGY

January tends to see continued weakness in crude oil (page 143) and in natural gas (page 145) before the typical bottom is posted in February. Traders should prepare for the strongest buy month for oil and natural gas (pages 26, 32, and 124). Heating Oil tends to decline in January into early February 69.7% of the time since 1980 with the exception of 2011 and 2012 (see pages 14, 124 and 147).

◆ METALS

Gold has a strong history of making a seasonal peak from mid- to late January into early February. Shorting gold during this time period has resulted in a cumulative profit of $45,480 over the past 38 years (page 124). Silver also has a tendency to peak in late February and follows gold price weakness into March (page 30). Copper tends to respect its seasonal December bottom to show mild strength in January (page 112).

◆ GRAINS

Soybeans tend to post a low in late January or early February (page 161). Wheat prices tend to see seasonal weakness in January as well (page 18). In fact, this trade boasts a 69.8% success rate, with 30 years up and 13 down. Corn prices tend to buck that trend, as we enter into the new marketing year (page 158).

◆ SOFTS

Cocoa shows signs of strength in January and continues higher until March (page 34). Coffee tends to show a mixed performance in the month of January, giving back some of December's gains (page 170). Sugar tends to show a mixed performance in January, as beet and continued sugar cane harvest in the southeast United States and India puts pressure on prices (page 173).

◆ MEATS

Live cattle prices tend to follow December's strength (page 176), and hog prices tend to remain under pressure from making any significant moves up until March (page 179).

◆ CURRENCIES

The euro has a short life span since beginning in 1999. However, since inception, it has a stellar trade by going short on the third trading day and holding for 24 days. It has been up 11 and registered three losses (page 16). The Swiss franc and the British pound both show a strong seasonal tendency to continue lower from late December. The yen also demonstrates weakness from December into February.

JANUARY STRATEGY CALENDAR*

Symbol	B	M	E
SP	L/S		
US	L/S		
CL	L/S		
NG	L/S		
HO	L/S		
HG	L/S		
GC	L/S		
SI	L/S		
C	L/S		
S	L/S		
W	L/S		
CC	L/S		
KC	L/S		
SB	L/S		
LC	L/S		
LH	L/S		
BP	L/S		
EC	L/S		
SF	L/S		
JY	L/S		

*Graphic representation of the Commodity Seasonality Percentage Plays on pages 124–125.
L = Long Trade, S = Short Trade. See pages 131–137 for contract symbols.

DECEMBER 2012/JANUARY 2013

MONDAY
31
FN: HG, GC, SI, S
LT: HO

Of a stock's move, 31% can be attributed to the general stock market, 12% to the industry influence, 37% to the influence of other groupings, and the remaining 20% is peculiar to the one stock.
— Benjamin F. King (*Market and Industry Factors in Stock Price Behavior, Journal of Business*, January 1966)

New Years Day (Market Closed)

TUESDAY
1

There's nothing wrong with cash. It gives you time to think.
— Robert Prechter, Jr. (*Elliott Wave Theorist*)

End Long Euro(H) (Oct. 24, 2012)
End Long Swiss Franc(H) (Nov. 27, 2012)

WEDNESDAY
2

The principles of successful stock speculation are based on the supposition that people will continue in the future to make the mistakes that they have made in the past.
— Thomas F. Woodlock (Wall Street Journal editor & columnist, quoted in Reminiscences of a Stock Operator, 1866–1945)

Start Short Heating Oil(J)—69.7% Accuracy Since 1980—End Feb. 15—Page 14

THURSDAY
3
FN: HO

Only those who will risk going too far can possibly find out how far one can go.
— T.S. Eliot (English poet, essayist and critic, *The Wasteland*, 1888–1965)

Start Short Euro(H)—78.6% Accuracy Since 1999—End Feb. 8—Page 16
Start Short Wheat(N)—69.8% Accuracy Since 1970—End May 8—Page 18

FRIDAY
4
OE: CC, LC, BP, EC, SF, JY

When I talk to a company that tells me the last analyst showed up three years ago, I can hardly contain my enthusiasm.
— Peter Lynch (Fidelity Investments, *One Up On Wall Street*, b. 1944)

SATURDAY
5

SUNDAY
6

SHORT HEATING OIL IN EARLY JANUARY

Heating oil prices typically track closely with crude oil prices. After the summer driving season is over, refiners focus more on building up inventory levels of heating oil. This drives both heating oil and crude oil to a seasonal peak in September followed by a low in December. After a brief relief at yearend both oils exhibit weakness in January and February. This sets up a high probability trade. Selling short April heating Oil on the second trading day of January and holding for 30 days boasts a 69.7% accuracy rate and cumulative gains of $34,184 dating back to 1980.

However, there are times when the byproduct's pricing decouples from crude oil price trends; when inventories for crude oil are inverted due to the demand for the products. This occurs at certain times of the year, typically in peak heating season, which is defined by the EIA (U.S. Energy Information Administration) as October through March.

In fact, this trade did not work in the last two years. During both January 2011 and 2012, prices of crude oil declined due to a build in inventories and China's economy was suspected of contracting giving the perception of a decline in demand. At the same time snow storms and frigid temperatures moved into the North East section of the U.S. causing a spike in demand for heating oil.

At points A and B in the chart below heating oil prices spike while crude oil prices moved lower as marked at points B and D. This situation seems to be more of an isolated incidence as our research shows. The lower quadrant of the chart shows the seasonal trend of heating oil, which shows the typical trend is to decline from January into mid-February as illustrated at points E and F. The point here is to remember that all years are not created equal and one still needs to use confirming indicators and risk management when using seasonal analysis.

	ENTRY		EXIT		PROFIT/
YEAR	DATE	CLOSE	DATE	CLOSE	LOSS
1980	1/3	86.60	2/14	75.50	$4,662
1981	1/6	105.80	2/18	97.85	3,339
1982	1/5	91.58	2/17	80.96	4,460
1983	1/4	78.69	2/15	73.13	2,335
1984	1/4	75.65	2/15	75.64	4
1985	1/3	68.09	2/14	70.66	−1,079
1986	1/3	67.31	2/14	49.00	7,690
1987	1/5	47.83	2/17	47.64	80
1988	1/5	48.38	2/17	44.82	1,495
1989	1/4	46.67	2/15	47.23	−235
1990	1/3	62.50	2/14	57.26	2,201
1991	1/3	65.13	2/14	58.30	2,869
1992	1/3	52.75	2/14	54.15	−588
1993	1/5	55.13	2/17	54.46	281
1994	1/4	45.30	2/15	44.16	479
1995	1/4	49.33	2/15	47.02	970
1996	1/3	52.76	2/15	51.91	357
1997	1/3	65.63	2/14	58.83	2,856
1998	1/5	48.38	2/18	46.10	958
1999	1/5	34.90	2/18	31.56	1,403
2000	1/5	62.17	2/17	72.17	−4,200
2001	1/3	77.21	2/15	74.10	1,306
2002	1/3	55.89	2/15	56.10	−88
2003	1/3	82.59	2/18	97.32	−6,187
2004	1/6	90.29	2/19	90.13	67
2005	1/4	118.91	2/16	132.35	−5,645
2006	1/4	183.19	2/16	165.35	7,493
2007	1/4	160.86	2/16	166.65	−2,432
2008	1/3	266.66	2/15	262.49	1,751
2009	1/5	156.25	2/18	114.14	17,686
2010	1/5	219.96	2/18	206.22	5,771
2011	1/4	251.53	2/16	278.09	−11,155
2012	1/4	306.48	2/17	317.72	−4,721
				33-Year Gain	$34,184

JANUARY SHORT HEATING OIL (APRIL) TRADING DAY: 2-HOLD: 30 DAYS

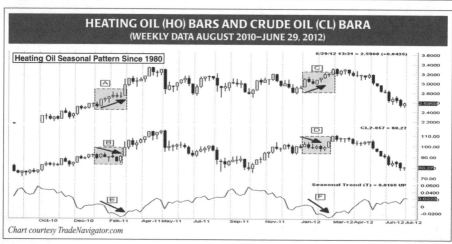

HEATING OIL (HO) BARS AND CRUDE OIL (CL) BARA
(WEEKLY DATA AUGUST 2010–JUNE 29, 2012)

Heating Oil Seasonal Pattern Since 1980

Chart courtesy TradeNavigator.com

JANUARY

Anyone who believes that exponential growth can go on forever in a finite world is either a madman or an economist.
— Kenneth Ewart Boulding (Economist, activist, poet, scientist, philosopher, cofounder General Systems Theory, 1910–1993)

End Long Wheat(K) (Dec. 7, 2012)

TUESDAY
8

If investing is entertaining, if you're having fun, you're probably not making any money. Good investing is boring.
— George Soros (Financier, philanthropist, political activist, author and philosopher, b. 1930)

WEDNESDAY
9

No other country can substitute for the U.S. The U.S. is still No. 1 in military, No. 1 in economy, No. 1 in promoting human rights and No. 1 in idealism. Only the U.S. can lead the world. No other country can.
— Senior Korean official (to Thomas L. Friedman *NY Times* Foreign Affairs columnist, 2/25/2009)

THURSDAY
10

Behold, my son, with what little wisdom the world is ruled.
— Count Axel Gustafsson Oxenstierna (1648 letter to his son at conclusion of Thirty Years War, 1583–1654)

End Long Corn(N) (Dec. 10, 2012)

FRIDAY
11
OE: KC

For want of a nail, the shoe was lost. For want of a shoe, the horse was lost. For want of a horse, the rider was lost. For want of a rider, the battle was lost. For want of a battle, the kingdom was lost. And all for the want of a nail!
— English proverb

SATURDAY
12

SUNDAY
13

EURO PEAKS AGAINST U.S. DOLLAR

The euro currency was first introduced to the world markets in 1999 and was finally launched with bank notes and physical coins in 2002. As of June 2011, the following countries use the euro as their currency: Andorra, Austria, Belgium, Cyprus, Estonia, Finland, France, Germany, Greece, Ireland, Italy, Kosovo, Luxembourg, Malta, Monaco, Montenegro, Netherlands, Portugal, San Marino, Slovakia, Slovenia, Spain, and Vatican City.

The European Central Bank dictates monetary policy and puts more emphasis on inflation concerns rather than on economic contraction. We have seen in the past that the ECB would rather maintain steady interest rates than stoke the flames of inflationary pressures. As a result, the ECB is less likely to adjust interest rates compared to its peers. An ongoing European sovereign debt crisis left the ECB with more than just an interest rate adjustment agenda. The crisis has also negatively impacted this trade in the past two years.

Despite this wall of worry, seasonally speaking, we do see in the 14-year history of the euro a tendency for prices to head lower against the U.S. dollar on or about the third trading day in January through the first week of February. Theory suggests this has worked in the past due to the fact that multinational conglomerate corporations based here in the United States repatriate funds after the New Year, and this has a tendency to depress prices in the first quarter.

There are several ways to take advantage of this market—in particular, through an ETF that tracks the euro directly (FXE). By examining the chart below you will see the euro currency futures contract mirrors the line chart based on the closing prices of the CurrencyShares euro (FXE). See pages 131–137 for additional correlated trades.

JANUARY SHORT EURO (MARCH)
TRADING DAY: 3–HOLD: 24 DAYS

YEAR	ENTRY DATE	ENTRY CLOSE	EXIT DATE	EXIT CLOSE	PROFIT/ LOSS
1999	1/6	116.42	2/10	113.63	$3,488
2000	1/5	103.69	2/9	99.45	5,300
2001	1/4	95.24	2/8	91.85	4,238
2002	1/4	89.27	2/8	87.20	2,587
2003	1/6	104.42	2/10	107.32	−3,625
2004	1/6	127.37	2/10	126.94	538
2005	1/5	132.74	2/9	127.98	5,950
2006	1/5	121.53	2/9	119.91	2,025
2007	1/4	131.31	2/8	130.61	875
2008	1/4	147.77	2/8	144.92	3,563
2009	1/6	134.92	2/10	128.59	7,912
2010	1/6	144.08	2/10	137.35	8,413
2011	1/5	131.46	2/9	137.18	−7,150
2012	1/5	127.92	2/9	132.90	−6,225
				14-Year Gain	**$27,888**

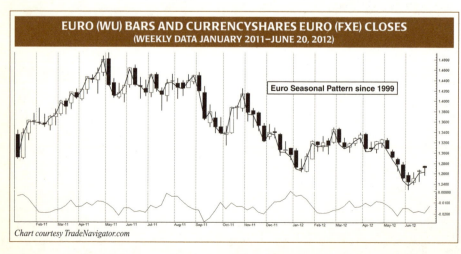

EURO (WU) BARS AND CURRENCYSHARES EURO (FXE) CLOSES
(WEEKLY DATA JANUARY 2011–JUNE 20, 2012)

Euro Seasonal Pattern since 1999

Chart courtesy TradeNavigator.com

JANUARY

MONDAY
14
LT: S

At the age of 24, I began setting clear, written goals for each area of my life. I accomplished more in the following year than I had in the previous 24.
— Brian Tracy (Motivational speaker)

TUESDAY
15
OE: SB

Chance favors the informed mind.
— Louis Pasteur (French chemist, founder of microbiology, 1822–1895)

WEDNESDAY
16
OE: CL

Small volume is usually accompanied by a fall in price; large volume by a rise in price.
— Charles C. Ying ("Stock Market Prices and Volumes of Sales," *Econometrica*, July 1966)

THURSDAY
17

Cooperation is essential to address 21st-century challenges; you can't fire cruise missiles at the global financial crisis.
— Nicholas D. Kristof (*NY Times* columnist, 10/23/2008)

FRIDAY
18
OE: SP

Averaging down in a bear market is tantamount to taking a seat on the down escalator at Macy's.
— Richard Russell (*Dow Theory Letters*, 1984)

SATURDAY
19

SUNDAY
20

WHEAT TURNS TO CHAFF

Winter wheat (traded at the CME Group) is typically planted in the September through October time frame. Traders anticipate the crop size, and this puts pressure on prices. In addition, the Southern Hemisphere crops are working through the export process, adding new supplies to the market. As the Southern Hemisphere supply is consumed, prices tend to climb until the size and health of the newly planted crop is known. These events help explain how the seasonal peak is made in January (page 164).

Wheat is not a homogeneous crop, due to the many different classes that are grown (i.e. soft red winter wheat [SRW], hard red spring wheat [HRS], and durum wheat). All have different protein contents and are used for different purposes.

SRW has a lower protein content and is used for cracker-type products. This is the wheat that is deliverable through the old CBOT or CME Group. HRS wheat has a higher protein content and is used in baking products; durum wheat is very high in protein and is used in pasta and noodles. As winter wheat is planted in the fall, corn is harvested, and wheat that may be used as feed can be substituted with less expensive corn, in most years.

Traders can look to take advantage of this seasonality by selling on or about January 4 and holding until on or about May 8. This trade has worked 30 times in the last 43 years, for a success rate of 69.8%. Also consider Ralcorp (RAH), makers of Post Cereals' Shredded Wheat and the former "human food" division of Ralston Purina, which tends to lag the seasonal price swings in Wheat. See pages 131–137 for additional correlated trades.

JANUARY SHORT WHEAT (JULY)
TRADING DAY: 3–HOLD: 85 DAYS

YEAR	ENTRY DATE	ENTRY CLOSE	EXIT DATE	EXIT CLOSE	PROFIT/ LOSS
1970	1/7	138 5/8	5/08	137 3/8	$63
1971	1/6	161 1/8	50/7	151 3/8	488
1972	1/5	148 1/4	5/05	144	213
1973	1/4	235 1/2	5/08	233 1/8	119
1974	1/4	467 1/2	5/08	352	5,775
1975	1/6	411	5/07	312 1/2	4,925
1976	1/6	355 3/4	5/06	339 3/4	800
1977	1/5	287 1/4	5/09	253 1/2	1,688
1978	1/5	284 1/4	5/08	300 1/4	−800
1979	1/4	313 1/4	5/07	356 1/2	−2,163
1980	1/4	464 3/4	5/08	432	1,638
1981	1/6	499 3/4	5/07	433 3/4	3,300
1982	1/6	412 3/4	5/07	358 1/2	2,713
1983	1/5	342 3/4	5/06	362 3/4	−1,000
1984	1/5	342 3/4	5/07	341 1/2	63
1985	1/4	330 1/2	5/07	324 3/4	288
1986	1/6	278 1/4	5/07	273 1/4	250
1987	1/6	239 1/2	5/07	290 1/2	−2,550
1988	1/6	319 1/4	5/06	307 1/2	588
1989	1/5	400 1/4	5/08	418 1/2	−913
1990	1/4	360 1/2	5/07	352 3/4	388
1991	1/4	271 1/4	5/07	288 1/4	−850
1992	1/6	341 1/2	5/08	369 3/4	−1,413
1993	1/6	318	5/07	293	1,250
1994	1/5	342 1/2	5/09	325 1/2	850
1995	1/5	347 1/4	5/08	356 3/4	−475
1996	1/4	441	5/06	556 1/2	−5,775
1997	1/6	346 3/4	5/07	404 1/4	−2,875
1998	1/6	339 1/2	5/08	312 1/4	1,363
1999	1/6	307 1/2	5/10	264	2,175
2000	1/5	271	5/08	268 3/4	113
2001	1/4	305 3/4	5/08	266 3/4	1,950
2002	1/4	298	5/08	272 1/4	1,288
2003	1/6	311 3/4	5/08	298 1/2	663
2004	1/6	382 1/4	5/07	403	−1,038
2005	1/5	314	5/09	313 1/2	25
2006	1/5	358 3/4	5/09	384 3/4	−1,300
2007	1/5	477	50/9	482	−250
2008	1/4	817 1/4	5/07	807 1/2	488
2009	1/6	668	5/08	591	3,850
2010	1/6	589 1/2	5/10	492 3/4	4,838
2011	1/5	846 1/4	5/09	790 1/2	2,788
2012	1/5	664 3/4	5/09	600	3,238
43-Year Gain					**$26,769**

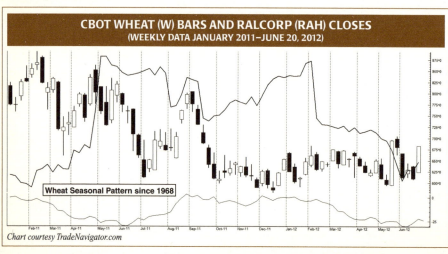

CBOT WHEAT (W) BARS AND RALCORP (RAH) CLOSES
(WEEKLY DATA JANUARY 2011–JUNE 20, 2012)

Wheat Seasonal Pattern since 1968

Chart courtesy TradeNavigator.com

JANUARY

Martin Luther King Jr. Day (Market Closed)

MONDAY
21

You may not have started out life in the best of circumstances. But if you can find a mission in life worth working for and believe in yourself, nothing can stop you from achieving success.
— Kemmons Wilson (Holiday Inn founder)

TUESDAY
22
LT: CL

If there is something you really want to do, make your plan and do it. Otherwise, you'll just regret it forever.
— Richard Rocco (PostNet franchisee, Entrepreneur Magazine 12/2006, b. 1946)

Start Long S&P 500(H)—73.3% Accuracy Since 1983—End Feb. 1—Page 22

WEDNESDAY
23

Based on my own personal experience—both as an investor in recent years and an expert witness in years past—rarely do more than three or four variables really count. Everything else is noise.
— Martin J. Whitman (Founder Third Avenue Funds, b. 1924)

THURSDAY
24
FN: CL

History must repeat itself because we pay such little attention to it the first time.
— Blackie Sherrod (Sportswriter, b. 1919)

FRIDAY
25
OE: US, C, S, W

No one ever claimed that managed care was either managed or cared.
— Anonymous

SATURDAY
26

SUNDAY
27

FEBRUARY ALMANAC

FEBRUARY						
S	M	T	W	T	F	S
					1	2
3	4	5	6	7	8	9
10	11	12	13	14	15	16
17	18	19	20	21	22	23
24	25	26	27	28		

◆ STOCKS AND BONDS

S&P 500 has shown a tendency to decline before Presidents' Day weekend holiday, and as our seasonal pattern shows (page 138), the S&P 500 tends to continue that decline into March in recent years. 30-year Treasury bond prices have a tendency to continue their decline in February, as we hold a short position from November (page 106).

MARCH						
S	M	T	W	T	F	S
					1	2
3	4	5	6	7	8	9
10	11	12	13	14	15	16
17	18	19	20	21	22	23
24	25	26	27	28	29	30
31						

◆ ENERGY

Crude oil makes a strong seasonal bottom, registering a whopping 82.8% success rate with 24 gains in 29 years (pages 26 and 126). February marked the annual low in 2009 and a seasonal low in 2010 and 2011 (page 143). Natural gas also generates a stellar trade from its mid-winter bottom with a 72.7% success rate, gaining 16 out of the last 22 years (page 32). Cover Short Heating Oil from January and look to enter long position on the 8th trading day headed into mid-April through peak heating season. This trade boasts a 78.8% success rate since 1980.

◆ METALS

Gold has demonstrated a tradable seasonal downturn from late February to mid-March (page 124). In 2009, gold peaked at $1013 on February 20 and traded towards $870 by April 6. Silver tends to make price declines in sympathy with gold's seasonal declines. In the past 40 years, silver has declined 30 years for a 75.0% success rate (page 30). Copper prices tend to move in the opposite direction of gold and silver. However, the best trade from December suggests exiting longs on strength during February on or about the 25th of the month (page 112).

◆ GRAINS

Soybeans register a recovery rally from January's break that lasts into the May peak. Soybeans have seen price advances from mid-February to late May, 24 out of the last 44 years, for a 54.5% success rate (page 24). Corn has a tendency to move higher in sympathy with soybeans (page 158). Wheat marches to a different beat and generally sees price declines during February (pages 18 and 164).

◆ SOFTS

Cocoa prices tend to pause in February before advancing and peaking out in March (page 34). Coffee prices see average gains in February lasting though mid- to end of May (page 52). Sugar prices tend to peak in mid-month, triggering a 57.5% win statistic with 23 years out of 40 performing well, including four of the last five years (pages 124 and 173).

◆ MEATS

Live cattle prices have a tendency to see further price gains following January's strength. However, March is a tough month for beef prices. Buyers beware as the bottom generally does not come until June (page 60). Lean hog prices tend to move lower in February and into March, which is the time when one wants to be long headed toward Memorial Day weekend (page 179).

◆ CURRENCIES

The euro tends to be flat during February, but we do see the market correct from January's decline. Our best trade short position is covered on or about the 8th of the month (page 16). The Swiss franc also sees price corrections, and this is the time to cover short positions from the December best trade on or about February 28 (page 116). The British pound tends to remain in a downtrend until mid-March (page 36). Look for continued weakness in February (page 182). The yen posts a secondary low in February, creating a long opportunity on or about February 8 through early May (page 124).

FEBRUARY STRATEGY CALENDAR*

Symbol	B	M	E
SP	L / S		
US	L / S		
CL	L / S		
NG	L / S		
HO	L / S		
HG	L / S		
GC	L / S		
SI	L / S		
C	L / S		
S	L / S		
W	L / S		
CC	L / S		
KC	L / S		
SB	L / S		
LC	L / S		
LH	L / S		
BP	L / S		
EC	L / S		
SF	L / S		
JY	L / S		

*Graphic representation of the Commodity Seasonality Percentage Plays on pages 124–125.
L = Long Trade, S = Short Trade. See pages 131–137 for contract symbols.

JANUARY/FEBRUARY

MONDAY
28
OE: HO, NG, HG, GC, SI

Take care of your employees and they'll take care of your customers.
— John W. Marriott (Founder Marriott International, 1900–1985)

TUESDAY
29
LT: NG, HG, GC, SI

But how do we know when irrational exuberance has unduly escalated asset values, which then become subject to unexpected and prolonged contractions as they have in Japan over the past decade?
— Alan Greenspan (Fed Chairman 1987–2006, 12/5/96 speech to American Enterprise Institute, b. 1926)

WEDNESDAY
30
FN: NG

Buy a stock the way you would buy a house. Understand and like it such that you'd be content to own it in the absence of any market.
— Warren Buffett (CEO Berkshire Hathaway, investor and philanthropist, b. 1930)

THURSDAY
31
FN: HG, GC, SI
LT: HO

Today's Ponzi-style acute fragility and speculative dynamics dictate that he who panics first panics best.
— Doug Noland (Prudent Bear Funds, *Credit Bubble Bulletin*, 10/26/07)

End Long S&P 500(H) (Jan. 23)

FRIDAY
1
OE: CC, LC

The only function of economic forecasting is to make astrology look respectable.
— John Kenneth Galbraith (Canadian/American economist and diplomat, 1908–2006)

SATURDAY
2

SUNDAY
3

END OF JANUARY LONG S&P 500 TRADE

The best six months for owning stocks begins in November and runs until April. However, after the first trading day in January, the market tends to take a breather. It is at this time that we tend to see some profit taking for tax deferment purposes.

By the third week of the month, we have had major economic reports, such as the employment situation and inflation figures; and traders and investors have had a chance to regain a celebratory mood, as the Martin Luther King holiday weekend comes to a close. Traders come back feeling rejuvenated and see the dip in the market as an opportunity to put money back to work.

Buying this "January Dip" has a 73.3% success rate, registering 22 gains with only 8 losses in its 30-year history. The key is to enter a long position on or about January 23 and exit on or about February 1.

Even in early 2009, during the worst bear market since the Great Depression, this trade gained $2,000. More surprising is the fact that this trade's best performance came in 2008, just as the bear market was beginning in earnest.

There are several ways to take advantage of this "January Dip". One is through the futures markets traded at the CME. Stock traders may wish to explore trading the SPDR S&P 500 exchange-traded fund (SPY), which allows one to use options. The chart below displays the direct correlation of the front-month S&P 500 futures contract to SPY. See pages 131–137 for additional correlated trades.

	JANUARY LONG S&P 500 (MARCH) TRADING DAY: 15–HOLD: 7 DAYS				
YEAR	ENTRY DATE	ENTRY CLOSE	EXIT DATE	EXIT CLOSE	PROFIT/ LOSS
1983	1/21	143.90	2/01	143.25	−$163
1984	1/23	167.00	2/01	165.10	−475
1985	1/22	177.15	1/31	180.45	825
1986	1/22	202.80	1/31	213.05	2,563
1987	1/22	276.40	2/02	277.35	238
1988	1/22	248.10	2/02	255.85	1,938
1989	1/23	286.85	2/01	299.00	3,037
1990	1/22	331.40	1/31	330.50	−225
1991	1/22	329.85	1/31	344.65	3,700
1992	1/22	419.25	1/31	408.60	−2,662
1993	1/22	436.65	2/02	443.05	1,600
1994	1/21	473.60	2/01	479.90	1,575
1995	1/23	468.10	2/01	471.90	950
1996	1/22	613.70	1/31	637.95	6,063
1997	1/22	791.60	1/31	787.50	−1,025
1998	1/23	964.40	2/03	1010.70	11,575
1999	1/25	1243.50	2/03	1278.50	8,750
2000	1/24	1411.80	2/02	1415.50	925
2001	1/23	1366.00	2/01	1382.50	4,125
2002	1/23	1129.00	2/01	1123.40	−1,400
2003	1/23	883.00	2/03	858.50	−6,125
2004	1/23	1140.20	2/03	1133.00	−1,800
2005	1/24	1166.20	2/02	1193.20	6,750
2006	1/24	1270.40	2/02	1271.90	375
2007	1/24	1446.20	2/02	1453.10	1,725
2008	1/23	1341.50	2/01	1397.10	13,900
2009	1/23	823.50	2/03	831.50	2,000
2010	1/25	1092.60	2/03	1096.40	950
2011	1/24	1288.50	2/02	1300.00	2,875
2012	1/24	1311.40	2/02	1322.70	2,825
				30-Year Gain	$65,388

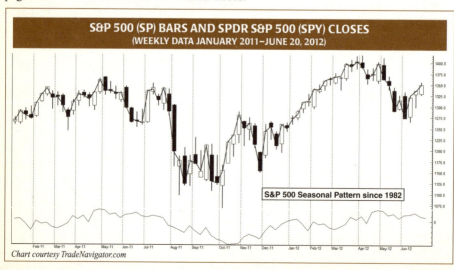

S&P 500 (SP) BARS AND SPDR S&P 500 (SPY) CLOSES
(WEEKLY DATA JANUARY 2011–JUNE 20, 2012)

S&P 500 Seasonal Pattern since 1982

Chart courtesy TradeNavigator.com

FEBRUARY

In the stock market those who expect history to repeat itself exactly are doomed to failure.
— Yale Hirsch (Creator of *Stock Trader's Almanac*, b. 1923)

Start Short 30-Year Bond(M)—65.7% Accuracy Since 1978—End Apr. 10—Page 124

TUESDAY

5

The worst mistake investors make is taking their profits too soon, and their losses too long.
— Michael Price (Mutual Shares Fund)

WEDNESDAY

6

The man who can master his time can master nearly anything.
— Winston Churchill (British statesman, 1874–1965)

End Long Cattle(J) (Jun. 20, 2012)
End Short Yen(H) (Oct. 16, 2012)

THURSDAY

7

Try to surround yourself with people who can give you a little happiness, because you can only pass through this life once, Jack. You don't come back for an encore.
— Elvis Presley (1935–1977)

End Short Euro(H) (Jan. 4)
Start Long Yen(M)—55.6% Accuracy Since 1977—End May 9—Page 124

FRIDAY

8

OE: KC, BP, EC, SF, JY

An economist is someone who sees something happen, and then wonders if it would work in theory.
— Ronald Reagan (40th U.S. President, 1911–2004)

SATURDAY

9

SUNDAY

10

STRENGTH IN SOYBEANS

Soybeans have seen price advances from mid-February to the end of May, 24 out of the last 44 years, for a 54.5% success rate. Generally, we have heavier livestock demand, as animals consume more food during cold winter months. It is well after harvest, and inventories have started to decline. After the New Year, export business begins to pick up again.

It is usually after the January crop production report that traders get a better indication of what supply estimates are. Transportation during harsh winter months can hinder deliveries, causing price spikes. In addition, supplies from the Southern Hemisphere regions are at their lowest levels.

Another event that can and has weighed in on our export business is the value of the U.S. dollar. Since the U.S. dollar has been on a massive decline after reaching a peak in 2002, our exports have been strong. However, sluggish global growth could damper U.S. soybean exports.

Soy meal is used as an animal feed and is not a storable commodity. Therefore demand for soybeans to crush into meal is strong during this period. Demand lasts well into May, as we go through the planting process and potential delays from wet spring. South American harvest gets underway and puts pressure on prices in late May, which is why our exit period is on or about May 30.

Stock traders can consider Bunge Ltd. (BG), one of the world's largest soybean crushers, buyers, sellers, transporters, and commercial hedgers, as it tracks soybeans well. See pages 131–137 for additional correlated trades.

FEBRUARY LONG SOYBEANS (JULY)
TRADING DAY: 9–HOLD: 73 DAYS

YEAR	ENTRY DATE	ENTRY CLOSE	EXIT DATE	EXIT CLOSE	PROFIT/ LOSS
1969	2/13	268 3/4	6/02	266 1/2	−$113
1970	2/12	260 7/8	5/28	271	506
1971	2/11	313	5/27	311 3/4	−63
1972	2/11	324 3/8	5/26	352 1/8	1,388
1973	2/13	525 1/4	5/30	1018	24,638
1974	2/14	654 3/4	5/31	547	−5,388
1975	2/13	614	5/30	502 3/4	−5,563
1976	2/12	499 1/4	5/27	576	3,838
1977	2/11	740 1/2	5/31	960	10,975
1978	2/13	576 1/2	5/30	745 1/4	8,438
1979	2/13	754	5/30	736	−900
1980	2/13	712 3/4	5/29	624	−4,438
1981	2/12	789 1/2	5/29	764 3/4	−1,238
1982	2/11	664 1/4	5/27	643 1/2	−1,038
1983	2/11	623	5/27	610 1/2	−625
1984	2/13	725 3/4	5/29	867	7,063
1985	2/13	602 3/4	5/30	563 1/2	−1,963
1986	2/13	542 3/4	5/30	525 1/4	−875
1987	2/12	484 1/4	5/29	548 3/4	3,225
1988	2/11	637 1/4	5/26	754	5,838
1989	2/13	741	5/30	717	−1,200
1990	2/13	588 1/4	5/30	605 1/4	850
1991	2/13	601 1/2	5/30	578 1/4	−1,163
1992	2/13	587	6/02	630	2,150
1993	2/11	574 1/4	5/27	609	1,738
1994	2/11	692 1/2	5/31	701	425
1995	2/13	572 1/2	5/30	579 3/4	363
1996	2/13	739 1/2	5/29	775	1,775
1997	2/13	764 1/2	5/30	880 1/2	5,800
1998	2/12	689 3/4	5/29	618 1/2	−3,563
1999	2/11	506 3/4	5/27	457 1/4	−2,475
2000	2/11	523 1/4	5/26	534 1/4	550
2001	2/13	457 1/2	5/30	437 1/2	−1,000
2002	2/13	447 1/2	5/30	501 1/4	2,688
2003	2/13	569	5/30	624 1/2	2,775
2004	2/12	808 3/4	5/27	822	663
2005	2/11	527 3/4	5/27	667 3/4	7,000
2006	2/13	607	5/30	583 1/2	−1,175
2007	2/13	783 3/4	5/31	806 1/4	1,125
2008	2/13	1356 1/4	5/29	1322 3/4	−1,675
2009	2/12	976	5/26	1185 1/2	10,475
2010	2/11	958 3/4	5/27	951 3/4	−350
2011	2/11	1437	5/27	1379 3/4	−2,863
2012	2/14	1271 1/4	5/30	1373 1/4	5,100
				44-Year Gain	**$71,719**

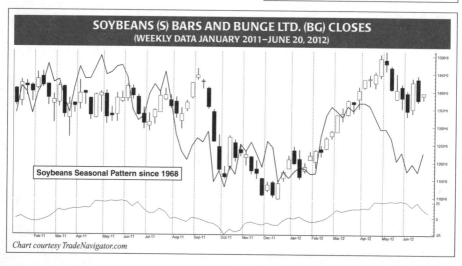

SOYBEANS (S) BARS AND BUNGE LTD. (BG) CLOSES
(WEEKLY DATA JANUARY 2011–JUNE 20, 2012)

Soybeans Seasonal Pattern since 1968

Chart courtesy TradeNavigator.com

MONDAY
11

A weakened White House creates uncertainty on Wall Street.
— Robert D. Hormats (Under Secretary of State Economic, Energy and Agricultural 2009-, Goldman Sachs 1982–2009, CNN 10/28/2005, b.1943)

Start Long Heating Oil(N)—78.8% Accuracy Since 1980—End May 13—Page 124

TUESDAY
12

It's not what you say. It's what they hear.
— (A sign in an advertising office)

Ash Wednesday
Start Long Soybeans(N)—54.5% Accuracy Since 1969—End May 30—Page 24

WEDNESDAY
13

Today's generation of young people holds more power than any generation before it to make a positive impact on the world.
— William J. Clinton (42nd U.S. President, Clinton Global Initiative, b. 1946)

Valentine's Day ♥
Start Long Crude Oil(N)—82.8% Accuracy Since 1984—End May 13—Page 26

THURSDAY
14
FN: CC
LT: LH
OE: CL, LH

When a falling stock becomes a screaming buy because it cannot conceivably drop further, try to buy it 30 percent lower.
— Al Rizzo (1986)

End Short Heating Oil(J) (Jan. 3)

FRIDAY
15
OE: SP, SB

A person's greatest virtue is his ability to correct his mistakes and continually make a new person of himself.
— Yang-Ming Wang (Chinese philosopher, 1472–1529)

SATURDAY
16

SUNDAY
17

CRUDE OIL STRIKES A WINNER IN FEBRUARY

Crude oil has a tendency to bottom in early February and then rally through mid-May. It is that early February break that can give traders an edge by buying low in a seasonally strong period. In the 29-year history, this trade has worked 24 years for an 82.8% win ratio.

The seasonal influence that causes crude oil to move higher in this time period is partly due to continuing demand for heating oil and diesel fuel in the northern states and partly due to the shut down of refinery operations in order to switch production facilities from producing heating oil to reformulated unleaded gasoline in anticipation of heavy demand for the upcoming summer driving season. This has refiners buying crude oil in order to ramp up the production for gasoline.

When the futures markets seem hazardous and unstable, there are other alternatives. One such opportunity is to trade the smaller-sized electronic futures contract (symbol QM), or one can use options on the futures. Stock traders can use the exchange-traded funds (ETFs), United States Oil Fund (USO) or Select SPDR Energy (XLE), or options on these ETFs. One other aspect is to look for highly correlated stocks, like Exxon (XOM) or other refinery stocks that have a direct price correlation to the underlying futures market and trade those markets under the seasonal aspects.

Notice the direct correlation between crude oil futures and the price value of USO in the chart below. The bottom line shows the seasonal tendencies for oil dating back to 1983. See pages 131–137 for additional correlated trades.

FEBRUARY LONG CRUDE OIL (JULY)
TRADING DAY: 10–HOLD: 60 DAYS

YEAR	ENTRY DATE	ENTRY CLOSE	EXIT DATE	EXIT CLOSE	PROFIT/ LOSS
1984	2/14	29.18	5/10	30.37	$1,190
1985	2/14	25.86	5/13	27.03	1,170
1986	2/14	16.38	5/13	15.21	−1,170
1987	2/13	17.57	5/12	18.93	1,360
1988	2/12	16.55	5/10	17.61	1,060
1989	2/14	15.98	5/11	18.83	2,850
1990	2/14	21.37	5/11	19.34	−2,030
1991	2/14	18.50	5/13	20.96	2,460
1992	2/14	19.72	5/12	21.08	1,360
1993	2/12	20.02	5/12	20.41	390
1994	2/14	15.09	5/12	17.70	2,610
1995	2/14	17.95	5/11	19.24	1,290
1996	2/14	17.60	5/10	20.14	2,540
1997	2/14	21.20	5/13	21.28	80
1998	2/13	17.00	5/12	15.93	−1,070
1999	2/12	12.33	5/11	17.99	5,660
2000	2/14	26.51	5/10	28.05	1,540
2001	2/14	28.31	5/11	29.08	770
2002	2/14	21.56	5/13	27.62	6,060
2003	2/14	31.57	5/13	28.08	−3,490
2004	2/13	32.42	5/11	39.97	7,550
2005	2/14	47.88	5/11	51.95	4,070
2006	2/14	63.22	5/11	74.68	11,460
2007	2/14	60.34	5/11	64.12	3,780
2008	2/14	94.89	5/12	124.10	29,210
2009	2/13	48.14	5/12	59.71	11,570
2010	2/12	76.08	5/11	80.22	4,140
2011	2/14	95.58	5/11	98.77	3,190
2012	2/15	103.60	5/11	96.49	−7,110
29-Year Gain					**$92,490**

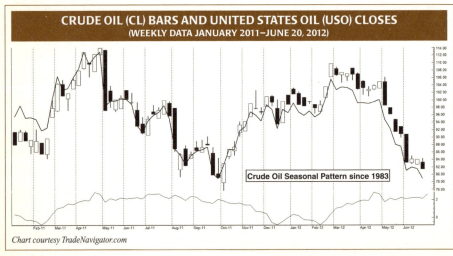

CRUDE OIL (CL) BARS AND UNITED STATES OIL (USO) CLOSES
(WEEKLY DATA JANUARY 2011–JUNE 20, 2012)

Crude Oil Seasonal Pattern since 1983

Chart courtesy TradeNavigator.com

FEBRUARY

Presidents' Day (Market Closed)

MONDAY

18

Civility is not a sign of weakness, and sincerity is always subject to proof. Let us never negotiate out of fear. But let us never fear to negotiate.
— John F. Kennedy (35th U.S. President, Inaugural Address 1/20/1961, 1917–1963)

TUESDAY

19

Liberals have practiced tax and tax, spend and spend, elect and elect but conservatives have perfected borrow and borrow, spend and spend, elect and elect.
— George Will (*Newsweek*, 1989)

Start Short Gold(J)—63.2% Accuracy Since 1975—End Mar. 15—Page 124
Start Short Silver(K)—75.0% Accuracy Since 1973—End Apr. 25—Page 30

WEDNESDAY

20

FN: KC
LT: CL

The most dangerous thing that takes place [in companies] is that success breeds arrogance, and arrogance seems to make people stop listening to their customers and to their employees. And that is the beginning of the end. The challenge is not to be a great company; the challenge is to remain a great company.
— George Fisher (Motorola)

Start Short Sugar(N)—57.5% Accuracy Since 1973—End Apr. 18—Page 124

THURSDAY

21

The more feted by the media, the worse a pundit's accuracy.
— Sharon Begley (Senior editor *Newsweek*, 2/23/2009, referencing Philip E. Tetlock's 2005 *Expert Political Judgment*)

FRIDAY

22

FN: CL
OE: US, C, S, W

The usual bull market successfully weathers a number of tests until it is considered invulnerable, whereupon it is ripe for a bust.
— George Soros (Financier, philanthropist, political activist, author and philosopher, b. 1930)

SATURDAY

23

SUNDAY

24

MARCH ALMANAC

MARCH						
S	M	T	W	T	F	S
					1	2
3	4	5	6	7	8	9
10	11	12	13	14	15	16
17	18	19	20	21	22	23
24	25	26	27	28	29	30
31						

APRIL						
S	M	T	W	T	F	S
	1	2	3	4	5	6
7	8	9	10	11	12	13
14	15	16	17	18	19	20
21	22	23	24	25	26	27
28	29	30				

◆ STOCKS AND BONDS

S&P 500 has shown a tendency to see strength after February weakness. March marks the end of the first quarter; we have seen funds taking profits prior to the end of the quarter, adding to potential late month weakness (page 138). Beware the Ides of March because St. Patrick's Day mid-month bullishness typically fades as the month concludes. 30-year Treasury bond price has a tendency to continue its decline (page 140) and trade in synch with stock prices, as the quarter draws to a close. Historically, this is still the time to be short by selling into mid-month strength.

◆ ENERGY

After January and February weakness, crude oil begins to strengthen in March at the outset of its best seven months, March–September. The seasonal best trade from February is still long through mid-May (pages 26 and 143). Natural gas prices also remain firm through March; the seasonal best trade from February is still long as well, heading into late April (page 32). Heating Oil remains in a seasonally strong period we are holding a long position from February. Late comers can look for a late-month break near St. Patrick's Day to enter a long position lasting into mid-April.

◆ METALS

Gold posts bottoms during March, and this is the time to cover the seasonal best trade short position from February (page 124). Silver is still in decline, as our seasonal best trade is holding a short position until late April (page 30). Copper prices can run higher in March and April, depending on the price gains from December through late February, which is our best trade time frame to be long (page 112). Look for a seasonal peak in April or May (page 48) to make trading decisions.

◆ GRAINS

Soybeans during March are still in our best trade long scenario (page 24), but this month can produce consolidation or a pause in any strong price gain due to anticipation of the quarterly grain stocks report and the farmer planting intentions report. Wheat prices are still in a seasonal decline mode heading into the June harvest lows (page 18). Corn has weakened in March in recent years, down 8 of the last 12 years (page 160).

◆ SOFTS

Cocoa begins a seasonal decline, instituting a short position in our seasonal best trade category (page 34). Coffee prices tend to see corrections after big up moves in February. This is the "frost scare" season in South America. Coffee is susceptible to higher prices until the seasonal peak in May (pages 52 and 170). Sugar prices continue to decline (page 173).

◆ MEATS

Front-month live cattle prices tend to post a seasonal high in March. Producers are liquidating inventories because packers and processors are preparing for BBQ season (pages 60 and 176). Lean hog prices tend to rise during March because demand for ham increases for Easter (page 179).

◆ CURRENCIES

The euro currency has revealed a tendency to decline during the second half of March, 8 out of 14 years (page 124). The Swiss franc also has a tendency to see price declines from mid-March through mid-May (page 187). The British pound has a distinct pattern of doing the opposite of the euro and Swiss franc; it has a strong tendency to move up against the U.S. dollar in mid- March (pages 36 and 182). The yen has a strong seasonal tendency to sell off in mid-March through early April (page 124).

MARCH STRATEGY CALENDAR*

Symbol	B	M	E
SP	L/S		
US	L/S		
CL	L/S		
NG	L/S		
HO	L/S		
HG	L/S		
GC	L/S		
SI	L/S		
C	L/S		
S	L/S		
W	L/S		
CC	L/S		
KC	L/S		
SB	L/S		
LC	L/S		
LH	L/S		
BP	L/S		
EC	L/S		
SF	L/S		
JY	L/S		

* Graphic representation of the Commodity Seasonality Percentage Plays on pages 124–125.
L = Long Trade, S = Short Trade. See pages 131–137 for contract symbols.

28

FEBRUARY/MARCH

Start Long Natural Gas(N)—72.7% Accuracy Since 1991—End Apr. 24—Page 32
End Long Copper(K) (Dec. 14, 2012)

MONDAY
25

OE: HO, NG, HG, GC, SI

I would rather be positioned as a petrified bull rather than a penniless bear.
— John L. Person (Professional trader, author, speaker, *Commodity Trader's Almanac*, nationalfutures.com, 11/3/2010, b. 1961)

TUESDAY
26

LT: NG, HG, GC, SI

Don't compete. Create. Find out what everyone else is doing and then don't do it.
— Joel Weldon

WEDNESDAY
27

FN: NG

I measure what's going on, and I adapt to it. I try to get my ego out of the way. The market is smarter than I am so I bend.
— Martin Zweig (Fund manager, *Winning on Wall Street*)

End Short Swiss Franc(H) (Dec. 28, 2012)

THURSDAY
28

FN: US, HG, GC, SI, C, S, W
LT: HO, SB, LC

Today we deal with 65,000 more pieces of information each day than did our ancestors 100 years ago.
— Dr. Jean Houston (A founder of the Human Potential Movement, b. 1937)

FRIDAY
1

FN: SB
OE: CC, LC

Laws are like sausages. It's better not to see them being made.
— Otto von Bismarck (German-Prussian politician, 1st Chancellor of Germany, 1815–1898)

SATURDAY
2

SUNDAY
3

SILVER TARNISHES IN FEBRUARY

Over the years silver has peaked in February, most notably so in 1980 when the Hunt Brothers' plot to corner the silver market was foiled. Our seasonal study shows that selling on or about February 20 and holding until about April 25 has worked 30 times in the last 40 years, for a win probability of 75.0%. As you can see in the short silver table, the usual February silver break was trumped by the overarching precious metal bull market of 2002–2012 three times in the last ten years.

After suffering declines for two years in a row, this trade returned to success with its second best performance in 2012 as most of the commodity sector weakened on slowing global growth.

Silver is considered the "poor man's" gold, and it does in fact tend to mirror the price move of gold. It is an industrial metal, so in periods of declining economic conditions silver can remain weak. However, it does have a demand base for jewelry, and it is also used in the electronics industry because of its high electrical conductivity and its extreme resistance to corrosion. It is still used in some photo processing applications, but demand in this area has declined with the rise of the digital age of computer imaging.

The chart below of silver has the closing price of ASA Limited (ASA), a mining company that produces silver, overlaid on top. The bottom line is the average seasonal tendency of silver. ASA fairly closely mirrors silver's price moves. See pages 131–137 for additional correlated trades.

FEBRUARY SHORT SILVER (MAY)
TRADING DAY: 13–HOLD: 45 DAYS

YEAR	ENTRY DATE	ENTRY CLOSE	EXIT DATE	EXIT CLOSE	PROFIT/ LOSS
1973	2/21	230.4	4/26	212.4	$900
1974	2/21	579.2	4/26	551.3	1,395
1975	2/21	464.0	4/28	435.0	1,450
1976	2/19	424.0	4/23	439.5	−775
1977	2/17	458.1	4/25	475.7	−880
1978	2/21	511.3	4/26	493.9	870
1979	2/20	792.2	4/25	755.5	1,835
1980	2/20	3485.0	4/24	1415.0	103,500
1981	2/19	1363.0	4/24	1125.0	11,900
1982	2/18	856.8	4/23	726.0	6,540
1983	2/17	1477.5	4/25	1230.0	12,375
1984	2/17	933.5	4/24	926.5	350
1985	2/20	634.8	4/25	628.5	315
1986	2/20	596.7	4/25	509.0	4,385
1987	2/19	553.5	4/24	904.5	−17,550
1988	2/18	643.6	4/22	641.5	105
1989	2/17	604.4	4/25	579.5	1,245
1990	2/20	542.9	4/25	492.2	2,535
1991	2/20	372.3	4/25	389.7	−870
1992	2/20	415.6	4/24	396.5	955
1993	2/18	365.8	4/23	395.5	−1,485
1994	2/17	527.0	4/25	513.0	700
1995	2/17	482.3	4/25	571.7	−4,470
1996	2/20	558.3	4/24	529.2	1,455
1997	2/20	527.8	4/25	472.0	2,790
1998	2/19	676.4	4/24	622.5	2,695
1999	2/18	549.3	4/23	514.5	1,740
2000	2/17	529.8	4/24	495.3	1,725
2001	2/20	446.6	4/25	436.5	505
2002	2/20	441.4	4/25	462.0	−1,030
2003	2/20	467.2	4/25	463.2	200
2004	2/19	667.7	4/23	616.3	2,570
2005	2/17	741.2	4/25	726.0	760
2006	2/17	950.0	4/25	1256.0	−15,300
2007	2/20	1396.3	4/25	1376.5	990
2008	2/20	1786.7	4/24	1666.0	6,035
2009	2/19	1397.2	4/24	1292.0	5,260
2010	2/18	1608.5	4/23	1819.2	−10,535
2011	2/17	3158.1	4/25	4714.9	−77,840
2012	2/21	3450.0	4/25	3032.6	20,870
				40-Year Gain	**$68,215**

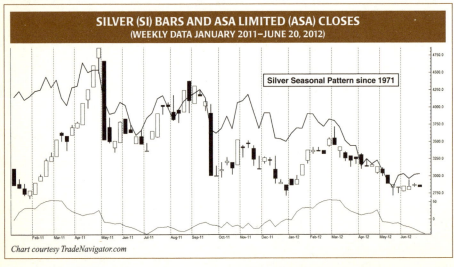

SILVER (SI) BARS AND ASA LIMITED (ASA) CLOSES
(WEEKLY DATA JANUARY 2011–JUNE 20, 2012)

Silver Seasonal Pattern since 1971

Chart courtesy TradeNavigator.com

MONDAY

4

FN: HO

The cause of the Dark Ages can be traced to the Y1K problem.
— (A voice on the Internet)

TUESDAY

5

All a parent can give a child is roots and wings.
— Chinese proverb

WEDNESDAY

6

Your organization will never get better unless you are willing to admit that there is something wrong with it.
— General Norman Schwartzkof (Ret. Commander of Allied Forces in 1990–1991 Gulf War)

THURSDAY

7

We are handicapped by policies based on old myths rather than current realities.
— James William Fulbright (U.S. Senator Arkansas 1944–1974, 1905–1995)

FRIDAY

8

OE: KC, BP, EC, SF, JY

I'm very big on having clarified principles. I don't believe in being reactive. You can't do that in the markets effectively. I can't. I need perspective. I need a game plan.
— Ray Dalio (Money manager, founder Bridgewater Associates, *Fortune* 3/16/2009, b. 1949)

SATURDAY

9

Daylight Saving Time Begins

SUNDAY

10

NATURAL GAS SURGES

Our long natural gas trade from late February to late April boasts a 72.7% success rate, gaining 16 out of the last 22 years. One of the factors in this seasonal price gain is consumption driven by demand for heating homes and businesses in the northern cold weather areas in the United States. In particular, when December and January are colder than normal, we see depletions in inventories through February. This has a tendency to cause price spikes lasting through mid-April.

This best trade scenario has a holding period of approximately 41 trading days lasting until on or about April 24. It is at this time that inventories start to replenish and demand tapers off until mid-July, when demand for generating electricity is highest in order to run air conditioners during heat spells.

The chart below is natural gas (NG) with the United States Natural Gas (UNG) ETF overlaid, displaying the strong correlation in price moves. In addition, the bottom line shows the average seasonal price tendency since 1990, illustrating the bottom that occurs in February. See pages 131–137 for additional correlated trades.

FEBRUARY LONG NATURAL GAS (JULY)
TRADING DAY: 16–HOLD: 41 DAYS

YEAR	ENTRY DATE	ENTRY CLOSE	EXIT DATE	EXIT CLOSE	PROFIT/ LOSS
1991	2/25	1.446	4/24	1.399	−$470
1992	2/25	1.205	4/23	1.400	1,950
1993	2/23	1.725	4/23	2.453	7,280
1994	2/23	2.130	4/22	2.169	390
1995	2/23	1.590	4/24	1.727	1,370
1996	2/23	1.949	4/23	2.300	3,510
1997	2/25	1.950	4/24	2.137	1,870
1998	2/24	2.308	4/23	2.408	1,000
1999	2/23	1.813	4/22	2.271	4,580
2000	2/23	2.605	4/20	3.102	4,970
2001	2/23	5.265	4/24	5.177	−880
2002	2/25	2.536	4/24	3.465	9,290
2003	2/25	5.529	4/24	5.630	1,010
2004	2/24	5.179	4/22	5.773	5,940
2005	2/23	6.628	4/22	7.359	7,310
2006	2/23	7.973	4/24	8.031	580
2007	2/23	8.059	4/24	7.863	−1,960
2008	2/25	9.353	4/23	11.084	17,310
2009	2/24	4.500	4/23	3.662	−8,380
2010	2/23	5.032	4/22	4.330	−7,020
2011	2/23	4.126	4/21	4.535	4,090
2012	2/24	2.980	4/24	2.180	−8,000
				22-Year Gain	**$45,740**

Since the summer of 2008, the natural gas bear market, caused by a glut in the United States from increased supplies and decreased demand due to ideal weather conditions, has put a damper on this trade in three of the last four years. Using risk management techniques, such as stop loss orders and options strategies, should have prevented catastrophic losses from occurring. Furthermore, utilizing technical timing tools, as we illustrate on pages 120–123, should not only improve results but also help keep you out of the seasonal trade when macro trends override seasonality.

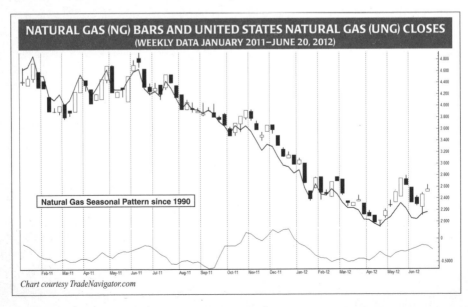

NATURAL GAS (NG) BARS AND UNITED STATES NATURAL GAS (UNG) CLOSES
(WEEKLY DATA JANUARY 2011–JUNE 20, 2012)

Natural Gas Seasonal Pattern since 1990

Chart courtesy TradeNavigator.com

TRY IT FREE for 1 WEEK!
>go to **stocktradersalmanac.com/freeweek**

- ☑ Model Portfolio up 292% since inception
- ☑ 40+ years of proven market analysis
- ☑ Trading Alerts reveal opportunities/dangers
- ☑ And much more!

GET THE STA iPhone APP!

Get key technical analysis notifications right on your phone! The *Stock Trader's Almanac* app will alert you when major seasonal triggers are reached. The app also provides access to free, daily market insights and more.

Get the app by going to stocktradersalmanac.com/app

MARCH

MONDAY

11

Another factor contributing to productivity is technology, particularly the rapid introduction of new microcomputers based on single-chip circuits. ... The results over the next decade will be a second industrial revolution.
— Yale Hirsch (Creator of *Stock Trader's Almanac, Smart Money Newsletter* 9/22/1976, b. 1923)

TUESDAY

12

The greatest lie ever told: Build a better mousetrap and the world will beat a path to your door.
— Yale Hirsch (Creator of *Stock Trader's Almanac*, b. 1923)

WEDNESDAY

13

LT: CC

All there is to investing is picking good stocks at good times and staying with them as long as they remain good companies.
— Warren Buffett (CEO Berkshire Hathaway, investor & philanthropist, b. 1930)

Start Short Cocoa(N)—77.5% Accuracy Since 1973—End Apr. 17—Page 34
Start Short Yen(M)—72.2% Accuracy Since 1977—End Apr. 4—Page 124

THURSDAY

14

LT: SP, C, S, W
OE: SP

Never tell people how to do things. Tell them what to do and they will surprise you with their ingenuity.
— General George S. Patton, Jr. (U.S. Army field commander WWII, 1885–1945)

End Short Gold(J) (Feb. 20)
Start Short Euro(M)—57.1% Accuracy Since 1999—End Mar. 28—Page 124

 **FRIDAY**

15

OE: CL, SB

We're not believers that the government is bigger than the business cycle.
— David Rosenberg (Economist, Merrill Lynch, *Barron's* 4/21/2008)

SATURDAY

16

St. Patrick's Day ☘

SUNDAY

17

COCOA PEAKS BEFORE ST. PATRICK'S DAY

Cocoa begins a seasonal decline, instituting a short position in our seasonal best trade category. Selling on or about March 14, right before St. Patrick's Day, and holding until on or about April 17, for an average holding period of 23 trading days, has been a winner 31 of the past 40 years. Even in the face of the 2008 great commodity bull run, this seasonal tendency worked with a potential profit per contract of $1,730.

Cocoa has two main crop seasons. The main crop, from the Ivory Coast and Ghana in Africa, accounts for 75% of the world production runs from January through March. As inventories are placed on the market, this has a tendency to depress prices, especially when demand starts to fall for hot chocolate drinks and chocolate candy in the spring and summer time.

For stock traders, here is an interesting comparison. The chart below is Hershey Foods (HSY) with cocoa prices overlaid and the historic seasonal tendency of Hershey on the bottom. Notice the inverse relationship. See pages 131–137 for additional correlated trades.

When cocoa prices rise, Hershey prices decline; and then as cocoa prices decline in March, we see a small advance in the stock price. Investors should be aware of the price swings of the underlying product that companies need to manufacture goods in order to obtain a decent profit margin.

MARCH SHORT COCOA TRADING (JULY)
TRADING DAY: 10–HOLD: 23 DAYS

YEAR	ENTRY DATE	CLOSE	EXIT DATE	CLOSE	PROFIT/ LOSS
1973	3/14	806	4/16	940	–$1,340
1974	3/14	1422	4/17	1916	–4,940
1975	3/14	1320	4/17	1184	1,360
1976	3/12	1367	4/14	1657	–2,900
1977	3/14	3929	4/15	3523	4,060
1978	3/14	3401	4/17	3389	120
1979	3/14	3304	4/17	3086	2,180
1980	3/14	2976	4/17	2804	1,720
1981	3/13	2101	4/15	2070	310
1982	3/12	1976	4/15	1651	3,250
1983	3/14	1869	4/15	1807	620
1984	3/14	2517	4/16	2451	660
1985	3/14	2080	4/17	2255	–1,750
1986	3/14	2080	4/17	1938	1,420
1987	3/13	1909	4/15	2004	–950
1988	3/14	1581	4/15	1543	380
1989	3/14	1396	4/17	1255	1,410
1990	3/14	1083	4/17	1285	–2,020
1991	3/14	1221	4/17	1112	1,090
1992	3/13	1093	4/15	968	1,250
1993	3/12	897	4/15	960	–630
1994	3/14	1271	4/15	1150	1,210
1995	3/14	1365	4/17	1318	470
1996	3/14	1243	4/17	1352	–1,090
1997	3/14	1464	4/17	1451	130
1998	3/13	1663	4/16	1586	770
1999	3/12	1242	4/15	1102	1,400
2000	3/14	909	4/14	846	630
2001	3/14	1052	4/17	989	630
2002	3/14	1547	4/17	1537	100
2003	3/14	1941	4/16	1847	940
2004	3/12	1415	4/15	1376	390
2005	3/14	1788	4/15	1533	2,550
2006	3/14	1467	4/17	1460	70
2007	3/14	1783	4/17	1989	–2,060
2008	3/14	2914	4/17	2741	1,730
2009	3/13	2383	4/16	2381	20
2010	3/12	2946	4/15	2890	560
2011	3/14	3359	4/17	3127	2,320
2012	3/14	2338	4/17	2281	570
40-Year Gain					**$16,640**

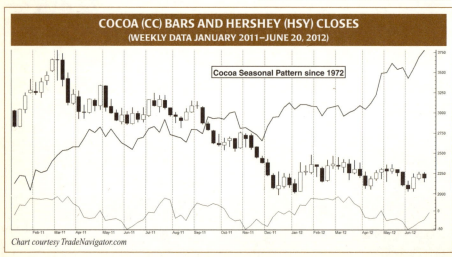

COCOA (CC) BARS AND HERSHEY (HSY) CLOSES
(WEEKLY DATA JANUARY 2011–JUNE 20, 2012)

Cocoa Seasonal Pattern since 1972

Chart courtesy TradeNavigator.com

MARCH

MONDAY
18
LT: KC, BP, EC, SF, JY

As for it being different this time, it is different every time. The question is in what way, and to what extent.
— Tom McClellan (*The McClellan Market Report*)

TUESDAY
19
LT: US

We may face more inflation pressure than currently shows up in formal data.
— William Poole (Economist, president Federal Reserve Bank St. Louis 1998–2008, June 2006 speech, b. 1937)

WEDNESDAY
20
LT: CL

Oil has fostered massive corruption in almost every country that has been "blessed" with it, and the expectation that oil wealth will transform economies has lead to disastrous policy choices.
— Ted Tyson (Chief Investment Officer, Mastholm Asset Management)

Start Long British Pound(M)—73% Accuracy Since 1976—End Apr. 23—Page 36
End Short British Pound(M) (Dec. 28, 2012)

THURSDAY
21

Nothing is more uncertain than the favor of the crowd.
— Marcus Tullius Cicero (Great Roman Orator, Politician, 106–43 B.C.)

FRIDAY
22
FN: CL
OE: US, C, S, W

Small business has been the first rung on the ladder upward for every minority group in the nation's history.
— S. I. Hayakawa (1947, U.S. Senator California 1977–1983, 1906–1992)

SATURDAY
23

SUNDAY
24

MARCH BRITISH POUND INVASION

The British pound has a distinct pattern of doing the opposite of the euro and Swiss franc. It has a strong tendency to move up against the U.S. dollar from mid-March through the latter part of April. In fact, in the 37-year history, it has been positive 27 times, for a success rate of 73.0%.

Entering on or about March 21, holding a long position for 22 trading days, and exiting on or about April 23 has had a string of winners the last seven years in a row, starting in 2005. Perhaps the fact that Britain's fiscal year begins in April helps to push the pound's value up against the U.S. dollar, as money moves back overseas. Cross transactions between the pound versus the euro currency and the pound versus the yen may help influence the rise in the pound's value relative to the U.S. dollar.

The weekly chart below depicts the British pound with the exchange-traded fund (ETF) on the British pound (FXB) overlaid to illustrate how the two instruments trade in tandem. Traders also have the ability to trade foreign currencies on a regulated marketplace, such as the CME Group's futures and options exchanges that provide more electronic access than ETFs afford. Investors who require less leverage will find the FXB an adequate trading vehicle. Either way, the seasonal tendency is quite strong for the pound to move up in this time frame. See pages 131–137 for additional correlated trades.

MARCH LONG BRITISH POUND (JUNE) TRADING DAY: 15–HOLD: 22 DAYS

YEAR	ENTRY DATE	CLOSE	EXIT DATE	CLOSE	PROFIT/ LOSS
1976	3/19	188.90	4/21	182.60	−$3,938
1977	3/21	169.00	4/21	171.10	1,313
1978	3/21	190.00	4/21	181.65	−5,219
1979	3/21	203.40	4/23	206.65	2,031
1980	3/21	219.00	4/23	227.10	5,063
1981	3/20	226.65	4/22	219.65	−4,375
1982	3/19	181.10	4/21	178.35	−1,719
1983	3/21	147.00	4/21	154.40	4,625
1984	3/21	143.70	4/23	142.05	−1,031
1985	3/21	117.45	4/23	123.70	3,906
1986	3/21	150.60	4/23	152.40	1,125
1987	3/20	159.25	4/22	162.20	1,844
1988	3/21	182.20	4/21	189.25	4,406
1989	3/21	171.58	4/21	170.48	−688
1990	3/21	156.88	4/23	161.92	3,150
1991	3/21	177.64	4/23	169.88	−4,850
1992	3/20	168.66	4/22	174.56	3,688
1993	3/19	148.34	4/21	153.42	3,175
1994	3/21	148.44	4/20	149.02	363
1995	3/21	158.56	4/21	160.96	1,500
1996	3/21	153.56	4/22	151.10	−1,538
1997	3/21	160.24	4/21	162.14	1,187
1998	3/20	166.20	4/22	166.78	363
1999	3/19	162.70	4/21	160.58	−1,325
2000	3/21	157.38	4/20	157.94	350
2001	3/21	142.88	4/23	143.76	550
2002	3/21	141.82	4/23	144.24	1,513
2003	3/21	155.48	4/23	158.10	1,638
2004	3/19	181.80	4/21	176.51	−3,306
2005	3/21	189.01	4/21	190.34	831
2006	3/21	174.98	4/21	178.26	2,050
2007	3/21	196.80	4/20	200.29	2,181
2008	3/24	197.06	4/23	197.30	150
2009	3/20	144.40	4/22	145.03	394
2010	3/19	151.00	4/20	153.61	1,631
2011	3/21	163.02	4/20	163.97	594
2012	3/21	158.49	4/20	161.03	1,588
				37-Year Gain	$23,219

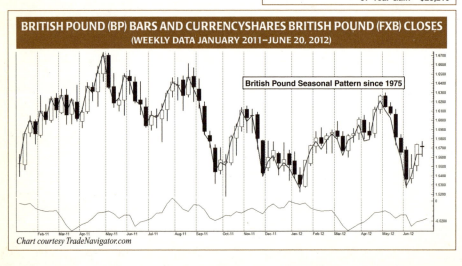

BRITISH POUND (BP) BARS AND CURRENCYSHARES BRITISH POUND (FXB) CLOSES
(WEEKLY DATA JANUARY 2011–JUNE 20, 2012)

British Pound Seasonal Pattern since 1975

Chart courtesy TradeNavigator.com

MARCH

If you torture the data long enough, it will confess to anything.
— Darrell Huff (*How to Lie With Statistics*, 1954)

Passover

The greatest discovery of my generation is that human beings can alter their lives by altering their attitudes.
— William James (Philosopher, psychologist, 1842–1910)

In the course of evolution and a higher civilization we might be able to get along comfortably without Congress, but without Wall Street, never.
— Henry Clews (1900)

End Short Euro(M) (Mar. 15)

No horse gets anywhere until he is harnessed. No steam or gas ever drives anything until it is confined. No Niagara is ever turned into light and power until it is tunneled. No life ever grows great until it is focused, dedicated, disciplined.
— Harry Emerson Fosdick (Protestant minister, author, 1878–1969)

Good Friday (Market Closed)

We pay the debts of the last generation by issuing bonds payable by the next generation.
— Lawrence J. Peter

Easter

APRIL ALMANAC

APRIL						
S	M	T	W	T	F	S
	1	2	3	4	5	6
7	8	9	10	11	12	13
14	15	16	17	18	19	20
21	22	23	24	25	26	27
28	29	30				

◆ STOCKS AND BONDS

S&P 500 has shown a tendency to see price declines ahead of mid-month tax deadlines and then a month-end recovery. April is considered one of the best six months to be long, according to the *Stock Traders Almanac*. 30-year Treasury bond price has a tendency to make a seasonal low towards the end of the month (page 42).

MAY						
S	M	T	W	T	F	S
				1	2	3	4
5	6	7	8	9	10	11
12	13	14	15	16	17	18
19	20	21	22	23	24	25
26	27	28	29	30	31	

◆ ENERGY

Crude oil has a tendency to continue rallying through April into mid-May, as we are long crude from our seasonal best trade in February (pages 26 and 124). This is still one of the best seven months to be long: from March through September. Natural gas prices tend to peak in mid- to late April. Our best seasonal long trade from February signals an exit on or about April 24 (page 32). Heating oil prices can remain firm through end of month, but on average, demand declines as heating season ends. We exit our long heating oil trade in May (page 124), but aggressive traders should be looking to sell rallies against a monthly pivot or resistance level.

◆ METALS

Gold has a tendency to decline in April, as tax-related selling pressures prices (page 40). Our best seasonal short trade for silver from February signals an exit on or about April 25 (page 30). Copper tends to form a seasonal high toward the end of April and the first part of May (pages 112 and 149).

◆ GRAINS

Soybeans in April still see upside, as planting concerns and demand for both meal and oil remain strong, U.S. inventories decline, and new supplies are not yet ready since South America's harvest is just beginning (page 161). Wheat is still under pressure, as harvest adds fresh inventories that outweigh demand (page 164). Corn has a tendency to remain strong, especially as April can lead to planting delays in cool, wet spring conditions. In addition, April tax season has passed, and farmers tend to start focusing on production rather than marketing, allowing inventories to build up on farm locations (page 158).

◆ SOFTS

Cocoa's best seasonal short trade from March signals an exit on or about April 17 (pages 34 and 124). Coffee prices are seasonally strong, as this is still just short of the Columbian and Brazilian harvest. It is also the time when the threat of frost damaging the South American crop is high (page 170). Sugar tends to remain weak during this time frame due to inventory from sugar cane harvests in the U.S. Southeast and Brazil (page 173).

◆ MEATS

Live cattle prices are in a seasonally weak period through mid-June, but we do see times when prices consolidate, especially if the month prior showed significant price declines (page 176). Ranchers tend to pay more attention to breeding in the spring rather than bringing livestock to market. Lean hog prices, on the other hand, continue to remain firm in April from a seasonal perspective (page 179). As corn prices increase feed costs, hog producers have shifted towards liquidating inventories and are preparing for breeding. Furthermore, competing pork producers from Canada have had more incentives to market their product with the increase in value of the Canadian dollar. This has magnified the seasonal peak which comes in late May.

◆ CURRENCIES

The euro has weakened in April for three of the past four years (page 186). The Swiss franc continues its seasonally flat period from March until the first part of August (page 187). The British pound best seasonal long trade from March signals an exit on or about April 23 (page 36). The yen best seasonal short trade from March signals an exit on or about April 4 (page 124).

APRIL STRATEGY CALENDAR*

Symbol	B	M	E
SP	L/S		
US	L/S		
CL	L/S		
NG	L/S		
HO	L/S		
HG	L/S		
GC	L/S		
SI	L/S		
C	L/S		
S	L/S		
W	L/S		
CC	L/S		
KC	L/S		
SB	L/S		
LC	L/S		
LH	L/S		
BP	L/S		
EC	L/S		
SF	L/S		
JY	L/S		

*Graphic representation of the Commodity Seasonality Percentage Plays on pages 124–125.
L = Long Trade, S = Short Trade. See pages 131–137 for contract symbols.

38

APRIL

MONDAY
1

I am young, powerful and successful, and I produce at least $10,000 a month.
— (Mantra of Suze Orman, *The 9 Steps to Financial Freedom*, as a young Merrill Lynch broker)

TUESDAY
2

FN: HO

Don't worry about people stealing your ideas. If the ideas are any good, you'll have to ram them down people's throats.
— Howard Aiken (U.S. computer scientist, 1900–1973)

WEDNESDAY
3

Markets are constantly in a state of uncertainty and flux and money is made by discounting the obvious and betting on the unexpected.
— George Soros (Financier, philanthropist, political activist, author and philosopher, b. 1930)

End Short Yen(M) (Mar. 14)

THURSDAY
4

Benjamin Graham was correct in suggesting that while the stock market in the short run may be a voting mechanism, in the long run it is a weighing mechanism. True value will win out in the end.
— Burton G. Malkiel (Economist, April 2003 Princeton Paper, *A Random Walk Down Wall Street*, b. 1932)

FRIDAY
5

OE: CC, LC, BP, EC, SF, JY

I will never knowingly buy any company that has a real time quote of their stock price in the building lobby.
— Robert Mahan (A trader commenting on Enron)

SATURDAY
6

SUNDAY
7

APRIL TAX TIME TAKES A BITE OUT OF GOLD

Gold has a tendency to continue the seasonal decline that begins in January, leaving April vulnerable to price declines. April tends to see tax-related selling pressure on gold prices along with other financial markets, specifically the U.S. stock markets, and more predominantly, in the technology sector as represented by the NASDAQ 100. It seems that some investors raise capital to pay the IRS by liquidating portions of assets, such as gold and stocks (see *Stock Traders Almanac 2013*, page 38).

Generally speaking, April is also a weak month from a demand perspective. The two forces of increased sales (supply) and no major demand cause the downside price pressure on gold during April. The monthly percentage changes show a distinct gold price decline (page 154).

The weekly chart below shows the price comparison of gold to a gold mining stock, Newmont Mining (NEM). NEM is a major producer of gold and other metals. This company manages properties in the United States, Australia, Peru, Indonesia, Ghana, Canada, Bolivia, New Zealand, and Mexico. The company was founded in 1916 and is based in Denver, Colorado. Not only are they diversified in various countries, but they also have a long history of being in business. This stock also trades well over an average of six million shares per day.

As you can see, the April selloff is predominant not only in the price of gold but also in the shares of this company. The bottom chart shows the average seasonality since 1975 of gold futures prices making declines in the month of April. Here again is another example of trading opportunities using seasonalities of commodities that have direct correlation to other markets, allowing you to trade that product under the seasonal aspects. Newmont Mining is one such example that mirrors the price movement of gold.

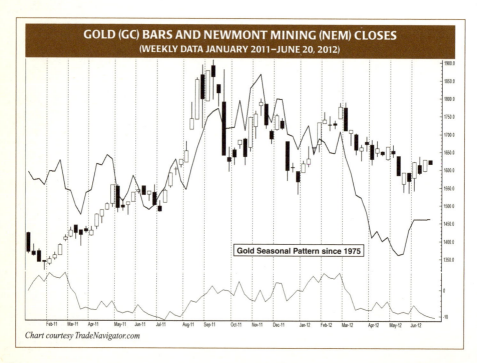

GOLD (GC) BARS AND NEWMONT MINING (NEM) CLOSES
(WEEKLY DATA JANUARY 2011–JUNE 20, 2012)

Gold Seasonal Pattern since 1975

Chart courtesy TradeNavigator.com

MONDAY

8

FN: LC

I had an unshakable faith. I had it in my head that if I had to, I'd crawl over broken glass. I'd live in a tent—it was gonna happen. And I think when you have that kind of steely determination...people get out of the way.
— Rick Newcombe (Syndicator, *Investor's Business Daily*)

TUESDAY

9

Life does not consist mainly of facts and happenings. It consists mainly of the storm of thoughts that are forever blowing through one's mind.
— Mark Twain (1835–1910, pen name of Samuel Longhorne Clemens, American novelist and satirist)

End Short 30-Year Bond(M) (Feb. 5)

WEDNESDAY

10

We can guarantee cash benefits as far out and at whatever size you like, but we cannot guarantee their purchasing power.
— Alan Greenspan (Fed Chairman 1987–2006, on funding Social Security to Senate Banking Committee 2/15/05)

THURSDAY

11

People who can take a risk, who believe in themselves enough to walk away [from a company] are generally people who bring about change.
— Cynthia Danaher (Exiting GM of Hewlett-Packard's Medical Products Group, *Newsweek*)

FRIDAY

12

LT: LH
OE: KC, LH

A successful man is one who can lay a firm foundation with the bricks that others throw at him.
— Sidney Greenberg (Rabbi, author, 1918–2003)

SATURDAY

13

SUNDAY

14

BONDS CAN GO UP WHEN STOCKS GO DOWN

The vast majority of investors do not understand the nature of trading Treasury bond futures. There exists an inverse relationship between yield and price. When yield or rates go up, bond prices go down and vice versa. When investors feel threatened with a potential decline in the stock market, they allocate more money into bonds. This is often referred to as the "flight to safety" trade. Investors will also allocate more money to bonds when they believe the yield is more attractive than other shorter-term investment options.

There is no doubt that both of those conditions were met in late 2008 through early 2009. However, even in that unprecedented time, 30-year bond price action did respect a seasonal supply-demand cycle. By going long the September 30-year bond on or about April 24 and exiting the position on or about August 19, we discovered in the last 34 years a solid 70.6% success rate. This trade has a history of 24 wins with only 10 losses; the largest win was $20,250 in 2011, and the largest loss was $5,906 in 1999.

The 2009 stock rally off the bottom of the worst bear market since the Depression drove bonds lower. However, if one waited and used timing tools, losses could have been averted, and gains achieved. In 2012, as we were working on this edition, this trade was conforming to the seasonality, as stocks succumbed to a decline. Investors were in fact seeking safety and flocked to buy bonds.

Stock traders may consider the exchange-traded fund, iShares Barclays 20+ Year Bond (TLT), as a replacement for this futures contract. See pages 134–137 for additional correlated trades.

APRIL LONG 30-YR BOND (SEPTEMBER)
TRADING DAY: 18–HOLD: 81 DAYS

YEAR	ENTRY DATE	CLOSE	EXIT DATE	CLOSE	PROFIT/ LOSS
1978	4/26	94'270	8/21	95'020	$219
1979	4/26	88'260	8/21	90'190	1,781
1980	4/25	76'010	8/20	74'000	−2,031
1981	4/27	64'010	8/20	60'110	−3,688
1982	4/27	64'050	8/20	69'000	4,844
1983	4/27	77'270	8/22	72'160	−5,344
1984	4/26	65'000	8/21	66'230	1,719
1985	4/25	69'260	8/20	77'100	7,500
1986	4/24	97'240	8/19	102'080	4,500
1987	4/27	90'070	8/20	89'210	−563
1988	4/27	87'190	8/22	84'190	−3,000
1989	4/26	89'190	8/21	96'150	6,875
1990	4/26	88'110	8/21	89'190	1,250
1991	4/24	95'110	8/19	97'110	2,000
1992	4/28	97'040	8/21	105'220	8,563
1993	4/27	109'090	8/20	117'090	8,000
1994	4/26	105'210	8/22	102'040	−3,531
1995	4/27	104'280	8/22	110'060	5,313
1996	4/24	109'070	8/19	110'290	1,688
1997	4/24	106'280	8/19	114'060	7,313
1998	4/27	118'160	8/20	124'170	6,031
1999	4/26	120'280	8/19	114'310	−5,906
2000	4/27	96'020	8/22	99'290	3,844
2001	4/26	100'310	8/21	104'300	3,969
2002	4/24	100'200	8/19	108'290	8,281
2003	4/25	112'030	8/20	106'220	−5,406
2004	4/27	106'240	8/23	110'160	3,750
2005	4/26	113'240	8/19	116'080	2,500
2006	4/27	106'170	8/22	109'280	3,344
2007	4/25	111'160	8/21	110'200	−875
2008	4/24	114'315	8/19	117'185	2,594
2009	4/27	123'220	8/20	120'095	−3,391
2010	4/26	115'260	8/19	134'110	18,531
2011	4/27	119'290	8/22	140'050	20,250
				34-Year Gain	**$100,922**

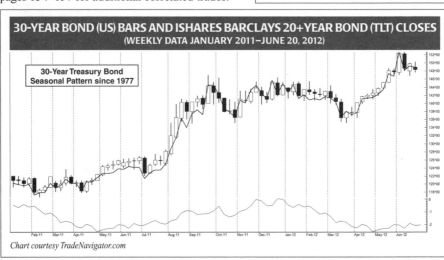

30-YEAR BOND (US) BARS AND ISHARES BARCLAYS 20+YEAR BOND (TLT) CLOSES
(WEEKLY DATA JANUARY 2011–JUNE 20, 2012)

30-Year Treasury Bond Seasonal Pattern since 1977

Chart courtesy TradeNavigator.com

APRIL

Income Tax Deadline

MONDAY
15
OE: SB

Taxes are what we pay for civilized society.
— Oliver Wendell Holmes Jr. (U.S. Supreme Court Justice 1902–1932, "The Great Dissenter," inscribed above IRS HQ entrance, 1841–1935)

TUESDAY
16

Three passions, simple but overwhelmingly strong, have governed my life: the longing for love, the search for knowledge, and unbearable pity for the suffering of mankind.
— Bertrand Russell (British mathematician and philosopher, 1872–1970)

End Short Cocoa(N) (Mar. 14)

WEDNESDAY
17
FN: CC
OE: CL

When new money is created on a grand scale, it must go somewhere and have some major consequences. One of these will be greatly increased volatility and instability in the economy and financial system.
— J. Anthony Boeckh, Ph.D (Chairman Bank Credit Analyst 1968–2002, *The Great Reflation, Boeckh Investment Letter*)

End Short Sugar(N) (Feb. 21)

THURSDAY
18

Develop interest in life as you see it; in people, things, literature, music—the world is so rich, simply throbbing with rich treasures, beautiful souls and interesting people. Forget yourself.
— Henry Miller (American writer, *Tropic of Cancer, Tropic of Capricorn,* 1891–1980)

 FRIDAY
19
OE: SP

The future now belongs to societies that organize themselves for learning. What we know and can do holds the key to economic progress.
— Ray Marshall (b. 1928) and Marc Tucker (b. 1939) (*Thinking for a Living: Education and the Wealth of Nations*, 1992)

SATURDAY
20

SUNDAY
21

BEEF PRICES HEAD SOUTH BEFORE SUMMER

Live cattle prices tend to post a seasonal high in early May. Between the supplies of fattened beef coming out of feed lots from the cold winter months to competing meat products like poultry and pork, supply tends to outpace demand, and we see a strong seasonal tendency for beef prices to decline, starting on or about May 2 through mid-June. In the past 36 years ending in 2011, this trade has worked 23 times for a 63.9% success rate.

At present, there is currently no ETF that is outright geared towards beef prices, but investors do have other options besides outright futures contract positions to trade this commodity's seasonality. Investors can start examining which companies have not only a like or tandem price relationship, but also an inverse relationship with seasonal price moves in the underlying commodity markets, as is the case with live cattle and McDonald's (page 60). Another possibility is the ETN, iPath DJ-UBS Livestock Total Return Sub-Index (COW).

However, the chart below is of the ETF Market Vectors Agribusiness (MOO), which tracks beef prices closely, as it contains many stocks related to the cattle ranching business. See pages 131–137 for additional correlated trades. At press time, both live cattle and MOO had already declined substantially by mid-June 2012, after establishing a peak seasonal high in late February.

MAY SHORT LIVE CATTLE (OCTOBER) TRADING DAY: 2–HOLD: 30 DAYS

YEAR	ENTRY DATE	ENTRY CLOSE	EXIT DATE	EXIT CLOSE	PROFIT/ LOSS
1976	5/4	45.675	6/16	45.200	190
1977	5/3	43.125	6/15	38.650	1,790
1978	5/2	52.625	6/14	50.050	1,030
1979	5/2	72.450	6/14	65.500	2,780
1980	5/2	61.500	6/16	65.100	−1,440
1981	5/4	65.550	6/16	65.300	100
1982	5/4	63.525	6/16	59.425	1,640
1983	5/3	60.825	6/15	59.000	730
1984	5/2	62.625	6/14	62.225	160
1985	5/2	62.100	6/14	62.725	−250
1986	5/2	52.325	6/16	49.950	950
1987	5/4	62.775	6/16	61.700	430
1988	5/3	68.150	6/15	63.950	1,680
1989	5/2	69.500	6/14	71.750	−900
1990	5/2	74.125	6/14	76.025	−760
1991	5/2	76.000	6/14	75.325	270
1992	5/4	70.525	6/16	71.175	−260
1993	5/4	74.300	6/16	75.100	−320
1994	5/3	70.675	6/15	67.875	1,120
1995	5/2	61.950	6/14	62.325	−150
1996	5/2	63.800	6/14	67.250	−1,380
1997	5/2	69.075	6/16	67.425	660
1998	5/4	69.675	6/16	65.400	1,710
1999	5/4	63.700	6/16	65.675	−790
2000	5/2	72.100	6/14	70.225	750
2001	5/2	73.525	6/14	74.475	−380
2002	5/2	65.875	6/14	64.575	520
2003	5/2	71.225	6/16	68.525	1,080
2004	5/4	84.450	6/17	86.925	−990
2005	5/3	86.200	6/15	82.750	1,380
2006	5/2	81.075	6/14	83.300	−890
2007	5/2	96.075	6/15	94.675	560
2008	5/2	104.400	6/16	110.575	−2,470
2009	5/4	86.550	6/16	85.775	310
2010	5/4	96.450	6/16	90.425	2,410
2011	5/3	118.050	6/15	111.025	2,810
				36-Year Gain	**$14,080**

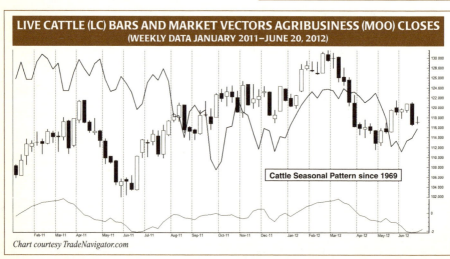

LIVE CATTLE (LC) BARS AND MARKET VECTORS AGRIBUSINESS (MOO) CLOSES
(WEEKLY DATA JANUARY 2011–JUNE 20, 2012)

Cattle Seasonal Pattern since 1969

Chart courtesy TradeNavigator.com

MONDAY

22

FN: KC
LT: CL

I'm not nearly so concerned about the return on my capital as I am the return of my capital.
— Will Rogers (American humorist and showman, 1879–1935)

End Long British Pound(M) (Mar. 21)

TUESDAY

23

The heights by great men reached and kept, were not attained by sudden flight, but they, while their companions slept, were toiling upward in the night.
— Henry Wadsworth Longfellow

End Long Natural Gas(N) (Feb. 25)
Start Long 30-Year Bond(U)—70.6% Accuracy Since 1978—End Aug. 19—Page 42
Start Long S&P 500(U)—66.7% Accuracy Since 1982—End Jun. 4—Page 124

WEDNESDAY

24

FN: CL

The choice of starting a war this [pre-election] spring was made for political as well as military reasons…
[The president] cleary does not want to have a war raging on the eve of his presumed reelection campaign.
— Senior European diplomat (*NY Times* 3/14/03)

End Short Silver(K) (Feb. 20)

THURSDAY

25

OE: HO, NG, HG, GC, SI

The true mystery of the world is the visible, not the invisible.
— Oscar Wilde (Irish-born writer and wit, 1845–1900)

End Short 30-Year Bond(M) (Nov. 20, 2012)

FRIDAY

26

LT: NG, HG, GC, SI
OE: US, C, S, W

It is better to be out wishing you were in, than in wishing you were out.
— Albert W. Thomas (Trader, investor, *Over My Shoulder*, mutualfundmagic.com, *If It Doesn't Go Up, Don't Buy It!*, b. 1927)

SATURDAY

27

SUNDAY

28

MAY ALMANAC

MAY						
S	M	T	W	T	F	S
			1	2	3	4
5	6	7	8	9	10	11
12	13	14	15	16	17	18
19	20	21	22	23	24	25
26	27	28	29	30	31	

JUNE						
S	M	T	W	T	F	S
						1
2	3	4	5	6	7	8
9	10	11	12	13	14	15
16	17	18	19	20	21	22
23	24	25	26	27	28	29
30						

◆ STOCKS AND BONDS

S&P's have shown a tendency to see price declines—as the saying goes "sell in May and go away." However, no one said it was the beginning of the month. In recent years we start to see stocks peak in mid- to end of month, as illustrated in our seasonal chart (page 138). 30-year Treasury bonds prices continue their bottoming process in May, as seen in our seasonal chart (pages 42 and 140).

◆ ENERGY

Liquidate crude oil long from February on or about May 13 (page 26). Natural gas generally consolidates during the month of May prior to forming a mid-June peak, followed by early summer weakness (page 145). Exit the long heating oil trade from February 14 on or about May 13 (page 124).

◆ METALS

Gold continues to remain weak from a seasonal perspective headed into the early summer month trading doldrums. Silver sees a strong tendency to peak—look to sell silver on or about May 14 and hold through June 25 for a 66.7% win ratio and a cumulative gain of $60,495 the last 39 years, and a six-year win steak from 2006–2011 (page 50). Getting short copper on or about May 10 and exiting on or about May 30 has produced 25 wins out of 40 years. 2012 had the best gain with $7,513 in profits (page 48).

◆ GRAINS

Soybeans tend to peak out and start a seasonal decline towards the end of the month in most normal weather years, as planting is well established and the crop growing season is well underway. This lasts through early August when "drought scares" develop. This is the time to take advantage of any further seasonal strength to liquidate long positions from February on or about May 30 (page 24). Wheat prices continue to trend lower under normal crop years before the harvest lows are made in June (page 164). Corn tends to move sideways in May. Don't look to short corn until the seasonal peak in June (page 62).

◆ SOFTS

Cocoa sees some price consolidation, as it heads toward its seasonal low in June (pages 125 and 167). Coffee has its best seasonal trade, as it typically hits a seasonal high in May; look to sell short on or about May 22 (page 52). Sugar sees some price consolidation, as it also tends to hit a seasonal low in June (pages 58 and 173).

◆ MEATS

Live cattle prices generally trend lower in May heading into June when they typically establish their average seasonal low (page 176). Look to sell on the second trading day and hold for 30 days. This trade has a 63.9% win probability (page 126). Cattle prices then tend to bottom in mid- to late June when it typically establishes a seasonal low (page 60). Lean hogs usually peak in May (page 179).

◆ CURRENCIES

The euro has no real meaningful trend direction or influences from one particular seasonal factor during the month of May. The Swiss franc also drifts sideways, with a tendency to post a seasonal bottom in May, but typically does not advance higher against the U.S. dollar until August. The British pound can be shorted on or about May 29 and held through June 10. This trade worked 24 of 37 years, for a cumulative gain of $15,463 (page 124). The yen should rally, giving traders a chance to liquidate the seasonal best long trade from February, on or about May 9 (page 124).

MAY STRATEGY CALENDAR*

Symbol		B	M	E
SP	L/S			
US	L/S			
CL	L/S			
NG	L/S			
HO	L/S			
HG	L/S			
GC	L/S			
SI	L/S			
C	L/S			
S	L/S			
W	L/S			
CC	L/S			
KC	L/S			
SB	L/S			
LC	L/S			
LH	L/S			
BP	L/S			
EC	L/S			
SF	L/S			
JY	L/S			

* Graphic representation of the Commodity Seasonality Percentage Plays on pages 124–125.
L = Long Trade, S = Short Trade. See pages 131–137 for contract symbols.

APRIL/MAY

MONDAY

29

FN: NG

The highest reward for a person's toil is not what they get for it, but what they become by it.
— John Ruskin (English writer)

TUESDAY

30

FN: HG, GC, SI, C, S, W
LT: HO, SB, LC

The investor who concentrated on the 50 stocks in the S&P 500 that are followed by the fewest Wall Street analysts wound up with a rousing 24.6% gain in [2006 versus] 13.6% [for] the S&P 500.
— Rich Bernstein (Chief Investment Strategist, Merrill Lynch, *Barron's* 1/8/07)

WEDNESDAY

1

FN: SB

What lies behind us and what lies before us are tiny matters, compared to what lies within us.
— Ralph Waldo Emerson (American author, poet and philosopher, *Self-Reliance*, 1803–1882)

Start Short Cattle(V)—63.9% Accuracy Since 1976—End Jun. 14—Page 44

THURSDAY

2

FN: HO

"Sell in May and go away." However, no one ever said it was the beginning of the month.
— John L. Person (Professional trader, author, speaker, *Commodity Trader's Almanac*, nationalfutures.com, 6/19/2009, b. 1961)

FRIDAY

3

OE: CC, LC, BP, EC, SF, JY

A market is the combined behavior of thousands of people responding to information, misinformation and whim.
— Kenneth Chang (*NY Times* journalist)

SATURDAY

4

SUNDAY

5

COPPER TOPS IN MAY

Copper prices tend to peak out when construction season is underway. Supplies have built up, but demand tends to decline. Producers have a tendency to ship inventories when prices are the highest during periods of strong demand (page 149). However, builders order hand-to-mouth rather than stockpile copper tubing for plumbing installations when prices get too high. This could be one explanation for this short term seasonal tendency.

Traders can look to sell copper on or about May 10, and then exit on or about May 30. This trade has racked up 25 wins out of the last 40 years. Impressively, 2007 and 2008 totaled $10,163 in profits. However, the global economic rebound and growth in China in 2009 created a demand spike causing copper prices to rise during this seasonally weak period.

In 2010, this trade proved successful as slowing growth gave rise to double-dip recession fears. However, in 2011, it was not, resulting in the worst loss ever. Always evaluate technical timing indicators, macroeconomic trends, and fundamentals before executing any trade, especially seasonal trades. The best gain ever in 2012, handily offset last year's losses.

Besides selling a futures contract, one way to capitalize on this event is to look at iShares DJ US Basic Materials (IYM), which contains natural resource companies that mine iron ore, aluminum, and, of course, copper among other metals. Notice the striking similarities of the seasonal tendencies between the price moves of this ETF in relation to the price of copper. See pages 131–137 for additional correlated trades.

MAY SHORT COPPER (JULY) TRADING DAY: 8–HOLD: 13 DAYS					
	ENTRY		EXIT		PROFIT/
YEAR	DATE	CLOSE	DATE	CLOSE	LOSS
1973	5/10	65.90	5/30	71.05	−$1,288
1974	5/10	129.80	5/30	107.50	5,575
1975	5/12	55.30	5/30	54.70	150
1976	5/12	71.30	6/01	69.70	400
1977	5/11	66.00	5/31	60.40	1,400
1978	5/10	59.50	5/30	65.90	−1,600
1979	5/10	85.10	5/30	79.40	1,425
1980	5/12	88.60	5/30	93.40	−1,200
1981	5/12	82.10	6/01	81.50	150
1982	5/12	72.95	6/01	61.50	2,863
1983	5/11	80.80	5/31	78.35	613
1984	5/10	63.70	5/30	64.15	−113
1985	5/10	65.50	5/30	60.75	1,188
1986	5/12	63.90	5/30	63.10	200
1987	5/12	66.95	6/01	66.90	12
1988	5/11	94.40	5/31	91.30	775
1989	5/10	122.50	5/30	114.50	2,000
1990	5/10	118.40	5/30	111.50	1,725
1991	5/10	102.25	5/30	96.65	1,400
1992	5/12	101.10	6/01	102.30	−300
1993	5/12	82.25	6/01	80.40	462
1994	5/11	98.00	5/31	103.75	−1,438
1995	5/10	124.25	5/31	130.50	−1,563
1996	5/10	124.50	5/30	115.50	2,250
1997	5/12	113.30	5/30	119.10	−1,450
1998	5/12	79.30	6/01	75.95	837
1999	5/12	71.00	6/01	63.50	1,875
2000	5/10	82.85	5/30	81.15	425
2001	5/10	75.95	5/30	76.25	−75
2002	5/10	73.85	5/30	75.20	−338
2003	5/12	75.20	5/30	78.25	−762
2004	5/12	118.75	6/01	129.25	−2,625
2005	5/11	144.25	5/31	145.65	−350
2006	5/10	368.80	5/30	367.40	350
2007	5/10	356.65	5/30	330.35	6,575
2008	5/12	374.95	5/30	360.60	3,587
2009	5/12	208.60	6/01	231.90	−5,825
2010	5/12	318.80	6/01	306.30	3,125
2011	5/11	391.35	5/31	417.75	−6,600
2012	5/10	369.05	5/30	339.00	7,513
				40-Year Gain	$21,350

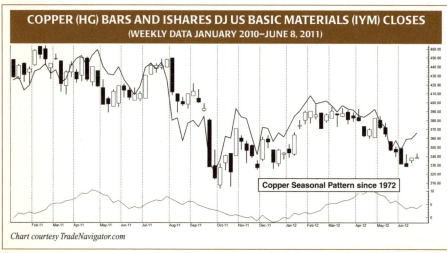

COPPER (HG) BARS AND ISHARES DJ US BASIC MATERIALS (IYM) CLOSES
(WEEKLY DATA JANUARY 2010–JUNE 8, 2011)

Copper Seasonal Pattern since 1972

Chart courtesy TradeNavigator.com

MONDAY

6

When a country lives on borrowed time, borrowed money and borrowed energy, it is just begging the markets to discipline it in their own way at their own time. Usually the markets do it in an orderly way—except when they don't.
— Thomas L. Friedman (*NY Times* Foreign Affairs columnist, , 2/24/05)

TUESDAY

7

What is it that attracts me to the young? When I am with mature people I feel their rigidities, their tight crystallizations. They have become...like the statues of the famous. Achieved. Final.
— Anaïs Nin (*The Diaries of Anaïs Nin, Vol. IV*, 1903–1977)

End Short Wheat(N) (Jan. 4)

WEDNESDAY

8

Interviewer: How is it possible to fight an enemy willing and ready to die for his cause? Accommodate him!
— General Norman Schwartzkof (Ret. commander of allied forces in 1990–1991 Gulf War, December 2001)

End Long Yen(M) (Feb. 8)

THURSDAY

9

We always live in an uncertain world. What is certain is that the United States will go forward over time.
— Warren Buffett (CEO Berkshire Hathaway, investor & philanthropist, CNBC 9/22/2010, b. 1930)

Start Short Copper(N)—62.5% Accuracy Since 1973—End May 30—Page 48

FRIDAY

10

OE: KC

Everything possible today was at one time impossible. Everything impossible today may at some time in the future be possible.
— Edward Lindaman (Apollo space project, president Whitworth College, 1920–1982)

SATURDAY

11

Mother's Day

SUNDAY

12

SILVER SLIPS IN MAY

Silver has a strong tendency to peak or continue lower in May, bottoming in late June. Traders can look to sell silver on or about May 13 and hold until on or about June 24. In the past 39 years, this trade has seen declines 26 times, for a success rate of 66.7%. At press time in mid-June of 2012, this trade was attempting to conform to typical seasonal price declines, but declines could be muted, as silver had already suffered a pullback.

The futures market has, without a doubt, been trading under extremely volatile conditions recently. This type of environment may not be suitable for all traders, especially those who cannot monitor positions closely. There are other products to trade, such as the exchange-traded fund, iShares Silver Trust (SLV), shown in the chart below. Notice the price action is identical on a closing basis between the underlying silver futures contract and SLV.

Each share represents one ounce of silver; the closing price of the ETF will represent, within reason, spot silver. As of June 20, 2012, SLV owned 315,766,825.1 ounces of silver with 325.45 million shares outstanding. Just like every other ETF, there is a premium or discount to net asset value (NAV), which accounts for the difference.

The bottom line of the chart below shows the 40-year historic average seasonal price tendency of silver as well as the decline typically seen from the highs in February until the lows are posted in late June into early July. This May silver short trade captures the tail end of silver's weak seasonal period. See pages 131–137 for additional correlated trades.

MAY SHORT SILVER (JULY) TRADING DAY: 10–HOLD: 29 DAYS				
	ENTRY		EXIT	PROFIT/
YEAR	DATE	CLOSE	DATE	CLOSE	LOSS
1973	5/14	246.2	6/25	268.3	–$1,105
1974	5/14	584.0	6/25	462.3	6,085
1975	5/14	462.7	6/25	455.2	375
1976	5/14	453.8	6/25	473.5	–985
1977	5/13	479.6	6/24	446.8	1,640
1978	5/12	508.8	6/23	531.6	–1,140
1979	5/14	848.5	6/25	870.5	–1,100
1980	5/14	1315.0	6/25	1575.0	–13,000
1981	5/14	1114.0	6/25	948.0	8,300
1982	5/14	689.0	6/25	517.5	8,575
1983	5/13	1331.0	6/24	1227.0	5,200
1984	5/14	895.5	6/25	834.5	3,050
1985	5/14	664.0	6/25	615.5	2,425
1986	5/14	508.0	6/25	511.0	–150
1987	5/14	887.0	6/25	685.5	10,075
1988	5/13	670.0	6/24	681.0	–550
1989	5/12	561.0	6/23	533.8	1,360
1990	5/14	512.5	6/25	482.2	1,515
1991	5/14	407.8	6/25	437.5	–1,485
1992	5/14	412.3	6/25	400.3	600
1993	5/14	446.3	6/25	449.0	–135
1994	5/13	543.5	6/24	540.0	175
1995	5/12	535.2	6/23	535.5	–15
1996	5/14	540.0	6/25	514.7	1,265
1997	5/14	483.8	6/25	475.5	415
1998	5/14	556.0	6/25	533.5	1,125
1999	5/14	539.0	6/25	506.5	1,625
2000	5/12	505.8	6/23	495.8	500
2001	5/14	435.7	6/25	429.8	295
2002	5/14	460.7	6/25	483.2	–1,125
2003	5/14	487.2	6/25	456.5	1,535
2004	5/14	572.8	6/28	589.8	–850
2005	5/13	694.0	6/24	728.0	–1,700
2006	5/12	1423.5	6/23	1028.5	19,750
2007	5/14	1323.5	6/26	1228.0	4,775
2008	5/14	1661.3	6/25	1650.3	550
2009	5/14	1404.0	6/25	1400.5	175
2010	5/14	1922.5	6/25	1911.0	575
2011	5/13	3501.3	6/24	3463.8	1,875
			39-Year Gain		**$60,495**

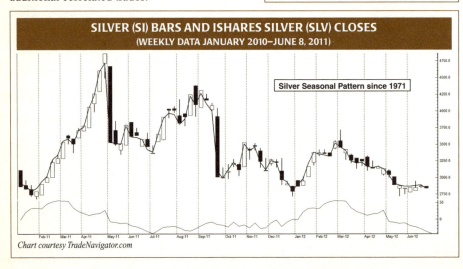

SILVER (SI) BARS AND ISHARES SILVER (SLV) CLOSES
(WEEKLY DATA JANUARY 2010–JUNE 8, 2011)

Silver Seasonal Pattern since 1971

Chart courtesy TradeNavigator.com

MAY

End Long Crude Oil(N) (Feb. 14)
End Long Heating Oil(N) (Feb. 12)

MONDAY
13

A cynic is a man who knows the price of everything and the value of nothing.
— Oscar Wilde (Irish-born writer and wit, 1845–1900)

Start Short Silver(N)—66.7% Accuracy Since 1973—End Jun. 25—Page 50

TUESDAY
14

LT: C, S, W, LH
OE: LH

Bear markets don't act like a medicine ball rolling down a smooth hill. Instead, they behave like a basketball bouncing down a rock-strewn mountainside; there's lots of movement up and sideways before the bottom is reached.
— Daniel Turov (*Turov on Timing, Barron's* May 21, 2001, b. 1947)

WEDNESDAY
15

LT: CC
OE: SB

Marx's great achievement was to place the system of capitalism on the defensive.
— Charles A. Madison (1977)

THURSDAY
16

OE: CL

What investors really get paid for is holding dogs. Small stocks tend to have higher average returns than big stocks, and value stocks tend to have higher average returns than growth stocks.
— Kenneth R. French (Economist, Dartmouth, NBER, b. 1954)

FRIDAY
17

OE: SP

Everyone blames the foreigners when the economy goes south. Always. It is human nature to blame others, and it is the same all over the world.
— Jim Rogers (Financier, *Adventure Capitalist*, b. 1942)

SATURDAY
18

SUNDAY
19

COFFEE BUZZ FADES IN SUMMER

Coffee typically posts a seasonal high in May. This creates coffee's most powerful seasonal play under normal weather conditions, which means a lack of frost in the Southern Hemisphere growing regions of Columbia and Brazil. Traders should look to sell short on or about May 22 and hold through August 8. This trade has worked 27 out of last 38 years with a 71.1% success rate.

However, this trade did not fare so well in 2006, 2007, and 2010. An explanation as to why this market defied the seasonal tendency to decline in this time period was that there was a lack of rain during the key flower pollination stage, resulting in a much smaller crop than expected in Brazil back in 2007. Trade estimates were looking for 50 million kg bags of production, but according to forecasts, that estimate backed down to 45 million kg bags of production. So in essence, supply declined due to poor weather conditions, while demand remained steady. Tight supplies and a falling dollar supported coffee in 2010 through early 2011.

Traders can sell futures or implement a bearish option position. As for other trading opportunities, the chart below shows the coffeehouse and distributor Starbucks' (SBUX) price line overlaid on the bar chart of coffee.

When coffee declines, historically we have seen a price increase for shares of (SBUX). The reverse is also true. If coffee prices have been up strong on or about May 22, and if SBUX is near its yearly or monthly lows, then traders may want to look to buy shares of SBUX or consider call options. See pages 131–137 for additional correlated trades.

MAY SHORT COFFEE (SEPTEMBER) TRADING DAY: 16–HOLD: 54 DAYS					
	ENTRY		EXIT		PROFIT/
YEAR	DATE	CLOSE	DATE	CLOSE	LOSS
1974	5/22	75.50	8/08	62.50	$4,875
1975	5/22	56.14	8/08	84.80	−10,748
1976	5/24	136.95	8/10	147.65	−4,013
1977	5/23	305.25	8/10	205.11	37,553
1978	5/22	153.11	8/08	126.69	9,908
1979	5/22	156.62	80/8	197.29	−15,251
1980	5/22	209.42	8/08	138.77	26,494
1981	5/22	115.82	8/10	117.32	−563
1982	5/24	119.46	8/10	126.86	−2,775
1983	5/23	127.75	8/09	126.17	592
1984	5/22	154.09	8/08	141.71	4,643
1985	5/22	146.81	8/09	134.68	4,549
1986	5/22	215.18	8/11	170.90	16,605
1987	5/22	123.23	8/10	103.80	7,286
1988	5/23	133.85	8/09	118.34	5,816
1989	5/22	128.59	8/08	83.03	17,085
1990	5/22	99.11	8/08	91.85	2,723
1991	5/22	89.05	8/09	81.15	2,963
1992	5/22	65.50	8/10	53.25	4,594
1993	5/24	63.25	8/10	74.95	−4,388
1994	5/23	136.65	8/09	182.30	−17,119
1995	5/22	165.10	8/09	144.75	7,631
1996	5/22	119.60	8/09	115.10	1,688
1997	5/22	229.95	8/08	205.85	9,038
1998	5/22	134.00	8/10	134.20	−75
1999	5/24	120.50	8/10	93.75	10,031
2000	5/22	105.80	8/09	79.50	9,863
2001	5/22	67.90	8/08	49.65	6,844
2002	5/22	53.40	8/09	47.55	2,194
2003	5/22	68.00	8/08	63.70	1,613
2004	5/24	78.75	8/11	67.10	4,369
2005	5/23	121.15	8/09	102.60	6,956
2006	5/22	102.50	8/08	107.10	−1,725
2007	5/22	114.30	8/09	119.50	−1,950
2008	5/22	136.60	8/11	135.85	281
2009	5/22	136.90	8/10	135.85	394
2010	5/24	133.65	8/10	169.65	−13,500
2011	5/23	265.50	8/09	234.75	11,531
				38-Year Gain	$146,010

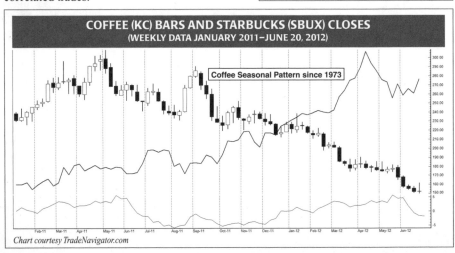

COFFEE (KC) BARS AND STARBUCKS (SBUX) CLOSES
(WEEKLY DATA JANUARY 2011–JUNE 20, 2012)

Coffee Seasonal Pattern since 1973

Chart courtesy TradeNavigator.com

MAY

MONDAY
20
LT: KC

I was in search of a one-armed economist so that the guy could never make a statement and then say: "on the other hand."
— Harry S. Truman (33rd U.S. President, 1884–1972)

TUESDAY
21
LT: CL

The dissenter (or "contrary investor") is every human at those moments of his life when he resigns momentarily from the herd and thinks for himself.
— Archibald MacLeish (American poet, writer and political activist, 1892–1982)

Start Short Coffee(U)—71.1% Accuracy Since 1974—End Aug. 8—Page 52

WEDNESDAY
22

Make money and the whole nation will conspire to call you a gentleman.
— George Bernard Shaw (Irish dramatist, 1856–1950)

THURSDAY
23
FN: CL

If you create an act, you create a habit. If you create a habit, you create a character. If you create a character, you create a destiny.
— André Maurois (Novelist, biographer, essayist, 1885–1967)

FRIDAY
24
OE: US, C, S, W

There's no trick to being a humorist when you have the whole government working for you.
— Will Rogers (American humorist and showman, 1879–1935)

SATURDAY
25

SUNDAY
26

JUNE ALMANAC

JUNE

S	M	T	W	T	F	S
						1
2	3	4	5	6	7	8
9	10	11	12	13	14	15
16	17	18	19	20	21	22
23	24	25	26	27	28	29
30						

JULY

S	M	T	W	T	F	S
	1	2	3	4	5	6
7	8	9	10	11	12	13
14	15	16	17	18	19	20
21	22	23	24	25	26	27
28	29	30	31			

◆ STOCKS AND BONDS

S&P's often exhibit weakenss mid- to end-of-month, especially after June's quarterly quadruple witching, as illustrated in our seasonal chart (page 138). 30-year Treasury bond prices are weak in June, but tend to recover towards the end of the month from early month losses. Watch for this mid-month reversal, especially when stocks start to make an end-of-month selloff. Buy bonds on second trading day and hold for 10 days. This has a 67.6% win probability with 23 wins in 34 years (page 125). We are still holding onto our top seasonal long from April until late August (page 42).

◆ ENERGY

Seasonally, this is still one of the best seven months, March to September, to be long crude oil. However, June tends to see price consolidations after major price moves in May (page 143). Natural gas prices tend to move lower in June until mid-July, when we typically see the market make its average seasonal low (page 68). Heating oil prices continue to remain in a seasonally weak period, but if we see early-month-weakness prices can post short-term bottoms at month end lasting into mid-July.

◆ METALS

Most years gold prices continue in a downtrend, as it is in its seasonally weak price period until July–August (page 78). Cover short silver position from May 14 on or about June 25 (page 50). Copper tends to have counter seasonal rallies in June (page 149).

◆ GRAINS

Soybeans' seasonal peak, sell on June 7; hold until end of July (page 56). Wheat often makes a seasonal low in June. Enter long position around June 10 and exit near November 6 (page 125). Corn is in the middle of seasonal decline, especially in normal or above-average weather conditions. Enter short positions by selling on or about June 26 and holding through the end of July. The last 42 years, this trade has worked 64.3% of the time, for a cumulative profit of $25,506 (page 62).

◆ SOFTS

Enter new long cocoa position on or about June 4; exit on or about July 9. This trade worked 25 of 39 years for cumulative profits of $16,380 (page 125). Coffee continues its downtrend, as it is in the seasonally weak price period (page 52). Sugar tends to post a seasonal low in June, giving us a sweet long trade through the end of July (page 58).

◆ MEATS

This is seasonally the best time to go long cattle. Short-term traders can buy the August contract, and for our top seasonal longer-term play, traders can enter a long position in the April contract of the following year on or about June 20 and exit around February 7. 66.7% win probability; cumulative profits are $41,320 (page 60). Hogs continue their downtrend, as they are in their seasonally weak price period (page 179).

◆ CURRENCIES

The euro tends to trend lower into the end of the third quarter (page 185). Swiss francs generally move lower into August (page 187). Cover short British pound position from May 29 on or about June 10 (page 46). In the past 36 years, reversing positions and going long on or about June 28 and holding into late July has produced 26 years of successful trades, for a success rate of 70.3%. The cumulative profit is $31,831 (page 125). The yen tends to trend lower into August (page 190).

JUNE STRATEGY CALENDAR*

Symbol	B	M	E
SP	L / S		
US	L / S		
CL	L / S		
NG	L / S		
HO	L / S		
HG	L / S		
GC	L / S		
SI	L / S		
C	L / S		
S	L / S		
W	L / S		
CC	L / S		
KC	L / S		
SB	L / S		
LC	L / S		
LH	L / S		
BP	L / S		
EC	L / S		
SF	L / S		
JY	L / S		

*Graphic representation of the Commodity Seasonality Percentage Plays on pages 124–125.
L = Long Trade, S = Short Trade. See pages 131–137 for contract symbols.

54

MAY/JUNE

Memorial Day (Market Closed)

Experience is helpful, but it is judgment that matters.
— General Colin Powell (Chairman Joint Chiefs 1989–93, Secretary of State 2001–05, *NY Times* 10/22/2008, b. 1937)

TUESDAY

28

OE: HO, NG, HG, GC, SI

With respect to trading Sugar futures, if they give it away for free at restaurants you probably don't want to be trading it.
— John L. Person (Professional trader, author, speaker, *Commodity Trader's Almanac*, nationalfutures.com, 2/22/2011 TradersExpo, b. 1961)

Start Short British Pound(U)—64.9% Accuracy Since 1975—End Jun. 10—Page 124

WEDNESDAY

29

LT: NG, HG, GC, SI

There is a habitual nature to society and human activity. People's behavior and what they do with their money and time bears upon economics and the stock market.
— Jeffrey A. Hirsch (Editor, *Stock Trader's Almanac*, b. 1966)

End Long Soybeans(N) (Feb. 13)
End Short Copper(N) (May 10)

THURSDAY

30

FN: NG

The market can stay irrational longer than you can stay solvent.
— John Maynard Keynes (British economist, 1883–1946)

FRIDAY

31

FN: US, HG, GC, SI
LT: HO
OE: CC, LC

So at last I was going to America! Really, really going, at last! The boundaries burst. The arch of heaven soared! A million suns shone out for every star. The winds rushed in from outer space, roaring in my ears, "America! America!"
— Mary Antin (1881–1949, Immigrant writer, *The Promised Land*, 1912)

SATURDAY

1

SUNDAY

2

SHORT SOYBEANS
FOR SUMMER

After planting season has finished through the bean belt of Illinois and up through Minnesota, soybeans tend to post a seasonal peak. Once the crop is actually planted, the fear of a reduced crop size due to planting delays from late spring storms has abated. When the crop is in the ground, traders start focusing on the potential size of the new crop. In addition, supplies are available from the South American harvest, and this puts additional pressure on prices.

By mid-June, we have a good understanding of the crop size due to what was planted. Under ideal weather conditions, traders tend to sell the market, as producers and grain elevators start hedging or forward contracting out their crops production. This marketing effort can last through harvest time.

The genetically modified (GMO) seed, Roundup Ready by Monsanto (MON), is more resistant than ever to insects and drought or heat stress. In addition, there has been more worldwide acceptance of this technology. U.S. farmers have increased usage and production to over 85% of this variety. This may explain why, under normal weather growing years, prices tend to decline, as there is a better estimate of the crop size.

The chart below shows the price line of the fertilizer company Mosaic (MOS) overlaid on the bar chart of soybeans. Traders looking to capture moves in soybeans may want to explore taking out positions in companies such as Mosaic that tend to correlate to the commodity's seasonal price moves. See pages 131–137 for additional correlated trades.

JUNE SHORT SOYBEANS (SEPTEMBER) TRADING DAY: 5–HOLD: 36 DAYS					
	ENTRY		EXIT		PROFIT/
YEAR	DATE	CLOSE	DATE	CLOSE	LOSS
1970	6/5	266 1/4	7/28	286	−988
1971	6/7	310 1/2	7/28	331 1/4	−1,038
1972	6/7	339 3/4	7/28	337 1/2	113
1973	6/7	853	8/01	872	−950
1974	6/7	537 1/2	7/30	865	−16,375
1975	6/6	478	7/29	627	−7,450
1976	6/7	609	7/28	631 1/2	−1,125
1977	6/7	832 1/2	7/28	577 1/4	12,763
1978	6/7	666 1/2	7/28	621 3/4	2,238
1979	6/7	753	7/30	711	2,100
1980	6/6	631 1/2	7/29	762 1/4	−6,538
1981	6/5	727 3/4	7/28	746 1/2	−938
1982	6/7	642 1/2	7/28	602 3/4	1,988
1983	6/7	626	7/28	720	−4,700
1984	6/7	755 1/4	7/30	609 1/2	7,288
1985	6/7	580 3/4	7/30	519 1/4	3,075
1986	6/6	513	7/29	503 1/2	475
1987	6/5	570	7/28	534 3/4	1,763
1988	6/7	886 1/2	7/28	748 1/2	6,900
1989	6/7	647 3/4	7/28	604 1/4	2,175
1990	6/7	612 1/4	7/30	593 3/4	925
1991	6/7	587 1/4	7/30	580	363
1992	6/5	614 1/2	7/28	559 3/4	2,738
1993	6/7	587 3/4	7/28	690	−5,113
1994	6/7	646	7/28	572 1/2	3,675
1995	6/7	602 1/2	7/28	627	−1,225
1996	6/7	752 1/2	7/30	744 3/4	388
1997	6/6	720 1/2	7/29	675 1/2	2,250
1998	6/5	586 1/2	7/28	572	725
1999	6/7	473	7/28	424 1/4	2,438
2000	6/7	526 3/4	7/28	447 3/4	3,950
2001	6/7	447 1/4	7/30	504	−2,838
2002	6/7	484 1/2	7/30	531 1/2	−2,350
2003	6/6	602 1/2	7/29	527 1/4	3,763
2004	6/7	718	7/29	590	6,400
2005	6/7	679 3/4	7/28	689	−463
2006	6/7	610 1/2	7/28	584	1,325
2007	6/7	847	7/30	831	800
2008	6/6	1446 1/2	7/30	1395 1/2	2,550
2009	6/5	1101	7/28	968	6,650
2010	6/7	904 1/4	7/28	985	−4,038
2011	6/7	1387	7/28	1362 1/2	1,225
				42-Year Gain	$24,913

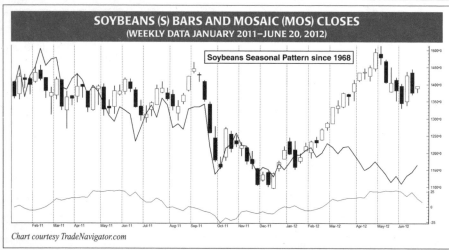

SOYBEANS (S) BARS AND MOSAIC (MOS) CLOSES
(WEEKLY DATA JANUARY 2011–JUNE 20, 2012)

Soybeans Seasonal Pattern since 1968

Chart courtesy TradeNavigator.com

MONDAY

3

If you live each day as if it was your last, someday you'll most certainly be right.
— Favorite quote of Steve Jobs (CEO Apple & Pixar, Stanford University commencement address, 6/15/05)

TUESDAY

4

FN: HO

End Long S&P 500(U) (Apr. 24)
Start Long 30-Year Bond(U)—67.6% Accuracy Since 1978—End Jun. 18—Page 125
Start Long Cocoa(U)—64.1% Accuracy Since 1973—End Jul. 9—Page 125

I'm not better than the next trader, just quicker at admitting my mistakes and moving on to the next opportunity.
— George Soros (Financier, philanthropist, political activist, author and philosopher, b. 1930)

WEDNESDAY

5

When Amercia sneezes, the rest of the word catches cold.
— Anonymous (circa 1929)

THURSDAY

6

In nature there are no rewards or punishments; there are consequences.
— Horace Annesley Vachell (English writer, *The Face of Clay*, 1861–1955)

FRIDAY

7

OE: CC, LC, BP, EC, SF, JY

Start Short Soybeans Peak(U)—64.3% Accuracy Since 1970—End Jul. 30—Page 56

If you are ready to give up everything else – to study the whole history and background of the market and all the principal companies… as carefully as a medical student studies anatomy – … and, in addition, you have the cool nerves of a great gambler, the sixth sense of a clairvoyant, and the courage of a lion, you have a ghost of a chance.
— Bernard Baruch (Financier, speculator, statesman, presidential adviser, 1870–1965)

SATURDAY

8

SUNDAY

9

SUGAR'S SUMMER SWEET SPOT

Due to the many regions on the planet that produce sugar, it goes through several seasonal price swings. However, it makes a sweet tradable seasonal low in mid-June. Sugarcane harvesting in the tropics and sugar beet planting in the Northern Hemisphere in the May/June time frame create uncertainty as to the size of the coming sugar crop, and prices tend to rally.

Over the past 37 years, going long sugar on or about June 17 and holding for about 32 days has delivered gains 23 times, for a success rate of 61.2% and a total gain of $20,026. A worldwide bull market in sugar, due to heavy demand from ethanol and some adverse (wet) weather conditions, pushed sugar prices to all-time highs in early 2011. This contributed to sizeable gains for this trade in the past five years straight.

Granted this trade worked very well the past several year, however, using trailing stops and managing this trade would have given traders even more bang. Our 2011 exit date trade price was 28.97, but the contracts actual closing high was not reached until August 19 at 30.96.

Using technical timing tools can not only get you into this trade at more profitable entry points, but more importantly, they can help you increase gains by keeping you in a winning trade longer during strong bullish trends. It is crucial to implement technical trading techniques in conjunction with seasonal patterns.

Alternatively, you can the ETN, iPath DJ-UBS Sugar (SGG). IPSU stock price sticks closely to sugar prices throughout the year. The chart below shows direct correlation between SGG and sugar, with sugar's seasonal price pattern since 1972 in the bottom section. See pages 131–137 for additional correlated trades.

	ENTRY		EXIT		PROFIT/
YEAR	**DATE**	**CLOSE**	**DATE**	**CLOSE**	**LOSS**
1975	6/16	12.34	7/31	16.54	$4,704
1976	6/15	13.63	7/30	12.42	−1,355
1977	6/15	8.52	8/2	8.09	−482
1978	6/15	7.18	8/1	6.41	−862
1979	6/15	8.95	8/1	8.91	−45
1980	6/16	35.86	7/31	30.62	−5,869
1981	6/15	15.83	7/30	16.64	907
1982	6/15	7.23	7/30	7.72	549
1983	6/15	11.26	8/1	12.08	918
1984	6/15	6.10	8/1	4.53	−1,758
1985	6/17	3.16	8/2	4.79	1,826
1986	6/16	6.81	8/1	6.49	−358
1987	6/15	7.22	7/30	5.95	−1,422
1988	6/15	9.84	8/1	11.63	2,005
1989	6/15	12.71	8/1	14.12	1,579
1990	6/15	12.50	8/1	10.55	−2,184
1991	6/17	8.73	8/2	9.59	963
1992	6/15	9.85	7/30	9.48	−414
1993	6/15	11.17	7/30	9.36	−2,027
1994	6/15	12.41	8/1	11.70	−795
1995	6/15	10.29	8/2	10.56	302
1996	6/17	11.23	8/2	11.71	538
1997	6/16	11.28	7/31	11.68	448
1998	6/15	7.84	7/30	8.84	1,120
1999	6/15	5.61	7/30	5.98	414
2000	6/15	8.50	8/2	10.79	2,565
2001	6/15	8.72	8/1	7.91	−907
2002	6/17	5.02	8/2	5.78	851
2003	6/16	6.42	7/31	7.21	885
2004	6/16	7.58	8/2	8.39	907
2005	6/15	8.78	8/1	9.96	1,322
2006	6/15	15.33	8/1	14.90	−482
2007	6/15	8.98	8/1	10.28	1,456
2008	6/16	12.27	8/1	14.13	2,083
2009	6/15	15.90	7/30	18.75	3,192
2010	6/15	15.95	7/30	19.57	4,054
2011	6/15	24.15	8/1	28.97	$5,398
				37-Year Gain	**$20,026**

**JUNE LONG SUGAR (OCTOBER)
TRADING DAY: 11–HOLD: 32 DAYS**

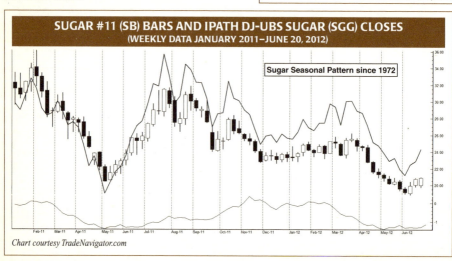

SUGAR #11 (SB) BARS AND IPATH DJ-UBS SUGAR (SGG) CLOSES
(WEEKLY DATA JANUARY 2011–JUNE 20, 2012)

Sugar Seasonal Pattern since 1972

Chart courtesy TradeNavigator.com

JUNE

End Short British Pound(U) (May 29)
Start Long Wheat(Z)—54.8% Accuracy Since 1970—End Nov. 6—Page 125

MONDAY
10
FN: LC

It isn't the incompetent who destroy an organization. It is those who have achieved something and want to rest upon their achievements who are forever clogging things up.
— Charles E. Sorenson (Danish-American engineer, officer, director of Ford Motor Co. 1907–1950, helped develop 1st auto assembly line, 1881–1968)

TUESDAY
11

When investment decisions need to consider the speed of light, something is seriously wrong.
— Frank M. Bifulco (Senior Portfolio Manager Alcott Capital Management, *Barron's Letters to the Editor*, 5/24/2010)

WEDNESDAY
12

The best minds are not in government. If any were, business would hire them away.
— Ronald Reagan (40th U.S. President, 1911–2004)

THURSDAY
13
OE: KC

There is a perfect inverse correlation between inflation rates and price/earnings ratios...When inflation has been very high...P/E has been [low].
— Liz Ann Sonders (Chief Investment Strategist Charles Schwab, June 2006)

End Short Cattle(V) (May 2)

FRIDAY
14
LT: LH
OE: LH

Government is like fire—useful when used legitimately, but dangerous when not.
— David Brooks (*NY Times* columnist, 10/5/07)

SATURDAY
15

Father's Day

SUNDAY
16

SUMMER BBQ SEASON GIVES BEEF A BOUNCE

This is seasonally the best time to buy live cattle. Fundamentally, beef consumption starts to decline in hot weather, but so does supply, as feed lots are short on inventory. Cash grain prices tend to remain high, as supply decreases before harvest season. This supply/demand imbalance creates a bid under the market. Then before school season begins, federal government subsidies for school lunch programs kick in for beef purchases.

As winter and the holiday season approach, consumption increases. This helps keep a floor of support in cattle futures through mid-February (page 176). Enter long positions on or about June 20; then exit on or about February 7. Out of the past 42 years, this trade has worked 28 times for a 66.7% success rate.

The chart below has McDonald's (MCD) closing prices overlaid on the front contract live cattle futures, with the seasonal price move of the futures on the bottom. It is interesting to note that while beef has a tendency to rise from June through August, MCD has a tendency to decline during this same time period on average since 1970. In recent years, this relationship has been less pronounced due to MCD's global growth success.

Traders may want to look at long futures strategies on beef in June, and stock traders certainly want to look for companies that would benefit, or in this case, see price weakness due to a commodity market move, such as this inverse relationship between MCD and beef prices. See pages 131–137 for additional correlated trades.

JUNE LONG LIVE CATTLE (APRIL)
TRADING DAY: 14–HOLD: 160 DAYS

YEAR	ENTRY DATE	ENTRY CLOSE	EXIT DATE	EXIT CLOSE	PROFIT/ LOSS
1970	6/18	29.400	2/05	32.050	$1,060
1971	6/18	31.450	2/04	34.750	1,320
1972	6/20	35.250	2/12	43.775	3,410
1973	6/20	46.525	2/07	50.850	1,730
1974	6/20	37.000	2/07	36.150	−340
1975	6/19	41.050	2/06	39.175	−750
1976	6/18	45.975	2/07	39.075	−2,760
1977	6/20	42.050	2/07	44.250	880
1978	6/20	53.475	2/08	66.250	5,110
1979	6/20	69.650	2/07	71.175	610
1980	6/19	67.300	2/09	67.925	250
1981	6/18	68.750	2/04	63.200	−2,220
1982	6/18	59.525	2/03	62.150	1,050
1983	6/20	60.800	2/07	67.600	2,720
1984	6/20	65.600	2/06	68.200	1,040
1985	6/20	64.200	2/06	60.600	−1,440
1986	6/19	54.650	2/05	63.300	3,460
1987	6/18	65.525	2/04	70.925	2,160
1988	6/20	73.350	2/06	76.450	1,240
1989	6/20	73.600	2/06	77.275	1,470
1990	6/20	76.125	2/06	77.875	700
1991	6/20	75.700	2/06	77.675	790
1992	6/18	70.650	2/04	77.900	2,900
1993	6/18	75.925	2/03	74.350	−630
1994	6/20	70.975	2/06	73.975	1,200
1995	6/20	64.550	2/06	64.175	−150
1996	6/20	66.200	2/06	65.925	−110
1997	6/19	72.520	2/06	65.770	−2,700
1998	6/18	68.850	2/05	67.750	−4400
1999	6/18	69.100	2/07	72.750	1,460
2000	6/20	75.325	2/07	78.800	1,390
2001	6/20	76.750	2/11	75.975	−310
2002	6/20	69.600	2/10	77.900	3,320
2003	7/21	75.875	3/09	79.425	1,420
2004	6/21	86.250	2/08	88.800	1,020
2005	6/20	85.350	2/07	89.775	1,770
2006	6/20	87.100	2/08	94.875	3,110
2007	6/20	97.525	2/07	96.050	−590
2008	6/19	116.750	2/09	87.750	−11,600
2009	6/18	91.175	2/05	90.400	−310
2010	6/18	94.850	2/04	133.025	15,270
2011	6/20	119.500	2/08	128.800	3,720
				42-Year Gain	**$41,230**

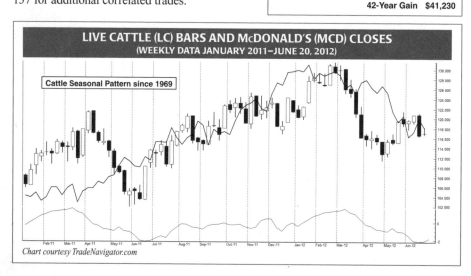

LIVE CATTLE (LC) BARS AND McDONALD'S (MCD) CLOSES
(WEEKLY DATA JANUARY 2011–JUNE 20, 2012)

Cattle Seasonal Pattern since 1969

Chart courtesy TradeNavigator.com

JUNE

Start Long Sugar(V)—62.2% Accuracy Since 1975—End Aug. 1—Page 58

MONDAY

17

FN: CC
LT: BP, EC, SF, JY
OE: CL, SB

The government would not look fondly on Caesar's Palace if it opened a table for wagering on corporate failure. It should not give greater encouragement for Goldman Sachs [et al] to do so.
— Roger Lowenstein (Financial journalist and author, *End of Wall Street, NY Times* OpEd 4/20/2010, b. 1954)

End Long 30-Year Bond(U) (Jun. 4)

TUESDAY

18

A senior European diplomat said he was convinced that the choice of starting a war this spring was made for political as well as military reasons. [The President] clearly does not want to have a war raging on the eve of his presumed reelection campaign.
— Reported by Steven R. Weisman (*NY Times* 3/14/03)

WEDNESDAY

19

LT: US

Six words that spell business success: create concept, communicate concept, sustain momentum.
— Yale Hirsch (Creator of *Stock Trader's Almanac*, b. 1923)

Start Long Cattle(J)—66.7% Accuracy Since 1970—End Feb. 7 , 2014—Page 60

THURSDAY

20

FN: KC
LT: SP, CL
OE: SP

From very early on, I understood that you can touch a piece of paper once…if you touch it twice, you're dead. Therefore, paper only touches my hand once. After that, it's either thrown away, acted on or given to somebody else.
— Manuel Fernandez (Businessman, *Investor's Business Daily*)

FRIDAY

21

OE: US, C, S, W

The knowledge of past times… is both an ornament and nutriment to the human mind.
— Leonardo da Vinci (Italian Renaissance polymath, 1452–1519)

SATURDAY

22

SUNDAY

23

MOTHER NATURE MAKES CORN POP

Corn tends to peak in June under normal crop years, as planting is complete and farmers are looking for cooperation from Mother Nature to produce increased production yields. Look to sell on or about June 26 and hold through August 1. This is when we typically get a "drought scare" or mid-summer rally. The 42-year history of this timing strategy shows a win in 27 of those years, for a success rate of 64.3%.

With the price increase in corn headed into summer, we normally see the market settle back, as farmers have a better idea of their crop size and start to hedge or forward contract sales out to lock in a profit. Depending on the levels of volatility, traders can look to sell futures or buy put options, or once again, look for alternative trading opportunities.

The chart below has Deere & Co. (DE) overlaid with corn prices and the bottom line showing the seasonal tendency of corn prices since 1970. As you can see, there is a high correlation of the price of corn and the share price of DE. One can look to sell DE, buy puts, or write calls in the seasonally weak time frame that starts in June and goes into July. See pages 131–137 for additional correlated trades.

JUNE SHORT CORN (SEPTEMBER)
TRADING DAY: 18–HOLD: 25 DAYS

YEAR	ENTRY DATE	ENTRY CLOSE	EXIT DATE	EXIT CLOSE	PROFIT/LOSS
1970	6/24	133 1/4	7/30	130 5/8	$131
1971	6/24	154 1/4	7/30	132 1/2	1,088
1972	6/26	122 3/8	8/01	126 5/8	−213
1973	6/26	210 1/4	8/01	278	−3,388
1974	6/26	291 3/4	8/01	369 1/2	−3,888
1975	6/25	262 1/2	7/31	287	−1,225
1976	6/24	294 3/4	7/30	280 1/4	725
1977	6/24	228 1/2	8/01	195	1,675
1978	6/26	257 1/4	8/01	225 1/2	1,588
1979	6/26	315 1/4	8/01	288 1/2	1,338
1980	6/25	290 1/2	7/31	335 1/4	−2,238
1981	6/24	347	7/30	335 1/4	588
1982	6/24	271 1/4	7/30	245 3/4	1,275
1983	6/24	304 1/4	8/01	330 1/4	−1,300
1984	6/26	322 1/2	8/01	293 1/4	1,463
1985	6/26	257	8/01	232	1,250
1986	6/25	189 3/4	7/31	165 1/4	1,225
1987	6/24	196 1/2	7/30	162 1/2	1,700
1988	6/24	347 1/2	8/01	290	2,875
1989	6/26	244 1/4	8/01	222 1/2	1,088
1990	6/26	283 3/4	8/01	255 1/2	1,413
1991	6/26	237 1/4	8/01	262 1/2	−1,263
1992	6/24	253 3/4	7/30	221 3/4	1,600
1993	6/24	226 1/4	7/30	235 3/4	−475
1994	6/24	250 1/2	8/01	217 3/4	1,638
1995	6/26	272 1/2	8/01	282 1/2	−500
1996	6/26	388 3/4	8/01	360 1/2	1,413
1997	6/25	242 1/4	7/31	265 1/2	−1,163
1998	6/24	265 3/4	7/30	220 1/4	2,275
1999	6/24	216 1/2	7/30	203 1/4	663
2000	6/26	202 3/4	8/01	179 3/4	1,150
2001	6/26	193 1/4	8/01	215 1/4	−1,100
2002	6/26	229	8/01	249 1/4	−1,013
2003	6/25	234 3/4	7/31	206	1,438
2004	6/25	280 1/2	8/02	218 1/4	3,113
2005	6/24	242	8/01	231 3/4	513
2006	6/26	234 1/2	8/01	240 1/2	−300
2007	6/26	367	8/01	319	2,400
2008	6/25	744 1/2	8/01	565	8,975
2009	6/24	395	7/30	332 1/4	3,138
2010	6/24	353 3/4	7/30	392 3/4	−1,950
2011	6/24	657	8/01	681 1/4	−1,213
				42-Year Gain	**$26,506**

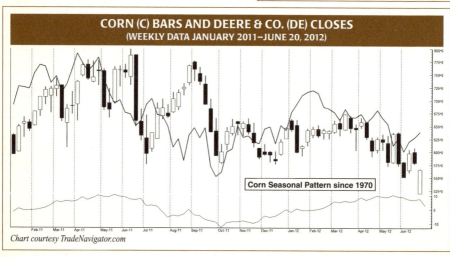

CORN (C) BARS AND DEERE & CO. (DE) CLOSES
(WEEKLY DATA JANUARY 2011–JUNE 20, 2012)

Corn Seasonal Pattern since 1970

Chart courtesy TradeNavigator.com

JUNE

One only gets to the top rung on the ladder by steadily climbing up one at a time, and suddenly all sorts of powers, all sorts of abilities, which you thought never belonged to you-suddenly become within your own possibility....
— Margaret Thatcher (British, prime minister, 1979–1990, b. 1925)

End Short Silver(N) (May 14)

I have noticed over the years the difficulty some people have in cutting losses, admitting an error, and moving on. I am rather frequently—and on occasion, quite spectacularly—wrong. However, if we expect to be wrong, then there should be no ego tied up in admitting the error, honoring the stop loss, selling the loser—and preserving your capital.
— Barry L. Ritholtz (CEO Fusion IQ, *Bailout Nation*, The Big Picture blog, 8/12/2010, b. 1961)

Start Short Corn(U)—64.3% Accuracy Since 1970—End Aug. 1—Page 62

Regulatory agencies within five years become controlled by industries they were set up to regulate.
— Gabriel Kolko

If you can buy more of your best idea, why put [the money] into your 10th-best idea or your 20th-best idea? The more positions you have, the more average you are.
— Bruce Berkowitz (Fairholme Fund, *Barron's* 3/17/08)

Start Long British Pound(U)—70.3% Accuracy Since 1975—End Jul. 23—Page 125

War is God's way of teaching Americans geography.
— Ambrose Bierce (Writer, satirist, Civil War hero, *The Devil's Dictionary*, 1842–1914?)

JULY ALMANAC

JULY						
S	M	T	W	T	F	S
	1	2	3	4	5	6
7	8	9	10	11	12	13
14	15	16	17	18	19	20
21	22	23	24	25	26	27
28	29	30	31			

◆ STOCKS AND BONDS

S&P 500 tends to see follow-through weakness in July. Tech stocks generally sell off in July, as this month marks the start of the NASDAQ's worst four months. This weakness weighs on the performance of the S&P 500. In the last 30-year history, selling September S&P 500 on or about the 10th trading day and holding for 7 trading days has reaped a cumulative profit of $44,488, with 19 wins, but 6 losses the last 7 years (page 66). Weakness prevails from month end through October (page 138). 30-year Treasury bond prices are flat to weak, but have tendencies to rally, especially when stocks take a sharp nose dive in July.

AUGUST						
S	M	T	W	T	F	S
				1	2	3
4	5	6	7	8	9	10
11	12	13	14	15	16	17
18	19	20	21	22	23	24
25	26	27	28	29	30	31

◆ ENERGY

Crude oil continues to stay supportive during the month of July. Seasonally, this is one of the best months to get long natural gas. Buy November natural gas futures on or about July 24 and hold until about October 21. In the past 22 years, this trade has worked 12 times, for a success rate of 54.5%. The cumulative profit totals $21,720. Though since it's best gain in 2005 this trade has been a big loser 5 of the last 6 years (page 68). Over the last five years heating oil prices have a tendency to decline from mid-month into early October (page 147). Refineries shutting down for maintenance can create occasional price spikes.

◆ METALS

Seasonally, the end of July begins a strong price period for gold until early October (page 152). Silver can follow gold's strength in July (page 155). Copper prices tend to make counter-seasonal uptrends in July, as summer construction season is underway (page 149).

◆ GRAINS

Soybeans are seasonally in a weak period; cover the short position from June (page 56) on or about July 30. Soybeans can remain weak under normal weather markets until the harvest lows in late October (page 94), but as August approaches, hot, dry weather conditions can create a panic short-covering rally. Wheat remains in a strong uptrend after harvest lows are posted in June (page 125). Even though corn is in a seasonally weak time period, there are times when we see counter-seasonal rallies due to weather scares. Look at the past history of price moves in corn (page 158). End-of-month weakness in corn prices gives us an opportunity to cover the short corn position from June (page 62).

◆ SOFTS

Liquidate long cocoa trades from June on or about July 9 (page 125). This is also the month to reverse the position toward the end of the month. Seasonally, we see downturns lasting into early November. Short December cocoa on or about July 25 and hold until around November 1 (page 76). Coffee prices tend to remain under pressure until early August when we have a best seasonal trade (page 74). Sugar prices tend to be choppy during the month of July, as the market is trying to post a seasonal low (page 173). This is the peak harvest time in Brazil and India.

◆ MEATS

Seasonally, this is a strong price period for live cattle until February (page 176). We are holding a long position from June (page 60). Lean hogs are in a seasonally weak period until late October to early November (page 179).

◆ CURRENCIES

The euro tends to consolidate into early September. July can produce rallies (page 185), but the overall trend remains down against the dollar. The Swiss franc seasonally enters a strong period, since this currency correlates well with gold's price moves and gold is strong in this period. Traders may want to watch this relationship between gold and the Swiss franc. August tends to produce the best seasonal trades (page 70) for the "Swissie". Exit the British pound long position from June (page 125) on or about July 23. The yen continues to historically show weakness through the early part of August (page 190).

JULY STRATEGY CALENDAR*

Symbol		B	M	E
SP	L–S			
US	L–S			
CL	L–S			
NG	L–S			
HO	L–S			
HG	L–S			
GC	L–S			
SI	L–S			
C	L–S			
S	L–S			
W	L–S			
CC	L–S			
KC	L–S			
SB	L–S			
LC	L–S			
LH	L–S			
BP	L–S			
EC	L–S			
SF	L–S			
JY	L–S			

*Graphic representation of the Commodity Seasonality Percentage Plays on pages 124–125.
L = Long Trade, S = Short Trade. See pages 131–137 for contract symbols.*

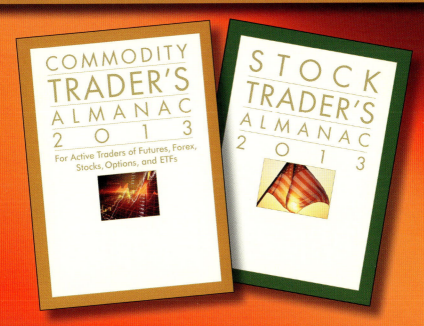

The perfect companion to *Stock Trader's Almanac*

CAPITALIZE ON POST-ELECTION YEAR MARKET TRENDS

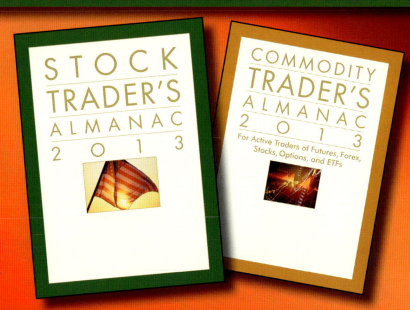

PROVEN RESULTS YEAR AFTER YEAR.

Your Guide to the 2013 market, economy and political environment, including key insights into the post- election year markets:

- Based on history, understand the impact of the 2012 presidential and congressional elections on the stock market.
- Learn why the Dow has posted full-year gains in only 9 of 19 post-election years when a sitting president had just completed his re-election bid.
- Discover why the historically best scenario for all investors has been a Democrat in the White House and Republican control of Congress with average gains of 19.5%.
- Understand why more times than not, difficult tasks are not begun until after the Inaugural Ball which frequently impact the market negatively.

Plus...

- New tactics for implementing the Best Six Months Strategies with ETFs and mutual funds, renowned as one of the best indicators of the market's direction.

As a loyal and valued *Commodity Trader's Almanac* reader you will receive **20% off your 2013 Stock Trader's Almanac purchase!**

ORDER TODAY!

Visit www.wiley.com or call 1800 356 5016 to place your order. (Reference code CTA13)

JULY

MONDAY

1

FN: SB

Establish a no excuse environment – you will find your own quality will increase as well.
— Jordan Kimmel (Portfolio manager Magnet AE Fund, b. 1958)

TUESDAY

2

FN: HO

To me, the "tape" is the final arbiter of any investment decision. I have a cardinal rule: Never fight the tape!
— Martin Zweig (Fund manager, *Winning on Wall Street*)

(Shortened Trading Day)

WEDNESDAY

3

Discipline always makes hard work easy.
— Jordan Kimmel (Portfolio manager Magnet AE Fund, b. 1958)

Independence Day
(Market Closed)

THURSDAY

4

Politics ought to be the part-time profession of every citizen who would protect the rights and privileges of free people and who would preserve what is good and fruitful in our national heritage.
— Dwight D. Eisenhower (34th U.S. President, 1890–1969)

FRIDAY

5

OE: CC, LC, BP, EC, SF, JY

There is no one who can replace America. Without American leadership, there is no leadership. That puts a tremendous burden on the American people to do something positive. You can't be tempted by the usual nationalism.
— Lee Hong-koo (South Korean prime minister 1994–1995 and ambassador to U.S. 1998–2000, *NY Times* 2/25/2009)

SATURDAY

6

SUNDAY

7

LAST-HALF OF JULY SHORT S&P 500

Active traders looking for a high probability play should pay heed to this potential market move. Sell the September S&P 500 on or about July 15 and hold until on or about July 24. This trade has a 63.3% success rate, registering 19 wins against 11 losses in the last 30 years. The best win was $19,150 in 2002, and the worst loss was in 2009, posting a $12,650 bereavement.

Looking at the chart on page 138, you will see the average price tendency is for a mid-summer sell-off. Part of the reason is perhaps due to the fact that July starts the worst four months of the year in the NASDAQ and also falls in the middle of the worst six months for the Dow and S&P 500 indices.

Mid-July is also when we typically kick off earnings season, where a strong early month rally can fade, as active traders may have "bought the rumor" or bought ahead on anticipation of good earnings expectations and then turn around and "sell the fact" once the news hits the street.

Watch for an early month rally, and pay close attention, especially if we trade near the monthly predicted resistance level using Pivot Point analysis (2010 edition, pages 6–9). Market conditions that tend to start out strong early in the month tend to fade towards the middle to end of month. Executing this trade to the letter has resulted in losses in six of the last seven years. However, using the timing tools detailed on pages 6–9 in the 2010 and 2011 editions could have turned those losses into profits with a little extra effort.

Active traders can also consider the electronic e-mini Futures (ES), and stock traders can use the exchange-traded fund SPDR S&P 500 (SPY) and/or trade options on any of these equities. See pages 131–137 for additional correlated trades.

JULY SHORT S&P 500 (SEPTEMBER)
TRADING DAY: 10–HOLD: 7 DAYS

YEAR	ENTRY DATE	ENTRY CLOSE	EXIT DATE	EXIT CLOSE	PROFIT/ LOSS
1982	7/15	113.50	7/26	111.20	$575
1983	7/15	165.15	7/26	171.40	−1,563
1984	7/16	153.65	7/25	150.35	825
1985	7/15	194.05	7/24	191.90	538
1986	7/15	235.05	7/24	238.40	−837
1987	7/15	312.20	7/24	310.30	475
1988	7/15	272.80	7/26	266.15	1,663
1989	7/17	335.60	7/26	340.60	−1,250
1990	7/16	372.30	7/25	359.65	3,163
1991	7/15	384.50	7/24	380.75	938
1992	7/15	417.20	7/24	411.25	1,488
1993	7/15	449.75	7/26	449.05	175
1994	7/15	454.80	7/26	453.95	213
1995	7/17	565.45	7/26	564.05	350
1996	7/15	630.25	7/24	630.70	−113
1997	7/15	931.75	7/24	945.85	−3,525
1998	7/15	1183.40	7/24	1147.40	9,000
1999	7/15	1419.40	7/26	1354.80	16,150
2000	7/17	1522.00	7/26	1469.00	13,250
2001	7/16	1210.50	7/25	1191.50	4,750
2002	7/15	920.60	7/24	844.00	19,150
2003	7/15	1000.90	7/24	980.30	5,150
2004	7/15	1103.40	7/26	1082.90	5,125
2005	7/15	1231.20	7/26	1235.00	−950
2006	7/17	1240.50	7/26	1273.20	−8,175
2007	7/16	1559.70	7/25	1524.70	8,750
2008	7/15	1211.50	7/24	1253.80	−10,575
2009	7/15	927.20	7/24	977.80	−12,650
2010	7/15	1090.40	7/26	1109.50	−4,775
2011	7/15	1314.90	7/26	1326.20	−2,825
				30-Year Gain	**$44,488**

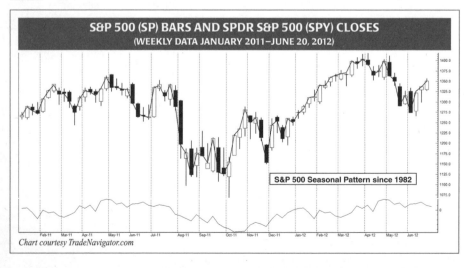

S&P 500 (SP) BARS AND SPDR S&P 500 (SPY) CLOSES
(WEEKLY DATA JANUARY 2011–JUNE 20, 2012)

S&P 500 Seasonal Pattern since 1982

Chart courtesy TradeNavigator.com

MONDAY
8

When a company reports higher earnings for its first quarter (over its previous year's first quarter), chances are almost five to one it will also have increased earnings in its second quarter.
— Niederhoffer, Cross & Zeckhauser

End Long Cocoa(U) (Jun. 4)

TUESDAY
9

Every time everyone's talking about something, that's the time to sell.
— George Lindemann (Billionaire, *Forbes*)

WEDNESDAY
10

A bank is a place where they lend you an umbrella in fair weather and ask for it back again when it begins to rain.
— Robert Frost (American poet, 1874–1963

THURSDAY
11

Self-discipline is a form of freedom. Freedom from laziness and lethargy, freedom from expectations and demands of others, freedom from weakness and fear—and doubt.
— Harvey A. Dorfman (Sports psychologist, *The Mental ABC's of Pitching*, b. 1935)

FRIDAY
12

LT: C, S, W
OE: KC

When you're one step ahead of the crowd, you're a genius. When you're two steps ahead, you're a crackpot.
— Shlomo Riskin (Rabbi, author, b. 1940)

SATURDAY
13

SUNDAY
14

SUMMER AIR CONDITIONING HEATS UP NATURAL GAS

Seasonally, July is a good month to get long natural gas ahead of its best five months, August through December. Buy natural gas futures on or about July 24 and hold until about October 21. In the past 22 years, this trade has worked 12 times, for a success rate of 54.5%. Mild winter weather and ample supplies have led to a glut in natural gas in recent years, resulting in losses for this trade in five of the last six years. Approach this trade with caution.

This unique commodity has a dual demand season based on hot and cold weather temperatures. In the United States, natural gas, coal, and refined petroleum products are used as substitutes in electric power generation. Electric power generators switch back and forth, preferring to use whichever energy source is less expensive.

Natural gas is a cleaner burning fuel source, and as crude oil has risen sharply, the less expensive product has been natural gas. But this has pushed prices higher in recent years. In addition, the effect of higher crude oil has caused demand to spike for natural gas, thus magnifying seasonal price moves.

The seasonal spikes in demand are obvious in the chart below, as increased summer electricity demand from air conditioning lift prices in mid-July. As we exit the summer season, weather can still play a role in September, when hurricanes can and have threatened production in the Gulf of Mexico, as occurred with Hurricane Katrina.

JULY LONG NATURAL GAS (NOVEMBER) TRADING DAY: 17–HOLD: 62 DAYS				
	ENTRY		EXIT	PROFIT/
YEAR	DATE	CLOSE	DATE	CLOSE	LOSS
1990	7/25	1.775	10/22	1.970	$1,950
1991	7/24	1.670	10/21	2.013	3,430
1992	7/24	1.975	10/21	2.488	5,130
1993	7/26	2.344	10/21	2.126	−2,180
1994	7/26	2.066	10/21	1.597	−4,690
1995	7/27	1.699	10/24	1.772	730
1996	7/25	2.250	10/22	2.625	3,750
1997	7/24	2.273	10/21	3.404	11,310
1998	7/24	2.310	10/21	2.180	−1,300
1999	7/26	2.734	10/21	3.064	3,300
2000	7/27	3.951	10/24	4.820	8,690
2001	7/25	3.583	10/25	2.938	−6,450
2002	7/25	3.243	10/22	4.110	8,670
2003	7/24	4.981	10/21	4.875	−1,060
2004	7/26	6.366	10/21	7.697	13,310
2005	7/26	8.101	10/21	12.872	47,710
2006	7/27	8.858	10/24	7.091	−17,670
2007	7/25	7.228	10/22	6.891	−3,370
2008	7/24	9.833	10/21	6.844	−29,890
2009	7/24	4.760	10/21	5.100	3,400
2010	7/26	4.853	10/21	3.368	−14,850
2011	7/26	4.450	10/21	3.630	−8,200
				22-Year Gain	$21,720

Besides options on futures, traders can take advantage of these seasonal price moves through options on the ETF, U.S. Natural Gas (UNG), or stocks of companies that find, produce, develop, and distribute natural gas. One in particular is Devon Energy (DVN), which correlates very closely with natural gas futures, as shown in the chart below. See pages 131–137 for additional correlated trades.

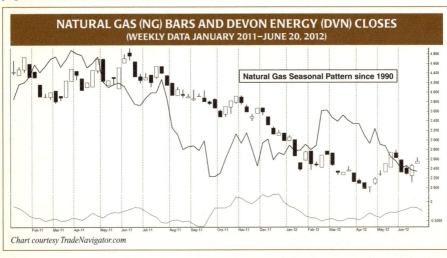

NATURAL GAS (NG) BARS AND DEVON ENERGY (DVN) CLOSES
(WEEKLY DATA JANUARY 2011–JUNE 20, 2012)

Natural Gas Seasonal Pattern since 1990

Chart courtesy TradeNavigator.com

JULY

Start Short S&P 500(U)—63.3% Accuracy Since 1982—End Jul. 24—Page 66

MONDAY

15

LT: LH
OE: SB, LH

The stock market is that creation of man which humbles him the most.
— Anonymous

TUESDAY

16

LT: CC

Prosperity is a great teacher; adversity a greater.
— William Hazlitt (English essayist, 1778–1830)

WEDNESDAY

17

OE: CL

The game is lost only when we stop trying.
— Mario Cuomo (Former NY Governor, *C-Span*)

THURSDAY

18

Companies that announce mass layoffs or a series of firings underperform the stock market over a three-year period.
— Bain & Company (*Smart Money Magazine*, August 2001)

 FRIDAY

19

LT: KC
OE: SP

Explosive growth of shadow banking was about the invisible hand having a party, a non-regulated drinking party, with rating agencies handing out fake IDs.
— Paul McCulley (Economist, bond investor, PIMCO, coined "shadow banking" in 2007, *NY Times* 4/26/2010, b. 1957)

SATURDAY

20

SUNDAY

21

SWISS FRANC FOLLOWS GOLD HIGHER

The Swiss franc correlates well with gold's price moves. Gold is strong in this time period, so traders may want to watch this relationship between gold and the Swiss franc.

The "Swissie," which is trader talk for the currency, has been a safe haven currency in the past, especially during times of financial and geopolitical instability. Due to this country's neutral stance and ability to close its borders, it has been well protected, as history shows.

However, under normal market conditions or a normal trading environment, the "Swissie" does tend to have seasonal forces against the U.S. dollar. One tendency for a relatively predictable move is in August. Traders want to go long on this seasonal best trade on or about August 8 and hold until on or about October 16. In the last 37-year history of this trade, it has worked 26 years, for a success rate of 70.3%. This trade's worst loss, in 2011, was the result of central bank intervention and could have been avoided through the use of technical indicators.

The chart below shows the Swiss franc overlaid with the price of the exchange-traded fund, CurrencyShares Swiss Franc (FXF), demonstrating how closely the two trading instruments are correlated. The line at the bottom shows the 37-year average seasonal price move. As you can see, the August through October period (page 187) tends to lead prices higher versus the U.S. dollar. See pages 131–137 for additional correlated trades.

	AUGUST LONG SWISS FRANC (DECEMBER) TRADING DAY: 6–HOLD: 48 DAYS				
	ENTRY		**EXIT**		**PROFIT/**
YEAR	**DATE**	**CLOSE**	**DATE**	**CLOSE**	**LOSS**
1975	8/08	37.48	10/16	38.12	$800
1976	8/09	40.69	10/15	41.10	513
1977	8/08	41.92	10/14	44.41	3,112
1978	8/08	60.95	10/16	67.55	8,250
1979	8/08	62.58	10/16	61.97	−762
1980	8/08	61.56	10/16	61.21	−438
1981	8/10	46.82	10/16	53.87	8,813
1982	8/09	48.03	10/15	46.87	−1,450
1983	8/08	46.97	10/14	47.72	938
1984	8/08	41.88	10/16	39.27	−3,263
1985	8/08	43.29	10/16	45.64	2,938
1986	8/08	60.50	10/16	61.96	1,825
1987	8/10	64.26	10/16	67.71	4,312
1988	8/08	63.89	10/14	66.22	2,913
1989	8/08	61.75	10/16	61.36	−488
1990	8/08	74.54	10/16	78.45	4,888
1991	8/08	66.08	10/16	66.69	762
1992	8/10	74.84	10/16	75.34	625
1993	8/09	66.21	10/15	69.83	4,525
1994	8/08	75.06	10/14	79.37	5,388
1995	8/08	86.57	10/16	87.35	975
1996	8/08	83.58	10/16	79.39	−5,238
1997	8/08	67.19	10/17	68.27	1,350
1998	8/10	67.75	10/19	75.79	10,050
1999	8/09	67.85	10/18	68.71	1,075
2000	8/08	59.10	10/17	56.93	−2,713
2001	8/08	58.60	10/18	61.18	3,225
2002	8/08	66.23	10/17	66.27	50
2003	8/08	73.68	10/17	75.26	1,975
2004	8/09	80.13	10/18	81.46	1,663
2005	8/08	80.24	10/17	77.90	−2,925
2006	8/08	82.80	10/17	79.32	−4,350
2007	8/08	84.40	10/17	85.01	762
2008	8/08	92.64	10/17	88.34	−5,375
2009	8/10	92.22	10/16	98.28	7,575
2010	8/09	95.46	10/15	104.26	11,000
2011	8/08	132.65	10/14	112.09	−25,700
			37-Year Gain		**$37,600**

SWISS FRANC (SF) BARS AND CURRENCYSHARES SWISS FRANC (FXF) CLOSES
(WEEKLY DATA JANUARY 2011–JUNE 20, 2012)

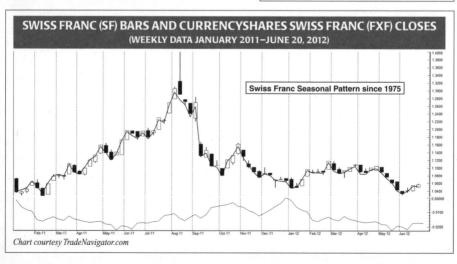

Swiss Franc Seasonal Pattern since 1975

Chart courtesy TradeNavigator.com

JULY

MONDAY
22
LT: CL

*In democracies, nothing is more great or brilliant than commerce; it attracts the attention of the public
and fills the imagination of the multitude; all passions of energy are directed towards it.*
— Alexis de Tocqueville (Author, *Democracy in America* 1840, 1805–1859)

End Long British Pound(U) (Jun. 28)

TUESDAY
23

That's the American way. If little kids don't aspire to make money like I did, what the hell good is this country?
— Lee Iacocca (American industrialist, Former Chrysler CEO, b. 1924)

End Short S&P 500(U) (Jul. 15)
Start Long Natural Gas(X)—54.5% Accuracy Since 1990—End Oct. 21—Page 68

WEDNESDAY
24
FN: CL

*At a time of war, we need you to work for peace. At a time of inequality, we need you to work for
opportunity. At a time of so much cynicism and so much doubt, we need you to make us believe again.*
— Barack H. Obama (44th U.S. President, Commencement Wesleyan University 5/28/2008, b. 1961)

Start Short Cocoa(Z)—69.2% Accuracy Since 1973—End Nov. 1—Page 76

THURSDAY
25
OE: HG, GC, SI

Every successful enterprise requires three people—a dreamer, a businessman, and a son-of-a-bitch.
— Peter McArthur (1904)

FRIDAY
26
OE: US, HO, NG, C, S, W

In the realm of ideas, everything depends on enthusiasm; in the real world, all rests on perseverance.
— Johann Wolfgang von Goethe (German poet and polymath, 1749–1832)

SATURDAY
27

SUNDAY
28

AUGUST ALMANAC

AUGUST						
S	M	T	W	T	F	S
				1	2	3
4	5	6	7	8	9	10
11	12	13	14	15	16	17
18	19	20	21	22	23	24
25	26	27	28	29	30	31

SEPTEMBER						
S	M	T	W	T	F	S
1	2	3	4	5	6	7
8	9	10	11	12	13	14
15	16	17	18	19	20	21
22	23	24	25	26	27	28
29	30					

◆ STOCKS AND BONDS

S&P 500 has shown a tendency to see strength lasting into early September (page 138). In 2010, stocks posted typical declines in August that proved to be the launching pad for the strongest "Best Six Months" since 1998. 30-year Treasury bond prices are flat to weak but have tendencies to rally, especially when stocks take sharp nose dives.

◆ ENERGY

Crude oil continues to stay supportive during the month of August, but beware of late month declines. Seasonally, this is one of the best five months to be long natural gas, from late July through December. Best seasonal trade is long natural gas from about July 24 (page 68). Heating Oil remains under pressure, except for a sympathy rally or reactions to strength in crude oil due to hurricane scares caused by refinery outages in the Gulf region.

◆ METALS

Seasonally, this is still in a strong price period for gold until October. Traders should be long from our seasonal best trade (page 78). Silver follows gold's strength, seasonally speaking (page 155). Copper prices tend to continue the seasonal downturn in August, as the dog days of summer cause a decline in demand and the construction season slows to a crawl (page 149).

◆ GRAINS

Soybeans are seasonally still in a weak period under normal weather markets until the harvest lows in October (page 94). Wheat remains in a strong uptrend after harvest lows are posted in June (page 125). Even though corn is in a seasonally weak time period, there are times when we see counterseasonal rallies due to weather scares (page 158).

◆ SOFTS

Cocoa encounters a countertrend seasonal trade (page 76). This is a potential conflict with the short position established in July. Cocoa is volatile during mid-crop harvest. Active traders can look to take a countertrend long trade on or about August 20 through September. Cover short coffee position from May on or about August 8 (page 52). Enter new long trade on or about August 16. This trade has worked 26 times in its 38-year history, with a 68.4% success rate (page 74). Sugar prices tend to be choppy during the month of August, as the market tries to post a seasonal low. Exit the long sugar trade from June on or about August 1 (page 58). This is the end of harvest time in Brazil and India. Seasonal bottoms are typically posted in September (page 173).

◆ MEATS

Live cattle continue in their seasonally strong price period until February (page 60). Lean hogs continue to see weakness in August (page 179).

◆ CURRENCIES

The euro has a tendency to continue to decline against the U.S. dollar headed into Labor Day weekend. However, the first part of September marks a short-term seasonal buying opportunity (page 125). Go long the December Swiss franc contract for its seasonal best trade on or about August 8, and hold until about October 16 (page 70). The British pound tries to post a bottom in August into September (page 84). The yen has a strong seasonal tendency to post bottoms against the U.S. dollar in late August to early October, as it marks the halfway point in Japan's fiscal year, which runs April–March (page 190).

AUGUST STRATEGY CALENDAR*

Symbol		B	M	E
SP	L/S			
US	L/S			
CL	L/S			
NG	L/S			
HO	L/S			
HG	L/S			
GC	L/S			
SI	L/S			
C	L/S			
S	L/S			
W	L/S			
CC	L/S			
KC	L/S			
SB	L/S			
LC	L/S			
LH	L/S			
BP	L/S			
EC	L/S			
SF	L/S			
JY	L/S			

* Graphic representation of the Commodity Seasonality Percentage Plays on pages 124–125.
L = Long Trade, S = Short Trade. See pages 131–137 for contract symbols.

JULY/AUGUST

Anytime there is change there is opportunity. So it is paramount that an organization get energized rather than paralyzed.
— Jack Welch (GE CEO, *Fortune*)

End Short Soybeans Peak(U) (Jun. 7)

The first panacea for a mismanaged nation is inflation of the currency; the second is war. Both bring a temporary prosperity; both bring a permanent ruin. But both are the refuge of political and economic opportunists.
— Ernest Hemingway (American writer, 1954 Nobel Prize, 1899–1961)

What's going on… is the end of Silicon Valley as we know it. The next big thing ain't computers… it's biotechnology.
— Larry Ellison (Oracle CEO, quoted in *The Wall Street Journal*, April 8, 2003)

End Short Corn(U) (Jun. 26)
End Long Sugar(V) (Jun. 17)

A weak currency is the sign of a weak economy, and a weak economy leads to a weak nation.
— H. Ross Perot (American businessman, *The Dollar Crisis*, 2-time 3rd-party presidential candidate 1992 & 1996, b. 1930)

We are like tenant farmers chopping down the fence around our house for fuel when we should be using Nature's inexhaustible sources of energy—sun, wind and tide. I'd put my money on the sun and solar energy. What a source of power! I hope we don't have to wait until oil and coal run out before we tackle that.
— Thomas Alva Edison (American inventor, 1093 patents, 1847–1931)

AUGUST GIVES COFFEE A LIFT

Coffee has increased in popularity on an international scale in the last few decades. Most consumption had been from the United States, parts of Europe, and Canada. Many Europeans have switched from tea to coffee, and with the introduction in late 2005 of Starbucks coffee in Europe and in Asia, more and more people are consuming "Vente Lattes."

Demand is improving, especially for higher grade and quality coffee. With increasing global consumption habits, if there are threats of supply disruptions or production declines for higher grade coffee, the futures market can be prone to extreme price moves.

Coffee typically tends to start a seasonal bottoming process before distributors begin buying ahead of anticipated demand in the upcoming cold winter months. This is the time to cover the best seasonal trade short position from May on or about August 8. It is also a time to look for a short-term trade opportunity from the buy side. Traders should look to enter a new long position on or about August 16 and hold this position until about September 5. This trade usually falls right around Labor Day.

This trade has worked 26 times in the last 38 years, for a success rate of 68.4%. The chart below shows the way the market traded in 2011–2012 along with Green Mountain Coffee Roasters (GMCR) as well as the 38-year average seasonal trading pattern. Despite its issues, GMCR remains highly correlated with coffee's seasonal moves. See pages 131–137 for additional correlated trades.

AUGUST LONG COFFEE (DECEMBER)
TRADING DAY: 12–HOLD: 13 DAYS

YEAR	ENTRY DATE	CLOSE	EXIT DATE	CLOSE	PROFIT/ LOSS
1974	8/16	56.25	9/05	55.60	−$244
1975	8/18	85.73	9/05	81.35	−1,643
1976	8/17	153.75	9/03	153.85	37
1977	8/16	193.50	9/02	183.81	−3,634
1978	8/16	128.50	9/05	150.38	8,205
1979	8/16	195.50	9/05	208.09	4,721
1980	8/18	154.16	9/05	135.34	−7,058
1981	8/18	114.57	9/04	107.29	−2,730
1982	8/17	125.70	9/03	126.95	469
1983	8/16	129.45	9/02	130.37	345
1984	8/16	142.25	9/05	144.80	956
1985	8/16	138.70	9/05	136.75	−731
1986	8/18	180.93	9/05	203.32	8,396
1987	8/18	106.25	9/04	116.80	3,956
1988	8/16	120.69	9/02	123.17	930
1989	8/16	79.26	9/05	83.45	1,571
1990	8/16	98.20	9/05	103.70	2,063
1991	8/16	82.75	9/05	90.20	2,794
1992	8/18	53.20	9/04	54.50	487
1993	8/17	74.00	9/03	76.25	844
1994	8/16	197.00	9/02	209.90	4,838
1995	8/16	146.35	9/05	149.10	1,031
1996	8/16	111.55	9/05	111.60	19
1997	8/18	162.95	9/05	188.85	9,713
1998	8/18	113.00	9/04	112.85	−56
1999	8/17	92.40	9/03	92.30	−38
2000	8/16	82.90	9/05	78.50	−1,650
2001	8/16	52.85	9/05	52.10	−281
2002	8/16	50.35	9/05	56.70	2,381
2003	8/18	62.25	9/05	66.35	1,538
2004	8/17	72.45	9/03	72.20	−94
2005	8/16	101.45	9/02	103.05	600
2006	8/16	108.60	9/05	110.30	638
2007	8/16	115.25	9/05	116.05	300
2008	8/18	137.95	9/05	142.65	1,763
2009	8/18	128.25	9/04	124.10	−1,556
2010	8/17	178.30	9/03	186.95	3,244
2011	8/16	255.00	9/02	288.05	12,394
				38-Year Gain	**$54,518**

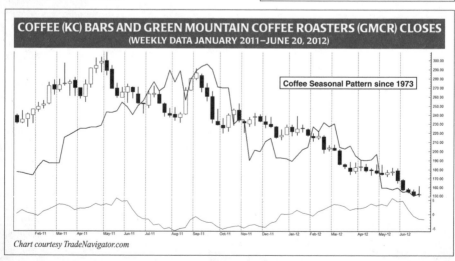

COFFEE (KC) BARS AND GREEN MOUNTAIN COFFEE ROASTERS (GMCR) CLOSES
(WEEKLY DATA JANUARY 2011–JUNE 20, 2012)

Coffee Seasonal Pattern since 1973

Chart courtesy TradeNavigator.com

AUGUST

MONDAY
5
FN: LC

Under capitalism man exploits man: under socialism the reverse is true.
— Polish proverb

TUESDAY
6

It is not how right or how wrong you are that matters, but how much money you make when right and how much you do not lose when wrong.
— George Soros (Financier, philanthropist, political activist, author and philosopher, b. 1930)

WEDNESDAY
7

I have a simple philosophy. Fill what's empty. Empty what's full. And scratch where it itches.
— Alice Roosevelt Longworth

End Short Coffee(U) (May 22)
Start Long Swiss Franc(Z)—70.3% Accuracy Since 1975—End Oct. 16—Page 70

THURSDAY
8

If you don't know who you are, the stock market is an expensive place to find out.
— George Goodman (*Institutional Investor, New York*, "Adam Smith", *The Money Game*, b. 1930)

FRIDAY
9
OE: KC, BP, EC, SF, JY

Writing a book is an adventure. To begin with it is a toy, an amusement; then it is a mistress, and then a master, and then a tyrant.
— Winston Churchill (British statesman, 1874–1965)

SATURDAY
10

SUNDAY
11

TWIN COCOA CROPS CREATE TWIN SUMMERTIME TRADES

Cocoa is split between two harvested crops. The so-called mid-crop begins in May and can last until August. The main crop is between October and March. This accounts for the fact that we see, from a seasonal perspective, downturns lasting into early November.

But as harvest is underway in the mid-crop, the market is vulnerable to volatility created by harvest and/or shipping delays caused by weather conditions. Looking at this situation from a historical perspective, we have found, that in the last 39 years, selling cocoa on or about July 25 and holding until around November 1 has worked 27 times.

Active traders can look to take a secondary long trade on or about August 20 and exit on approximately September 24. In the past 39 years this trade has worked 25 times, providing a success rate of 64.1%.

The weekly chart below shows the inverse price relationship of cocoa and chocolate titan Hershey (HSY). The graph in the bottom section shows the 39-year average seasonal price tendency. From June to November cocoa goes through a period of increased volatility during the mid-crop harvest. See pages 131–137 for additional correlated trades.

JULY SHORT COCOA (DECEMBER) TRADING DAY: 18–HOLD: 70 DAYS

YEAR	ENTRY DATE	ENTRY CLOSE	EXIT DATE	EXIT CLOSE	PROFIT/ LOSS
1973	7/27	1613	11/7	1321	$2,920
1974	7/25	1585	11/4	1898	−3,130
1975	7/25	1272	11/5	1385	−1,130
1976	7/27	1946	11/5	3084	−11,380
1977	7/28	4057	11/7	3963	940
1978	7/27	3143	11/6	3811	−6,680
1979	7/26	3061	11/2	2695	3,660
1980	7/25	2336	11/3	2095	2,410
1981	7/27	2087	11/3	1956	1,310
1982	7/27	1451	11/4	1350	1,010
1983	7/27	2404	11/3	2032	3,720
1984	7/26	2097	11/2	2295	−1,980
1985	7/26	2185	11/6	2039	1,460
1986	7/28	2028	11/4	1889	1,390
1987	7/27	2050	11/3	1819	2,310
1988	7/27	1504	11/3	1309	1,950
1989	7/27	1311	11/3	964	3,470
1990	7/26	1313	11/2	1147	1,660
1991	7/26	1086	11/4	1200	−1,140
1992	7/27	1072	11/3	949	1,230
1993	7/27	970	11/3	1097	−1,270
1994	7/27	1500	11/3	1319	1,810
1995	7/28	1282	11/6	1329	−470
1996	7/26	1394	11/4	1325	690
1997	7/25	1556	11/3	1578	−220
1998	7/27	1601	11/3	1508	930
1999	7/27	1068	11/4	836	2,320
2000	7/28	882	11/6	743	1,390
2001	7/26	930	11/8	1099	−1,690
2002	7/26	1796	11/4	1806	−100
2003	7/25	1447	11/3	1422	250
2004	7/27	1618	11/3	1460	1,580
2005	7/27	1488	11/3	1376	1,120
2006	7/27	1531	11/3	1484	470
2007	7/26	2037	11/2	1970	670
2008	7/25	2828	11/3	1969	8,590
2009	7/27	2900	11/3	3274	−3,740
2010	7/27	3003	11/3	2764	2,390
2011	7/27	3073	11/3	2720	3,530
				39-Year Gain	**$22,250**

AUGUST LONG COCOA (DECEMBER) TRADING DAY: 14–HOLD: 24 DAYS

YEAR	ENTRY DATE	ENTRY CLOSE	EXIT DATE	EXIT CLOSE	PROFIT/ LOSS
1973	8/20	1393	9/24	1549	$1,560
1974	8/20	1662	9/24	1694	320
1975	8/20	1151	9/24	1220	690
1976	8/19	2174	9/23	2436	2,620
1977	8/18	3814	9/22	4075	2,610
1978	8/18	3257	9/22	3804	5,470
1979	8/20	2991	9/24	3068	770
1980	8/20	2130	9/24	2328	1,980
1981	8/20	2109	9/24	2103	−60
1982	8/19	1506	9/23	1538	320
1983	8/18	2165	9/22	2115	−500
1984	8/20	2016	9/24	2418	4,020
1985	8/20	2174	9/24	2305	1,310
1986	8/20	1957	9/24	2000	430
1987	8/20	1932	9/24	1940	80
1988	8/18	1390	9/22	1216	−1,740
1989	8/18	1178	9/22	1054	−1,240
1990	8/20	1178	9/24	1295	1,170
1991	8/20	1010	9/24	1204	1,940
1992	8/20	1073	9/24	957	−1,160
1993	8/19	1029	9/23	1174	1,450
1994	8/18	1459	9/22	1337	−1,220
1995	8/18	1334	9/22	1295	−390
1996	8/20	1430	9/24	1366	−640
1997	8/20	1569	9/24	1691	1,220
1998	8/20	1576	9/24	1527	−490
1999	8/19	961	9/23	969	80
2000	8/18	796	9/22	812	160
2001	8/20	1007	9/28	1077	700
2002	8/20	1917	9/24	2120	2,030
2003	8/20	1542	9/24	1637	950
2004	8/19	1731	9/23	1522	−2,090
2005	8/18	1398	9/22	1342	−560
2006	8/18	1545	9/22	1499	−460
2007	8/20	1759	9/24	2011	2,520
2008	8/20	2659	9/24	2757	980
2009	8/20	2915	9/24	3066	1,510
2010	8/19	2892	9/23	2780	−1,120
2011	8/18	2985	9/22	2680	−3,050
				39-Year Gain	**$22,170**

COCOA (CC) BARS & HERSHEY (HSY) CLOSES
(WEEKLY DATA JANUARY 2011–JUNE 20, 2012)

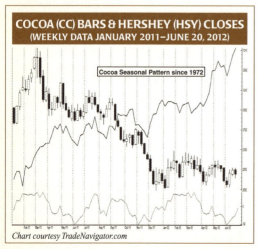

Cocoa Seasonal Pattern since 1972

Chart courtesy TradeNavigator.com

AUGUST

MONDAY

12

Even being right 3 or 4 times out of 10 should yield a person a fortune, if he has the sense to cut his losses quickly on the ventures where he has been wrong.
— Bernard Baruch (Financier, speculator, statesman, presidential adviser, 1870–1965)

TUESDAY

13

The Clairvoyant Society of London will not meet Tuesday because of unforeseen circumstances.
— Advertisement in the London Financial Times

WEDNESDAY

14

LT: S, LH
OE: LH

Banking establishments are more dangerous than standing armies; and that the principle of spending money to be paid by posterity, under the name of funding, is but swindling futurity on a large scale.
— Thomas Jefferson (3rd U.S. President, 1743–7/4/1826, 1816 letter to John Taylor of Caroline)

THURSDAY

15

OE: CL, SB

Over the last 25 years, computer processing capacity has risen more than a millionfold, while communication capacity has risen over a thousandfold.
— Richard Worzel (Futurist, *Facing the Future*, b. 1950)

Start Long Coffee(Z)—68.4% Accuracy Since 1974—End Sep. 5—Page 74

FRIDAY

16

OE: SP

In investing, the return you want should depend on whether you want to eat well or sleep well.
— J. Kenfield Morley

SATURDAY

17

SUNDAY

18

GOLD GLITTERS MID-SUMMER

Seasonally, this is a strong price period for gold until late September or early October. Look to enter long positions on or about August 26 and hold until October 1. In the last 37 years, this trade has worked 22 times, for a success rate of 59.5%. The ten years prior to 2011 had provided an amazing cumulative profit of $32,280 per futures contract.

The chart below is a weekly chart of the price of gold with the exchange-traded fund (ETF) known as the SPDR Gold Shares Trust (GLD) overlaid to show the direct price correlation between the two trading vehicles. The line on the bottom section is the 37-year average seasonal tendency showing the market directional price trend.

SPDR Gold Shares (GLD) was the first ETF to own physical gold in the U.S. Each share represents 1/10 ounce of gold and the closing price of the ETF will represent, within reason, spot gold divided by 10. As of June 20, 2012, GLD owned 41,205,335.16 ounces of gold with 424.5 million shares outstanding. Just like every other ETF, a premium or discount to net asset value (NAV) can exist. See pages 131–137 for additional correlated trades, such as stocks of gold mining and producing companies that track the underlying commodity rather closely.

AUGUST LONG GOLD (DECEMBER)
TRADING DAY: 18–HOLD: 25 DAYS

YEAR	ENTRY DATE	ENTRY CLOSE	EXIT DATE	EXIT CLOSE	PROFIT/ LOSS
1975	8/26	165.6	10/01	144.2	−$2,140
1976	8/25	106.1	9/30	116.1	1,000
1977	8/24	146.9	9/29	156.0	910
1978	8/24	204.8	9/29	220.9	1,610
1979	8/24	320.7	10/01	424.5	10,380
1980	8/26	651.0	10/01	696.5	4,550
1981	8/26	430.5	10/01	440.0	950
1982	8/25	417.0	9/30	404.8	−1,220
1983	8/24	433.4	9/29	411.5	−2,190
1984	8/24	362.3	10/01	350.9	−1,140
1985	8/26	342.9	10/01	327.1	−1,580
1986	8/26	385.6	10/01	429.2	4,360
1987	8/26	465.8	10/01	459.7	−610
1988	8/24	444.4	9/29	401.6	−4,280
1989	8/24	370.6	9/29	372.0	140
1990	8/27	396.2	10/02	393.9	−230
1991	8/26	360.3	10/01	357.3	−300
1992	8/26	340.9	10/01	349.1	820
1993	8/25	375.5	9/30	357.1	−1,840
1994	8/24	388.6	9/29	398.7	1,010
1995	8/24	387.9	9/29	386.5	−140
1996	8/26	394.5	10/01	381.0	−1,350
1997	8/26	329.0	10/01	336.1	710
1998	8/26	285.9	10/01	302.1	1,620
1999	8/25	254.2	9/30	299.5	4,530
2000	8/24	277.5	9/29	276.9	−60
2001	8/24	274.9	10/03	291.6	1,670
2002	8/26	311.0	10/01	322.2	1,120
2003	8/26	366.8	10/01	385.0	1,820
2004	8/25	410.0	9/30	420.4	1,040
2005	8/24	442.2	9/29	475.8	3,360
2006	8/24	628.5	9/29	604.2	−2,430
2007	8/24	677.5	10/01	754.1	7,660
2008	8/26	828.1	10/01	887.3	5,920
2009	8/26	945.8	10/01	1000.7	5,490
2010	8/25	1243.3	9/30	1309.6	6,630
2011	8/24	1757.3	9/29	1617.3	−14,000
				37-Year Gain	**$33,790**

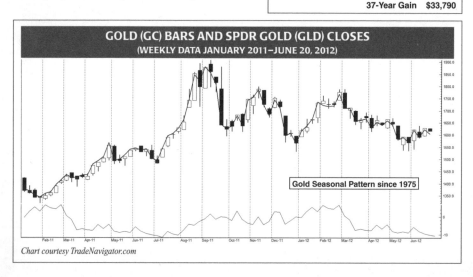

GOLD (GC) BARS AND SPDR GOLD (GLD) CLOSES
(WEEKLY DATA JANUARY 2011–JUNE 20, 2012)

Gold Seasonal Pattern since 1975

Chart courtesy TradeNavigator.com

AUGUST

End Long 30-Year Bond(U) (Apr. 24)

There has never been a commercial technology like this (Internet) in the history of the world, whereby the minute you adopt it, it forces you to think and act globally.
— Robert D. Hormats (Under Secretary of State Economic, Energy and Agricultural 2009-, Goldman Sachs 1982–2009, b.1943)

Start Long Cocoa(Z)—64.1% Accuracy Since 1973—End Sep. 24—Page 76

TUESDAY
20
LT: CL

Any human anywhere will blossom in a hundred unexpected talents and capacities simply by being given the opportunity to do so.
— Doris Lessing (British novelist, born in Persia 1919)

WEDNESDAY
21

I don't believe in intuition. When you get sudden flashes of perception, it is just the brain working faster than usual.
— Katherine Anne Porter (American author, 1890–1980)

THURSDAY
22
FN: CL, KC

You can't grow long-term if you can't eat short-term. Anybody can manage short. Anybody can manage long. Balancing those two things is what management is.
— Jack Welch (CEO of General Electric, *Business Week*, June 8, 1998)

FRIDAY
23
OE: US, C, S, W

I write an email about every week to ten days...and within about 24 hours everyone will have read it. The amazing thing is how I can change the direction of the entire company within 24 hours. Ten years ago I couldn't do that.
— Michael Marks (CEO Flextronics, *Forbes*, 7/7/03)

SATURDAY
24

SUNDAY
25

SEPTEMBER ALMANAC

SEPTEMBER						
S	M	T	W	T	F	S
1	2	3	4	5	6	7
8	9	10	11	12	13	14
15	16	17	18	19	20	21
22	23	24	25	26	27	28
29	30					

◆ STOCKS AND BONDS

S&P's have shown a tendency to see mid-month selloffs lasting into early October (page 138). Even during the big rebound in 2009, S&P's posted a mid-September high and declined until October 2. 30-year Treasury bonds tend to rise when stock prices tend to decline (page 142).

OCTOBER						
S	M	T	W	T	F	S
		1	2	3	4	5
6	7	8	9	10	11	12
13	14	15	16	17	18	19
20	21	22	23	24	25	26
27	28	29	30	31		

◆ ENERGY

Crude oil tops out in September with the peak driving and hurricane seasons behind us. Refineries begin to focus on the production of heating oil and less on gasoline, thereby reducing the amount of crude oil inventories. Selling the February futures contract on or before September 12 and holding until on or about December 10 has produced 18 winning trades in the last 29 years (page 82). Natural gas is in the midst of its best two-month span from September through October (page 145). In mild hurricane seasons, heating oil prices see declines towards mid-month as threats of damage and refinery disruptions dissipate. Traders should prepare to go short as October marks seasonal peaks from pre-winter inventory buildup (page 92).

SEPTEMBER STRATEGY CALENDAR*

Symbol		B	M	E
SP	L			
	S			
US	L			
	S			
CL	L			
	S			
NG	L			
	S			
HO	L			
	S			
HG	L			
	S			
GC	L			
	S			
SI	L			
	S			
C	L			
	S			
S	L			
	S			
W	L			
	S			
CC	L			
	S			
KC	L			
	S			
SB	L			
	S			
LC	L			
	S			
LH	L			
	S			
BP	L			
	S			
EC	L			
	S			
SF	L			
	S			
JY	L			
	S			

◆ METALS

Liquidate the long gold position from August (page 78) near month end. Silver has a tendency to follow gold higher during the month (page 155). Copper prices tend to stabilize in September but still lean toward a seasonal downturn until mid-December (Page 149).

◆ GRAINS

Soybeans are in a weak period under normal weather markets until the harvest lows come by late October (page 94). Wheat continues to remain in an uptrend, but prices have a tendency to stall or correct mid-month (page 164). Corn continues a seasonal decline in normal weather conditions apart from any early frost scare. Generally, the corn crop is made by now, and prices tend to decline until the seasonal harvest lows are posted in late October or early November (page 158).

◆ SOFTS

Exit the long cocoa trade from August 20 on or about September 24. In addition, we have a trading opportunity that overlaps this trade and the July short (page 76), which is to sell a December futures contract short on or about September 16 and hold until on or about October 31. In the last 39-years, this trade has worked 27 times, for a success rate of 69.2% (page 125). We also exit the long coffee trade from August 16, on or about September 5 (page 74). Sugar bottoms are typically posted in late August to early October (page 173).

◆ MEATS

Live cattle prices tend to press higher through year-end, as demand tends to rise in the fall. Fostering the bullish bias is the fact that people generally eat more meat in cooler temperatures. Also bullish for cattle prices, with children back in school, government-sponsored lunch programs reinforce the demand outlook (page 176). Lean hog prices continue their seasonal decline, typically lasting to November (page 102).

◆ CURRENCIES

The euro tends to rally after Labor Day, from approximately September 9 until about October 1. In the 13-year history, this trade has worked 11 times, good for a cumulative profit of $22,775 (page 125). The Swiss franc is still in an uptrend until on or about October 16 (page 70). British pound is a buy in September. Look to go long around September 18, holding until about November 4 (page 84). The yen has a strong seasonal tendency to continue rallying against the U.S. dollar (page 190).

* Graphic representation of the Commodity Seasonality Percentage Plays on pages 124–125.
L = Long Trade, S = Short Trade. See pages 131–137 for contract symbols.

80

AUGUST/SEPTEMBER

Start Long Gold(Z)—59.5% Accuracy Since 1975—End Oct. 1—Page 78

MONDAY

26

In politics as in chess, or in the military or in business, when you have the advantage you must press it quickly – or lose it. For the first time in history, we are in a position to checkmate tyranny. Momentum is largely on the side of democracy.
— Garry Kasparov (World Chess Champion 1985–2000)

TUESDAY

27

OE: HO, NG, HG, GC, SI

All great truths begin as blasphemies.
— George Bernard Shaw (Irish dramatist, 1856–1950)

WEDNESDAY

28

LT: NG, HG, GC, SI

If the market does not rally, as it should during bullish seasonal periods, it is a sign that other forces are stronger and that when the seasonal period ends those forces will really have their say.
— Edson Gould (Stock market analyst, *Findings & Forecasts*, 1902–1987)

THURSDAY

29

FN: NG

It isn't as important to buy as cheap as possible as it is to buy at the right time.
— Jesse Livermore (Early 20th century stock trader and speculator, *How to Trade in Stocks*, 1877–1940)

FRIDAY

30

FN: US, HG, GC, SI, C, S, W
LT: HO, LC

Let me end my talk by abusing slightly my status as an official representative of the Federal Reserve. I would like to say to Milton [Friedman]: regarding the Great Depression, you're right; we did it. We're very sorry. But thanks to you, we won't do it again.
— Ben Bernanke (Fed Chairman 2006-, 11/8/02 speech as Fed Govenor)

SATURDAY

31

SUNDAY

1

CRUDE OIL TAKES A BREATHER

In most years, crude oil prices make significant price gains in the summer, as vacationers and the annual trek of students returning to college in August create increased demand for unleaded gasoline. The market also prices in a premium for supply disruptions due to threats of hurricanes in the Gulf of Mexico. However, towards mid-September, we see a seasonal tendency of prices to peak out, as the driving and hurricane seasons are behind us.

Selling on or before September 12 and holding until on or about December 10 has produced 18 winning trades in the last 29 years. This gives us a 62.1% success rate and total gains of $55,100 per futures contract.

Below is a chart of crude oil overlaid with the price of Frontline Limited (FRO), a company that primarily transports crude oil. What better way to follow the price of a commodity that needs to be transported? This company's stock price does reflect the fact that when demand goes up, prices rise for both crude oil and the stock due to the need for increased shipments. In this scenario, the company should profit. However, as demand for crude oil declines, there is less need for shipping, and the company's revenues should also decline.

This ebb and flow of supply and demand tendencies are correlated, as the chart shows, with the price of crude oil, FRO, and the seasonal historic price of the company at the bottom. Frontline highly correlates to the seasonal price swings in crude oil. See pages 131–137 for additional correlated trades.

SEPTEMBER SHORT CRUDE OIL (FEBRUARY) TRADING DAY: 8–HOLD: 62 DAYS

YEAR	ENTRY DATE	ENTRY CLOSE	EXIT DATE	EXIT CLOSE	PROFIT/ LOSS
1983	9/13	30.93	12/12	28.98	$1,950
1984	9/13	29.65	12/12	26.80	2,850
1985	9/12	26.28	12/11	25.79	490
1986	9/11	14.76	12/10	15.24	−480
1987	9/11	19.00	12/10	18.16	840
1988	9/13	14.51	12/12	15.72	−1,210
1989	9/13	18.88	12/11	20.51	−1,630
1990	9/13	28.11	12/11	25.88	2,230
1991	9/12	21.16	12/10	19.46	1,700
1992	9/11	21.51	12/10	19.38	2,130
1993	9/13	18.11	12/10	15.36	2,750
1994	9/13	17.67	12/12	16.95	720
1995	9/13	17.74	12/12	18.42	−680
1996	9/12	22.23	12/11	22.93	−700
1997	9/11	19.62	12/10	18.41	1,210
1998	9/11	15.20	12/10	11.21	3,990
1999	9/13	22.54	12/10	24.71	−2,170
2000	9/13	31.24	12/12	29.10	2,140
2001	9/18	27.55	12/17	19.52	8,030
2002	9/12	28.05	12/11	27.42	630
2003	9/11	28.01	12/10	31.76	−3,750
2004	9/13	42.42	12/10	41.36	1,060
2005	9/13	65.19	12/12	62.26	2,930
2006	9/13	67.51	12/12	61.99	5,520
2007	9/13	76.05	12/11	89.92	−13,870
2008	9/11	101.94	12/09	44.66	57,280
2009	9/11	71.14	12/09	72.55	−1,410
2010	9/13	80.37	12/09	88.88	−8,510
2011	9/13	90.66	12/09	99.60	−8,940
				29-Year Gain	**$55,100**

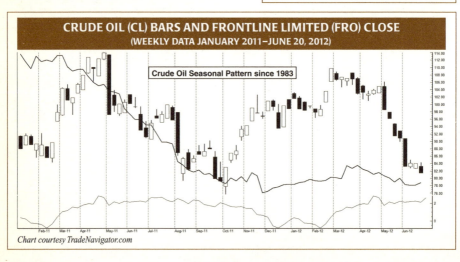

CRUDE OIL (CL) BARS AND FRONTLINE LIMITED (FRO) CLOSE
(WEEKLY DATA JANUARY 2011–JUNE 20, 2012)

Crude Oil Seasonal Pattern since 1983

Chart courtesy TradeNavigator.com

SEPTEMBER

Labor Day (Market Closed)

What's money? A man is a success if he gets up in the morning and goes to bed at night and in between does what he wants to do.
— Bob Dylan (American singer-songwriter, musician and artist, b. 1941)

TUESDAY
3

New indicator: CFO Magazine gave Excellence awards to WorldCom's Scott Sullivan (1998), Enron's Andrew Fastow (1999), and to Tyco's Mark Swartz (2000). All were subsequently indicted.
— Roger Lowenstein (Financial journalist and author, *Origins Of The Crash*, b. 1954)

WEDNESDAY
4
FN: HO

Financial markets will find and exploit hidden flaws, particularly in untested new innovations—and do so at a time that will inflict the most damage to the most people.
— Raymond F. DeVoe, Jr. (Market strategist Jesup & Lamont, *The DeVoe Report*, 3/30/07)

Rosh Hashanah
End Long Coffee(Z) (Aug. 16)

THURSDAY
5

We prefer to cut back exposure on what's going against us and add exposure where it's more favorable to our portfolio. This way, we're always attempting to tilt the odds in our favor. This is the exact opposite of a long investor that would average down. Averaging down is a very dangerous practice.
— John Del Vecchio & Brad Lamensdorf (Portfolio managers Active Bear ETF, 5/10/12 *Almanac Investor* Interview)

FRIDAY
6
OE: CC, LC, BP, EC, SF, JY

The wisdom of the ages is the fruits of freedom and democracy.
— Lawrence Kudlow (Economist, 24th Annual Paulson SmallCap Conference, Waldorf Astoria NYC, 11/8/01)

SATURDAY
7

SUNDAY
8

BRITISH POUND AUTUMN RALLY

Great Brittan is a multi-trillion-dollar economy, and its largest city, London, is considered the world's top financial trading center. Many market factors can influence the floating value of the pound versus other currencies such as the euro. However, when we compare the pound in terms of the U.S. dollar, we see several trading opportunities throughout the year.

Here is an interesting, relatively short-term trade, one that seems to have the same reaction with the trade direction in the yen, Swiss franc, and euro currencies during this time period. The British pound has a seasonal tendency to decline just ahead of the end of the third quarter and reach a bottom near mid-September.

We typically see rallies in October through the end of the calendar year. After that, the market starts to fade against the dollar again, before posting a bottom shortly before Britain's fiscal year begins in April. Seasonally speaking, the pound tends to trade higher in value against the U.S. dollar from about September 18 until about November 4. In the last 37 years, this trade has worked 25 times, for a success rate of 67.6%.

The chart below shows the pound with the exchange-traded fund, CurrencyShares British Pound (FXB), overlaid to illustrate the close correlation to price movement of these two trading vehicles. Technical timing tools could have improved the results from 2008 and 2009, boosting the potential profit of this seasonal trading opportunity. See pages 131–137 for additional correlated trades.

SEPTEMBER LONG BRITISH POUND (DECEMBER) TRADING DAY: 12–HOLD: 33 DAYS				
	ENTRY		EXIT	PROFIT/
YEAR	DATE CLOSE	DATE	CLOSE	LOSS
1975	9/17 205.65	11/3	206.50	$1,062
1976	9/17 169.60	11/4	160.90	−10,875
1977	9/19 174.10	11/3	179.95	7,312
1978	9/19 194.40	11/3	196.00	2,000
1979	9/19 213.25	11/5	207.10	−7,688
1980	9/17 237.20	11/3	244.35	8,938
1981	9/17 184.50	11/3	189.30	6,000
1982	9/17 171.40	11/3	167.40	−5,000
1983	9/19 151.65	11/3	148.95	−3,375
1984	9/19 123.85	11/5	126.85	3,750
1985	9/18 132.30	11/4	143.50	14,000
1986	9/17 146.15	11/3	140.45	−7,125
1987	9/17 163.85	11/3	173.90	12,563
1988	9/19 166.32	11/3	176.96	13,300
1989	9/19 155.34	11/3	155.90	700
1990	9/19 185.46	11/5	196.32	13,575
1991	9/18 170.90	11/4	176.58	7,100
1992	9/17 174.66	11/3	154.22	−25,550
1993	9/17 152.24	11/3	147.82	−5,525
1994	9/19 156.72	11/3	161.66	6,175
1995	9/19 154.26	11/3	157.72	4,325
1996	9/18 156.00	11/4	164.44	10,550
1997	9/17 159.56	11/4	168.26	10,875
1998	9/17 167.54	11/4	165.76	−2,225
1999	9/17 162.38	11/4	162.14	−300
2000	9/19 141.20	11/6	143.02	2,275
2001	9/20 145.90	11/7	145.92	25
2002	9/18 154.12	11/5	155.86	2,175
2003	9/17 159.98	11/4	167.56	9,475
2004	9/17 178.07	11/4	183.72	7,063
2005	9/19 180.07	11/4	175.03	−6,300
2006	9/19 188.34	11/6	189.72	1,725
2007	9/19 199.77	11/6	208.45	10,850
2008	9/17 181.56	11/4	158.92	−28,288
2009	9/17 164.47	11/3	163.33	−1,425
2010	9/17 156.24	11/3	161.09	6,062
2011	9/19 156.78	11/3	160.31	4,413
			37-Year Gain	$62,613

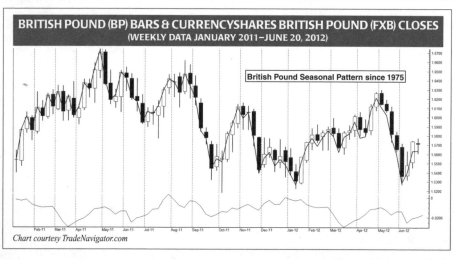

BRITISH POUND (BP) BARS & CURRENCYSHARES BRITISH POUND (FXB) CLOSES
(WEEKLY DATA JANUARY 2011–JUNE 20, 2012)

British Pound Seasonal Pattern since 1975

Chart courtesy TradeNavigator.com

SEPTEMBER

Start Long Euro(Z)—84.6% Accuracy Since 1999—End Oct. 1—Page 125

MONDAY
9

Brazil is the country of the future and always will be.
— (Brazilian joke)

TUESDAY
10

Executives owe it to the organization and to their fellow workers not to tolerate nonperforming individuals in important jobs.
— Peter Drucker (Austria-born pioneer management theorist, 1909–2005)

WEDNESDAY
11

"In Memory"

[A contrarian's opportunity] If everybody is thinking alike, then somebody isn't thinking.
— General George S. Patton, Jr. (U.S. Army field commander WWII, 1885–1945)

Start Short Crude Oil(G)—62.1% Accuracy Since 1983—End Dec. 10—Page 82

THURSDAY
12

Entrepreneurs who believe they're in business to vanquish the competition are less successful than those who believe their goal is to maximize profits or increase their company's value.
— Kaihan Krippendorff (Business consultant, strategist, author, *The Art of the Advantage*, The Strategic Learning Center, b. 1971)

FRIDAY
13

LT: C, S, W, CC
OE: KC

640K ought to be enough for anybody.
— William H. Gates (Microsoft founder, 1981, Try running Microsoft Vista on less than a Gig)

Yom Kippur

SATURDAY
14

SUNDAY
15

SILVER SLUMPS IN OCTOBER

Silver has a tendency to move up in September, as jewelers and manufacturers accumulate inventories in preparation for increased demand for jewelry during the year-end holiday season. In addition, the harvest season in India is underway, where tradition has been that farmers sell grain and buy precious metals, including silver, in preparation for their wedding season. Once this demand has been satisfied, silver tends to peak in early October.

This trade goes short silver on or about October 4 until about October 29. In the last 40 years this trade has worked 23 times, for a success rate of 57.5%. The over-arching precious metals bull market of 2002–2012, negatively impacted this trade in seven of the last ten years.

The weekly chart below shows Newmont Mining (NEM) stock prices overlaid on the price of silver. This company's main business is mining precious metals, such as gold and silver. As you can see, the stock price does move in close correlation with the price of silver, and the line on the bottom shows the seasonal tendency for silver prices to move lower through the month of October.

Traders have several ways to take advantage of this seasonal tendency, with an outright short position in silver futures, options on the futures, shares in the exchange-traded fund, iShares Silver Trust (SLV), and stocks or options on stocks like Newmont Mining that correlate well with the underlying commodity price moves. See pages 131–137 for additional correlated trades.

OCTOBER SHORT SILVER (DECEMBER) TRADING DAY: 4–HOLD: 17 DAYS

YEAR	ENTRY DATE	ENTRY CLOSE	EXIT DATE	EXIT CLOSE	PROFIT/ LOSS
1972	10/5	178.0	11/01	185.5	−$375
1973	10/4	275.5	10/31	288.1	−630
1974	10/4	513.0	10/30	489.0	1,200
1975	10/6	446.5	10/30	422.5	1,200
1976	10/6	431.7	10/29	433.2	−75
1977	10/6	469.0	10/31	489.2	−1,010
1978	10/5	588.5	10/30	636.5	−2,400
1979	10/4	1691.0	10/29	1665.0	1,300
1980	10/6	2165.0	10/29	1943.0	11,100
1981	10/6	968.0	10/29	938.0	1,500
1982	10/6	833.0	10/29	1009.0	−8,800
1983	10/6	1042.0	10/31	863.0	8,950
1984	10/4	773.5	10/29	723.0	2,525
1985	10/4	640.0	10/29	625.0	750
1986	10/6	581.5	10/29	563.0	925
1987	10/6	773.5	10/29	692.5	4,050
1988	10/6	637.0	10/31	634.8	110
1989	10/5	524.3	10/30	528.3	−200
1990	10/4	473.0	10/29	415.7	2,865
1991	10/4	417.0	10/29	411.5	275
1992	10/6	375.5	10/29	376.5	−50
1993	10/6	428.7	10/29	436.7	−400
1994	10/6	566.5	10/31	526.2	2,015
1995	10/5	530.7	10/30	534.3	−180
1996	10/4	487.5	10/29	482.0	275
1997	10/6	520.7	10/29	479.5	2,060
1998	10/6	509.0	10/29	507.5	75
1999	10/6	553.0	10/29	518.0	1,750
2000	10/5	493.8	10/30	477.0	840
2001	10/4	466.5	10/29	424.3	2,110
2002	10/4	449.0	10/29	451.0	−100
2003	10/6	481.5	10/29	514.2	−1,635
2004	10/6	724.5	10/29	730.5	−300
2005	10/6	759.5	10/31	758.0	75
2006	10/5	1107.0	10/30	1225.0	−5,900
2007	10/4	1350.0	10/29	1443.0	−4,650
2008	10/6	1128.5	10/29	980.5	7,400
2009	10/6	1729.5	10/29	1665.5	3,200
2010	10/6	2304.3	10/29	2456.4	−7,605
2011	10/6	3200.5	10/31	3435.4	−11,745
				40-Year Gain	**$10,495**

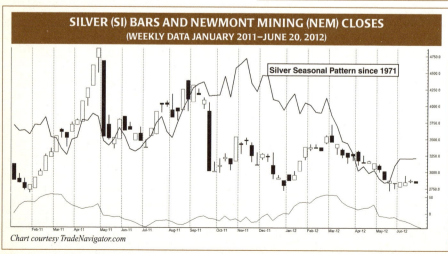

SILVER (SI) BARS AND NEWMONT MINING (NEM) CLOSES
(WEEKLY DATA JANUARY 2011–JUNE 20, 2012)

Silver Seasonal Pattern since 1971

Chart courtesy TradeNavigator.com

SEPTEMBER

Start Short Cocoa(Z)—69.2% Accuracy Since 1973—End Oct. 31—Page 125

MONDAY
16
LT: BP, EC, SF, JY
OE: SB

I went to a restaurant that serves "breakfast at any time." So I ordered French toast during the Renaissance.
— Steven Wright (Comedian, b. 1955)

TUESDAY
17
OE: CL

The way a young man spends his evenings is a part of that thin area between success and failure.
— Robert R. Young (U.S. financier and railroad tycoon, 1897–1958)

Start Long British Pound(Z)—67.6% Accuracy Since 1975—End Nov. 4—Page 84

WEDNESDAY
18
LT: KC

A president is elected and tries to get rid of the dirty stuff in the economy as quickly as possible, so that by the time the next election comes around, he looks like a hero. The stock market is reacting to what the politicians are doing.
— Yale Hirsch (Creator of *Stock Trader's Almanac, NY Times* 10/10/2010, b. 1923)

THURSDAY
19
LT: SP, US
OE: SP

It's better to have your enemies inside the tent pissing out than outside pissing in.
— Lyndon B. Johnson (36th U.S. President, 1908–1973)

FRIDAY
20
LT: CL
OE: US, C, S, W

The political problem of mankind is to combine three things: economic efficiency, social justice, and individual liberty.
— John Maynard Keynes (British economist, 1883–1946)

SATURDAY
21

SUNDAY
22

JAPANESE YEN DIVES AGAINST THE DOLLAR

The Japanese economy runs on a fiscal year running from April through March. The midpoint of the second half of their fiscal year is in October. Accounting and balance sheet adjustments are made at these points in time and are responsible for large currency transactions that have a seasonal influence on prices. Some years, of course, are more dramatic that others, but in normal economic times, we see a seasonal weakness that prevails in the yen versus the dollar.

Traders need to be aware of several key elements at hand that can cause values to move violently. For one, intervention plays a role in the currencies. In past years, the Central Bank of Japan (BOJ) has been known for intervention on behalf of managing the yen's value versus the U.S. dollar.

Traders should be aware of these tendencies and the history of actions taken with respect to certain central bankers. If the yen does manage to overstep its value relative to the dollar, beware that the BOJ can and has stepped in.

Based on our seasonal studies, traders can look to sell the yen on or about October 16 and hold until about February 7. In the 36-year history of this trade, it has worked 23 years, for a success rate of 63.9%. Massive declines in the value of the U.S. dollar, since its peak in 2002, have adversely affected this trade six times over the last ten years, so it is crucial to use technical timing tools.

The chart below shows the exchange-traded fund, Currency-Shares Japanese Yen (FXY) overlaid on the front-month yen futures contract. FXY is highly correlated with the underlying commodity price moves. See pages 131–137 for additional correlated trades.

OCTOBER SHORT YEN (MARCH)
TRADING DAY: 12–HOLD: 78 DAYS

YEAR	ENTRY DATE	ENTRY CLOSE	EXIT DATE	EXIT CLOSE	PROFIT/ LOSS
1976	10/18	34.08	2/08	34.79	−$888
1977	10/18	40.25	2/08	41.54	−1,613
1978	10/17	56.62	2/09	50.67	7,437
1979	10/16	44.18	2/07	41.92	2,825
1980	10/16	48.55	2/10	49.45	−1,125
1981	10/16	44.80	2/08	42.91	2,363
1982	10/18	37.73	2/07	42.19	−5,575
1983	10/18	43.53	2/09	42.85	850
1984	10/16	40.98	2/06	38.55	3,038
1985	10/16	46.48	2/06	52.51	−7,538
1986	10/16	65.09	2/06	64.88	263
1987	10/16	71.40	2/08	77.69	−7,862
1988	10/18	79.95	20/8	77.64	2,888
1989	10/17	70.73	2/07	68.81	2,400
1990	10/16	78.80	2/06	78.00	1,000
1991	10/16	76.55	2/06	79.41	−3,575
1992	10/16	83.64	2/08	80.81	3,538
1993	10/18	93.44	2/07	92.05	1,738
1994	10/18	103.59	2/08	101.43	2,700
1995	10/17	102.23	2/07	94.93	9,125
1996	10/16	90.98	2/07	81.73	11,563
1997	10/17	84.68	2/11	81.43	4,063
1998	10/19	89.03	2/10	87.81	1,525
1999	10/19	97.32	2/10	92.25	6,337
2000	10/18	95.27	2/09	85.50	12,213
2001	10/17	83.26	2/11	75.06	10,250
2002	10/17	80.68	2/11	82.65	−2,463
2003	10/17	91.83	2/11	94.99	−3,950
2004	10/19	93.02	2/10	94.72	−2,125
2005	10/19	88.17	2/13	85.26	3,638
2006	10/18	85.84	2/09	82.61	4,038
2007	10/17	87.29	2/11	93.73	−8,050
2008	10/17	99.46	2/10	110.62	−13,950
2009	10/16	110.17	2/09	111.57	−1,750
2010	10/18	123.36	2/8	121.37	2,487
2011	10/18	130.64	2/9	128.81	$2,287
				36-Year Gain	**$38,100**

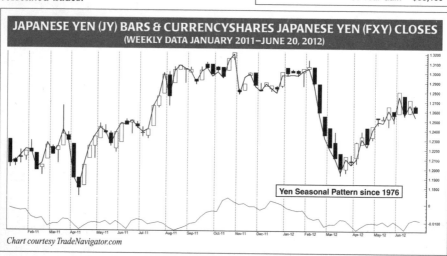

JAPANESE YEN (JY) BARS & CURRENCYSHARES JAPANESE YEN (FXY) CLOSES
(WEEKLY DATA JANUARY 2011–JUNE 20, 2012)

Yen Seasonal Pattern since 1976

Chart courtesy TradeNavigator.com

SEPTEMBER

MONDAY
23

There are two kinds of people who lose money: those who know nothing and those who know everything.
— Henry Kaufman (German-American economist, b. 1927, to Robert Lenzner in Forbes 10/19/98 who added, "With two Nobel Prize winners in the house, Long-Term Capital clearly fits the second case.")

End Long Cocoa(Z) (Aug. 20)

TUESDAY
24
FN: CL

If buying equities seem the most hazardous and foolish thing you could possibly do, then you are near the bottom that will end the bear market.
— Joseph E. Granville

WEDNESDAY
25
OE: HO NG, HG, GC, SI

It was never my thinking that made the big money for me. It was always my sitting. Got that? My sitting tight!
— Jesse Livermore (Early 20th century stock trader & speculator, *How to Trade in Stocks*, 1877–1940)

THURSDAY
26
LT: NG, HG, GC, SI

The first human who hurled an insult instead of a stone was the founder of civilization.
— Sigmund Freud (Austrian neurologist, psychiatrist, "father of psychoanalysis," 1856–1939)

FRIDAY
27
FN: NG

Let's roll!
— Todd Beamer (Passenger on United Airlines Flight 93 just before foiling the hijackers, September 11, 2001)

SATURDAY
28

SUNDAY
29

OCTOBER ALMANAC

OCTOBER

S	M	T	W	T	F	S
		1	2	3	4	5
6	7	8	9	10	11	12
13	14	15	16	17	18	19
20	21	22	23	24	25	26
27	28	29	30	31		

◆ STOCKS AND BONDS

S&P's have shown a tendency to see major bottoms in October, kicking off what is dubbed the "Best Six Months", according to *Stock Traders Almanac*. Our best seasonal percentage play gets long the March futures contract on or about the 25th and holds until December 24. This trade has a cumulative gain from the last 30 years of $231,888 (page 100). 30-year Treasuries tend to move in tandem with equities during this time of year (page 140).

NOVEMBER

S	M	T	W	T	F	S
					1	2
3	4	5	6	7	8	9
10	11	12	13	14	15	16
17	18	19	20	21	22	23
24	25	26	27	28	29	30

◆ ENERGY

Crude oil continues its seasonally weak period. We remain short from September, holding until about December 10 (page 82). Liquidate the natural gas long position from July, on or about October 21 (page 68). Heating oil prices see price surges as wholesalers begin to market to consumers, colder than normal temperatures add support as we begin the heating season. Traders can sell this strength by going short December heating oil around the 14th and hold until around Thanksgiving. This trade has a success rate of 62.5% over the past 32 years with a total gain of $51,652.

◆ METALS

Gold tends to remain under pressure in October. Silver tends to follow gold's lead, and traders can enter a short December futures position on or about October 4, holding until on or about October 29. In the last 40 years, this trade has worked 23 times, for a success rate of 57.5% and a cumulative gain of $10,495 (page 86). Copper continues its seasonal downtrend, as new construction begins to wind down for the winter months (page 149).

◆ GRAINS

Look to go long January soybeans on or about October 22, holding until about November 7 (page 94). Wheat prices generally consolidate, as harvest and new crop corn and soybean products dominate the trade (page 164). Corn's tends to post a harvest low in October (page 158).

◆ SOFTS

Cocoa is wrapping up its weak period. We are still holding the short December contract from September (page 76). Coffee prices tend to stabilize, as cold weather increases consumption, but not enough to offset inventories; thus, there is no significant price move during this month (page 170). Sugar generally maintains its seasonal uptrend (page 173).

◆ MEATS

Live cattle prices remain in a seasonal uptrend, as farmers and ranchers are focusing on the grain harvest business. Demand for beef continues to rise, as the temperature falls (page 176). Lean hogs prices remain in a seasonal downtrend. Producers are feeding newly harvested corn to fatten hogs. Weights are generally up, leading to a seasonal glut in pork through November (page 179).

◆ CURRENCIES

The euro is typically weak in October. However, we are in the beginning of a seasonally strong period until January. We have a strong seasonal bottom that we want to take advantage of by going long a March futures contract on or about the 24th and holding until January (page 96). Liquidate the long Swiss franc from August, on or about October 16 (page 70). The British pound is in a period of rising prices; maintain the long trade position from September 18 until on or about November 4 (page 84). The yen's seasonal weakness prevails versus the dollar. Traders can look to short the March yen futures contract on or about October 16, holding that position until on or about February 7 (page 88).

OCTOBER STRATEGY CALENDAR*

Symbol	B	M	E
SP	L S		
US	L S		
CL	L S		
NG	L S		
HO	L S		
HG	L S		
GC	L S		
SI	L S		
C	L S		
S	L S		
W	L S		
CC	L S		
KC	L S		
SB	L S		
LC	L S		
LH	L S		
BP	L S		
EC	L S		
SF	L S		
JY	L S		

* Graphic representation of the Commodity Seasonality Percentage Plays on pages 124–125.
L = Long Trade, S = Short Trade. See pages 131–137 for contract symbols.

MONDAY

30

FN: HG, GC, SI
LT: HO, SB

Let me tell you the secret that has led me to my goal. My strength lies solely in my tenacity.
— Louis Pasteur (French chemist, founder of microbiology, 1822–1895)

End Long Gold(Z) (Aug. 26)
End Long Euro(Z) (Sep. 9)

TUESDAY

1

FN: SB

Being uneducated is sometimes beneficial. Then you don't know what can't be done.
— Michael Ott (Venture capitalist)

WEDNESDAY

2

FN: HO

Get inside information from the president and you will probably lose half your money. If you get it from the chairman of the board, you will lose all your money.
— Jim Rogers (Financier, b. 1942)

THURSDAY

3

History is a collection of agreed upon lies.
— Voltaire (French philosopher, 1694–1778)

Start Short Silver(Z)—57.5% Accuracy Since 1972—End Oct. 29—Page 86

FRIDAY

4

OE: CC, LC, BP, EC, SF, JY

I cannot give you a formula for success but I can give you a formula for failure: Try to please everybody.
— Herbert Swope (American Journalist, 1882–1958)

SATURDAY

5

SUNDAY

6

PRE-WINTER PREP PRESSURES HEATING OIL

Somewhat counter intuitively, heating oil prices usually make a seasonal high well ahead of the peak demand time of the year. Refiners, retailers, and consumers are highly trained to stock up on heating oil months before the dead of winter when temperatures are coldest and the need for heat the greatest. In line with its parent crude oil, heating oil has a penchant for topping out in mid-October.

This sets up an autumn short trade opportunity. For the past 32 years, selling December heating oil short on or about October 14 and holding until around Thanksgiving has been profitable 62.5% of the time, posting gains in 20 of these years for a cumulative gain of $51,652 per contract. This trade runs contiguous to the crude oil short from September to December on page 82.

In the chart below, the ELEMENTS Rogers International Commodity Energy ETN (RJN) is plotted against heating oil. Despite the fact that RJN is composed of a basket of six different energy futures (47.7% crude oil, 31.8% Brent crude oil, 6.8% natural gas, 6.8% RBOB gasoline, 4.1% heating oil, and 2.7% gas oil), it is extremely closely correlated to the price trend of heating oil.

There are not many liquid stocks or exchange trade products that track heating oil well. RJN is an exchange trade note (ETN). Like ETFs, ETNs trade intraday on a major exchange like a stock, but they are an unsecured, unsubordinated, debt security. However, the credit rating of the issuer of RJN, the reputation of renowned investor Jim Rogers, whose name is on the fund, the relatively robust liquidity of RJN, and the fact that it has options make RJN one of the best equity-oriented alternatives for trading heating oil futures.

OCTOBER SHORT HEATING OIL (DECEMBER) TRADING DAY: 10–HOLD: 29 DAYS

YEAR	ENTRY DATE	ENTRY CLOSE	EXIT DATE	EXIT CLOSE	PROFIT/ LOSS
1980	10/14	83.00	11/25	90.00	−$2,940
1981	10/14	99.81	11/24	101.49	−706
1982	10/14	103.61	11/26	85.85	7,459
1983	10/14	82.86	11/28	80.67	920
1984	10/12	79.75	11/26	75.32	1,861
1985	10/14	82.21	11/22	89.34	−2,995
1986	10/14	40.90	11/24	41.90	−420
1987	10/14	56.25	11/24	55.46	332
1988	10/14	44.06	11/28	48.65	−1,928
1989	10/13	61.29	11/24	61.41	−50
1990	10/12	106.06	11/23	88.66	7,308
1991	10/14	69.94	11/22	62.06	3,310
1992	10/14	65.36	11/24	56.50	3,721
1993	10/14	56.32	11/24	50.06	2,629
1994	10/14	47.56	11/28	50.58	−1,268
1995	10/13	49.52	11/27	53.42	−1,638
1996	10/14	73.68	11/22	72.79	374
1997	10/14	58.17	11/24	55.60	1,079
1998	10/14	39.63	11/24	33.29	2,663
1999	10/14	59.09	11/24	69.84	−4,515
2000	10/13	101.99	11/27	108.52	−2,743
2001	10/12	64.76	11/26	52.17	5,288
2002	10/14	81.47	11/22	76.64	2,029
2003	10/14	88.21	11/24	82.03	2,596
2004	10/14	155.10	11/24	145.16	4,175
2005	10/14	199.04	11/28	163.56	14,902
2006	10/13	176.11	11/27	170.52	2,348
2007	10/12	226.69	11/23	270.42	−18,367
2008	10/14	228.82	11/24	178.44	21,160
2009	10/14	197.39	11/24	194.97	1,016
2010	10/14	230.27	11/24	232.55	−958
2011	10/14	304.66	11/25	292.73	5,011
				32-Year Gain	**$51,652**

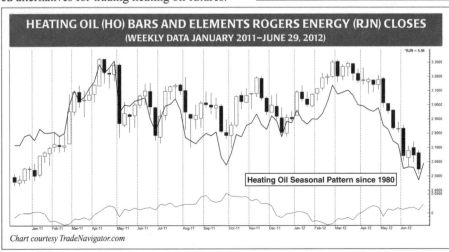

HEATING OIL (HO) BARS AND ELEMENTS ROGERS ENERGY (RJN) CLOSES
(WEEKLY DATA JANUARY 2011–JUNE 29, 2012)

Heating Oil Seasonal Pattern since 1980

Chart courtesy TradeNavigator.com

OCTOBER

MONDAY

7

FN: LC

When Paris sneezes, Europe catches cold.
— Prince Klemens Metternich (Austrian statesman, 1773–1859)

TUESDAY

8

One machine can do the work of fifty ordinary men. No machine can do the work of one extraordinary man.
— Elbert Hubbard (American author, *A Message To Garcia*, 1856–1915)

WEDNESDAY

9

Age is a question of mind over matter. If you don't mind, it doesn't matter.
— Leroy Robert "Satchel" Paige (Negro League and Hall of Fame Pitcher, 1906–1982)

THURSDAY

10

When the S&P Index Future premium over "Cash" gets too high, I sell the future and buy the stocks. If the premium disappears, well, buy the future and sell the stocks.
— Neil Elliott (Fahnestock)

FRIDAY

11

OE: KC

My best shorts come from research reports where there are recommendations to buy stocks on weakness; also, where a brokerage firm changes its recommendation from a buy to a hold.
— Marc Howard (Hedge fund manager, *New York Magazine* 1976, b. 1941)

SATURDAY

12

SUNDAY

13

SOYBEAN'S HARVEST LOWS OFFER POTENTIAL FREE MEAL

This is generally not the time to sell short, especially after a prolonged decline from a peak in price at the June highs. Traders should not be looking to sell on any further weakness in early October; in fact, this is the time to cover short bean positions. Typically, this is the time of year when soybeans post what is known as their harvest lows.

Soybeans are a cash commodity because end users with feed operations that use soy meal to feed livestock and poultry must purchase hand-to-mouth, as soy meal does not have a long shelf life. Fresh new product is being rushed to cattle and hog feed lots as well as to poultry operations, and exports of soybeans are being marketed. This wave of demand starts to create a floor of support in prices (page 161).

To take advantage of this seasonal trend, traders can go long soybeans on or about October 24 and hold until around November 7. In the last 44 years, this trade has worked 27 times, for a 61.4% success rate.

The chart below shows the price of Monsanto (MON) overlaid on the price of soybeans. MON makes Roundup Ready soybean seed and has a joint venture with Cargill to commercialize a proprietary grain processing technology under the name Extrax.

Monsanto correlates very well with the price direction of soybeans. It also forms its average seasonal low in October. See pages 131–137 for additional correlated trades.

OCTOBER LONG SOYBEANS (JANUARY) TRADING DAY: 16–HOLD: 12 DAYS

YEAR	ENTRY DATE	ENTRY CLOSE	EXIT DATE	EXIT CLOSE	PROFIT/ LOSS
1968	10/22	255	11/08	261 1/4	$313
1969	10/22	250	11/07	249 1/2	−25
1970	10/22	306 1/4	11/10	308	88
1971	10/22	327 3/4	11/09	320 7/8	−344
1972	10/23	342 3/8	11/09	356 1/4	694
1973	10/23	554	11/08	556 1/2	125
1974	10/22	867	11/08	863	−200
1975	10/22	517 1/2	11/07	504 3/4	−638
1976	10/22	658	11/10	675	850
1977	10/24	535 3/4	11/09	595 1/2	2,988
1978	10/23	681 1/2	11/09	669	−625
1979	10/22	673 3/4	11/07	667	−338
1980	10/22	922 1/2	11/10	911	−575
1981	10/22	667 3/4	11/09	667 1/4	−25
1982	10/22	543 1/4	11/10	578 1/4	1,750
1983	10/24	841	11/09	872 1/2	1,575
1984	10/22	634 1/2	11/07	639	225
1985	10/22	522 1/4	11/07	527	238
1986	10/22	493 1/2	11/07	500 1/4	338
1987	10/22	544 3/4	11/09	553 1/4	425
1988	10/24	780 1/2	11/09	808 1/4	1,388
1989	10/23	575 1/4	11/08	576 3/4	75
1990	10/22	625 1/2	11/07	597 1/2	−1,400
1991	10/22	567	11/07	557	−500
1992	10/22	552 3/4	11/09	551	−88
1993	10/22	629 1/2	11/09	639	475
1994	10/24	564 1/4	11/09	572	388
1995	10/23	678 1/4	11/08	689 3/4	575
1996	10/22	690	11/07	685 3/4	−213
1997	10/22	704 3/4	11/07	739 1/2	1,738
1998	10/22	565	11/09	573 1/2	425
1999	10/22	484 1/2	11/09	479	−275
2000	10/23	473 1/2	11/08	484	525
2001	10/22	426 3/4	11/07	441 1/4	725
2002	10/22	548 1/4	11/07	568 1/4	1,000
2003	10/22	752	11/07	748 1/2	−175
2004	10/22	532	11/09	510 1/2	−1,075
2005	10/24	587 1/2	11/09	588 1/2	50
2006	10/23	630 1/2	11/08	678	2,375
2007	10/22	993 3/4	11/07	1038 1/2	2,238
2008	10/22	864 3/4	11/07	921	2,813
2009	10/22	1007	11/09	972	−1,750
2010	10/22	1211 1/2	11/09	1329	5,875
2011	10/24	1235 1/4	11/09	1185 1/2	−2,488

44-Year Gain $19,538

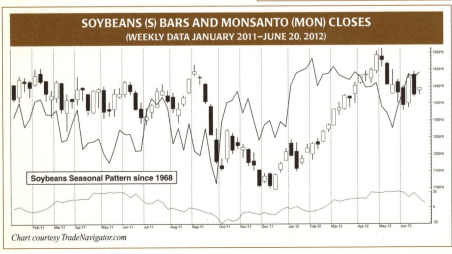

SOYBEANS (S) BARS AND MONSANTO (MON) CLOSES
(WEEKLY DATA JANUARY 2011–JUNE 20, 2012)

Soybeans Seasonal Pattern since 1968

Chart courtesy TradeNavigator.com

OCTOBER

Columbus Day (Bond Market Closed)
Start Short Heating Oil(Z)—62.5% Accuracy Since 1980—End Nov. 22—Page 92

MONDAY

14
LT: LH
OE: LH

The authority of a thousand is not worth the humble reasoning of a single individual.
— Galileo Galilei (Italian physicist and astronomer, 1564–1642)

TUESDAY

15
OE: SB

Wall Street's graveyards are filled with men who were right too soon.
— William Peter Hamilton (Editor, *Wall Street Journal, The Stock Market Barometer*, 1922, 1867–1929)

End Long Swiss Franc(Z) (Aug. 8)
Start Short Yen(H)—63.9% Accuracy Since 1976—End Feb. 7, 2014—Page 88

WEDNESDAY

16

It's a lot of fun finding a country nobody knows about. The only thing better is finding a country everybody's bullish on and shorting it.
— Jim Rogers (Financier, *Investment Biker*, b. 1942)

THURSDAY

17
OE: CL

A government which robs Peter to pay Paul can always depend on the support of Paul.
— George Bernard Shaw (Irish dramatist, 1856–1950)

FRIDAY

18
OE: SP

It is totally unproductive to think the world has been unfair to you. Every tough stretch is an opportunity.
— Charlie Munger (Vice-Chairman Berkshire Hathaway, 2007 Wesco Annual Meeting, b. 1924)

SATURDAY

19

SUNDAY

20

TWO-MONTH YEAR-END EURO RALLY

Here is one of our best foreign currency (FX) plays. We had a hard time deciding whether or not share it. The euro is weak in the beginning of October and then, towards the end of the month, begins a seasonally strong period. Since it is a trade phenomenon that has been shared at several conferences in the past, after long discussions, we decided to add the trade in the 2010 edition. This, of course, jinxed the trade.

In the short history of the euro currency, the market seems to make a bottom around the third week of October; then we see a tendency to make a price gain against the U.S. dollar by year's end. Many factors could be at play to explain this, such as multi-conglomerate U.S. corporations' need to make fiscal year-end book adjustments as well as to make foreign payroll and bonuses.

The trade itself begins by going long on or about October 24 and holding until about January 2. Due to the expiration of the December futures contract, we ran the statistics using the March futures contract. Overall we have a 61.5% success rate with 8 wins and 5 losses. The best win was in 2000 with a whopping $14,813 gain. Once again in 2011, European sovereign debt concerns trumped seasonal tendency.

OCTOBER LONG EURO (MARCH) TRADING DAY: 18 – HOLD : 47 DAYS					
	ENTRY		EXIT		PROFIT/
YEAR	DATE	CLOSE	DATE	CLOSE	LOSS
1999	10/28	106.22	1/6	103.49	–$3,413
2000	10/26	83.39	1/4	95.24	14,813
2001	10/24	88.92	1/3	89.74	1,025
2002	10/25	97.15	1/6	104.42	9,087
2003	10/27	116.98	1/6	127.37	12,988
2004	10/27	127.05	1/5	132.74	7,113
2005	10/27	122.35	1/6	122.03	–400
2006	10/26	127.78	1/4	131.31	4,413
2007	10/25	143.37	1/4	147.77	5,500
2008	10/27	125.23	1/5	135.73	13,125
2009	10/26	148.50	1/4	144.10	–5,500
2010	10/26	138.20	1/3	133.62	–5,725
2011	10/26	138.88	1/4	129.44	–11,800
			13-Year Gain		$41,225

Traders can use the spot FX markets, which would eliminate the need to buy a far out futures contract month. Stock traders can look at the exchange-traded fund, CurrencyShares Euro (FXE), or trade options on this instrument. In addition, the International Securities Exchange has a Euro Currency Index quoted in dollars per euro, symbol (EUI). It is accessible through your stock options broker; it is an exchange-listed security and is cash-settled in U.S. dollars with a European style exercise. See pages 131–137 for additional correlated trades.

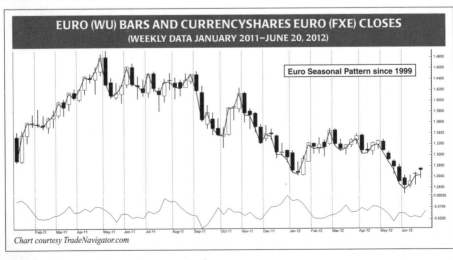

EURO (WU) BARS AND CURRENCYSHARES EURO (FXE) CLOSES
(WEEKLY DATA JANUARY 2011–JUNE 20, 2012)

Euro Seasonal Pattern since 1999

Chart courtesy TradeNavigator.com

End Long Natural Gas(X) (Jul. 24)

MONDAY

21

You have to keep digging, keep asking questions, because otherwise you'll be seduced or brainwashed into the idea that it's somehow a great privilege, an honor, to report the lies they've been feeding you.
— David Halberstam (Amercian writer, war reporter, 1964 Pulitzer Prize, 1934–2007)

Start Long Soybeans(F)—61.4% Accuracy Since 1968—End Nov. 7—Page 94

TUESDAY

22

LT: CL

The biggest change we made was the move to a boundary-less company. We got rid of the corner offices, the bureaucracy, and the not-invented-here syndrome. Instead we got every mind in the game, got the best out of all our people.
— Jack Welch (retiring CEO of General Electric, *Business Week*, September 10, 2001)

WEDNESDAY

23

Cannot people realize how large an income is thrift?
— Marcus Tullius Cicero (Great Roman Orator, Politician, 106–43 B.C.)

Start Long Euro(H)—61.5% Accuracy Since 1999—End Jan. 2, 2014—Page 96

THURSDAY

24

FN: CL

A "tired businessman" is one whose business is usually not a successful one.
— Joseph R. Grundy (U.S. Senator Pennsylvania 1929–1930, businessman, 1863–1961)

Start Long S&P 500(H)—73.3% Accuracy Since 1982—End Dec. 24—Page 100

FRIDAY

25

OE: US, C, S, W

Brilliant men are often strikingly ineffectual; they fail to realize that the brilliant insight is not by itself achievement. They never have learned that insights become effectiveness only through hard systematic work.
— Peter Drucker (Austrian-born pioneer management theorist, 1909–2005)

SATURDAY

26

SUNDAY

27

NOVEMBER ALMANAC

NOVEMBER						
S	M	T	W	T	F	S
					1	2
3	4	5	6	7	8	9
10	11	12	13	14	15	16
17	18	19	20	21	22	23
24	25	26	27	28	29	30

◆ STOCKS AND BONDS

We are holding our best seasonal percentage play, which is long the S&P's March futures contract from October 25 and holding until December 24 (page 100). Short-term traders watch for a rally the day before Thanksgiving and the day after, known as "Black Friday." 30-year Treasury bond prices tend to decline in late November. We have a seasonal short play selling the June futures contract on or about November 20 and holding through April 28 the following year (page 106).

DECEMBER						
S	M	T	W	T	F	S
1	2	3	4	5	6	7
8	9	10	11	12	13	14
15	16	17	18	19	20	21
22	23	24	25	26	27	28
29	30	31				

◆ ENERGY

Crude oil continues to be in a seasonally weak period. We are still short from September, holding that position until about December 10 (page 82). November is a mixed month for natural gas, depending on the temperatures in the Midwest. Beginning in October, if weather patterns are mild, then we see less demand; prices tend to consolidate (page 145). Heating Oil has closed lower in November from October's close 17 of the past 32 years (page 148).

◆ METALS

Look to go long a gold February futures contract on or about November 19 until about December 4 (page 104). The long trade was outstanding, as gold posted an interim high on December 3, before giving back all November's gains. Aggressive traders can look to go long December silver in tandem with gold (page 155). Copper's seasonal downtrend continues through December (page 149).

◆ GRAINS

Liquidate the long soybeans positions from October, on or about November 7 (page 94). Also liquidate the long wheat position from June, on or about November 6 (page 125). Corn is just beginning its seasonally strong period after the harvest lows (page 158).

◆ SOFTS

Cover the short cocoa position from July, on or about November 1 (page 76). Enter a long March cocoa position on or about November 6 and hold until on or about December 26. This trade has worked 21 of 40 years, for a success rate of 52.5%, and has had a cumulative profit of $15,720, suffering this trade's worst loss in 2011 (page 125). Coffee prices continue to stabilize, as cold weather increases consumption, but November rarely sees significant price moves (page 170). Sugar prices tend to peak out, but don't offer any solid trading opportunities (page 173).

◆ MEATS

Live cattle prices exhibit a push higher toward the middle of the month, but consumer demand declines, as the turkey-centric Thanksgiving holiday diminishes beef sales. This can cause a short-term glut of inventory that can push prices lower through the first part of December (page 176). Buy February lean hogs on or about November 4 and exit on or before November 21 (page 102).

◆ CURRENCIES

Over the last 13 years, the euro has rallied through year-end eight times. Our best year-end rally play in the euro is still long (page 96). Look to go long the Swiss franc on or about November 26 and hold through year end (page 125). Liquidate the long British pound position from September on or about November 4 (page 84). The yen remains in a seasonal weak period versus the U.S. dollar. Maintain a short position from about October 16 until about February 7 (page 88).

NOVEMBER STRATEGY CALENDAR*

Symbol	B	M	E
SP	L / S		
US	L / S		
CL	L / S		
NG	L / S		
HO	L / S		
HG	L / S		
GC	L / S		
SI	L / S		
C	L / S		
S	L / S		
W	L / S		
CC	L / S		
KC	L / S		
SB	L / S		
LC	L / S		
LH	L / S		
BP	L / S		
EC	L / S		
SF	L / S		
JY	L / S		

* Graphic representation of the Commodity Seasonality Percentage Plays on pages 124–125.
L = Long Trade, S = Short Trade. See pages 131–137 for contract symbols.

98

OCTOBER/NOVEMBER

MONDAY

28

OE: HO, NG, HG, GC, SI

We will have to pay more and more attention to what the funds are doing. They are the ones who have been contributing to the activity, especially in the high-fliers.
— Humphrey B. Neill (Investor, analyst, author, *NY Times* 6/11/1966, 1895–1977)

End Short Silver(Z) (Oct. 4)

TUESDAY

29

LT: NG, HG, GC, SI

When teachers held high expectations of their students that alone was enough to cause an increase of 25 points in the students' IQ scores.
— Warren Bennis (Author, *The Unconscious Conspiracy: Why Leaders Can't Lead*, 1976)

WEDNESDAY

30

FN: NG

If you are not willing to study, if you are not sufficiently interested to investigate and analyze the stock market yourself, then I beg of you to become an outright long-pull investor, to buy good stocks, and hold on to them; for otherwise your chances of success as a trader will be nil.
— Humphrey B. Neill ((Investor, analyst, author, *Tape Reading and Market Tactics*, 1931, 1895–1977)

Halloween 🎃

End Short Cocoa(Z) (Sep. 16)

THURSDAY

31

FN: HG, GC, SI, S
LT: HO, LC

Friendship renders prosperity more brilliant, while it lightens adversity by sharing it and making its burden common.
— Marcus Tullius Cicero (Great Roman Orator, Politician, 106–43 B.C.)

End Short Cocoa(Z) (Jul. 25)

FRIDAY

1

OE: CC, LC

To achieve satisfactory investment results is easier than most people realize. The typical individual investor has a great advantage over the large institutions.
— Benjamin Graham (Economist, investor, *Securities Analysis* 1934, *The Intelligent Investor* 1949, 1894–1976)

SATURDAY

2

Daylight Saving Time Ends

SUNDAY

3

MASSIVE S&P 500 GAINS HALLOWEEN TO CHRISTMAS

Here it is folks, the beginning of the best six months of the year to go long equities. October has been considered, on average, the best time to go long stocks with the reputation of having tremendous crashes, "acting as the bear market killer."

October has a spooky history that has scared many strong-willed and financially sound investors and traders with the likes of the fabled Friday the 13th crash in 1989, or the earlier double whammy, back to back debacles in 1978 and 1979. Once again, as an avid futures trader who was around and trading during the crash in 1987, John can testify that October can be a scary month, yet a lucrative one for the well-informed trader.

As is published in the *Stock Traders Almanac*, October can be a time to buy depressed stocks. This may be what helps in this situation, going long the March futures contract on or about October 25 and holding until December 24. Once again, due to the length of the holding period, we have featured this trade entering the next-month futures contract as opposed to the front-month December contract, which one would need to roll into the March contract due to expiration.

The success rate is a whopping 73.3%, registering a cumulative gain of $231,888 per one lot futures contract. This is the *Commodity Trader Almanac's* highest dollar amount winner by far. In fact, even during the worst of times in 2008, we registered a nice return of $7,825. The best gain was in 1999 with a profit of $38,975, and the worst loser was in 2000 with a loss of only $13,600. In the last 30 years, we have had 22 wins and only 8 losses. Europe's debt crisis spoiled the trade in 2011.

This is a trade well worth considering, and of course, there are several ways to participate: full-futures contracts, the e-mini electronic futures, the exchange-traded fund, SPDR S&P 500 (SPY), or in fact, devising a bullish option strategy on these products. See pages 131–137 for additional correlated trades.

OCTOBER LONG S&P 500 MARCH) TRADING DAY: 19 – HOLD : 41 DAYS

YEAR	ENTRY DATE	ENTRY CLOSE	EXIT DATE	EXIT CLOSE	PROFIT/ LOSS
1982	10/27	135.75	12/27	144.70	$2,238
1983	10/27	169.10	12/28	167.40	−425
1984	10/25	171.95	12/24	171.15	−200
1985	10/25	189.05	12/24	209.25	5,050
1986	10/27	240.05	12/24	248.30	2,063
1987	10/27	229.75	12/24	253.30	5,888
1988	10/27	282.15	12/27	280.00	−537
1989	10/26	343.65	12/26	350.45	1,700
1990	10/25	314.10	12/24	331.20	4,275
1991	10/25	387.60	12/24	400.90	3,325
1992	10/27	418.30	12/24	440.65	5,587
1993	10/27	466.65	12/27	471.65	1,250
1994	10/27	470.40	12/27	466.00	−1,100
1995	10/26	583.35	12/26	619.55	9,050
1996	10/25	711.75	12/24	759.05	11,825
1997	10/27	884.40	12/24	942.20	14,450
1998	10/27	1084.10	12/24	1239.50	38,850
1999	10/27	1321.90	12/27	1477.80	38,975
2000	10/26	1391.30	12/26	1336.90	−13,600
2001	10/25	1104.70	12/24	1147.20	10,625
2002	10/25	898.50	12/24	891.50	−1,750
2003	10/27	1029.20	12/24	1092.90	15,925
2004	10/27	1126.00	12/27	1208.40	20,600
2005	10/27	1189.70	12/27	1264.00	18,575
2006	10/26	1404.70	12/26	1428.80	6,025
2007	10/25	1534.90	12/24	1506.60	−7,075
2008	10/27	833.70	12/24	865.00	7,825
2009	10/27	1055.50	12/24	1122.00	16,625
2010	10/27	1173.50	12/27	1253.30	19,950
2011	10/27	1276.60	12/27	1260.20	−4,100
30-Year Gain					**$231,888**

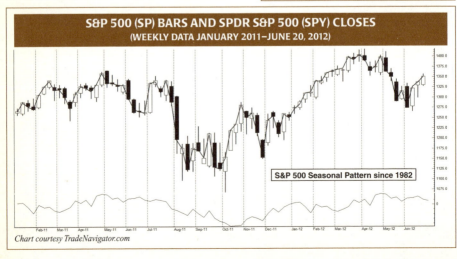

S&P 500 (SP) BARS AND SPDR S&P 500 (SPY) CLOSES
(WEEKLY DATA JANUARY 2011–JUNE 20, 2012)

S&P 500 Seasonal Pattern since 1982

Chart courtesy TradeNavigator.com

NOVEMBER

End Long British Pound(Z) (Sep. 18)
Start Long Lean Hogs(G)—67.4% Accuracy Since 1969—End Nov. 21—Page 102

MONDAY
4
FN: HO

Those that forget the past are condemned to repeat its mistakes, and those that mis-state the past should be condemned.
— Eugene D. Cohen (Letter to the Editor Financial Times 10/30/06)

Election Day

TUESDAY
5

I know nothing grander, better exercise...more positive proof of the past, the triumphant result of faith in humankind, than a well-contested American national election.
— Walt Whitman (American poet, 1819–1892)

End Long Wheat(Z) (Jun. 10)
Start Long Cocoa(H)—52.5% Accuracy Since 1972—End Dec. 26—Page 125

WEDNESDAY
6

If all the economists in the world were laid end to end, they still wouldn't reach a conclusion.
— George Bernard Shaw (Irish dramatist, 1856–1950)

End Long Soybeans(F) (Oct. 22)

THURSDAY
7

In an uptrend, if a higher high is made but fails to carry through, and prices dip below the previous high, the trend is apt to reverse. The converse is true for downtrends.
— Victor Sperandeo (*Trader Vic—Methods of a Wall Street Master*)

FRIDAY
8
OE: KC, BP, EC, SF, JY

The reading of all good books is indeed like a conversation with the noblest men of past centuries, in which they reveal to us the best of their thoughts.
— René Descartes (French philosopher, mathematician & scientist, 1596–1650)

SATURDAY
9

SUNDAY
10

LEAN HOGS FATTEN UP BEFORE THANKSGIVING

Demand for pork increases, as consumers switch meat products when beef prices are too high. In addition, Canadian imports have started to fall off, and now we begin a cycle of demand outpacing inventories.

Seasonally, we have a low posted in the hog market in November, so traders should look to buy lean hogs on or about November 4 and exit on or about November 21. In the last 43 years, this trade has provided 29 years of gains, for a success rate of 67.4%. The cumulative profit is $16,350. Again, using some simple timing techniques should have had you exiting after Thanksgiving at even more favorable prices in 2010.

The chart below is of Hormel Foods (HRL), overlaid on the lean hogs front-month futures contract to illustrate the correlation in the price action. This company is in the business of processing pork and producing hogs, both here in the United States and abroad.

As you can see, Hormel has a strong correlation to the price of hog futures. The price move of HRL and lean hog futures in 2011–2012 is rather similar to the historical seasonal price pattern of lean hogs, shown in the bottom line on the chart. Another company traders can follow based on hog price moves is Smithfield Foods (SFD), a pork product producer. These two stocks frequently move in tandem with hogs. See pages 131–137 for additional correlated trades and page 179 for more hog seasonalities.

NOVEMBER LONG LEAN HOGS (FEBRUARY)
TRADING DAY: 2–HOLD: 13 DAYS

YEAR	ENTRY DATE	CLOSE	EXIT DATE	CLOSE	PROFIT/ LOSS
1969	11/4	25.550	11/21	27.050	$600
1970	11/4	17.000	11/23	17.250	100
1971	11/2	22.175	11/19	23.425	500
1972	11/2	29.350	11/22	29.200	−60
1973	11/2	46.075	11/21	48.750	1,070
1974	11/4	43.650	11/22	44.075	170
1975	11/4	50.450	11/21	53.225	1,110
1976	11/3	29.925	11/22	33.300	1,350
1977	11/2	36.875	11/21	38.350	590
1978	11/2	49.400	11/22	53.700	1,720
1979	11/2	40.800	11/21	45.250	1,780
1980	11/5	55.575	11/24	55.450	−50
1981	11/3	49.000	11/20	46.300	−1,080
1982	11/2	53.825	11/19	56.750	1,170
1983	11/2	46.700	11/21	46.175	−210
1984	11/2	51.000	11/21	53.475	990
1985	11/4	46.125	11/21	46.300	70
1986	11/4	48.625	11/21	51.425	1,120
1987	11/3	41.275	11/20	43.750	990
1988	11/2	45.825	11/21	42.625	−1,280
1989	11/2	46.625	11/21	50.625	1,600
1990	11/2	50.050	11/21	51.725	670
1991	11/4	42.175	11/21	42.750	230
1992	11/3	42.925	11/20	44.225	520
1993	11/2	49.875	11/19	47.425	−980
1994	11/2	36.800	11/21	34.950	−740
1995	11/2	46.200	11/21	46.950	300
1996	11/4	75.950	11/21	76.275	130
1997	11/4	62.825	11/21	61.775	−420
1998	11/3	42.625	11/20	36.650	−2,390
1999	11/2	49.700	11/19	54.925	2,090
2000	11/2	53.700	11/21	56.850	1,260
2001	11/2	54.700	11/21	53.600	−440
2002	11/4	50.450	11/21	52.750	920
2003	11/4	58.550	11/21	54.075	−1,790
2004	11/2	69.725	11/19	73.400	1,470
2005	11/2	65.925	11/21	64.625	−520
2006	11/2	67.800	11/21	66.550	−500
2007	11/2	59.875	11/21	62.750	1,150
2008	11/4	61.850	11/21	64.100	900
2009	11/3	64.525	11/20	64.375	−60
2010	11/2	72.375	11/19	76.850	1,790
2011	11/2	89.725	11/21	91.000	510

43-Year Gain $16,350

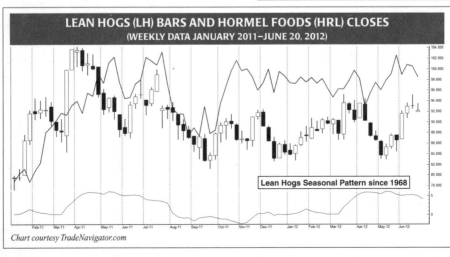

LEAN HOGS (LH) BARS AND HORMEL FOODS (HRL) CLOSES
(WEEKLY DATA JANUARY 2011–JUNE 20, 2012)

Lean Hogs Seasonal Pattern since 1968

Chart courtesy TradeNavigator.com

NOVEMBER

Veterans' Day

MONDAY
11

Change is the law of life. And those who look only to the past or present are certain to miss the future.
— John F. Kennedy (35th U.S. President, 1917–1963)

TUESDAY
12

A national debt, if it is not excessive, will be to us a national blessing.
— Alexander Hamilton (U.S. Treasury Secretary 1789–1795, The Federalist 1788, in April 30, 1781 letter to Robert Morris)

WEDNESDAY
13

In my experience, selling a put is much safer than buying a stock.
— Kyle Rosen (Boston Capital Mgmt., *Barron's* 8/23/04)

THURSDAY
14
LT: S

It's not the strongest of the species (think "traders") that survive, nor the most intelligent, but the one most responsive to change.
— Charles Darwin

FRIDAY
15
FN: CC
OE: SP, CL, SB

Our firm conviction is that, sooner or later, capitalism will give way to socialism... We will bury you.
— Nikita Khrushchev (Soviet leader 1953–1964, 1894–1971)

SATURDAY
16

SUNDAY
17

GOLD BUGS GET A TREAT FOR THE HOLIDAYS

Gold prices tend to move up prior to the holidays, and the trend has worked especially well over the last 12 years. Seasonally speaking, it is best for traders to go long on or about November 19 and hold until about December 4. Over the last 37 years, this trade has worked 21 times, for a success rate of 56.8%. The cumulative profit tallies up to $31,490. What is interesting is that this trade has had a 12-year win streak, starting from 2000. The longer-term record of this trade is not eye-popping, but with growing inflation concerns due to a global debt crisis and deficit spending, we would look for the current winning streak to continue in 2013 and beyond.

The chart below shows the correlation of gold with Freeport-McMoran Copper & Gold (FCX), a company in the business of the exploration and development of gold. The FCX stock price line chart is overlaid on the front-month gold futures contract. The line on the bottom section is the 37-year average seasonal price move for gold.

As you can see, both gold and FCX are highly correlated. What is important here is to see the seasonality of November's rally into December. Notice the price dip in November in gold and FCX. This price relationship between gold and producers should continue unless a gold producer begins an aggressive hedging operation, which entails selling gold in the futures to lock in production profits. In this scenario, if gold prices continue to rise during the seasonal buy period and a gold producer sells futures contracts to lock in a profit, the company could reduce its maximum profit exposure, and that is when trading a stock versus a commodity would not be effective. See pages 131–137 for additional correlated trades.

NOVEMBER LONG GOLD (FEBRUARY) TRADING DAY: 13–HOLD: 10 DAYS

YEAR	ENTRY DATE	ENTRY CLOSE	EXIT DATE	EXIT CLOSE	PROFIT/ LOSS
1975	11/21	142.6	12/8	136.9	–$570
1976	11/18	129.3	12/3	133.3	400
1977	11/17	162.6	12/2	160.1	–250
1978	11/20	201.8	12/5	199.1	–270
1979	11/19	399.0	12/4	438.5	3,950
1980	11/20	665.1	12/5	638.0	–2,710
1981	11/18	405.5	12/3	428.0	2,250
1982	11/18	419.6	12/3	447.8	2,820
1983	11/17	384.2	12/2	404.1	1,990
1984	11/19	348.5	12/4	334.1	–1,440
1985	11/19	328.8	12/4	325.7	–310
1986	11/19	392.1	12/4	391.7	–40
1987	11/18	470.8	12/3	493.8	2,300
1988	11/17	426.0	12/5	434.2	820
1989	11/17	401.0	12/4	406.6	560
1990	11/19	385.6	12/4	380.5	–510
1991	11/19	367.3	12/4	367.9	60
1992	11/18	336.5	12/3	336.4	–10
1993	11/17	379.2	12/3	378.6	–60
1994	11/17	389.7	12/5	379.0	–1,070
1995	11/17	389.1	12/5	388.7	–40
1996	11/19	380.2	12/5	373.0	–720
1997	11/17	306.3	12/5	290.5	–1,580
1998	11/18	300.3	12/4	294.3	–600
1999	11/17	297.5	12/3	282.1	–1,540
2000	11/17	268.9	12/5	273.3	440
2001	11/19	273.7	12/5	274.6	90
2002	11/19	319.8	12/5	325.6	580
2003	11/19	396.0	12/5	407.3	1,130
2004	11/17	447.2	12/3	457.8	1,060
2005	11/17	490.8	12/5	512.6	2,180
2006	11/17	628.7	12/5	647.9	1,920
2007	11/19	784.8	12/4	807.6	2,280
2008	11/18	736.0	12/4	765.5	2,950
2009	11/18	1142.7	12/3	1218.3	7,560
2010	11/17	1339.0	12/2	1389.3	5,030
2011	11/17	1722.9	12/2	1751.3	2,840
				37-Year Gain	$31,490

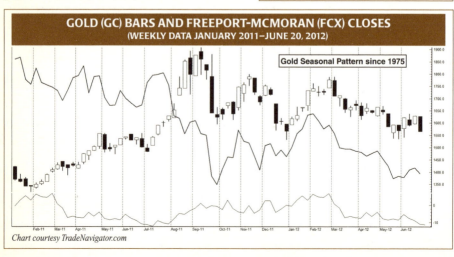

GOLD (GC) BARS AND FREEPORT-MCMORAN (FCX) CLOSES
(WEEKLY DATA JANUARY 2011–JUNE 20, 2012)

Gold Seasonal Pattern since 1975

Chart courtesy TradeNavigator.com

NOVEMBER

MONDAY
18

The advice of the elders to young men is very apt to be as unreal as a list of the best books.
— Oliver Wendell Holmes Jr. (U.S. Supreme Court Justice 1902–1932, *The Mind and Faith of Justice Holmes*, edited by Max Lerner, 1841–1935)

Start Long Gold(G)—56.8% Accuracy Since 1975—End Dec. 4—Page 104

TUESDAY
19

To succeed in the markets, it is essential to make your own decisions. Numerous traders cited listening to others as their worst blunder.
— Jack D. Schwager (Investment manager, author, *Stock Market Wizards: Interviews with America's Top Stock Traders*, b. 1948)

Start Short 30-Year Bond(M)—54.3% Accuracy Since 1977—End Apr. 28, 2014—Page 106

WEDNESDAY
20
FN: KC
LT: CL

There are very few instances in history when any government has ever paid off debt.
— Walter Wriston (Retired CEO of Citicorp and Citibank)

End Long Lean Hogs(G) (Nov. 4)

THURSDAY
21

We are nowhere near a capitulation point because it's at that point where it's despair, not hope, that reigns supreme, and there was scant evidence of any despair at any of the meetings I gave.
— David Rosenberg (Economist, Merrill Lynch, *Barron's* 4/21/2008)

End Short Heating Oil(Z) (Oct. 14)

FRIDAY
22
FN: CL
OE: US, C, S, W

Corporate guidance has become something of an art. The CFO has refined and perfected his art, gracefully leading on the bulls with the calculating grace and cunning of a great matador.
— Joe Kalinowski (I/B/E/S)

SATURDAY
23

SUNDAY
24

BONDS FREEZE UP IN WINTER

Typically, we see a seasonal tendency for bond prices to peak in November and then start a decline lasting into April, when we would be taking a seasonal long position, as covered on page 42.

Perhaps investors seeking a higher return feel more comfortable buying into the year-end stock market rally, so they sell bonds and reallocate funds into equities. Or perhaps end-of-year window dressing, or savvy traders wishing to take part in the up-coming January effect, play a role in the decline of bond prices.

In any event, this trade in the last 35 years has a 54.3% success rate. In late 2008, 30-year bonds made historic news with yields crashing and prices making all-time highs. The peak came on December 30, 2008, giving considerable heat to this trade. However, as time passed, this trade did unwind the massive equity loss, registering a small $578 decline.

Consider the fact that in late 2008, we were experiencing the worst financial debacle in history with the fall of Bear Stearns and Lehman Brothers as well as the discovery of history's most incredible Ponzi scheme artist, Bernie Madoff, who had scammed money from investors surpassing tens of billion of dollars. It is no wonder that this trade did not act perfectly, but over time and with proper risk management, active traders should be aware of the decoupling effect between bonds and stocks. So if stocks are rising in late November, consider taking a short bond position on or about November 20 and holding until approximately April 28. Europe's debt crisis stymied this trade in 2011–2012 as traders and investors sought the safety of Treasury bonds.

Stock traders may consider the exchange-traded fund PIMCO 25+ Year Zero Coupon U.S. Treasury (ZROZ) as a replacement for this futures contract. See pages 131–137 for additional correlated trades.

NOVEMBER SHORT 30-YR BOND (JUNE) TRADING DAY: 14–HOLD: 107 DAYS

YEAR	ENTRY DATE	ENTRY CLOSE	EXIT DATE	EXIT CLOSE	PROFIT/ LOSS
1977	11/18	101'070	4/25	95'240	$5,469
1978	11/21	93'080	4/26	88'190	4,656
1979	11/20	80'200	4/25	75'120	5,250
1980	11/21	69'230	4/29	62'180	7,156
1981	11/19	64'170	4/26	64'100	219
1982	11/19	77'140	4/26	77'300	−500
1983	11/18	69'220	4/24	65'080	4,438
1984	11/20	70'010	4/25	70'260	−781
1985	11/20	78'260	4/25	98'080	−19,438
1986	11/20	97'220	4/27	91'060	6,500
1987	11/19	87'130	4/25	88'210	−1,250
1988	11/18	87'040	4/25	89'210	−2,531
1989	11/20	98'270	4/25	89'060	9,656
1990	11/20	93'130	4/25	95'290	−2,500
1991	11/20	98'050	4/27	97'230	438
1992	11/19	101'130	4/26	111'110	−9,938
1993	11/18	113'260	4/21	105'250	8,031
1994	11/18	95'200	4/26	105'170	−9,906
1995	11/20	116'310	4/24	109'240	7,219
1996	11/21	114'210	4/29	108'300	5,719
1997	11/21	118'230	4/29	118'220	31
1998	11/20	127'160	4/27	121'230	5,781
1999	11/19	94'070	4/25	97'020	−2,844
2000	11/20	100'140	4/26	101'170	−1,094
2001	11/21	101'270	4/29	101'310	−125
2002	11/21	107'220	4/30	113'030	−5,406
2003	11/21	108'120	4/28	107'110	1,031
2004	11/19	110'280	4/26	114'020	−3,188
2005	11/21	112'130	4/27	106'220	5,719
2006	11/20	112'280	4/25	111'160	1,375
2007	11/21	115'270	4/28	116'010	−188
2008	11/20	123'095	4/28	123'260	−578
2009	11/19	118'190	4/26	116'280	1,719
2010	11/18	123'240	4/25	121'160	2,250
2011	11/18	141'130	4/25	141'300	−531
				35-Year Gain	$21,859

30-YEAR BOND (US) BARS AND PIMCO 25+ YEAR ZERO COUPON U.S. TREASURY (ZROZ) CLOSES
(WEEKLY DATA JANUARY 2011–JUNE 20, 2012)

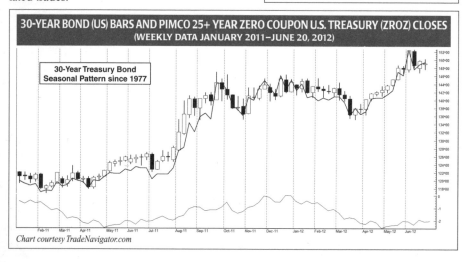

30-Year Treasury Bond Seasonal Pattern since 1977

Chart courtesy TradeNavigator.com

MONDAY

25

OE: HO, NG, HG, GC, SI

If a man can see both sides of a problem, you know that none of his money is tied up in it.
— Verda Ross

Start Long Swiss Franc(H)—54.1% Accuracy Since 1975—End Jan. 2 , 2014—Page 125

TUESDAY

26

LT: NG, HG, GC, SI

If you spend more than 14 minutes a year worrying about the market, you've wasted 12 minutes.
— Peter Lynch (Fidelity Investments, *One Up On Wall Street*, b. 1944)

WEDNESDAY

27

FN: NG

If you can buy all you want of a new issue, you do not want any; if you cannot obtain any, you want all you can buy.
— Rod Fadem (Stifel Nicolaus & Co., *Barron's* 1989)

Thanksgiving and Chanukah (Market Closed)

THURSDAY

28

There is a vitality, a life force, an energy, a quickening, that is translated through you into action, and because there is only one of you in all time, this expression is unique. And if you block it, it will never exist through any other medium and will be lost.
— Martha Graham (American choreographer, dancer, teacher)

(Shortened Trading Day)

FRIDAY

29

FN: US, HG, GC, SI, C, W
LT: HO

The world hates change, but it is the only thing that has brought progress.
— Charles Kettering (Inventor of electric ignition, founded Delco in 1909, 1876–1958)

SATURDAY

30

SUNDAY

1

DECEMBER ALMANAC

<table>
<tr><td colspan="7">DECEMBER</td></tr>
<tr><td>S</td><td>M</td><td>T</td><td>W</td><td>T</td><td>F</td><td>S</td></tr>
<tr><td>1</td><td>2</td><td>3</td><td>4</td><td>5</td><td>6</td><td>7</td></tr>
<tr><td>8</td><td>9</td><td>10</td><td>11</td><td>12</td><td>13</td><td>14</td></tr>
<tr><td>15</td><td>16</td><td>17</td><td>18</td><td>19</td><td>20</td><td>21</td></tr>
<tr><td>22</td><td>23</td><td>24</td><td>25</td><td>26</td><td>27</td><td>28</td></tr>
<tr><td>29</td><td>30</td><td>31</td><td></td><td></td><td></td><td></td></tr>
</table>

<table>
<tr><td colspan="7">JANUARY 2014</td></tr>
<tr><td>S</td><td>M</td><td>T</td><td>W</td><td>T</td><td>F</td><td>S</td></tr>
<tr><td></td><td></td><td></td><td>1</td><td>2</td><td>3</td><td>4</td></tr>
<tr><td>5</td><td>6</td><td>7</td><td>8</td><td>9</td><td>10</td><td>11</td></tr>
<tr><td>12</td><td>13</td><td>14</td><td>15</td><td>16</td><td>17</td><td>18</td></tr>
<tr><td>19</td><td>20</td><td>21</td><td>22</td><td>23</td><td>24</td><td>25</td></tr>
<tr><td>26</td><td>27</td><td>28</td><td>29</td><td>30</td><td>31</td><td></td></tr>
</table>

STOCKS AND BONDS

S&P's are prone to year-end buying pressure. Our best seasonal percentage play, which is long the March futures contract from October 25, exits on any strength from the "Santa Claus" rally by December 24 (page 100). 30-year Treasury bond prices are seasonally weak, as we are in a short June futures contract from November 20 and holding through April 28 (page 106).

ENERGY

Cover the short crude oil seasonal best trade from September on or about December 10 (page 82). Natural gas tends to see price declines, especially if inventories have not been worked off due to warmer than expected weather conditions (page 145). Heating oil has a tendency to see a relief rally lasting into the first of January, especially when we have early-month-weakness carried over from November.

METALS

Liquidate the long gold position from November on or about December 4 (page 104). Also, exit any complementary long silver positions that may have been established along side the November gold trade. Copper builds a solid base towards the middle to the end of the month. Go long May copper futures on or about December 13 and hold through on or about February 24 (page 112). The low in 2008 was made on December 26, and then prices made a rally into the first half of 2009. The trade worked even better the past three years.

GRAINS

The end-of-year marketing for soybeans is winding down, and farmers are reluctant to sell in front of end-of-year tax liabilities (page 161). December can see modest declines in the wheat market, which continues its seasonal downtrend (page 164). The corn market is in its seasonal period of strength, but much like soybeans, prices tend to consolidate due to year-end tax liabilities, as farmers tend to defer sales until after the New Year.

SOFTS

Exit the long cocoa position from November on or about December 26 (page 125). Coffee prices tend to rise through year-end, as cold northern winters help increase consumption (page 170). Sugar prices tend to decline by mid-December.

MEATS

Live cattle prices tend to stabilize, as holiday sales demand can put a floor of support under the market. In addition, farmers try to minimize their tax liabilities by deferring sales until the New Year (page 176). Lean hogs prices tend to flat line or consolidate, as producers work off inventories until prices begin to resume a seasonal uptrend in March (page 179).

CURRENCIES

The euro tends to rally through year-end (page 96). There is a seasonal short position for the Swiss franc, where we go short the March contract on or about December 27 until on or about February 27. This trade has worked 26 times in the last 37 years, for a success rate of 70.3% and a cumulative profit of $54,413 (page 116). Sell the June British pound on or around December 27 and hold until about March 20 (page 114). The yen is in a seasonal weak period versus the U.S. dollar. The trade is to be short from about October 16 and hold until about February 7 (page 88).

DECEMBER STRATEGY CALENDAR*

Symbol	B	M	E
SP L/S			
US L/S			
CL L/S			
NG L/S			
HO L/S			
HG L/S			
GC L/S			
SI L/S			
C L/S			
S L/S			
W L/S			
CC L/S			
KC L/S			
SB L/S			
LC L/S			
LH L/S			
BP L/S			
EC L/S			
SF L/S			
JY L/S			

* Graphic representation of the Commodity Seasonality Percentage Plays on pages 124–125.
L = Long Trade, S = Short Trade. See pages 131–137 for contract symbols.

DECEMBER

Whatever method you use to pick stocks..., your ultimate success or failure will depend on your ability to ignore the worries of the world long enough to allow your investments to succeed. It isn't the head but the stomach that determines the fate of the stockpicker.
— Peter Lynch (Fidelity Investments, *Beating the Street*, 1994)

We were fairly arrogant, until we realized the Japanese were selling quality products for what it cost us to make them.
— Paul A. Allaire (former Chairman of Xerox)

End Long Gold(G) (Nov. 19)

When someone told me "We're going with you guys because no one ever got fired for buying Cisco (products)." That's what they used to say in IBM's golden age.
— Mark Dickey (Former Cisco sales exec, then at SmartPipes, *Fortune* 5/15/00).

Don't be the last bear or last bull standing, let history guide you, be contrary to the crowd, and let the tape tell you when to act.
— Jeffrey A. Hirsch (Editor, *Stock Trader's Almanac*, b. 1966)

Start Long Wheat(K)—61.9% Accuracy Since 1970—End Jan. 7, 2014—Page 110

Doubt is the father of invention.
— Galileo Galilei (Italian physicist and astronomer, 1564–1642)

EAT YOUR WINTER WHEATIES

The wheat market has posted a tradable low in early December the past 24 years, since the effects of the big grain boom/bust cycle of the 1970s and 1980s wore off in 1987. We have included the trade results since 1970 to illustrate the impact of the overarching cycles on seasonality.

This commodity has a strong seasonal pattern (page 164), and in recent years, we have seen unprecedented price gains. In fact in February 2008, this market marked a record high of over $13.49 per bushel. This was an incredible move, partly due to what was suspected to be a speculative run on commodities from investors rather than a supply and demand imbalance.

CBOT wheat is considered winter wheat, as it is seeded in the September–October time frame and, during the winter, it enters its dormancy period. Southern Hemisphere supply puts pressure on prices into early December until the size and health of the newly planted Northern Hemisphere winter wheat crop is known, creating a seasonal peak in January.

Over the past 42 years, this trade has a 61.9% winning percentage with total gains of $9,462 per contract. But since 1987, this trade has produced gains in 20 of the last 25 years, for an 80% success rate and total gains of $15,063 per contract. Enter long positions on the May contract on or about December 7, and exit about 20 days later, when our January short wheat trade commences (page 18).

The chart below is of Kellogg (K), an end user or company that buys wheat to make cereals and snack cake items. Kellogg's line chart is overlaid on the price of wheat, and on the bottom is the seasonal price move of wheat. As you can see, wheat prices move mostly on an inverse relationship with this company. See pages 131–137 for additional correlated trades.

DECEMBER LONG CBOT WHEAT (MAY)
TRADING DAY: 5–HOLD: 20 DAYS

YEAR	ENTRY DATE	ENTRY CLOSE	EXIT DATE	EXIT CLOSE	PROFIT/ LOSS
1970	12/7	171 1/8	1/6	166 1/4	−$244
1971	12/7	150 5/8	1/6	156 1/2	294
1972	12/7	249 1/4	1/9	256 1/2	363
1973	12/7	507	1/9	547	2,000
1974	12/6	494 1/2	1/7	417 3/4	−3,838
1975	12/5	363 3/4	1/7	362 1/4	−75
1976	12/7	275 1/4	1/6	286 1/2	563
1977	12/7	274 1/2	1/6	282 3/4	413
1978	12/7	349 3/4	1/8	328	−1,088
1979	12/7	447 3/4	1/11	435 1/2	−613
1980	12/5	523 1/4	1/7	513 1/4	−500
1981	12/7	426 3/4	1/6	410 1/4	−825
1982	12/7	350 3/4	1/6	337 1/2	−663
1983	12/7	351 1/2	1/6	353 1/2	100
1984	12/7	341 3/4	1/8	334	−388
1985	12/6	322	1/7	311 3/4	−513
1986	12/5	267	1/6	255 1/4	−588
1987	12/7	313 1/4	1/6	330	838
1988	12/7	406 3/4	1/6	434 3/4	1,400
1989	12/7	385	1/8	389 1/4	213
1990	12/7	273 3/4	1/8	260 3/4	−650
1991	12/6	357 1/4	1/7	376 1/4	950
1992	12/7	342	1/6	343 1/4	63
1993	12/7	342	1/6	364 3/4	1,138
1994	12/7	373 1/2	1/6	374 1/4	38
1995	12/7	468 1/4	1/8	460	−413
1996	12/6	356 1/2	1/7	370	675
1997	12/5	367 1/4	1/6	332 1/4	−1,750
1998	12/7	294 3/4	1/6	297 3/4	150
1999	12/7	256	1/6	259 1/2	175
2000	12/7	281 1/2	1/8	294 1/2	650
2001	12/7	286 1/2	1/9	298	575
2002	12/6	344 1/4	1/8	331 3/4	−625
2003	12/5	397	1/6	397 3/4	38
2004	12/7	306	1/6	315 1/2	475
2005	12/7	322	1/6	340 3/4	938
2006	12/7	502 1/4	1/9	465 1/4	−1,850
2007	12/7	918 1/2	1/8	920 1/2	100
2008	12/5	488 1/2	1/6	656 1/2	8,400
2009	12/7	561	1/6	579 3/4	938
2010	12/7	805 1/2	1/5	835	1,475
2011	12/7	621 1/4	1/6	643 3/4	1,125
42-Year Gain					**$9,462**

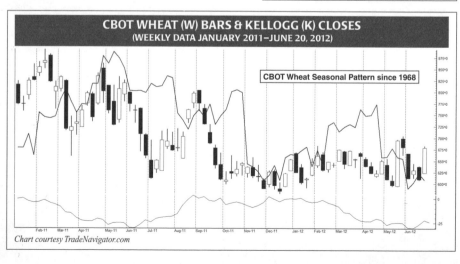

CBOT WHEAT (W) BARS & KELLOGG (K) CLOSES
(WEEKLY DATA JANUARY 2011–JUNE 20, 2012)

CBOT Wheat Seasonal Pattern since 1968

Chart courtesy TradeNavigator.com

110

Start Long Corn(N)—66.7% Accuracy Since 1970—End Jan. 10, 2014—Page 125

MONDAY

9

FN: LC

Three billion new people will be active on the Internet within ten years, as wireless broadband becomes ubiquitous.
— John Mauldin (Millennium Wave Advisors, 2000wave.com, 2/2/07)

End Short Crude Oil(G) (Sep. 12)

TUESDAY

10

Inflation is the modern way that governments default on their debt.
— Mike Epstein (MTA, MIT/Sloan Lab for Financial Engineering)

WEDNESDAY

11

Institutions tend to dump stock in a single transaction and buy, if possible, in smaller lots, gradually accumulating a position. Therefore, many more big blocks are traded on downticks than on upticks.
— Justin Mamis (Author, *The Mamis Letter, When To Sell*, b. 1929)

THURSDAY

12

If I had eight hours to chop down a tree, I'd spend six sharpening my axe.
— Abraham Lincoln (16th U.S. President, 1809–1865)

Start Long Copper(K)—70% Accuracy Since 1972—End Feb. 24, 2014—Page 112

FRIDAY

13

LT: C, W, CC, LH
OE: KC, LH

When everbody thinks alike, everyone is likely to be wrong.
— Humphrey B. Neill (Investor, analyst, author, *Art of Contrary Thinking* 1954, 1895–1977)

SATURDAY

14

SUNDAY

15

COPPER STARTS TO BUILD A BULLISH FOUNDATION

Copper prices tend to form seasonal bottoms during the month of December (page 149). Traders can look to go long on or about December 13 and hold until about February 24. This trade in the last 40-year history has worked 28 times, for a success rate of 70.0%.

Cumulative profit is a whopping $83,000. Nearly one-fourth of that profit came from 2007, as the cyclical boom in the commodity market magnified that seasonal price move. However, this trade has produced other big gains per single contract, such as an $14,475 gain in 2011, and even back in 1973, another substantial $9,475 gain. The biggest loss was for $5,000 back in 2006. These numbers show this trade can produce big wins and big losses.

The futures contract does have electronic access, and there are options on this commodity. But due to the potential volatility and thinness of the market, options are a consideration but are also not as actively traded as other commodities. Therefore, let's introduce a stock that mirrors the price moves of copper without the excess volatility. The chart below shows BHP Billiton's (BHP) prices overlaid on copper's. This company mines copper, silver, lead, and gold in Australia, Chile, Peru, and the United States.

Notice the price correlation to copper. The bottom line on the graph illustrates copper's average seasonal price moves, which BHP tracks rather closely. See pages 131–137 for additional correlated trades.

DECEMBER LONG COPPER (MAY)
TRADING DAY: 10–HOLD: 47 DAYS

YEAR	ENTRY DATE	CLOSE	EXIT DATE	CLOSE	PROFIT/ LOSS
1972	12/14	49.65	2/27	62.20	$3,138
1973	12/14	77.00	2/26	114.90	9,475
1974	12/13	57.00	2/24	58.50	375
1975	12/12	54.70	2/23	59.40	1,175
1976	12/14	60.50	2/22	67.00	1,625
1977	12/14	60.50	2/24	56.20	−1,075
1978	12/14	70.35	2/22	90.20	4,963
1979	12/14	101.00	2/25	121.00	5,000
1980	12/12	85.85	2/23	84.15	−425
1981	12/14	76.65	2/22	73.95	−675
1982	12/14	67.60	2/22	77.30	2,425
1983	12/14	66.65	2/22	66.35	−75
1984	12/14	60.35	2/25	58.00	−588
1985	12/13	64.35	2/21	64.65	75
1986	12/12	61.10	2/23	62.90	450
1987	12/14	97.70	2/22	89.60	−2,025
1988	12/14	125.10	2/22	129.25	1,038
1989	12/14	102.65	2/22	108.00	1,338
1990	12/14	106.00	2/25	109.70	925
1991	12/13	97.20	2/21	100.40	800
1992	12/14	99.70	2/22	99.50	−50
1993	12/14	79.80	2/22	86.75	1,738
1994	12/14	128.75	2/22	129.45	175
1995	12/14	122.70	2/23	114.20	−2,125
1996	12/13	96.20	2/21	109.70	3,375
1997	12/12	82.90	2/23	73.70	−2,300
1998	12/14	67.10	2/23	62.65	−1,113
1999	12/14	81.60	2/24	84.65	763
2000	12/14	88.60	2/23	80.10	−2,125
2001	12/14	68.50	2/26	70.85	587
2002	12/13	73.65	2/24	79.20	1,388
2003	12/12	98.40	2/25	131.25	8,213
2004	12/14	133.15	2/23	149.50	4,088
2005	12/14	191.30	2/23	219.95	7,162
2006	12/14	307.00	2/26	287.00	−5,000
2007	12/14	296.95	2/25	375.70	19,688
2008	12/12	144.10	2/23	145.75	413
2009	12/14	316.85	2/23	323.45	1,650
2010	12/14	420.05	2/22	436.30	4,063
2011	12/14	329.10	2/24	387.00	14,475
			40-Year Gain		**$83,000**

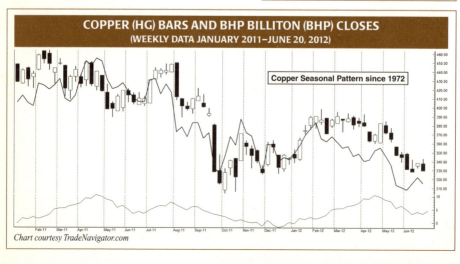

COPPER (HG) BARS AND BHP BILLITON (BHP) CLOSES
(WEEKLY DATA JANUARY 2011–JUNE 20, 2012)

Copper Seasonal Pattern since 1972

Chart courtesy TradeNavigator.com

DECEMBER

People do not change when you tell them they should; they change when they tell themselves they must.
— Michael Mandelbaum (Johns Hopkins foreign policy specialist, *NY Times*, 6/24/2009, b. 1946)

There are ways for the individual investor to make money in the securities markets. Buying value and holding long term while collecting dividends has been proven over and over again.
— Robert M. Sharp (Author, *The Lore and Legends of Wall Street*)

If you bet on a horse, that's gambling. If you bet you can make three spades, that's entertainment. If you bet cotton will go up three points, that's business. See the difference?
— Blackie Sherrod (Sportswriter, b. 1919)

Companies already dominant in a field rarely produce the breakthroughs that transform it.
— George Gilder

A.I. (artificial intelligence) is the science of how to get machines to do the things they do in the movies.
— Professor Astro Teller (Carnegie Mellon University)

BRITISH POUND INVASION FADES AWAY

We hear and see information daily on the values of currencies on CNBC, Bloomberg, Fox News, and in print journals, such as *The Wall Street Journal* or *Investors Business Daily*. Analysts and investors talk about the many ways currencies can affect everyday finances, one of which is the bottom line of a multinational corporation's earnings. Another ramification of currency value fluctuations is the effect they have on individuals through their impact on the cost of vacations and business travel abroad.

One currency, the British pound or "cable," as it is referred to, has a strong seasonal tendency to decline in December. The term cable refers to the British pound/U.S. dollar exchange rate. The term was derived from the method used to report the pound/dollar exchange rate. Back in the middle 1800s, the rate was quoted via the transatlantic cable. If you are an individual investor or just happening to visit London for the holidays, perhaps this statistical trading information will be of use. If you are traveling, I would suggest holding off buying pounds until late in December.

The British pound tends to show an average seasonal weakness from late December into March, partly because U.S. dollars tend to return to the U.S., and partly because there is some book squaring pressure prior to England's new fiscal year, which begins in April. Traders can look to sell on or about December 27 and hold until on or about March 20. This trade has worked in the past 37-year history 24 times, for a success rate of 64.9%.

The chart below shows the direct correlation between the British pound/U.S. dollar futures and CurrencyShares British Pound (FXB). The 37-year average seasonal price move is the bottom line of the chart and depicts the pound's tendency to peak in late December and decline through March. See pages 131–137 for additional correlated trades.

DECEMBER SHORT BRITISH POUND (JUNE)
TRADING DAY: 19–HOLD: 56 DAYS

YEAR	ENTRY DATE	CLOSE	EXIT DATE	CLOSE	PROFIT/ LOSS
1975	12/29	198.10	3/18	189.30	$11,000
1976	12/28	163.35	3/18	169.20	−7,312
1977	12/28	190.25	3/20	190.45	−250
1978	12/28	202.60	3/20	202.10	625
1979	12/31	219.00	3/20	219.45	−562
1980	12/29	239.50	3/19	228.00	14,375
1981	12/28	188.25	3/18	181.60	8,313
1982	12/28	162.20	3/17	149.90	15,375
1983	12/28	144.00	3/19	144.45	−562
1984	12/28	116.30	3/20	113.40	3,625
1985	12/27	142.15	3/19	147.40	−6,563
1986	12/26	142.80	3/18	159.50	−20,875
1987	12/28	185.25	3/17	182.45	3,500
1988	12/28	176.10	3/20	170.90	6,500
1989	12/28	155.18	3/20	157.48	−2,875
1990	12/28	188.28	3/20	176.22	15,075
1991	12/27	181.82	3/18	170.20	14,525
1992	12/28	146.88	3/18	147.74	−1,075
1993	12/28	149.62	3/17	148.82	1,000
1994	12/28	157.50	3/20	157.34	200
1995	12/28	154.14	3/19	153.12	1,275
1996	12/27	168.70	3/20	159.14	11,950
1997	12/26	166.58	3/19	165.90	850
1998	12/28	167.08	3/19	162.70	5,475
1999	12/28	161.54	3/17	157.30	5,300
2000	12/28	149.58	3/21	142.88	8,375
2001	12/28	143.64	3/21	141.82	2,275
2002	12/27	158.48	3/20	155.72	3,450
2003	12/26	174.74	3/18	181.92	−8,975
2004	12/28	191.16	3/18	191.08	100
2005	12/28	171.61	3/21	174.98	−4,212
2006	12/28	196.28	3/21	196.80	−650
2007	12/28	198.30	3/20	196.91	1,738
2008	12/26	146.51	3/19	145.15	1,700
2009	12/28	159.87	3/19	151.00	11,088
2010	12/28	153.47	3/18	161.99	−10,650
2011	12/28	154.25	3/21	158.49	−5,300
				37-Year Gain	**$77,825**

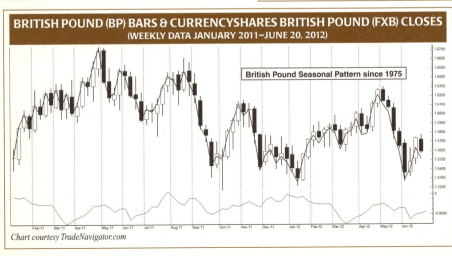

BRITISH POUND (BP) BARS & CURRENCYSHARES BRITISH POUND (FXB) CLOSES
(WEEKLY DATA JANUARY 2011–JUNE 20, 2012)

British Pound Seasonal Pattern since 1975

Chart courtesy TradeNavigator.com

DECEMBER

MONDAY

23

FN: CL

Capitalism is the legitimate racket of the ruling class.
— Al Capone (American gangster, 1899–1947)

(Shortened Trading Day)
End Long S&P 500(H) (Oct. 25)

TUESDAY

24

We are all born originals; why is it so many die copies?
— Edward Young (English poet, 1683–1765)

Christmas Day (Market Closed)

WEDNESDAY

25

I believe in the exceptional man—the entrepreneur who is always out of money, not the bureaucrat who generates cash flow and pays dividends.
— Armand Erpf (Investment banker, partner Loeb Rhoades, 1897–1971)

End Long Cocoa(H) (Nov. 6)

THURSDAY

26

OE: HO, NG, HG, GC, SI

There is no great mystery to satisfying your customers. Build them a quality product and treat them with respect. It's that simple.
— Lee Iacocca (American industrialist, Former Chrysler CEO, b. 1924)

Start Short British Pound(M)—64.9% Accuracy Since 1975—End Mar. 20, 2014—Page 114
Start Short Swiss Franc(H)—70.3% Accuracy Since 1975—End Feb. 27, 2014—Page 116

FRIDAY

27

LT: NG, HG, GC, SI
OE: US, C, S, W

I'd be a bum on the street with a tin cup, if the markets were always efficient.
— Warren Buffett (CEO Berkshire Hathaway, investor & philanthropist, b. 1930)

SATURDAY

28

SUNDAY

29

SWISS FRANC TRADES LIKE GOLD

As we covered on page 70, the "Swissie" has tracked the price movement of gold. In the past, this currency had been a safe haven in times of geopolitical tensions. However, this relationship has tended to depart from the norm since the introduction of the euro currency. Moreover, with the exposure of risk from a European sovereign debt crisis, Swiss banks have been perceived to be in jeopardy. This has put downward pressure on the Swiss franc versus the U.S. dollar, while gold prices increased during the first half of 2010. But do not rule out the flight of investors to the Swissie in times of trouble in the future.

There are periods of European upheavals, as occurred in 2004, when there was dissension among members of the European Union. In fact, there were riots in Paris, and some investors flocked to the Swiss franc as a short-term safe haven. A similar situation arose in 2011 when Greece's future in the EU was uncertain. This propped up the value of the Swissie against all major currencies, including the U.S. dollar.

One of our seasonal studies suggests that traders can establish a short position that correlates with the seasonal decline in gold in the New Year. Traders can look to go short the Swiss franc on or about December 27 and hold through the end of February.

In the 37-year history, this trade has worked 26 times, for a success rate of 70.3%. The seasonal chart of gold (page 152) closely correlates to the Swiss franc. Therefore, traders may want to take note that trading both gold and the Swiss franc simultaneously would not be considered diversified trading strategies. If the trade works, then that would be great; however, traders are exposed to double the risk.

There are several ways to take advantage of this situation, such as the trade strategies for gold mentioned on page 104, trading futures or a gold stock like Freeport-McMoran Copper & Gold (FCX), or this trade in the Swiss franc or the exchange-traded fund (ETF), CurrencyShares Swiss Franc (FXF). The chart below shows the direct correlation of the Swiss franc futures and the ETF. See pages 131–137 for additional correlated trades.

DECEMBER SHORT SWISS FRANC (MARCH)
TRADING DAY: 19–HOLD: 41 DAYS

YEAR	ENTRY DATE	ENTRY CLOSE	EXIT DATE	EXIT CLOSE	PROFIT/ LOSS
1975	12/29	38.32	2/26	39.07	−$938
1976	12/28	41.12	2/25	39.19	2,413
1977	12/28	49.89	2/27	54.35	−5,575
1978	12/28	63.34	2/27	60.35	3,738
1979	12/31	63.94	2/28	60.04	4,875
1980	12/29	57.81	2/26	51.26	8,188
1981	12/28	55.66	2/25	53.38	2,850
1982	12/28	50.65	2/24	49.15	1,875
1983	12/28	46.25	2/27	46.20	62
1984	12/28	38.94	2/27	35.44	4,375
1985	12/27	48.62	2/26	52.90	−5,350
1986	12/26	61.27	2/25	65.03	−4,700
1987	12/28	78.17	2/25	72.02	7,688
1988	12/28	66.70	2/27	64.44	2,825
1989	12/28	64.69	2/27	67.35	−3,325
1990	12/28	78.35	2/27	75.90	3,062
1991	12/27	73.39	2/26	66.80	8,238
1992	12/28	67.60	2/25	65.79	2,262
1993	12/28	69.35	2/24	69.74	−488
1994	12/28	77.13	2/27	80.62	−4,363
1995	12/28	87.24	2/27	84.78	3,075
1996	12/27	74.65	2/27	67.95	8,375
1997	12/26	70.41	2/26	68.24	2,713
1998	12/28	73.65	2/26	69.22	5,538
1999	12/28	63.16	2/25	60.68	3,100
2000	12/28	61.52	2/28	59.94	1,975
2001	12/28	59.72	2/28	58.91	1,013
2002	12/27	72.03	2/27	73.67	−2,050
2003	12/26	79.96	2/26	78.91	1,313
2004	12/28	88.48	2/25	86.03	3,063
2005	12/28	76.48	2/28	76.32	200
2006	12/28	82.40	2/28	82.25	188
2007	12/28	89.16	2/28	95.24	−7,600
2008	12/26	93.86	2/26	85.85	10,013
2009	12/28	96.65	2/26	93.08	4,463
2010	12/28	105.18	2/25	107.72	−3,175
2011	12/28	106.29	2/29	110.69	−5,500
				37-Year Gain	**$54,413**

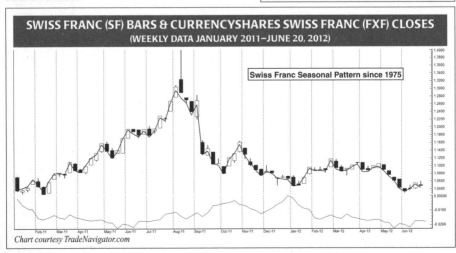

SWISS FRANC (SF) BARS & CURRENCYSHARES SWISS FRANC (FXF) CLOSES
(WEEKLY DATA JANUARY 2011–JUNE 20, 2012)

Swiss Franc Seasonal Pattern since 1975

Chart courtesy TradeNavigator.com

DECEMBER/JANUARY 2014

MONDAY
30
FN: NG

The fear of capitalism has compelled socialism to widen freedom, and the fear of socialism has compelled capitalism to increase equality.
— Will and Ariel Durant

TUESDAY
31
FN: HG, GC, SI, S
LT: HO, LC

If banking institutions are protected by the taxpayer and they are given free reign to speculate, I may not live long enough to see the crisis, but my soul is going to come back and haunt you.
— Paul A. Volcker (Fed Chairman 1979–1987, Chair Economic Recovery Advisory Board, 2/2/2010, b. 1927)

New Year's Day

WEDNESDAY
1

To an imagination of any scope the most far-reaching form of power is not money, it is the command of ideas.
— Oliver Wendell Holmes Jr. (U.S. Supreme Court Justice 1902–1932, *The Mind and Faith of Justice Holmes*, edited by Max Lerner, 1841–1935)

THURSDAY
2

The four most expensive words in the English language, "This time it's different."
— Sir John Templeton (Founder Templeton Funds, philanthropist, 1912–2008)

FRIDAY
3
FN: HO

It wasn't raining when Noah built the ark.
— Warren Buffett (CEO Berkshire Hathaway, investor & philanthropist, b. 1930)

SATURDAY
4

SUNDAY
5

2013 FUTURES AND OPTIONS EXPIRATION DATES

First Notice, Last Trade, and Option Expiration Days for all 20 markets included in the Almanac appear on the weekly calendar pages, where under the date you will see **FN** (First Notice), **LT** (Last Trade), and **OE** (Option Expiration) followed by the applicable futures code.

For example, "**FN**: S," on Thursday, February 28, 2013, is the First Notice Day of the March Soybeans contract. In order to leave more room for notes, we have omitted the contract month code "H" for March Soybeans. All First Notice, Last Trade and Option Expiration Dates refer to the front-month or near-term contract, so monthly codes are not necessary. Please refer to the contract specification pages 131–137 for an explanation of all the trading symbols and contract month codes.

As a handy cross-reference, all the important Futures and Option Expiration Dates are listed below and in the 2013 Strategy Calendar on pages 10–11. We hope you find these reference pages useful.

Aside from being aware of these key dates, traders must be well versed in the nuances of the nomenclature and implications of these events. Though not all markets have First Notice Dates, this is the point where all speculative longs need to be out of a specific contract; otherwise they risk getting a delivery notice. Last Trading Date refers to the date that the futures contract month is delisted and becomes a cash market.

Some New York markets, mainly the energy complex, list this the other way around. With the monthly expiration of crude oil, this information is helpful to traders by not establishing a new long position on or before Last Trading Day. Option Expiration Day is the last day on which an option may be exercised and exchanged for the underlying futures contract, stock, or ETF.

	FND	LTD	OED		FND	LTD	OED
S&P 500 (SP)				**30-Year Treasury Bond (US)**			
January	—	—	1/18/13	January	—	—	12/27/12
February	—	—	2/15/13	February	—	—	1/25/13
March	—	3/14/13	3/14/13	March	2/28/13	3/19/13	2/22/13
April	—	—	4/19/13	April	—	—	3/22/13
May	—	—	5/17/13	May	—	—	4/26/13
June	—	6/20/13	6/20/13	June	5/31/13	6/19/13	5/24/13
July	—	—	7/19/13	July	—	—	6/21/13
August	—	—	8/16/13	August	—	—	7/26/13
September	—	9/19/13	9/19/13	September	8/30/13	9/19/13	8/23/13
October	—	—	10/18/13	October	—	—	9/20/13
November	—	—	11/16/13	November	—	—	10/25/13
December	—	12/19/13	12/19/13	December	11/29/13	12/19/13	11/22/13
				Jan-14	—	—	12/27/13
Crude Oil (CL)				**Heating Oil (HO)**			
January	12/21/12	12/19/12	12/14/12	January	1/3/13	12/31/12	12/26/12
February	1/24/13	1/22/13	1/16/13	February	2/4/13	1/31/13	1/28/13
March	2/22/13	2/20/13	2/14/13	March	3/4/13	2/28/13	2/25/13
April	3/22/13	3/20/13	3/15/13	April	4/2/13	3/28/13	3/25/13
May	4/24/13	4/22/13	4/17/13	May	5/2/13	4/30/13	4/25/13
June	5/23/13	5/21/13	5/16/13	June	6/4/13	5/31/13	5/28/13
July	6/24/13	6/20/13	6/17/13	July	7/2/13	6/28/13	6/25/13
August	7/24/13	7/22/13	7/17/13	August	8/2/13	7/31/13	7/26/13
September	8/22/13	8/20/13	8/15/13	September	9/4/13	8/30/13	8/27/13
October	9/24/13	9/20/13	9/17/13	October	10/2/13	9/30/13	9/25/13
November	10/24/13	10/22/13	10/17/13	November	11/4/13	10/31/13	10/28/13
December	11/22/13	11/20/13	11/15/13	December	12/3/13	11/29/13	11/25/13
Jan-14	12/23/13	12/19/13	12/16/13	Jan-14	1/3/14	12/31/13	12/26/13
Natural Gas (NG)				**Copper (HG), Gold (GC) & Silver (SI)**			
January	12/28/12	12/27/12	12/26/12	January	12/31/12	1/29/13	12/26/12
February	1/30/13	1/29/13	1/28/13	February	1/31/13	2/26/13	1/28/13
March	2/27/13	2/26/13	2/25/13	March	2/28/13	3/26/13	2/25/13
April	3/27/13	3/26/13	3/25/13	April	3/28/13	4/26/13	3/25/13
May	4/29/13	4/26/13	4/25/13	May	4/30/13	5/29/13	4/25/13
June	5/30/13	5/29/13	5/28/13	June	5/31/13	6/26/13	5/28/13
July	6/27/13	6/26/13	6/25/13	July	6/28/13	7/29/13	6/25/13
August	7/30/13	7/29/13	7/26/13	August	7/31/13	8/28/13	7/25/13
September	8/29/13	8/28/13	8/27/13	September	8/30/13	9/26/13	8/27/13
October	9/27/13	9/26/13	9/25/13	October	9/30/13	10/29/13	9/25/13
November	10/30/13	10/29/13	10/28/13	November	10/31/13	11/26/13	10/28/13
December	11/27/13	11/26/13	11/25/13	December	11/29/13	12/27/13	11/25/13
Jan-14	12/30/13	12/27/13	12/26/13	Jan-14	12/31/13	1/29/14	12/26/13

2013 FUTURES AND OPTIONS EXPIRATION DATES

	FND	LTD	OED		FND	LTD	OED
Corn (C) & Wheat (W)				**Soybeans (S)**			
January	—	—	12/21/12	January	12/31/12	1/14/13	12/21/12
February	—	—	1/25/13	February	—	—	1/25/13
March	2/28/13	3/14/13	2/22/13	March	2/28/13	3/14/13	2/22/13
April	—	—	3/22/13	April	—	—	3/22/13
May	4/30/13	5/14/13	4/26/13	May	4/30/13	5/14/13	4/26/13
June	—	—	5/24/13	June	—	—	5/24/13
July	6/28/13	7/12/13	6/21/13	July	6/28/13	7/12/13	6/21/13
August	—	—	7/26/13	August	7/31/13	8/14/13	7/26/13
September	8/30/13	9/13/13	8/23/13	September	8/30/13	9/13/13	8/23/13
October	—	—	9/20/13	October	—	—	9/20/13
November	—	—	10/25/13	November	10/31/13	11/14/13	10/25/13
December	11/29/13	12/13/13	11/22/13	December	—	—	11/22/13
Jan-14	—	—	12/27/13	Jan-14	12/31/13	1/14/14	12/27/13
Cocoa (CC)				**Coffee (KC)**			
January	—	—	12/7/12	January	—	—	12/14/12
February	—	—	1/4/13	February	—	—	1/11/13
March	2/14/13	3/13/13	2/1/13	March	2/20/13	3/18/13	2/8/13
April	—	—	3/1/13	April	—	—	3/8/13
May	4/17/13	5/15/13	4/5/13	May	4/22/13	5/20/13	4/12/13
June	—	—	5/3/13	June	—	—	5/10/13
July	6/17/13	7/16/13	6/7/13	July	6/20/13	7/19/13	6/13/13
August	—	—	7/5/13	August	—	—	7/12/13
September	8/19/13	9/13/13	8/2/13	September	8/22/13	9/18/13	8/9/13
October	—	—	9/6/13	October	—	—	9/13/13
November	—	—	10/4/13	November	—	—	10/11/13
December	11/15/13	12/13/13	11/1/13	December	11/20/13	12/18/13	11/8/13
Jan-14	—	—	12/6/13	Jan-14	—	—	12/13/13
Sugar (SB)				**Live Cattle (LC)**			
January	—	—	12/17/12	January			1/4/13
February	—	—	1/15/13	February	2/4/13	2/28/13	2/1/13
March	3/1/13	2/28/13	2/15/13	March	—	—	3/1/13
April	—	—	3/15/13	April	4/8/13	4/30/13	4/5/13
May	5/1/13	4/30/13	4/15/13	May	—	—	5/3/13
June	—	—	5/15/13	June	6/10/13	6/28/13	6/7/13
July	7/1/13	6/28/13	6/17/13	July	—	—	7/5/13
August	—	—	7/15/13	August	8/5/13	8/30/13	8/2/13
September	—	—	8/15/13	September	—	—	9/6/13
October	10/1/13	9/30/13	9/16/13	October	10/7/13	10/31/13	10/4/13
November	—	—	10/15/13	November	—	—	11/1/13
December	—	—	11/15/13	December	12/9/13	12/31/13	12/6/13
Jan-14	—	—	12/16/13				
B. Pound (BP), Euro (EC), S. Franc (SF), J. Yen (JY)				**Lean Hogs (LH)**			
January	—	—	1/4/13	February	—	2/14/13	2/14/13
February	—	—	2/8/13	April	—	4/12/13	4/12/13
March	—	3/18/13	3/8/13	May	—	5/14/13	5/14/13
April	—		4/5/13	June	—	6/14/13	6/14/13
May	—		5/3/13	July	—	7/15/13	7/15/13
June	—	6/17/13	6/7/13	August	—	8/14/13	8/14/13
July	—		7/5/13	October	—	10/14/13	10/14/13
August	—		8/9/13	December	—	12/13/13	12/13/13
September	—	9/16/13	9/6/13				
October	—		10/4/13				
November	—		11/8/13				
December	—	12/16/13	12/6/13				

THE CRACK SPREAD CASE STUDY

The crack spread is a comparative strength chart that tracks the performance of crude oil versus the two main derivative products, namely gasoline and heating oil. This is a recognized spread for traders, and as a result is granted a special margin requirement through the commodity exchange.

Typically one uses the 3-2-1 ratio because it mirrors the refinery output ratio required to produce the byproducts from crude oil. This commonly used formula represents the theoretical refining margin that two barrels of unleaded gasoline and one barrel of heating oil are derived from three barrels of crude oil.

The crack spread often creates attractive trading opportunities. For example, if you believe that crude oil is expensive relative to the products, then you would sell crude oil and buy the products. One other useful tool is to use the crack spread chart to uncover hidden strength in the energy complex. If crude oil begins to strengthen relative to the products, then the crack spread will become less positive and the trend of the crack spread will weaken.

Notice in the chart below how in October 2011, crude oil prices climbed while both hearting oil and gasoline moved sideways and the crack spread moved lower. This was an indication that crude was outperforming the byproducts. As traders, we might not trade specific markets, but knowing the tools other traders use to make trading decisions may help give us an edge, especially if the markets are entering a seasonally strong or weak period. The crack spread can be instrumental as a confirming indicator, not only as a trading vehicle.

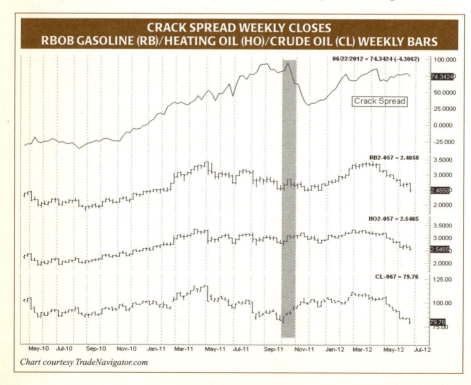

Chart courtesy TradeNavigator.com

THE "NOB" SPREAD CASE STUDY

The most commonly referenced and traded interest rate vehicles are the 10-year Treasury notes and the 30-year Treasury bonds. Ten-year notes reflect the value of the middle of the yield curve, and the 30-year bonds represent the long end of the yield curve. In most normal markets, as interest rates decline, Treasury prices rise. The longer-dated maturities are more sensitive to interest rate changes; therefore it is the long end of the yield curve that will move faster and further with a change in interest rates. Traders can look at a comparative strength chart or a spread chart comparing "notes-over-bonds," otherwise known as the *NOB spread*. This spread can be traded with a reduced margin requirement as it is recognized by the CME Group exchange. In addition, the spread chart can be used as an analysis tool to identify a change in trend direction in yields or interest rates.

In the chart below, the upper quadrant has the NOB spread; under that is the 10-year note, the 30-year bond, and in the lower quadrant, the Dow Jones Industrial Average. For the most part the notes and bonds trade in a parallel motion, whereas the spread tracks the difference of the actual performance. As interest rates decline, Treasury prices rise, but since the long end of the yield curve is more sensitive to these changes the 30-year bond outperforms the 10-year note. This causes the spread value to rise or become more positive. Momentum traders in a declining interest rate environment will buy the 30-year bond and sell the 10-year note as a spread to take advantage of the tendency of the long end of the yield curve to outperform the middle of the yield curve.

The NOB spread can also uncover another relationship change. Typically, when bonds go up stocks go down. Yale Hirsch's "Best Six Months Switching Strategy" as detailed in the *Stock Trader's Almanac*, now edited by Jeff Hirsch (also known by the adage "Sell in May and go away") manifests itself quite dramatically in the NOB spread. In late May 2009, the Dow stalled and declined into late July. At the same time, bond prices moved higher as the NOB spread did as well. This intermarket relationship was what we call "in-gear" or "in-synch." Fast forward to May 2010, the fabled flash-crash. Stocks were down, bonds went up, and the NOB spread moved higher or more positive. Again in May 2011, and again in May 2012, we experienced the same relationships. As a future guide, the NOB spread can act both as a trading instrument and, as the chart below depicts, as a confirming tool for other trade decisions.

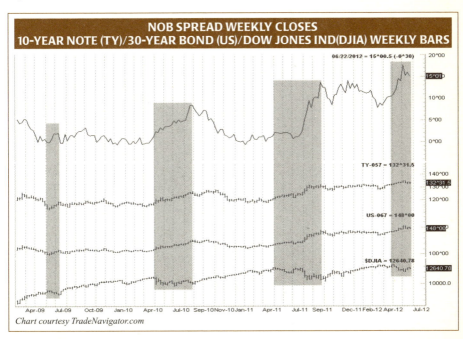

Chart courtesy TradeNavigator.com

A NEW MILLENNIUM "SELL IN MAY" SEASONAL TRADE

This case study describes an actual trade that was executed by taking advantage of a leveraged inverse ETF. These are the hybrid products of the 21st century. The market of interest was the *Direxion Daily Small Cap Bear 3X* (TZA), which means it correlates to three times the daily move of the small-cap index, but moves opposite to the underlying market. In this case it tracks the Russell 2000 index of small-cap stocks, which means if the stock index declined, then this ETF would move up in value.

John was looking for the best risk/reward opportunity to apply risk capital for a seasonal short trade for the overall stock market. The TZA came up on his radar screen. For starters, the Advanced-Decline (AD) line on the Russell 2000 was flashing a significant bearish divergence pattern. As the chart below shows, *iShares Russell 2000* (IWM) rose to a new yearly high in late March (point A), but the AD line made a lower high (point B).

In addition, the small-cap sector was significantly underperforming the overall market as the relative strength chart on page 9 of the IWM versus the SPDR S&P 500 (SPY) shows. Third, we entered the seasonally weak time period for stocks, the dreaded month of May. John applied one of the advanced options trading strategies covered on page 6, a vertical bull call spread, specifically the 18.00–20.00 strikes on TZA for the expiration in May.

This trade was put on for .63 cents or $63.00 per strategy on April 30 (point C). The analysis proved to be correct as the trade was closed out less than three weeks later before expiration for $1.14 or $114 per options strategy before commissions and fees. This gave just under a two-to-one risk-to-reward ratio. Granted, this was not the trade that we would retire on, but the case study is here to show you how traders can and do use seasonal analysis and apply it to various trading products and options strategies.

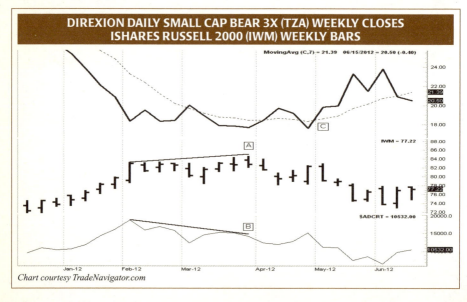

Chart courtesy TradeNavigator.com

POUNDING THE FACTS: JUNE LONG BRITISH POUND

Several times a year we attend and speak at the country's top investment conferences. In June 2012, we had the opportunity to speak at Moneyshow's Traders Expo in Dallas. One of the setups we were covering was the fact that seasonally the British pound enters a strong time frame that can last into August. This helps prove the point that one needs to stay on top of *all* of the markets, and, of course, follow the seasonal trends as illustrated in the *Commodity Traders Almanac.*

The reason we bring this up is that in June 2012 all eyes were focused on Greece, Spain, the Euro zone, and the Euro currency value—not the pound. At that conference, during several sessions we showed why the pound was a nice buy setup. We had a Persons High Close Doji pattern that created a buy signal, as the chart below shows at point A.

This setup provided traders with over a 200-point move in less than 7 trading days. Interestingly, the pattern occurred near the predicted Monthly Pivot Support level. If you are an avid reader and collect the *Almanacs*, if you pull out your 2010 copy, you will find this Doji pattern on page 7 with an explanation of Pivot Points on pages 8 and 9.

If this is your first year with us, congratulations, you can find this information on our website at *www.Personsplanet.com*. As we were putting together the finishing touches of the book, the pound remained above that buy level of 1.5500. We want you to know that the purpose of providing this case study is to share with you how we can take advantage of seasonal trades, and what other forms of market indicators and setups we look for to help enhance the performance of trades.

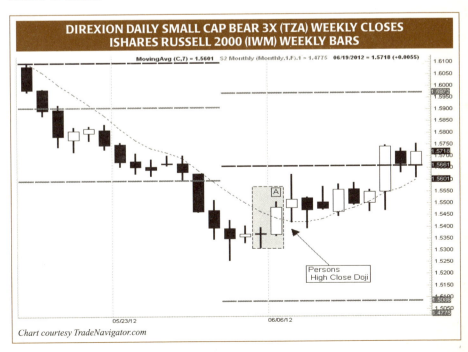

Chart courtesy TradeNavigator.com

COMMODITY SEASONALITY: TOP PERCENTAGE PLAYS

Below and continued on page 125 are the seasonal trades that are the backbone of the *Commodity Trader's Almanac*. After parsing the data compiled from the continuously linked, non-adjusted front-month contracts, seasonal strength and weakness was identified. Armed with these observations, the best contract to trade, the best time to execute, and the number of days to hold are determined for both the long and short. Inclusion of the trade is based primarily on the success rate, but new or developing trades are also included.

The hold period begins the day after the purchase. Hold days correlate to the trading days, not calendar days. Weekends and days on which the CME trading floor is closed, as depicted in the Strategy Calendar on pages 10–11 and throughout the Almanac on the weekly planner pages, are not counted in the hold period.

Whether you are buying or shorting the commodity or a correlating stock or ETF, the same logic applies; buy on or about the trading day listed and hold for the specified period. This is intended to be a guide for your trades, not gospel. If you are satisfied with your gain or have reached your threshold for losses, get out of the trade.

Results are based on trading one contract of the month specified; commissions, fees, and taxes are omitted. Moreover, when a trade results in no gain, it is counted as a loss. The trades are also conveniently mapped to the weekly planner pages to alert you of activity throughout the year.

A graphical representation of these trades is located on pages 126 and 127. A one month view of this graphic is also on each monthly almanac page. Each commodity has been listed in the same order as the databank, with their respective long and short trade opportunities mapped to provide a month-by-month snapshot of upcoming and currently active trades.

COMMODITY SEASONALITY: TOP PERCENTAGE PLAYS

Commodity	Contract	Years	Trading Day	Hold Days	Success Rate	# Gains	# Losses	Total Gain	Best Gain	Worst Loss
January										
Heating Oil Peaks (Short)	J	1980–2012	2	30	69.7%	23	10	$34,184	$17,686	$11,155
Euro Peaks (Short)	H	1999–2012	3	24	78.6	11	3	27,888	8,413	7,150
Wheat Peaks (Short)	N	1970–2012	3	85	69.8	30	13	26,769	5,775	5,775
S&P 500 Bottoms (Long)	H	1983–2012	15	7	73.3	22	8	65,388	13,900	6,125
February										
30-Year Bond Peaks (Short)	M	1978–2012	3	44	65.7	23	12	20,969	10,125	18,375
Yen Bottoms (Long)	M	1977–2012	6	62	55.6	20	16	9,988	22,350	10,688
Heating Oil Bottoms (Long)	N	1980–2012	8	62	78.8	26	7	122,006	44,339	9,468
Soybeans Bottom (Long)	N	1969–2012	9	73	54.5	24	20	71,719	24,638	5,563
Crude Oil Bottoms (Long)	N	1984–2012	10	60	82.8	24	5	92,490	29,210	7,110
Gold Peaks (Short)	J	1975–2012	13	17	63.2	24	14	45,480	14,300	6,170
Silver Peaks (Short)	K	1973–2012	13	45	75.0	30	10	68,215	103,500	77,840
Sugar Peaks (Short)	N	1973–2012	14	39	57.5	23	17	35,482	8,669	2,083
Natural Gas Bottoms (Long)	N	1991–2012	16	41	72.7	16	6	45,740	17,310	8,380
March										
Cocoa Peaks (Short)	N	1973–2012	10	23	77.5	31	9	16,640	4,060	4,940
Yen Peaks (Short)	M	1977–2012	10	14	72.2	26	10	19,000	4,963	7,713
Euro Peaks (Short)	M	1999–2012	11	9	57.1	8	6	5,462	4,938	4,013
British Pound Bottoms (Long)	M	1976–2012	15	22	73.0	27	10	23,219	5,063	5,219
April										
30-Year Bond Bottoms (Long)	U	1978–2011	18	81	70.6	24	10	100,922	20,250	5,906
S&P 500 Bottoms (Long)	U	1982–2011	18	28	66.7	20	10	24,800	23,075	33,175
May										
Cattle Peaks (Short)	V	1976–2011	2	30	63.9	23	13	14,080	2,808	2,470
Copper Peaks (Short)	N	1973–2012	8	13	62.5	25	15	21,350	7,513	6,600
Silver Peaks (Short)	N	1973–2011	10	29	66.7	26	13	60,495	19,750	13,000
Coffee Peaks (Short)	U	1974–2011	16	54	71.1	27	11	146,010	37,556	17,119
British Pound Peaks (Short)	U	1975–2011	20	8	64.9	24	13	15,463	7,125	1,938

(Continued on next page)

COMMODITY SEASONALITY: TOP PERCENTAGE PLAYS

(Continued from previous page)

COMMODITY SEASONALITY: TOP PERCENTAGE PLAYS

Commodity	Contract	Years	Trading Day	Hold Days	Success Rate	# Gains	# Losses	Total Gain	Best Gain	Worst Loss
June										
30-Year Bond Bottoms (Long)	U	1978–2011	2	10	67.6%	23	11	$22,547	$5,156	$2,828
Cocoa Bottoms (Long)	U	1973–2011	2	24	64.1	25	14	16,380	2,980	4,130
Soybeans Peak (Short)	U	1970–2011	5	36	64.3	27	15	24,913	12,763	16,375
Wheat Bottoms (Long)	Z	1970–2011	6	105	54.8	23	19	13,250	12,025	15,300
Sugar Bottoms (Long)	V	1975–2011	11	32	62.2	23	14	20,026	5,398	5,869
Cattle Bottoms (Long)	J	1970–2011	14	160	66.7	28	14	41,230	15,270	11,600
Corn Peaks (Short)	U	1970–2011	18	25	64.3	27	15	26,506	8,975	3,888
British Pound Bottoms (Long)	U	1975–2011	20	16	70.3	26	11	31,831	8,406	7,188
July										
S&P 500 Peaks (Short)	U	1982–2011	10	7	63.3	19	11	44,488	19,150	12,650
Natural Gas Bottoms (Long)	X	1990–2011	17	62	54.5	12	10	21,720	47,710	29,890
Cocoa Peaks (Short)	Z	1973–2011	18	70	69.2	27	12	22,250	8,590	11,380
August										
Swiss Franc Bottoms (Long)	Z	1975–2011	6	48	70.3	26	11	37,600	11,000	25,700
Coffee Bottoms (Long)	Z	1974–2011	12	13	68.4	26	12	54,518	12,394	7,058
Cocoa Bottoms (Long)	Z	1973–2011	14	24	64.1	25	14	22,170	5,470	3,050
Gold Bottoms (Long)	Z	1975–2011	18	25	59.5	22	15	33,790	10,380	14,000
September										
Euro Bottoms (Long)	Z	1999–2011	5	16	84.6	11	2	22,775	11,338	5,800
Crude Oil Peaks (Short)	G	1983–2011	8	62	62.1	18	11	55,100	57,280	13,870
Cocoa Peaks (Short)	Z	1973–2011	10	33	69.2	27	12	20,550	5,230	4,600
British Pound Bottoms (Long)	Z	1975–2011	12	33	67.6	25	12	62,613	14,000	28,288
October										
Silver Peaks (Short)	Z	1972–2011	4	17	57.5	23	17	10,495	11,100	11,745
Heating Oil Peaks (Short)	Z	1980–2011	10	29	62.5	20	12	51,652	21,160	18,367
Yen Peaks (Short)	H	1976–2011	12	78	63.9	23	13	38,100	12,213	13,950
Soybeans Bottom (Long)	F	1968–2011	16	12	61.4	27	17	19,538	5,875	2,488
Euro Bottoms (Long)	H	1999–2011	18	47	61.5	8	5	41,225	14,813	11,800
S&P 500 Bottoms (Long)	H	1982–2011	19	41	73.3	22	8	231,888	38,975	13,600
November										
Lean Hogs Bottoms (Long)	G	1969–2011	2	13	67.4	29	14	16,350	2,090	2,390
Cocoa Bottoms (Long)	H	1972–2011	4	34	52.5	21	19	15,720	6,920	5,130
Gold Bottoms (Long)	G	1975–2011	13	10	56.8	21	16	31,490	7,560	2,710
30-Year Bond Peaks (Short)	M	1977–2011	14	107	54.3	19	16	21,859	9,656	19,438
Swiss Franc Bottoms (Long)	H	1975–2011	18	24	54.1	20	17	44,950	11,400	4,438
December										
Wheat Bottoms (Long)	K	1970–2011	5	20	61.9	26	16	9,462	8,400	3,838
Corn Bottoms (Long)	N	1970–2011	6	22	66.7	28	14	16,644	4,063	1,213
Copper Bottoms (Long)	K	1972–2011	10	47	70.0	28	12	83,000	19,688	5,000
British Pound Peaks (Short)	M	1975–2011	19	56	64.9	24	13	77,825	15,375	20,875
Swiss Franc Peaks (Short)	H	1975–2011	19	41	70.3	26	11	54,413	10,013	7,600

Commodity Seasonality Strategy Calendar*

* Graphic representation of the Commodity Seasonality Percentage Plays on pages 126–127. L = Long Trade, S = Short Trade. See pages 131–137 for contract symbols.

Commodity Seasonality Strategy Calendar*

*Graphic representation of the Commodity Seasonality Percentage Plays on pages 126–127. L = Long Trade, S = Short Trade. See pages 131–137 for contract symbols.

CFTC COT REPORT–INSIDER'S LOOK GIVES TRADERS AN EDGE IN THE MARKET

We first introduced readers to the Commodity Futures Trading Commission's (CFTC) Commitment of Traders (COT) report available at *www.cftc.gov* and how to use it effectively in the *Commodity Trader's Almanac 2010*. It was a huge hit because readers learned this vital consensus report revealed who literally "owns" the market. In the 2011 edition, we illustrated how the small speculators take positions either way too early or way too late.

Since the COT report has proved to be such an instrumental tool we felt compelled to highlight its effectiveness in the 2012 edition and to continue do so on an ongoing basis. Just remember that the data in the COT report can help a trader determine if market participants are too heavily positioned on one side of the market in a long-term trend run. It is less effective as short-term indicator.

The data is collected at the close of business each Tuesday by the various futures exchanges and then turned over to the CFTC (the regulatory body overseeing commodity and futures trading). The CFTC releases the data on the following Friday at 3:30 PM ET for futures only.

This report breaks down the three main categories of traders and shows their overall net positions. The first group is called the *commercials* (the hedgers), the next group is called the *non-commercials* (the large specula-tors) and the third group is called the *non-reportable* (the small speculators).

The commercials are considered to be hedgers. They could be producers or users of a given product. Due to the fact that they do or will own the underlying product, they are trying to hedge their risk in the cash market from adverse price moves. They do this in the futures market, and they gener-ally receive a discount from the margin requirements set for speculators.

When commercial entities fill out their account application, they usually disclose the fact that they are hedging. The exchanges recognize that hedgers are on the other side of the market from a cash standpoint and can usually, financially speaking, support their futures position. Therefore they set lower margin rates for those accounts. Commercials are considered to be the "smart money" or the strong hands because they are in the business of that commodity. They are considered to have the "inside scoop."

Since money moves the market, banks and large professional traders are a bit savvier when it comes to their business. After all, one would think a bank has a good idea of what direction interest rates are going to take once a central bank meeting occurs, right?

This report reveals what the professionals are doing in relationship to the small speculators. If 80% of small speculators are accused of losing their money trading, then it would stand to reason that you would not want to be in the market on the side of the small speculator.

This report helps you to uncover imbalances in markets that have been trending in a particular direction for quite some time. This information can help you spot timing clues at market turning points and, therefore, can help you develop a game plan to enter or exit trades accordingly

Keep in mind the commercials are not in the market to time market turns. They are hedging their risk exposure in a cash position. Therefore, the non-commercials, professional speculators, and funds, in the short term, are considered the "smart money." Here are some general guidelines to follow:

- ✔ If non-commercials are net long, commercials are net long, and the non-reportable positions category are net short by at least a two-to-one margin, look at buying opportunities. In other words go long with the pros.

- ✔ If non-commercials are net short, commercials are net short, and the non-reportable positions category are net long by at least a two-to-one margin, look at selling opportunities.

- ✔ If non-commercials are net long, commercials are net short, and the non-reportable positions category are neutral, meaning not heavily net long or short, look at buying opportunities, and stick with the non-commercial "smart money."

On the next page, created using TradeNavigator® software, is a weekly chart on the E-mini S&P 500 futures contract. The bottom portion of the chart contains a COT indicator. There are three measurements plotted on a zero line histogram. Figures above the zero line indicate longs, and readings below the zero line indicate short positions.

The black histogram bars represent the small speculators position in the market. The gray line represents the large professional speculators and the black line represents the commercials or hedgers position. If the adage is true that 80 to 90 percent of small speculators lose in the markets then we want to track that group and do the opposite. Following that line of reasoning, let's focus on the small speculators (black histogram bars) using the E-mini S&P 500 futures contracts and combine our seasonal analysis with the COT data.

(continued on next page)

In 2010, small speculators were on the net short side of the market as it rallied in the beginning of the year. After a substantial rally, this group decided to get on the long side as shown at point "A" six weeks before the flash crash and the "sell in May" seasonal peak. In 2011, we had a slight different make up as small speculators were net short from the beginning of the year. This group continued to add to short positions. The market did not decline much in May. Unfortunately for the small speculators they covered shorts just weeks before the big mid-summer seasonal break in July as the chart shows at point "B." In 2012 this same group again held a net short position in the beginning of the year missing a nice trend up in stock prices. Finally, just weeks before the "sell in May" seasonal peak in prices this group decided to go net long at the top, and continued to add to losers, or their longs as prices continued lower.

If you refer to your 2010 edition you will see that we covered the fact that throughout most of decline in the stock market in 2008, small speculators were net long while professionals were net short. Then small speculators turned short (point C) just weeks before the March 2009 low was made and by the time the exact low was made they increased their net short holdings by the largest amount while the professional speculators increased their long positions by the largest margin. In 2013 watch out if the small speculators start going long a few weeks before the seasonal peak for prices May.

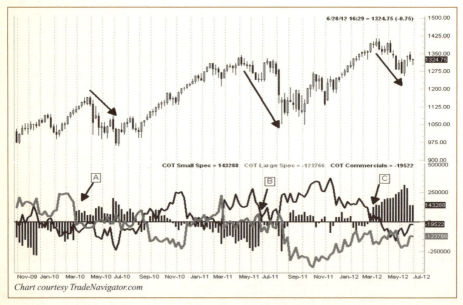

Chart courtesy TradeNavigator.com

COMMODITY AND RELATED SECURITIES SPECIFICATIONS

Contract/Security	Trading Symbol*	Exchange*	Trading Hours (ET)	Contract Size*	Unit Quoted*	Minimum Tick (Change)	Contract Months*
S&P 500 Futures	**SP**	**CME OC**	**9:30a–4:15p (M–F)**	**$250 x index**	**$/index**	**$0.10=$25.00**	**H,M,U,Z**
		Globex	4:30p–9:15a (M–Th)				
		Globex	6:00p–9:15a (Sun)				
		MSD	5:30p–6:00p				
E–mini S&P 500	ES	Globex	6:00 p–4:15p (M–Th)	$50 x index	$/index	$0.25=$12.50	H,M,U,Z
		Globex	4:30p–5:30p (M–Th)				
		Globex	6:00p–4:15p (Sun)				
		MSD	5:30p–6:00p				
iShares S&P 500	IVV	NYSE	9:30a–4:00p (M–F)	ETF	$	$0.01	ETF
S&P 500 SPDR	SPY	NYSE	9:30a–4:00p (M–F)	ETF	$	$0.01	ETF
30-Year Treasury	**US**	**CME OC**	**8:20a–3:00p (M–F)**	**$100,000**	**Pnt=$1000**	**.5 of 1/32=$15.625**	**H,M,U,Z**
	ZB	Globex	6:30p–5:00p (Su–F)				
iShares Barclays 20+yr Bond	TLT	NYSE	9:30a–4:00p (M–F)	ETF	$	$0.01	ETF
SPDR Barclays Long Term Treasury	TLO	NYSE	9:30a–4:00p (M–F)	ETF	$	$0.01	ETF
PIMCO 25+ Year Zero Coupon	ZROZ	NYSE	9:30a-4:00p (M-F)	ETF	$	$0.01	ETF
Vanguard Long–Term Bond	BLV	NYSE	9:30a–4:00p (M–F)	ETF	$	$0.01	ETF
Crude Oil	**CL**	**CME OC**	**9:00a–2:30p (M–F)**	**1000 bbl**	**$/bbl**	**$0.01=$10.00**	**All**
		Globex	6:00p–5:15p (Su–F)				
		MSD	5:15p–6:00p				
miNY Crude Oil	QM	CME	6:00p – 5:15p (Su–F)	500 bbl	$/bbl	$0.025=$12.50	All
		MSD	5:15p–6:00p				
ELEMENTS Rogers Int'l Energy	RJN	NYSE	9:30a-4:00p (M-F)	ETN	$	$0.01	ETN
iShares DJ US Energy	IYE	NYSE	9:30a–4:00p (M–F)	ETF	$	$0.01	ETF
iShares DJ US Oil & Gas Exp&Prod	IEO	NYSE	9:30a–4:00p (M–F)	ETF	$	$0.01	ETF
iShares DJ US Oil Equip & Serv	IEZ	NYSE	9:30a–4:00p (M–F)	ETF	$	$0.01	ETF
iShares GSCI Commodity	GSG	NYSE	9:30a–4:00p (M–F)	ETF	$	$0.01	ETF
iShares S&P Global Energy	IXC	NYSE	9:30a–4:00p (M–F)	ETF	$	$0.01	ETF
PowerShares DB Commodity	DBC	NYSE	9:30a–4:00p (M–F)	ETF	$	$0.01	ETF
PowerShares DB Energy	DBE	NYSE	9:30a–4:00p (M–F)	ETF	$	$0.01	ETF
PowerShares DB Oil	DBO	NYSE	9:30a–4:00p (M–F)	ETF	$	$0.01	ETF
PowerShares Oil Services	PXJ	NYSE	9:30a–4:00p (M–F)	ETF	$	$0.01	ETF
SPDR Energy	XLE	NYSE	9:30a–4:00p (M–F)	ETF	$	$0.01	ETF
SPDR Oil & Gas Equip & Service	XES	NYSE	9:30a–4:00p (M–F)	ETF	$	$0.01	ETF

(continued on next page)

* Month Codes: F = January, G = February, H = March, J = April, K = May, M = June, N = July, Q = August, U = September, V = October, X = November, Z = December I OC = Open Outcry,
DTH = Daily Trading Halts, MSD = Daily Maintenance Shutdown I oz = troy ounces, bu = bushels, lb = pounds, bbl = barrels, mmBtu = million British thermal units, mt = metric ton.
Stocks & ETFs trade at multiple exchanges. Different symbols can be assigned. All information obtained from sources believed to be reliable and subject to change. Check before trading.

COMMODITY AND RELATED SECURITIES SPECIFICATIONS

Contract/Security	Trading Symbol*	Exchange*	Trading Hours (ET)	Contract Size*	Unit Quoted*	Minimum Tick (Change)	Contract Months*
Crude Oil *(continued)*	CL	CME OC	9:00a–2:30p (M–F)	1000 bbl	$/bbl	$0.01=$10.00	All
SPDR Oil & Gas Explore & Prod	XOP	NYSE	9:30a–4:00p (M–F)	ETF	$	$0.01	ETF
United States 12 Month Oil Fund	USL	NYSE	9:30a–4:00p (M–F)	ETF	$	$0.01	ETF
United States Oil Fund	USO	NYSE	9:30a–4:00p (M–F)	ETF	$	$0.01	ETF
Vanguard Energy VIPERS	VDE	NYSE	9:30a–4:00p (M–F)	ETF	$	$0.01	ETF
Chesapeake Energy	CHK	NYSE	9:30a–4:00p (M–F)	STOCK	$	$0.01	STOCK
Chevron	CVX	NYSE	9:30a–4:00p (M–F)	STOCK	$	$0.01	STOCK
Conoco Phillips	COP	NYSE	9:30a–4:00p (M–F)	STOCK	$	$0.01	STOCK
Exxon Mobil	XOM	NYSE	9:30a–4:00p (M–F)	STOCK	$	$0.01	STOCK
Frontline Limited	FRO	NYSE	9:30a–4:00p (M–F)	STOCK	$	$0.01	STOCK
Marathon Oil	MRO	NYSE	9:30a–4:00p (M–F)	STOCK	$	$0.01	STOCK
Occidental Petroleum	OXY	NYSE	9:30a–4:00p (M–F)	STOCK	$	$0.01	STOCK
Heating Oil	HG	NYMEX OC	9:00a-2:30p (M-F)	42,000 gal	$/gal	$0.0001=$4.20	All
		Globex	6:00p-5:15p (Su-F)				
		MSD	5:15p-6:00p				
miNY Heating Oil	QH	NYMEX OC	9:00a-2:30p (M-F)	21,000 gal	$/gal	$0.001=$21.00	All
		Globex	6:00p-5:15p (Su-F)	21,000 gal	$/gal	$0.001=$21.00	All
		MSD	5:15p-6:00p				
ELEMENTS Rogers Int'l Energy	RJN	NYSE	9:30a-4:00p (M-F)	ETN	$	$0.01	ETN
United States Heating Oil Fund	UHN	NYSE	9:30a-4:00p (M-F)	ETF	$	$0.01	ETF
BP plc	BP	NYSE	9:30a-4:00p (M-F)	STOCK	$	$0.01	STOCK
Chevron	CVX	NYSE	9:30a-4:00p (M-F)	STOCK	$	$0.01	STOCK
ConocoPhillips	COP	NYSE	9:30a-4:00p (M-F)	STOCK	$	$0.01	STOCK
Exxon Mobil	XOM	NYSE	9:30a-4:00p (M-F)	STOCK	$	$0.01	STOCK
Marathon Oil	MRO	NYSE	9:30a-4:00p (M-F)	STOCK	$	$0.01	STOCK
Occidental Petroleum	OXY	NYSE	9:30a-4:00p (M-F)	STOCK	$	$0.01	STOCK
Sunoco	SUN	NYSE	9:30a-4:00p (M-F)	STOCK	$	$0.01	STOCK
Valero	VLO	NYSE	9:30a-4:00p (M-F)	STOCK	$	$0.01	STOCK
Natural Gas	NG	NYMEX OC	9:00a-2:30p (M-F)	10,000 mmBtu	$/mmBtu	$0.001=$10.00	All
		Globex	6:00p-5:15p (Su-F)				
		MSD	5:15p-6:00p				
miNY Natural Gas	QG	Globex	6:00p-5:15p (Su-F)	2,500 mmBtu	$/mmBtu	$0.005=$12.50	All
		MSD	5:15p-6:00p				
First Trust ISE–Revere Natural Gas	FCG	NYSE	9:30a-4:00p (M-F)	ETF	$	$0.01	ETF

* Month Codes: F = January, G = February, H = March, J = April, K = May, M = June, N = July, Q = August, U = September, V = October, X = November, Z = December / OC = Open Outcry,
DTH = Daily Trading Halts, MSD = Daily Maintenance Shutdown / oz = troy ounces, bu = bushels, lb = pounds, bbl = barrels, mmBtu = million British thermal units, mt = metric ton.
Stocks & ETFs trade at multiple exchanges. Different symbols can be assigned. All information obtained from sources believed to be reliable and subject to change. Check before trading.

COMMODITY AND RELATED SECURITIES SPECIFICATIONS

Contract/Security	Trading Symbol*	Exchange*	Trading Hours (ET)	Contract Size*	Unit Quoted*	Minimum Tick (Change)	Contract Months*
Natural Gas *(continued)*	**NG**	**NYMEX OC**	**9:00a-2:30p (M-F)**	**10,000 mmBtu**	**$/mmBtu**	**$0.001=$10.00**	**All**
ELEMENTS Rogers Int'l Energy	RJN	NYSE	9:30a-4:00p (M-F)	ETN	$	$0.01	ETN
iPath DJ-UBS Natural Gas	GAZ	NYSE	9:30a-4:00p (M-F)	ETN	$	$0.01	ETN
iShares DJ US Oil & Gas Exp&Prod	IEO	NYSE	9:30a-4:00p (M-F)	ETF	$	$0.01	ETF
SPDR Oil & Gas Equip & Service	XES	NYSE	9:30a-4:00p (M-F)	ETF	$	$0.01	ETF
SPDR Oil & Gas Explore & Prod	XOP	NYSE	9:30a-4:00p (M-F)	ETF	$	$0.01	ETF
United States Natural Gas Fund	UNG	NYSE	9:30a-4:00p (M-F)	ETF	$	$0.01	ETF
Apache	APA	NYSE	9:30a-4:00p (M-F)	STOCK	$	$0.01	STOCK
Devon Energy	DVN	NYSE	9:30a-4:00p (M-F)	STOCK	$	$0.01	STOCK
DTE Energy	DTE	NYSE	9:30a-4:00p (M-F)	STOCK	$	$0.01	STOCK
Noble	NE	NYSE	9:30a-4:00p (M-F)	STOCK	$	$0.01	STOCK
XTO Energy	XTO	NYSE	9:30a-4:00p (M-F)	STOCK	$	$0.01	STOCK
Copper	**HG**	**NYMEX OC**	**8:10a-1:00p (M-F)**	**25,000 lbs**	**¢/lb**	**¢0.05=$12.50**	**All**
		Globex	6:00p–5:15p (Su–F)				
		MSD	5:15p–6:00p				
miNY Copper *(Thinly Traded)*	QC	Globex	6:00p–5:15p (Su–F)	12,500 lbs	$/lb	$0.002=$25.00	All
		MSD	5:15p–6:00p				
Global X Copper Miners	COPX	NYSE	9:30a–4:00p (M–F)	ETF	$	$0.01	ETF
iShares DJ US Basic Materials	IYM	NYSE	9:30a–4:00p (M–F)	ETF	$	$0.01	ETF
PowerShares DB Base Metals	DBB	NYSE	9:30a–4:00p (M–F)	ETF	$	$0.01	ETF
BHP Billiton Ltd	BHP	NYSE	9:30a–4:00p (M–F)	STOCK	$	$0.01	STOCK
Southern Copper Corp	SCCO	NYSE	9:30a–4:00p (M–F)	STOCK	$	$0.01	STOCK
ISE Global Copper Index	CU	NASDAQ	9:30a-4:00p (M-F)	ETF	$	$0.01	ETF
Gold	**GC**	**NYMEX OC**	**8:20a-1:30p (M-F)**	**100 oz**	**$/oz**	**$0.10=$10.00**	**G,J,M,Q,V,Z**
		Globex	6:00p–5:15p (Su–F)				
		MSD	5:15p–6:00p				
E–mini Gold	YG	Globex	6:00p–5:15p (Su–F)	33 oz	$/oz	$0.10=$3.30	G,J,M,Q,V,Z
		MSD	5:15p–6:00p				
miNY Gold pretty liquid	QO	Globex	6:00p–5:15p (Su–F)	50 oz	$/oz	$0.25=$12.50	G,J,M,Q,V,Z
		MSD	5:15p–6:00p				
ETFS Gold	SGOL	NYSE	9:30a–4:00p (M–F)	ETF	$	$0.01	ETF
iShares Comex Gold	IAU	NYSE	9:30a–4:00p (M–F)	ETF	$	$0.01	ETF
Market Vectors Gold Miners	GDX	NYSE	9:30a–4:00p (M–F)	ETF	$	$0.01	ETF

(continued on next page)

* Month Codes: F = January, G = February, H = March, J = April, K = May, M = June, N = July, Q = August, U = September, V = October, X = November, Z = December I OC = Open Outcry, DTH = Daily Trading Halts, MSD = Daily Maintenance Shutdown I oz = troy ounces, bu = bushels, lb = pounds, bbl = barrels, mmBtu = million British thermal units, mt = metric ton. Stocks & ETFs trade at multiple exchanges. Different symbols can be assigned. All information obtained from sources believed to be reliable and subject to change. Check before trading.

COMMODITY AND RELATED SECURITIES SPECIFICATIONS

Contract/Security	Trading Symbol*	Exchange*	Trading Hours (ET)	Contract Size*	Unit Quoted*	Minimum Tick (Change)	Contract Months*
Gold *(continued)*	GC	NYMEX OC	8:20a–1:30p (M-F)	100 oz	$/oz	$0.10=$10.00	G,J,M,Q,V,Z
Market Vectors Jr Gold Miners	GDXJ	NYSE	9:30a–4:00p (M-F)	ETF	$	$0.01	ETF
PowerShares DB Gold	DGL	NYSE	9:30a–4:00p (M-F)	ETF	$	$0.01	ETF
PowerShares DB Precious Metals	DBP	NYSE	9:30a–4:00p (M-F)	ETF	$	$0.01	ETF
PowerShares Global Gold/Pre Metal	PSAU	NYSE	9:30a–4:00p (M-F)	ETF	$	$0.01	ETF
SPDR Gold	GLD	NYSE	9:30a–4:00p (M-F)	ETF	$	$0.01	ETF
Sprott Physical Gold	PHYS	NYSE	9:30a–4:00p (M-F)	ETF	$	$0.01	ETF
Agnico–Eagle Mines	AEM	NYSE	9:30a–4:00p (M-F)	STOCK	$	$0.01	STOCK
ASA Ltd.	ASA	NYSE	9:30a–4:00p (M-F)	STOCK	$	$0.01	STOCK
Barrick Gold	ABX	NYSE	9:30a–4:00p (M-F)	STOCK	$	$0.01	STOCK
Freeport–McMoRan Copper & Gold	FCX	NYSE	9:30a–4:00p (M-F)	STOCK	$	$0.01	STOCK
Newmont Mining	NEM	NYSE	9:30a–4:00p (M-F)	STOCK	$	$0.01	STOCK
Silver	SI	NYMEX OC	8:25a–1:25p (M-F)	5000 oz	¢/oz	¢0.5=$25.00	F,H,K,N,U,Z
		Globex	6:00p–5:15p (Su–F)				
		MSD	5:15p–6:00p				
E–mini Silver	YI	Globex	6:00p–5:15p (Su–F)	1000 oz	$/oz	$0.005=$5.00	F,H,K,N,U,Z
		MSD	5:15p–6:00p				
miNY Silver	QI	Globex	6:00p–5:15p (Su–F)	2500 oz	$/oz	$0.0125=$31.25	F,H,K,N,U,Z
		MSD	5:15p–6:00p				
ETFS Silver	SIVR	NYSE	9:30a–4:00p (M-F)	ETF	$	$0.01	ETF
Global X Silver Miners	SIL	NYSE	9:30a–4:00p (M-F)	ETF	$	$0.01	ETF
iShares Silver	SLV	NYSE	9:30a–4:00p (M-F)	ETF	$	$0.01	ETF
PowerShares DB Silver	DBS	NYSE	9:30a–4:00p (M-F)	ETF	$	$0.01	ETF
Mines Management	MGN	AMEX	9:30a–4:00p (M-F)	STOCK	$	$0.01	STOCK
Silver Wheaton	SLW	NYSE	9:30a–4:00p (M-F)	STOCK	$	$0.01	STOCK
Corn	C	CME OC	10:30a–2:15p (M-F)	5000 bu	¢/bu	¢0.25=$12.50	H,K,N,U,Z
	ZC	Globex	7:00p–7:00a (Su–F)				
		Globex	10:30a–2:15p (Su–F)				
Mini–Sized Corn	YC	CME OC	10:30a–2:45p (M-F)	1,000 bu	¢/bu	¢0.125=$1.25	H,K,N,U,Z
	XC	Globex	7:00p–7:00a (Su–F)				
		Globex	10:30a–2:45p (Su–F)				
Teucrium Corn	CORN	NYSE	9:30a–4:00p (M-F)	ETF	$	$0.01	ETF
iPath DJ-UBS Grains	JJG	NYSE	9:30a–4:00p (M-F)	ETN	$	$0.01	ETN
Jefferies TR/J CRB Global Ag	CRBA	NYSE	9:30a–4:00p (M-F)	ETF	$	$0.01	ETF

* Month Codes: F = January, G = February, H = March, J = April, K = May, M = June, N = July, Q = August, U = September, V = October, X = November, Z = December I OC = Open Outcry, DTH = Daily Trading Halts, MSD = Daily Maintenance Shutdown I oz = troy ounces, bu = bushels, lb = pounds, bbl = barrels, mmBtu = million British thermal units, mt = metric ton. Stocks & ETFs trade at multiple exchanges. Different symbols can be assigned. All information obtained from sources believed to be reliable and subject to change. Check before trading.

COMMODITY AND RELATED SECURITIES SPECIFICATIONS

Contract/Security	Trading Symbol*	Exchange*	Trading Hours (ET)	Contract Size*	Unit Quoted*	Minimum Tick (Change)	Contract Months*
Corn (continued)	**C**	**CME OC**	10:30a–2:15p (M–F)	5000 bu	¢/bu	¢0.25=$12.50	H,K,N,U,Z
Market Vectors Agribusiness	MOO	NYSE	9:30a–4:00p (M–F)	ETF	$	$0.01	ETF
Archer Daniels Midland	ADM	NYSE	9:30a–4:00p (M–F)	STOCK	$	$0.01	STOCK
Bunge Ltd.	BG	NYSE	9:30a–4:00p (M–F)	STOCK	$	$0.01	STOCK
Conagra	CAG	NYSE	9:30a–4:00p (M–F)	STOCK	$	$0.01	STOCK
Gruma S.A.B. de CV	GMK	NYSE	9:30a–4:00p (M–F)	STOCK	$	$0.01	STOCK
John Deere	DE	NYSE	9:30a–4:00p (M–F)	STOCK	$	$0.01	STOCK
Kellogg	K	NYSE	9:30a–4:00p (M–F)	STOCK	$	$0.01	STOCK
Monsanto	MON	NYSE	9:30a–4:00p (M–F)	STOCK	$	$0.01	STOCK
Mosaic	MOS	NYSE	9:30a–4:00p (M–F)	STOCK	$	$0.01	STOCK
Potash	POT	NYSE	9:30a–4:00p (M–F)	STOCK	$	$0.01	STOCK
Soybeans	**S**	**CME OC**	10:30a–2:15p (M–F)	5000 bu	¢/bu	¢0.25=$12.50	F,H,K,N,Q,U,X
	ZS	Globex	7:00p–7:00a (Su–F)				
		Globex	10:30a–2:15p (Su–F)				
Mini–Sized Soybeans	YK	CME OC	10:30a–2:45p (M–F)	1000 bu	¢/bu	¢0.125=$1.25	F,H,K,N,Q,U,X
	XK	Globex	7:00p–7:00a (Su–F)				
		Globex	10:30a–2:45p (Su–F)				
iPath DJ-UBS Grains	JJG	NYSE	9:30a-4:00p (M-F)	ETN	$	$0.01	ETN
Jefferies TR/J CRB Global Ag	CRBA	NYSE	9:30a–4:00p (M–F)	ETF	$	$0.01	ETF
Market Vectors Agribusiness	MOO	NYSE	9:30a–4:00p (M–F)	ETF	$	$0.01	ETF
Archer Daniels Midland	ADM	NYSE	9:30a–4:00p (M–F)	STOCK	$	$0.01	STOCK
Bunge Ltd.	BG	NYSE	9:30a–4:00p (M–F)	STOCK	$	$0.01	STOCK
Conagra	CAG	NYSE	9:30a–4:00p (M–F)	STOCK	$	$0.01	STOCK
John Deere	DE	NYSE	9:30a–4:00p (M–F)	STOCK	$	$0.01	STOCK
Monsanto	MON	NYSE	9:30a–4:00p (M–F)	STOCK	$	$0.01	STOCK
Mosaic	MOS	NYSE	9:30a–4:00p (M–F)	STOCK	$	$0.01	STOCK
Potash	POT	NYSE	9:30a–4:00p (M–F)	STOCK	$	$0.01	STOCK
Wheat	**W**	**CME OC**	10:30a–2:15p (M–F)	5000 bu	¢/bu	¢0.25=$12.50	H,K,N,U,Z
	ZW	Globex	7:00p–7:00a (Su–F)				
			10:30a–2:15p (Su–F)				
Mini–Sized Wheat	YW	CME OC	10:30a–2:45p (M–F)	1000 bu	¢/bu	¢0.125=$1.25	H,K,N,U,Z
		Globex	7:00p–7:00a (Su–F)				
			10:30a–2:45p (Su–F)				

(continued on next page)

---

* Month Codes: F = January, G = February, H = March, J = April, K = May, M = June, N = July, Q = August, U = September, V = October, X = November, Z = December I OC = Open Outcry,
DTH = Daily Trading Halts, MSD = Daily Maintenance Shutdown I oz = troy ounces, bu = bushels, lb = pounds, bbl = barrels, mmBtu = million British thermal units, mt = metric ton.
Stocks & ETFs trade at multiple exchanges. Different symbols can be assigned. All information obtained from sources believed to be reliable and subject to change. Check before trading.

COMMODITY AND RELATED SECURITIES SPECIFICATIONS

Contract/Security	Trading Symbol*	Exchange*	Trading Hours (ET)	Contract Size*	Unit Quoted*	Minimum Tick (Change)	Contract Months*
Wheat *(continued)*	W	CME OC	10:30a–2:15p (M–F)	5000 bu	¢/bu	¢0.25=$12.50	H,K,N,U,Z
iPath DJ-UBS Grains	JJG	NYSE	9:30a–4:00p (M–F)	ETN	$	$0.01	ETN
Jefferies TR/J CRB Global Ag	CRBA	NYSE	9:30a–4:00p (M–F)	ETF	$	$0.01	ETF
Market Vectors Agribusiness	MOO	NYSE	9:30a–4:00p (M–F)	ETF	$	$0.01	ETF
Archer Daniels Midland	ADM	NYSE	9:30a–4:00p (M–F)	STOCK	$	$0.01	STOCK
Bunge Ltd.	BG	NYSE	9:30a–4:00p (M–F)	STOCK	$	$0.01	STOCK
Conagra	CAG	NYSE	9:30a–4:00p (M–F)	STOCK	$	$0.01	STOCK
General Mills	GIS	NYSE	9:30a–4:00p (M–F)	STOCK	$	$0.01	STOCK
John Deere	DE	NYSE	9:30a–4:00p (M–F)	STOCK	$	$0.01	STOCK
Kellogg	K	NYSE	9:30a–4:00p (M–F)	STOCK	$	$0.01	STOCK
Monsanto	MON	NYSE	9:30a–4:00p (M–F)	STOCK	$	$0.01	STOCK
Mosaic	MOS	NYSE	9:30a–4:00p (M–F)	STOCK	$	$0.01	STOCK
Potash	POT	NYSE	9:30a–4:00p (M–F)	STOCK	$	$0.01	STOCK
Ralcorp Holdings	RAH	NYSE	9:30a–4:00p (M–F)	STOCK	$	$0.01	STOCK
Cocoa	CC	ICE	4:00a–2:00p (M–F)	10 mt	$/mt	$1.00=$10.00	H,K,N,U,Z
	CJ	Globex	6:00p–5:15p (Su–F)				
		MSD	5:15p–6:00p				
Hershey	HSY	NYSE	9:30a–4:00p (M–F)	STOCK	$	$0.01	STOCK
Coffee	KC	ICE	3:30a–2:00p (M–F)	37500 lbs	$/lb	$.0005=$18.75	H,K,N,U,Z
	KT	Globex	6:00p–5:15p (Su–F)				
		MSD	5:15p–6:00p				
Green Mountain Coffee Roasters	GMCR	NASDAQ	9:30a–4:00p (M–F)	STOCK	$	$0.01	STOCK
Starbucks	SBUX	NASDAQ	9:30a–4:00p (M–F)	STOCK	$	$0.01	STOCK
Sugar	SB	ICE	3:30a–2:00p (M–F)	112000 lbs	$/lb	$.0001=$11.20	H,K,N,V
	YO	Globex	6:00p–5:15p (Su–F)				
		MSD	5:15p–6:00p				
iPath DJ-UBS Sugar	SGG	NYSE	9:30a–4:00p (M–F)	ETN	$	$0.01	ETN
Live Cattle	LC	CME OC	10:05a–2:00p (M–F)	40000 lbs	¢/lb	$.00025=$10.00	G,J,M,Q,V,Z
	LE	Globex	10:05a M–2:55p F				
		DTH	5:00p–6–00p				
Market Vectors Agribusiness	MOO	NYSE	9:30a–4:00p (M–F)	ETF	$	$0.01	ETF
Burger King Holdings	BKC	NYSE	9:30a–4:00p (M–F)	STOCK	$	$0.01	STOCK
McDonalds	MCD	NYSE	9:30a–4:00p (M–F)	STOCK	$	$0.01	STOCK
Wendy's/Arby's Group	WEN	NYSE	9:30a–4:00p (M–F)	STOCK	$	$0.01	STOCK

* Month Codes: F = January, G = February, H = March, J = April, K = May, M = June, N = July, Q = August, U = September, V = October, X = November, Z = December I OC = Open Outcry, DTH = Daily Trading Halts, MSD = Daily Maintenance Shutdown I oz = troy ounces, bu = bushels, lb = pounds, bbl = barrels, mmBtu = million British thermal units, mt = metric ton. Stocks & ETFs trade at multiple exchanges. Different symbols can be assigned. All information obtained from sources believed to be reliable and subject to change. Check before trading.

COMMODITY AND RELATED SECURITIES SPECIFICATIONS

Contract/Security	Trading Symbol*	Exchange*	Trading Hours (ET)	Contract Size*	Unit Quoted*	Minimum Tick (Change)	Contract Months*
Lean Hogs	**LH**	**CME OC**	**10:05a–2:00p (M–F)**	**40000 lbs**	**¢/lb**	**$.00025=$10.00**	**G,J,K,M,N,Q,V,Z**
	HE	Globex	10:05a M–2:55p F				
		DTH	5:00p–6–00p				
Market Vectors Agribusiness	MOO	NYSE	9:30a–4:00p (M–F)	ETF	$	$0.01	ETF
Hormel Foods	HRL	NYSE	9:30a–4:00p (M–F)	STOCK	$	$0.01	STOCK
Smithfield Foods	SFD	NYSE	9:30a–4:00p (M–F)	STOCK	$	$0.01	STOCK
British Pound	**BP**	**CME OC**	**8:20a–3:00p (M–F)**	**62500 £**	**£$**	**$.0001=$6.25**	**H,M,U,Z**
	6B	Globex	6:00p–5:00p (Su–F)				
CurrencyShares British Pound	FXB	NYSE	9:30a–4:00p (M–F)	ETF	$	$0.01	ETF
Euro	**EC**	**CME OC**	**8:20a–3:00p (M–F)**	**125000 €**	**€/$**	**$.0001=$12.50**	**H,M,U,Z**
	6E	Globex	6:00p–5:00p (Su–F)				
E–Mini Euro	E7	Globex	6:00p–5:00p (Su–F)	62500 €	€/$	$.0001=$6.25	H,M,U,Z
CurrencyShares Euro	FXE	NYSE	9:30a–4:00p (M–F)	ETF	$	$0.01	ETF
WisdomTree Dreyfus Euro	EU	NYSE	9:30a–4:00p (M–F)	ETF	$	$0.01	ETF
Proshares UltraShort Euro	EUO	NYSE	9:30a-4:00p (M-F)	ETF	$	$0.01	ETF
Swiss Franc	**SF**	**CME OC**	**8:20a–3:00p (M–F)**	**125000 CHF**	**CHF/$**	**$.0001=$12.50**	**H,M,U,Z**
	6S	Globex	6:00p–5:00p (Su–F)				
CurrencyShares Swiss Franc	FXF	NYSE	9:30a–4:00p (M–F)	ETF	$	$0.01	ETF
Japanese Yen	**JY**	**CME OC**	**8:20a–3:00p (M–F)**	**12500000 ¥**	**¥/$**	**$.000001=$12.50**	**H,M,U,Z**
	6J	Globex	6:00p–5:00p (Su–F)				
E–Mini Yen	J7	Globex	6:00p–5:00p (Su–F)	6250000 ¥	¥/$	$.000001=$6.25	H,M,U,Z
CurrencyShares Japanese Yen	FXY	NYSE	9:30a–4:00p (M–F)	ETF	$	$0.01	ETF
WisdomTree Dreyfus Japanese Yen	JYF	NYSE	9:30a–4:00p (M–F)	ETF	$	$0.01	ETF
Proshares UltraShort Yen	YCS	NYSE	9:30a-4:00p (M-F)	ETF	$	$0.01	ETF
Dollar Index	**DX**	**ICE**	**8:00p-5:00, (Su-F)**	**$1,000 x Index**	**$**	**.005=$5.00**	**H,M,U,Z**
PowerShares USD Index Bullish	UUP	NYSE	9:30a-4:00p (M-F)	ETF	$	$0.01	ETF
PowerShares USD Index Bearish	UDN	NYSE	9:30a-4:00p (M-F)	ETF	$	$0.01	ETF
PowerShares 3X Long USD Index	UUPT	NYSE	9:30a-4:00p (M-F)	ETN	$	$0.01	ETN
PowerShares 3X Short USD Index	UDNT	NYSE	9:30a-4:00p (M-F)	ETN	$	$0.01	ETN

Month Codes: F = January, G = February, H = March, J = April, K = May, M = June, N = July, Q = August, U = September, V = October, X = November, Z = December / OC = Open Outcry, DTH = Daily Trading Halts, MSD = Daily Maintenance Shutdown / oz = troy ounces, bu = bushels, lb = pounds, bbl = barrels, mmBtu = million British thermal units, mt = metric ton. Stocks & ETFs trade at multiple exchanges. Different symbols can be assigned. All information obtained from sources believed to be reliable and subject to change. Check before trading.

S&P 500 CYCLE, SEASONAL PATTERN, AND TRADING GUIDE

Stock prices demonstrate predictable directional price swings throughout the year at certain times, as a function of the overall condition of the economy and the supply and demand of shares based on overall sector performance, and as a result of year-end window dressing and quarterly earnings reports.

There are other factors that can magnify or mute these price tendencies, as described for the past 46 years by Yale and Jeffrey Hirsch in the *Stock Traders Almanac*. The famed four-year Presidential Election/Stock Market cycle clearly shows the impact of politics on the market. There is also the January Barometer, which has a strong record for predicting the general course of stock prices for the year. Fiscal and monetary policy decisions, guided by the men in charge in Washington and Wall Street, have more to do with investors' confidence and, therefore, can be a catalyst for accelerating or putting the brakes on seasonal price moves as well.

Typically, October marks the best time of the year to buy stocks. This month has earned a reputation as a "bear killer," as 12 post–World War II bear markets were turned in October. The Santa Claus rally can spill into early January, but we do see some profit taking for tax deferment purposes, which can incite savvy traders to buy the "January Dip" and sell before the Presidents' Day holiday weekend. In April, we see an early month sell-off, as traders liquidate shares in order to pay taxes; this is where we see a typical top. This rally, spanning November to April, is the Best Six Months. As we hit mid- to late July, after second quarter earnings season, the market begins to fade; and aggressive traders may want to be short, while buyers may want to wait until the next cycle begins at the typical October low.

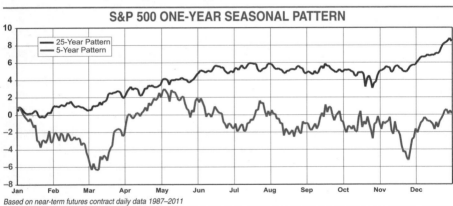

S&P 500 ONE-YEAR SEASONAL PATTERN

— 25-Year Pattern
— 5-Year Pattern

Based on near-term futures contract daily data 1987–2011

S&P 500 NEAR-TERM CONTRACT ANNUAL HIGHS, LOWS, AND CLOSES SINCE 1983

YEAR	HIGH DATE	HIGH CLOSE	LOW DATE	LOW CLOSE	YEAR CLOSE	YEAR	HIGH DATE	HIGH CLOSE	LOW DATE	LOW CLOSE	YEAR CLOSE
1983	10/10	174.05	01/03	139.00	167.30	1998	12/29	1254.60	01/09	929.50	1245.50
1984	09/17	173.00	07/24	148.85	170.20	1999	12/31	1484.20	01/14	1219.00	1484.20
1985	12/16	215.15	01/04	166.40	212.45	2000	03/24	1555.40	12/20	1279.60	1335.00
1986	12/04	254.65	01/22	202.80	242.15	2001	02/01	1382.50	09/21	973.00	1149.20
1987	08/25	338.40	10/19	201.50	246.75	2002	01/04	1175.30	10/09	777.80	878.90
1988	10/21	285.00	01/08	240.75	280.40	2003	12/31	1110.60	03/11	800.20	1110.60
1989	10/09	363.85	01/03	277.65	356.35	2004	12/29	1217.00	08/06	1063.60	1213.70
1990	07/16	372.30	10/11	297.35	330.65	2005	12/14	1282.10	04/20	1139.80	1254.80
1991	12/31	418.20	01/09	312.65	418.20	2006	12/14	1438.20	06/13	1232.40	1428.40
1992	12/22	441.95	04/08	395.25	437.65	2007	10/09	1576.20	03/05	1372.20	1477.20
1993	12/28	471.90	01/08	429.70	466.95	2008	01/03	1458.70	11/20	748.30	900.10
1994	02/02	482.30	04/04	439.25	461.35	2009	12/28	1123.10	03/09	675.90	1110.70
1995	12/14	623.75	01/03	461.45	618.45	2010	12/29	1255.70	07/02	1014.30	1253.00
1996	12/26	764.60	01/10	600.75	744.50	2011	04/29	1359.70	10/03	1086.30	1252.60
1997	10/07	989.60	04/11	738.50	979.10	2012*	03/26	1415.10	01/03	1272.10	AT PRESS TIME

*Through May 31, 2012

S&P 500 NEAR-TERM CONTRACT MONTHLY CLOSING PRICES

	Jan	Feb	Mar	Apr	May	Jun	Jul	Aug	Sep	Oct	Nov	Dec
1983	147.20	149.20	151.85	164.25	162.20	170.15	163.70	164.95	168.25	165.45	166.40	167.30
1984	165.50	157.15	161.05	161.40	150.80	154.85	152.25	167.40	170.10	168.60	164.55	170.20
1985	180.45	181.80	183.35	180.85	189.65	193.65	191.35	187.90	182.80	189.25	202.40	212.45
1986	213.05	226.00	241.00	234.80	247.55	252.25	235.95	252.65	230.60	244.70	248.65	242.15
1987	274.15	283.55	291.25	289.45	289.45	303.55	320.20	330.85	325.85	259.35	232.00	246.75
1988	257.05	267.30	259.05	261.00	262.95	275.40	273.25	261.60	274.15	279.10	273.05	280.40
1989	298.75	289.65	297.85	311.55	321.45	321.20	348.30	351.80	352.60	343.15	347.50	356.35
1990	330.50	332.95	341.45	332.10	361.75	362.35	358.60	322.55	306.75	306.80	324.05	330.65
1991	344.65	366.80	376.25	375.90	389.70	372.25	388.40	395.55	390.30	393.30	375.70	418.20
1992	408.60	412.35	404.20	414.80	414.90	409.50	423.90	414.15	418.35	417.80	430.95	437.65
1993	438.25	443.70	452.60	438.65	450.10	451.00	448.00	463.25	459.35	468.05	461.85	466.95
1994	481.70	466.15	446.75	450.35	456.20	445.05	458.90	474.10	463.25	472.45	453.95	461.35
1995	472.20	488.55	504.40	516.75	533.35	547.15	563.15	562.85	588.20	583.85	607.25	618.45
1996	637.95	638.25	651.25	654.85	666.95	676.80	642.40	651.35	691.40	709.65	758.25	744.50
1997	787.50	790.40	758.00	802.80	850.60	890.25	957.95	903.10	954.50	924.00	954.90	979.10
1998	987.80	1050.50	1110.50	1119.20	1090.80	1143.00	1123.00	954.00	1026.00	1105.20	1162.50	1245.50
1999	1281.50	1235.50	1293.30	1336.50	1297.20	1381.70	1331.80	1319.80	1298.20	1376.20	1391.50	1484.20
2000	1401.00	1372.00	1515.30	1460.00	1422.20	1468.10	1438.90	1521.20	1453.70	1440.20	1321.50	1335.00
2001	1372.90	1242.00	1169.20	1254.30	1257.40	1231.70	1215.30	1135.10	1043.70	1060.70	1140.00	1149.20
2002	1130.40	1106.90	1149.20	1077.20	1067.50	990.10	911.50	916.10	815.00	885.40	936.00	878.90
2003	854.70	840.90	847.00	916.10	963.30	973.30	989.30	1007.70	994.10	1049.50	1057.80	1110.60
2004	1129.90	1144.60	1124.90	1106.10	1120.30	1140.40	1101.10	1104.10	1114.90	1130.30	1174.10	1213.70
2005	1181.70	1204.10	1183.90	1158.50	1192.30	1195.50	1236.80	1221.40	1234.30	1209.80	1251.10	1254.80
2006	1283.60	1282.40	1303.30	1315.90	1272.10	1279.40	1281.80	1305.60	1345.40	1383.20	1402.90	1428.40
2007	1443.00	1408.90	1431.20	1488.40	1532.90	1515.40	1461.90	1476.70	1538.10	1554.90	1483.70	1477.20
2008	1379.60	1331.30	1324.00	1386.00	1400.60	1281.10	1267.10	1282.60	1167.40	967.30	895.30	900.10
2009	822.50	734.20	794.80	870.00	918.10	915.50	984.40	1019.70	1052.90	1033.00	1094.80	1110.70
2010	1070.40	1103.40	1165.20	1183.40	1088.50	1026.60	1098.30	1048.30	1136.70	1179.70	1179.60	1253.00
2011	1282.40	1326.10	1321.00	1359.70	1343.90	1315.50	1288.40	1217.70	1126.00	1249.30	1246.00	1252.60
2012	1308.20	1364.40	1403.20	1393.60	1309.20							

S&P 500 NEAR-TERM CONTRACT MONTHLY PERCENT CHANGES

	Jan	Feb	Mar	Apr	May	Jun	Jul	Aug	Sep	Oct	Nov	Dec	Year's Change
1983	3.8	1.4	1.8	8.2	−1.2	4.9	−3.8	0.8	2.0	−1.7	0.6	0.5	18.0
1984	−1.1	−5.0	2.5	0.2	−6.6	2.7	−1.7	10.0	1.6	−0.9	−2.4	3.4	1.7
1985	6.0	0.7	0.9	−1.4	4.9	2.1	−1.2	−1.8	−2.7	3.5	6.9	5.0	24.8
1986	0.3	6.1	6.6	−2.6	5.4	1.9	−6.5	7.1	−8.7	6.1	1.6	−2.6	14.0
1987	13.2	3.4	2.7	−0.6	N/C	4.9	5.5	3.3	−1.5	−20.4	−10.5	6.4	1.9
1988	4.2	4.0	−3.1	0.8	0.7	4.7	−0.8	−4.3	4.8	1.8	−2.2	2.7	13.6
1989	6.5	−3.0	2.8	4.6	3.2	−0.1	8.4	1.0	0.2	−2.7	1.3	2.5	27.1
1990	−7.3	0.7	2.6	−2.7	8.9	0.2	−1.0	−10.1	−4.9	0.02	5.6	2.0	−7.2
1991	4.2	6.4	2.6	−0.1	3.7	−4.5	4.3	1.8	−1.3	0.8	−4.5	11.3	26.5
1992	−2.3	0.9	−2.0	2.6	0.02	−1.3	3.5	−2.3	1.0	−0.1	3.1	1.6	4.7
1993	0.1	1.2	2.0	−3.1	2.6	0.2	−0.7	3.4	−0.8	1.9	−1.3	1.1	6.7
1994	3.2	−3.2	−4.2	0.8	1.3	−2.4	3.1	3.3	−2.3	2.0	−3.9	1.6	−1.2
1995	2.4	3.5	3.2	2.4	3.2	2.6	2.9	−0.1	4.5	−0.7	4.0	1.8	34.1
1996	3.2	0.1	2.0	0.6	1.8	1.5	−5.1	1.4	6.1	2.6	6.8	−1.8	20.4
1997	5.8	0.4	−4.1	5.9	6.0	4.7	7.6	−5.7	5.7	−3.2	3.3	2.5	31.5
1998	0.9	6.3	5.7	0.8	−2.5	4.8	−1.7	−15.0	7.5	7.7	5.2	7.1	27.2
1999	2.9	−3.6	4.7	3.3	−2.9	6.5	−3.6	−0.9	−1.6	6.0	1.1	6.7	19.2
2000	−5.6	−2.1	10.4	−3.6	−2.6	3.2	−2.0	5.7	−4.4	−0.9	−8.2	1.0	−10.1
2001	2.8	−9.5	−5.9	7.3	0.2	−2.0	−1.3	−6.6	−8.1	1.6	7.5	0.8	−13.9
2002	−1.6	−2.1	3.8	−6.3	−0.9	−7.3	−7.9	0.5	−11.0	8.6	5.7	−6.1	−23.5
2003	−2.8	−1.6	0.7	8.2	5.2	1.0	1.6	1.9	−1.3	5.6	0.8	5.0	26.4
2004	1.7	1.3	−1.7	−1.7	1.3	1.8	−3.4	0.3	1.0	1.4	3.9	3.4	9.3
2005	−2.6	1.9	−1.7	−2.1	2.9	0.3	3.5	−1.2	1.1	−2.0	3.4	0.3	3.40
2006	2.3	−0.1	1.6	1.0	−3.3	0.6	0.2	1.9	3.0	2.8	1.4	1.8	13.8
2007	1.0	−2.4	1.6	4.0	3.0	−1.1	−3.5	1.0	4.2	1.1	−4.6	−0.4	3.4
2008	−6.6	−3.5	−0.5	4.7	1.1	−8.5	−1.1	1.2	−9.0	−17.1	−7.4	0.5	−39.1
2009	−8.6	−10.7	8.3	9.5	5.5	−0.3	7.5	3.6	3.3	−1.9	6.0	1.5	23.4
2010	−3.6	3.1	5.6	1.6	−8.0	−5.7	7.0	−4.6	8.4	3.8	−0.01	6.2	12.8
2011	2.3	3.4	−0.4	2.9	−1.2	−2.1	−2.1	−5.5	−7.5	11.0	−0.3	0.5	−0.03
2012	4.4	4.3	2.8	−0.7	−6.1								
TOTALS	29.1	2.3	51.3	44.5	25.6	13.3	7.7	−9.9	−10.7	16.7	22.9	66.3	
AVG.	1.0	0.1	1.7	1.5	0.9	0.5	0.3	−0.3	−0.4	0.6	0.8	2.3	
# Up	20	18	21	19	19	18	12	17	15	18	18	25	
# Down	10	12	9	11	10	11	17	12	14	11	11	4	

139

30-YEAR TREASURY BOND CYCLE, SEASONAL PATTERN, AND TRADING GUIDE

Even though the 10-year note has become the benchmark yield instrument, the long end of the yield curve offers investors added volatility and much bigger price swings. Price is the opposite of yield; when prices move up, interest rates go down, and when prices decline, interest rates are rising. Moreover, Treasury issues, at times, have a decoupling relationship with stock price action. When stocks go up, investors sell bonds to raise cash to allocate back into equities and vice versa. In times of financial and economic upheaval, as was the case in late 2008, bond prices soar. However, we still see a seasonal cycle of supply and demand flows, as bond prices tend to peak towards mid-December when investors reallocate funds for year-end book adjustments. It is no coincidence that as stock prices are at their best, bond prices are beginning to peak. If that theory holds, then the opposite should be true.

Bond prices typically tend to make their seasonal bottom in late April to mid-June, as stocks tend to see summertime highs. Other factors that weigh on Treasury prices are the perception of inflation, whether real or not. Inflation, as well as increases in supply, reduce an investment instrument's long-term value. When we are in periods of rising inflation, we will see price declines (rising yields and interest rates). This accounts for the loss in the value of a bond today vis-a-vis the face value of the bond at maturity. A higher yield attracts an investor; in other words, higher interest rates help boost demand. The government spends money, and to raise capital they issue treasury bonds. This is done through quarterly refunding operations. Typically, the Treasury Department's borrowing estimates for the second quarter are announced around late January or early February, and this can add pressure to bond prices, where we see a seasonal decline lasting to the seasonal lows in June.

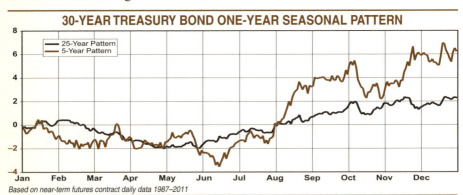

30-YEAR TREASURY BOND ONE-YEAR SEASONAL PATTERN

25-Year Pattern
5-Year Pattern

Based on near-term futures contract daily data 1987–2011

30-YEAR TREASURY BOND NEAR-TERM CONTRACT ANNUAL HIGHS, LOWS, AND CLOSES SINCE 1978

YEAR	HIGH DATE	HIGH CLOSE	LOW DATE	LOW CLOSE	YEAR CLOSE	YEAR	HIGH DATE	HIGH CLOSE	LOW DATE	LOW CLOSE	YEAR CLOSE
1978	01/04	98'310	12/28	90'060	90'110	1996	01/03	121'180	06/12	105'280	112'200
1979	07/02	92'090	11/07	78'060	82'060	1997	12/22	120'290	04/11	106'200	120'150
1980	06/16	86'000	02/21	64'130	71'120	1998	10/05	134'210	03/05	118'210	127'250
1981	01/05	72'290	09/29	55'260	61'290	1999	01/29	128'000	12/23	90'300	90'300
1982	11/04	79'030	02/09	57'030	76'200	2000	12/22	105'190	01/18	89'070	104'200
1983	05/04	79'220	08/08	68'220	70'010	2001	11/07	111'160	05/29	98'180	101'170
1984	12/18	72'220	05/30	59'080	71'020	2002	10/09	114'200	03/14	97'260	112'220
1985	12/27	85'100	03/18	67'170	85'070	2003	06/13	122'210	09/03	104'070	109'100
1986	04/16	104'270	01/13	81'250	98'060	2004	03/17	115'310	06/14	103'000	112'160
1987	01/09	101'190	10/19	77'250	87'310	2005	06/27	119'080	03/22	109'240	114'060
1988	02/10	95'010	08/22	83'310	89'040	2006	01/17	114'280	06/28	105'150	111'140
1989	08/01	100'120	03/20	86'160	98'210	2007	11/26	118'280	06/12	105'110	116'120
1990	01/02	98'130	08/24	87'050	95'230	2008	12/30	141'135	06/13	111'270	138'015
1991	12/31	104'240	06/12	92'090	104'240	2009	01/15	137'045	06/10	112'220	115'120
1992	09/08	106'290	03/16	97'090	104'210	2010	08/31	135'010	04/05	114'120	122'040
1993	10/15	121'300	01/12	103'210	114'160	2011	09/22	146'020	02/08	117'100	144'260
1994	01/28	117'140	11/11	96'020	99'050	2012*	05/31	149'230	03/19	135'120	AT PRESS TIME
1995	12/29	121'150	01/03	98'230	121'150						

*Through May 31, 2012

140

30-YEAR TREASURY BOND NEAR-TERM CONTRACT MONTHLY CLOSING PRICES

	Jan	Feb	Mar	Apr	May	Jun	Jul	Aug	Sep	Oct	Nov	Dec
1978	97'230	96'140	95'300	95'150	93'210	93'000	93'180	95'070	93'100	91'050	92'190	90'110
1979	91'160	89'210	90'050	88'060	89'270	91'270	90'170	89'110	87'250	79'300	82'130	82'060
1980	74'160	69'000	67'270	77'020	79'140	81'060	75'100	73'090	70'220	67'260	69'080	71'120
1981	69'090	65'310	67'020	61'280	65'260	64'120	61'010	58'080	56'000	58'220	65'200	61'290
1982	60'230	61'140	61'300	63'060	63'030	60'220	62'260	66'210	71'020	76'170	74'280	76'200
1983	73'110	76'220	75'310	78'300	74'020	74'140	69'300	69'070	72'230	70'220	71'020	70'010
1984	70'260	68'070	66'070	64'220	59'150	59'200	64'160	65'050	67'070	70'250	70'290	71'020
1985	73'060	67'280	69'230	70'240	76'130	77'020	75'060	76'010	75'190	78'170	80'160	85'070
1986	85'050	94'000	102'100	100'240	93'030	99'180	97'260	101'230	96'180	98'030	98'240	98'060
1987	99'220	100'140	98'150	93'020	91'020	91'160	89'160	86'170	81'220	87'180	86'240	87'310
1988	93'290	93'200	90'020	87'290	84'290	88'240	86'060	85'160	88'240	91'130	88'030	89'040
1989	90'260	88'060	88'130	90'060	93'000	97'300	99'240	96'070	95'270	99'110	99'150	98'210
1990	94'080	93'060	91'280	88'260	92'230	94'110	94'220	88'260	89'120	91'030	94'180	95'230
1991	96'100	95'170	95'150	96'130	94'310	93'200	94'270	97'080	100'000	99'260	98'260	104'240
1992	101'010	100'100	98'230	98'040	99'230	100'210	104'270	103'310	105'100	102'240	101'310	104'210
1993	107'060	109'200	109'170	110'050	109'050	113'300	115'160	118'130	118'170	118'240	114'070	114'160
1994	117'050	111'110	106'080	104'160	102'200	101'070	104'250	102'290	98'300	98'110	98'020	99'050
1995	101'150	103'140	103'290	105'110	112'210	113'170	111'070	112'240	114'110	117'020	119'050	121'150
1996	120'300	114'100	111'150	109'050	107'170	109'170	109'040	106'250	109'060	113'000	115'280	112'200
1997	111'140	110'140	107'070	109'090	109'200	111'020	116'240	112'240	115'090	118'150	119'010	120'150
1998	122'090	120'150	120'080	120'070	121'160	123'190	122'190	127'000	131'150	128'290	129'190	127'250
1999	128'000	120'310	120'180	120'060	117'150	115'290	114'310	113'310	113'300	113'190	93'020	90'300
2000	92'070	94'220	97'220	96'180	95'200	97'110	98'190	100'140	98'210	99'270	102'210	104'200
2001	104'020	105'090	104'060	100'150	99'180	100'100	104'010	105'100	105'160	110'140	103'220	101'170
2002	102'270	102'290	98'050	102'100	101'040	102'250	105'300	109'220	114'080	110'210	107'300	112'220
2003	112'060	114'150	112'240	114'010	119'070	117'110	105'200	106'000	112'050	108'230	107'270	109'100
2004	111'110	112'140	114'020	107'030	105'070	106'120	108'070	111'100	112'070	113'270	110'040	112'160
2005	114'270	112'110	111'120	114'270	117'140	118'240	115'100	118'010	114'130	111'310	112'010	114'060
2006	112'270	113'030	109'050	106'270	106'070	106'210	108'090	111'020	112'130	112'210	114'120	111'140
2007	110'040	112'300	111'080	111'240	109'040	107'240	110'020	111'180	111'110	112'190	117'060	116'120
2008	119'100	118'200	118'255	116'285	113'160	115'190	115'160	117'100	117'055	113'040	127'155	138'015
2009	126'225	123'110	129'225	122'180	117'210	118'115	119'000	119'240	121'120	120'050	122'230	115'120
2010	118'260	117'220	116'040	119'020	122'210	127'160	128'230	135'010	133'230	130'300	127'090	122'040
2011	120'200	120'110	120'060	122'120	124'270	123'010	128'040	136'010	142'200	139'010	141'120	144'260
2012	145'140	141'210	137'240	142'280	149'230							

30-YEAR TREASURY BOND NEAR-TERM CONTRACT MONTHLY PERCENT CHANGES

	Jan	Feb	Mar	Apr	May	Jun	Jul	Aug	Sep	Oct	Nov	Dec	Year's Change
1978	−1.8	−1.3	−0.5	−0.5	−1.9	−0.7	0.6	1.8	−2.0	−2.3	1.6	−2.4	−9.2
1979	1.3	−2.0	0.6	−2.2	1.9	2.2	−1.4	−1.3	−1.7	−8.9	3.1	−0.3	−9.0
1980	−9.4	−7.4	−1.7	13.6	3.1	2.2	−7.2	−2.7	−3.5	−4.10	2.1	3.1	−13.2
1981	−2.9	−4.8	1.7	−7.7	6.4	−2.2	−5.2	−4.6	−3.9	4.8	11.8	−5.7	−13.3
1982	−1.9	1.2	0.8	2.0	−0.1	−3.8	3.5	6.1	6.6	7.7	−2.2	2.3	23.8
1983	−4.3	4.6	−0.9	3.9	−6.2	0.5	−6.0	−1.0	5.1	−2.8	0.5	−1.5	−8.6
1984	1.1	−3.7	−2.9	−2.3	−8.1	0.3	8.2	1.0	3.2	5.3	0.2	0.2	1.5
1985	3.0	−7.3	2.7	1.5	8.0	0.9	−2.4	1.1	−0.6	3.9	2.5	5.9	19.9
1986	−0.1	10.4	8.8	−1.5	−7.6	6.9	−1.8	4.0	−5.1	1.6	0.7	−0.6	15.2
1987	1.5	0.8	−2.0	−5.5	−2.1	0.5	−2.2	−3.3	−5.6	7.2	−0.9	1.4	−10.4
1988	6.7	−0.3	−3.8	−2.4	−3.4	4.5	−2.9	−0.8	3.8	3.0	−3.6	1.2	1.3
1989	1.9	−2.9	0.2	2.0	3.1	5.3	1.9	−3.5	−0.4	3.7	0.1	−0.8	10.7
1990	−4.5	−1.1	−1.4	−3.3	4.4	1.8	0.4	−6.2	0.6	1.9	3.8	1.2	−3.0
1991	0.6	−0.8	−0.1	1.0	−1.5	−1.4	1.3	2.5	2.8	−0.2	−1.0	6.0	9.4
1992	−3.6	−0.7	−1.6	−0.6	1.6	0.9	4.2	−0.8	1.3	−2.4	−0.8	2.6	−0.1
1993	2.4	2.3	−0.1	0.6	−0.9	4.4	1.4	2.5	0.1	0.2	−3.8	0.2	9.4
1994	2.3	−5.0	−4.6	−1.6	−1.8	−1.4	3.5	−1.8	−3.9	−0.6	−0.3	1.1	−13.4
1995	2.3	1.9	0.5	1.4	6.9	0.8	−2.0	1.4	1.4	2.4	1.8	1.9	22.5
1996	−0.4	−5.5	−2.5	−2.1	−1.5	1.9	−0.4	−2.1	2.3	3.5	2.5	−2.8	−7.3
1997	−1.1	−0.9	−2.9	1.9	0.3	1.3	5.1	−3.4	2.2	2.8	0.5	1.2	7.0
1998	1.5	−1.5	−0.2	−0.03	1.1	1.7	−0.8	3.6	3.5	−1.9	0.5	−1.4	6.1
1999	0.2	−5.5	−0.3	−0.3	−2.3	−1.3	−0.8	−0.9	−0.03	−0.3	−18.1	−2.3	−28.8
2000	1.4	2.7	3.2	−1.2	−1.0	1.8	1.3	1.9	−1.8	1.2	2.8	1.9	15.1
2001	−0.5	1.2	−1.0	−3.6	−0.9	0.8	3.7	1.2	0.2	4.7	−6.1	−2.1	−3.0
2002	1.3	0.1	−4.6	4.2	−1.2	1.6	3.1	3.5	4.2	−3.1	−2.5	4.4	11.0
2003	−0.4	2.0	−1.5	1.1	4.5	−1.6	−10.0	0.4	5.8	−3.1	−0.8	1.4	−3.0
2004	1.9	1.0	1.4	−6.1	−1.8	1.1	1.7	2.9	0.8	1.4	−3.3	2.2	2.9
2005	2.1	−2.2	−0.9	3.1	2.3	1.1	−2.9	2.4	−3.1	−2.1	0.1	1.9	1.5
2006	−1.2	0.2	−3.5	−2.1	−0.6	0.4	1.5	2.6	1.2	0.2	1.5	−2.6	−2.4
2007	−1.2	2.6	−1.5	0.4	−2.3	−1.3	2.1	1.4	−0.2	1.1	4.1	−0.70	4.4
2008	2.5	−0.6	0.1	−1.6	−2.9	1.8	−0.1	1.6	−0.1	−3.5	12.7	8.3	18.6
2009	−8.2	−2.7	5.2	−5.5	−4.0	0.6	0.5	0.6	1.4	−1.0	2.1	−6.0	−16.4
2010	3.0	−0.9	−1.3	2.5	3.0	3.9	1.0	4.9	−1.0	−2.1	−2.8	−4.1	5.9
2011	−1.2	−0.2	−0.1	1.8	2.0	−1.5	4.1	6.2	4.8	−2.5	1.7	2.4	18.6
2012	0.4	−2.6	−2.8	3.7	4.8								
TOTALS	−5.3	−28.9	−17.5	−5.4	1.3	34.0	3.0	21.2	18.4	15.7	10.5	17.5	
AVG.	−0.2	−0.8	−0.5	−0.2	0.04	1.0	0.1	0.6	0.5	0.5	0.3	0.5	
# Up	19	13	11	16	15	25	19	21	19	18	21	20	
# Down	16	22	24	19	20	9	15	13	15	16	13	14	

CRUDE OIL CYCLE, SEASONAL PATTERN, AND TRADING GUIDE

Crude oil has shown strong seasonal bottoms in December and has a strong tendency to peak in September. One explanation for this is that refiners are building inventories ahead of the summer driving season and there is still a demand for heating oil as well as the competition from diesel and jet fuels. As the summer driving season ends, refiners focus more on increasing inventories for heating oil, and there is less demand for gasoline, so we have seen price weakness through the end of December into February.

One of the many aspects that resulted in the unprecedented price increase in crude oil in 2008 was the insatiable demand from China, India, and other developing nations. In addition, it is valued in terms of the U.S. dollar, so when we have periods of a weaker dollar against foreign currencies, this has helped support the value of crude oil prices, as occurred in late 2007 through mid-2008.

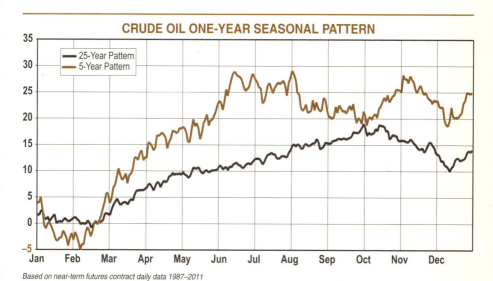

CRUDE OIL ONE-YEAR SEASONAL PATTERN

25-Year Pattern
5-Year Pattern

Based on near-term futures contract daily data 1987–2011

CRUDE OIL NEAR-TERM CONTRACT ANNUAL HIGHS, LOWS, AND CLOSES SINCE 1984

YEAR	HIGH DATE	HIGH CLOSE	LOW DATE	LOW CLOSE	YEAR CLOSE	YEAR	HIGH DATE	HIGH CLOSE	LOW DATE	LOW CLOSE	YEAR CLOSE
1984	05/16	31.22	12/20	26.33	26.41	1999	11/22	27.07	02/16	11.48	25.60
1985	11/25	31.01	12/17	25.09	26.30	2000	10/12	35.72	04/11	23.39	26.80
1986	01/06	26.57	03/31	10.42	17.94	2001	02/08	31.59	11/15	17.84	19.84
1987	08/03	22.16	12/18	15.40	16.70	2002	12/27	32.72	01/17	18.63	31.20
1988	04/26	18.60	10/05	12.60	17.24	2003	03/07	37.78	04/29	25.24	32.52
1989	12/26	21.91	02/14	16.81	21.82	2004	10/22	55.17	02/06	32.48	43.45
1990	10/09	40.40	07/06	16.47	28.44	2005	08/30	69.81	01/03	42.12	61.04
1991	01/16	30.29	02/22	17.91	19.12	2006	07/14	78.71	11/02	57.88	61.05
1992	06/24	22.89	01/09	17.86	19.50	2007	11/23	98.18	01/18	51.81	95.98
1993	03/04	21.07	12/28	14.11	14.17	2008	07/14	145.78	12/24	37.45	39.00
1994	08/01	20.55	03/28	14.08	17.76	2009	10/21	81.37	02/18	37.41	79.36
1995	05/01	20.50	07/20	16.77	19.55	2010	12/23	91.51	05/25	68.75	91.38
1996	12/31	25.92	01/29	17.45	25.92	2011	04/29	113.93	10/04	75.67	98.83
1997	01/08	26.62	12/30	17.60	17.64	2012*	02/24	109.77	05/31	86.53	AT PRESS TIME
1998	01/29	17.82	12/10	10.72	12.05						

*Through May 31, 2012

CRUDE OIL NEAR-TERM CONTRACT MONTHLY CLOSING PRICES

	Jan	Feb	Mar	Apr	May	Jun	Jul	Aug	Sep	Oct	Nov	Dec
1984	29.98	30.55	30.85	30.26	30.83	29.75	27.60	29.23	29.66	28.46	27.31	26.41
1985	26.41	26.73	28.29	27.63	27.84	26.87	27.12	28.08	29.08	30.38	29.75	26.30
1986	18.83	13.26	10.42	13.34	14.30	12.78	11.15	15.90	14.77	15.27	15.00	17.94
1987	18.75	16.60	18.83	18.73	19.38	20.29	21.37	19.73	19.59	19.96	18.51	16.70
1988	16.94	16.01	17.08	17.99	17.51	15.16	16.31	15.18	13.37	13.58	15.32	17.24
1989	17.03	18.15	20.19	20.42	19.90	20.27	18.31	18.83	20.13	19.94	19.89	21.82
1990	22.68	21.54	20.28	18.54	17.40	17.07	20.69	27.32	39.51	35.23	28.85	28.44
1991	21.54	19.16	19.63	20.96	21.13	20.56	21.68	22.26	22.23	23.37	21.48	19.12
1992	18.90	18.68	19.44	20.85	22.11	21.60	21.87	21.48	21.71	20.62	19.89	19.50
1993	20.26	20.60	20.44	20.53	20.02	18.85	17.88	18.29	18.79	16.92	15.43	14.17
1994	15.19	14.48	14.79	16.90	18.31	19.37	20.30	17.56	18.39	18.19	18.05	17.76
1995	18.39	18.49	19.17	20.38	18.89	17.40	17.56	17.84	17.54	17.64	18.18	19.55
1996	17.74	19.54	21.47	21.20	19.76	20.92	20.42	22.25	24.38	23.35	23.75	25.92
1997	24.15	20.30	20.41	20.21	20.88	19.80	20.14	19.61	21.18	21.08	19.15	17.64
1998	17.21	15.44	15.61	15.39	15.20	14.18	14.21	13.34	16.14	14.42	11.22	12.05
1999	12.75	12.27	16.76	18.66	16.84	19.29	20.53	22.11	24.51	21.75	24.59	25.60
2000	27.64	30.43	26.90	25.74	29.01	32.50	27.43	33.12	30.84	32.70	33.82	26.80
2001	28.66	27.39	26.29	28.46	28.37	26.25	26.35	27.20	23.43	21.18	19.44	19.84
2002	19.48	21.74	26.31	27.29	25.31	26.86	27.02	28.98	30.45	27.22	26.89	31.20
2003	33.51	36.60	31.04	25.80	29.56	30.19	30.54	31.57	29.20	29.11	30.41	32.52
2004	33.05	36.16	35.76	37.38	39.88	37.05	43.80	42.12	49.64	51.76	49.13	43.45
2005	48.20	51.75	55.40	49.72	51.97	56.50	60.57	68.94	66.24	59.76	57.32	61.04
2006	67.92	61.41	66.63	71.88	71.29	73.93	74.40	70.26	62.91	58.73	63.13	61.05
2007	58.14	61.79	65.87	65.71	64.01	70.68	78.21	74.04	81.66	94.53	88.71	95.98
2008	91.75	101.84	101.58	113.46	127.35	140.00	124.08	115.46	100.64	67.81	54.43	39.00
2009	41.70	44.76	49.66	51.15	66.31	69.89	69.30	69.96	70.61	77.00	77.28	79.36
2010	72.89	79.66	83.76	86.15	73.97	75.63	78.95	71.92	79.97	81.43	84.11	91.38
2011	92.19	96.97	106.72	113.93	102.70	95.42	95.70	88.81	79.20	93.19	100.36	98.83
2012	98.48	107.07	103.02	104.90	86.53							

CRUDE OIL NEAR-TERM CONTRACT MONTHLY PERCENT CHANGES

	Jan	Feb	Mar	Apr	May	Jun	Jul	Aug	Sep	Oct	Nov	Dec	Year's Change
1984	1.3	1.9	1.0	-1.9	1.9	-3.5	-7.2	5.9	1.5	-4.0	-4.0	-3.3	-10.8
1985	N/C	1.2	5.8	-2.3	0.8	-3.5	0.9	3.5	3.6	4.5	-2.1	-11.6	-0.4
1986	-28.4	-29.6	-21.4	28.0	7.2	-10.6	-12.8	42.6	-7.1	3.4	-1.8	19.6	-31.8
1987	4.5	-11.5	13.4	-0.5	3.5	4.7	5.3	-7.7	-0.7	1.9	-7.3	-9.8	-6.9
1988	1.4	-5.5	6.7	5.3	-2.7	-13.4	7.6	-6.9	-11.9	1.6	12.8	12.5	3.2
1989	-1.2	6.6	11.2	1.1	-2.5	1.9	-9.7	2.8	6.9	-0.9	-0.3	9.7	26.6
1990	3.9	-5.0	-5.8	-8.6	-6.1	-1.9	21.2	32.0	44.6	-10.8	-18.1	-1.4	30.3
1991	-24.3	-11.0	2.5	6.8	0.8	-2.7	5.4	2.7	-0.1	5.1	-8.1	-11.0	-32.8
1992	-1.2	-1.2	4.1	7.3	6.0	-2.3	1.3	-1.8	1.1	-5.0	-3.5	-2.0	2.0
1993	3.9	1.7	-0.8	0.4	-2.5	-5.8	-5.1	2.3	2.7	-10.0	-8.8	-8.2	-27.3
1994	7.2	-4.7	2.1	14.3	8.3	5.8	4.8	-13.5	4.7	-1.1	-0.8	-1.6	25.3
1995	3.5	0.5	3.7	6.3	-7.3	-7.9	0.9	1.6	-1.7	0.6	3.1	7.5	10.1
1996	-9.3	10.1	9.9	-1.3	-6.8	5.9	-2.4	9.0	9.6	-4.2	1.7	9.1	32.6
1997	-6.8	-15.9	0.5	-1.0	3.3	-5.2	1.7	-2.6	8.0	-0.5	-9.2	-7.9	-31.9
1998	-2.4	-10.3	1.1	-1.4	-1.2	-6.7	0.2	-6.1	21.0	-10.7	-22.2	7.4	-31.7
1999	5.8	-3.8	36.6	11.3	-9.8	14.5	6.4	7.7	10.9	-11.3	13.1	4.1	112.4
2000	8.0	10.1	-11.6	-4.3	12.7	12.0	-15.6	20.7	-6.9	6.0	3.4	-20.8	4.7
2001	6.9	-4.4	-4.0	8.3	-0.3	-7.5	0.4	3.2	-13.9	-9.6	-8.2	2.1	-26.0
2002	-1.8	11.6	21.0	3.7	-7.3	6.1	0.6	7.3	5.1	-10.6	-1.2	16.0	57.3
2003	7.4	9.2	-15.2	-16.9	14.6	2.1	1.2	3.4	-7.5	-0.3	4.5	6.9	4.2
2004	1.6	9.4	-1.1	4.5	6.7	-7.1	18.2	-3.8	17.9	4.3	-5.1	-11.6	33.6
2005	10.9	7.4	7.1	-10.3	4.5	8.7	7.2	13.8	-3.9	-9.8	-4.1	6.5	40.5
2006	11.3	-9.6	8.5	7.9	-0.8	3.7	0.6	-5.6	-10.5	-6.6	7.5	-3.3	0.02
2007	-4.8	6.3	6.6	-0.2	-2.6	10.4	10.7	-5.3	10.3	15.8	-6.2	8.2	57.2
2008	-4.4	11.0	-0.3	11.7	12.2	9.9	-11.4	-6.9	-12.8	-32.6	-19.7	-28.3	-59.4
2009	6.9	7.3	10.9	3.0	29.6	5.4	-0.8	1.0	0.9	9.0	0.4	2.7	103.5
2010	-8.2	9.3	5.1	2.9	-14.1	2.2	4.4	-8.9	11.2	1.8	3.3	8.6	15.1
2011	0.9	5.2	10.1	6.8	-9.9	-7.1	0.3	-7.2	-10.8	17.7	7.7	-1.5	8.2
2012	-0.4	8.7	-3.8	1.8	-17.5								
TOTALS	-7.8	5.0	103.9	82.7	20.7	8.1	34.3	83.2	72.2	-56.3	-73.2	-1.4	
AVG.	-0.3	0.2	3.6	2.9	0.7	0.3	1.2	3.0	2.6	-2.0	-2.6	-0.05	
# Up	16	17	20	18	14	14	20	16	16	12	10	14	
# Down	12	12	9	11	15	14	8	12	12	16	18	14	

144

NATURAL GAS CYCLE, SEASONAL PATTERN, AND TRADING GUIDE

Natural gas is really a fascinating energy source. It accounts for almost a quarter of total U.S. energy consumption. Its market share is likely to expand because of the favorable competitive position of gas in relation to other fuels and the tightening environmental standards for fuel combustion. Industrial users and electric utilities together account for 65% of the market; commercial and residential users combined are 35%. It is primarily methane, the lightest hydrocarbon molecule. It is burned to drive turbines in electrical-power-generation plants as well as to heat homes and businesses across the nation, and is used as a feedstock to produce the agricultural fertilizer ammonia. It is one of the most important economic commodities in the U.S. today after crude oil. Recent and substantial discoveries of shale gas have flooded the U.S. market with supply and kept prices weak.

This market has a strong seasonal tendency to bottom in July and then peak in December. The main reason for this can be explained by the fact that in cold weather it is used to heat homes, and business and production companies are building inventories ahead of this season.

Then, as production companies anticipate the needs for utility companies to produce more electricity to handle spikes in demand for air conditioning, we see prices rise in early summer and then continue to rise through year-end, when we begin the winter heating cycle.

NATURAL GAS ONE-YEAR SEASONAL PATTERN

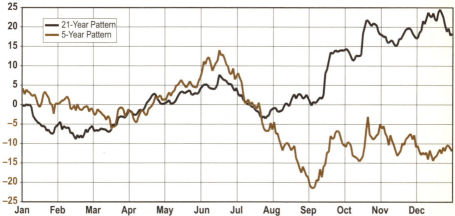

Based on near-term futures contract daily data 1991–2011

NATURAL GAS NEAR-TERM CONTRACT ANNUAL HIGHS, LOWS, AND CLOSES SINCE 1991

YEAR	HIGH DATE	HIGH CLOSE	LOW DATE	LOW CLOSE	YEAR CLOSE	YEAR	HIGH DATE	HIGH CLOSE	LOW DATE	LOW CLOSE	YEAR CLOSE
1991	10/17	2.186	06/24	1.118	1.343	2002	12/16	5.297	01/28	1.984	4.789
1992	09/23	2.593	02/14	1.079	1.687	2003	02/28	8.101	09/26	4.621	6.189
1993	04/23	2.514	01/19	1.508	1.997	2004	10/26	9.363	09/10	4.570	6.149
1994	02/01	2.639	09/02	1.560	1.725	2005	12/13	15.378	01/03	5.790	11.225
1995	12/27	2.868	01/13	1.323	2.619	2006	01/03	10.626	09/14	4.892	6.299
1996	12/20	3.920	09/04	1.764	2.757	2007	11/01	8.637	08/31	5.468	7.483
1997	10/27	3.836	03/03	1.803	2.264	2008	07/03	13.577	12/22	5.330	5.622
1998	04/08	2.689	09/02	1.652	1.945	2009	12/28	5.996	09/03	2.508	5.572
1999	10/27	3.223	02/26	1.628	2.329	2010	01/06	6.009	10/15	3.535	4.405
2000	12/29	9.775	01/05	2.168	9.775	2011	06/08	4.847	12/30	2.989	2.989
2001	01/09	9.819	10/01	2.208	2.570	2012*	01/06	3.040	04/17	1.951	AT PRESS TIME

*Through May 31, 2012

NATURAL GAS NEAR-TERM CONTRACT MONTHLY CLOSING PRICES

	Jan	Feb	Mar	Apr	May	Jun	Jul	Aug	Sep	Oct	Nov	Dec
1991	1.380	1.373	1.405	1.375	1.333	1.208	1.260	1.564	1.935	2.046	2.090	1.343
1992	1.180	1.171	1.357	1.422	1.625	1.518	1.892	2.112	2.515	2.295	2.087	1.687
1993	1.597	1.856	2.069	2.365	2.141	2.181	2.220	2.375	2.291	2.368	2.243	1.997
1994	2.554	2.208	2.075	2.067	1.917	2.184	1.893	1.586	1.657	1.950	1.695	1.725
1995	1.354	1.483	1.685	1.662	1.718	1.530	1.614	1.748	1.750	1.866	2.018	2.619
1996	2.658	2.236	2.336	2.224	2.406	2.911	2.163	1.859	2.214	2.728	3.497	2.757
1997	2.385	1.821	1.926	2.184	2.239	2.139	2.177	2.714	3.082	3.552	2.578	2.264
1998	2.257	2.321	2.522	2.221	2.170	2.469	1.844	1.752	2.433	2.275	1.976	1.945
1999	1.777	1.628	2.013	2.253	2.358	2.394	2.543	2.825	2.744	2.961	2.304	2.329
2000	2.662	2.761	2.945	3.141	4.356	4.476	3.774	4.782	5.186	4.490	6.589	9.775
2001	5.707	5.236	5.025	4.695	3.914	3.096	3.296	2.380	2.244	3.291	2.701	2.570
2002	2.138	2.357	3.283	3.795	3.217	3.245	2.954	3.296	4.138	4.156	4.200	4.789
2003	5.605	8.101	5.060	5.385	6.251	5.411	4.718	4.731	4.830	4.893	4.925	6.189
2004	5.397	5.416	5.933	5.862	6.442	6.155	6.112	5.074	6.795	8.725	7.620	6.149
2005	6.321	6.730	7.653	6.585	6.379	6.981	7.885	11.472	13.921	12.205	12.587	11.225
2006	9.316	6.714	7.210	6.555	6.384	6.104	8.211	6.048	5.620	7.534	8.844	6.299
2007	7.667	7.300	7.730	7.863	7.935	6.773	6.191	5.468	6.870	8.330	7.302	7.483
2008	8.074	9.366	10.101	10.843	11.703	13.353	9.119	7.943	7.438	6.783	6.51	5.622
2009	4.417	4.198	3.760	3.373	3.835	3.835	3.650	2.977	4.841	5.045	4.848	5.572
2010	5.131	4.813	3.869	3.920	4.341	4.616	4.923	3.816	3.872	4.038	4.180	4.405
2011	4.420	4.037	4.389	4.698	4.666	4.374	4.145	4.054	3.666	3.934	3.550	2.989
2012	2.503	2.625	2.120	2.285	2.422							

NATURAL GAS NEAR-TERM CONTRACT MONTHLY PERCENT CHANGES

	Jan	Feb	Mar	Apr	May	Jun	Jul	Aug	Sep	Oct	Nov	Dec	Year's Change
1991	−29.2	−0.5	2.3	−2.1	−3.1	−9.4	4.3	24.1	23.7	5.7	2.2	−35.7	−31.1
1992	−12.1	−0.8	15.9	4.8	14.3	−6.6	24.6	11.6	19.1	−8.7	−9.1	−19.2	25.6
1993	−5.3	16.2	11.5	14.3	−9.5	1.9	1.8	7.0	−3.5	3.4	−5.3	−11.0	18.4
1994	27.9	−13.5	−6.0	−0.4	−7.3	13.9	−13.3	−16.2	4.5	17.7	−13.1	1.8	−13.6
1995	−21.5	9.5	13.6	−1.4	3.4	−10.9	5.5	8.3	0.1	6.6	8.1	29.8	51.8
1996	1.5	−15.9	4.5	−4.8	8.2	21.0	−25.7	−14.1	19.1	23.2	28.2	−21.2	5.3
1997	−13.5	−23.6	5.8	13.4	2.5	−4.5	1.8	24.7	13.6	15.2	−27.4	−12.2	−17.9
1998	−0.3	2.8	8.7	−11.9	−2.3	13.8	−25.3	−5.0	38.9	−6.5	−13.1	−1.6	−14.1
1999	−8.6	−8.4	23.6	11.9	4.7	1.5	6.2	11.1	−2.9	7.9	−22.2	1.1	19.7
2000	14.3	3.7	6.7	6.7	38.7	2.8	−15.7	26.7	8.4	−13.4	46.7	48.4	319.7
2001	−41.6	−8.3	−4.0	−6.6	−16.6	−20.9	6.5	−27.8	−5.7	46.7	−17.9	−4.9	−73.7
2002	−16.8	10.2	39.3	15.6	−15.2	0.9	−9.0	11.6	25.5	0.4	1.1	14.0	86.3
2003	17.0	44.5	−37.5	6.4	16.1	−13.4	−12.8	0.3	2.1	1.3	0.7	25.7	29.2
2004	−12.8	0.4	9.5	−1.2	9.9	−4.5	−0.7	−17.0	33.9	28.4	−12.7	−19.3	−0.6
2005	2.8	6.5	13.7	−14.0	−3.1	9.4	12.9	45.5	21.3	−12.3	3.1	−10.8	82.6
2006	−17.0	−27.9	7.4	−9.1	−2.6	−4.4	34.5	−26.3	−7.1	34.1	17.4	−28.8	−43.9
2007	21.7	−4.8	5.9	1.7	0.9	−14.6	−8.6	−11.7	25.6	21.3	−12.3	2.5	18.8
2008	7.9	16.0	7.8	7.3	7.9	14.1	−31.7	−12.9	−6.4	−8.8	−4.0	−13.6	−24.9
2009	−21.4	−5.0	−10.4	−10.3	13.7	N/C	−4.8	−18.4	62.6	4.2	−3.9	14.9	−0.9
2010	−7.9	−6.2	−19.6	1.3	10.7	6.3	6.7	−22.5	1.5	4.3	3.5	5.4	−20.9
2011	0.3	−8.7	8.7	7.0	−0.7	−6.3	−5.2	−2.2	−9.6	7.3	−9.8	−15.8	−32.1
2012	−16.3	4.9	−19.2	7.8	6.0								
TOTALS	−130.9	−8.9	88.2	36.4	76.6	−9.9	−48.0	−3.2	264.7	178.0	−39.8	−50.5	
AVG	−6.0	−0.4	4.0	1.7	3.5	−0.5	−2.3	−0.2	12.6	8.5	−1.9	−2.4	
# Up	8	10	16	12	13	10	10	10	15	16	9	9	
# Down	14	12	6	10	9	10	11	11	6	5	12	12	

HEATING OIL CYCLE, SEASONAL PATTERN, AND TRADING GUIDE

Heating oil is vastly used for heating homes and office buildings as it heats boilers, which then radiate heat. It is classified as a distillate fuel that has a low-viscosity quality (light or watery substance). This fuel source accounts for 30% of the "cracking" or processing from crude oil, which is second to gasoline. Due to the late development of natural gas infrastructure, the main concentrated areas that use heating oil are in the Northeast section of the United States.

This commodity is an optionable product with listings on both the NYMEX through the Chicago Mercantile Exchange Group (CME) and the Intercontinental Commodity Exchange (ICE). The contract size is 42,000 gallons. It has a tick or each-trade value of .01 cents per gallon or $4.20. That means every 1.00 cent move represents a $420 value move per commodity contract.

Typically, heating oil trades near its peak in price around mid-October rather than in the dead of winter as many believe. The rationale behind this is that refineries have prepared for winter demand, wholesalers as well as residential customers have already placed orders, or the anticipated needs have been met. During mild winters, as occurred in 2012, we do not see significant declines in inventories as demand has weakened; therefore, we have increased carryover of inventories into the spring. This is a commodity that can go against the obvious, meaning that even if it is cold, demand is not necessarily high. Peak demand for heating oil is actually well ahead of the winter months.

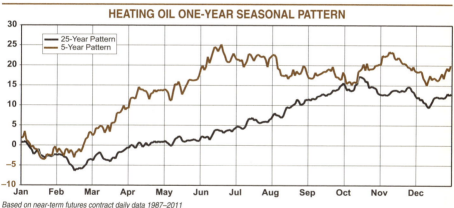

HEATING OIL ONE-YEAR SEASONAL PATTERN

25-Year Pattern
5-Year Pattern

Based on near-term futures contract daily data 1987–2011

HEATING OIL NEAR-TERM CONTRACT ANNUAL HIGHS, LOWS & CLOSES SINCE 1984

YEAR	HIGH DATE	HIGH CLOSE	LOW DATE	LOW CLOSE	YEAR CLOSE	YEAR	HIGH DATE	HIGH CLOSE	LOW DATE	LOW CLOSE	YEAR CLOSE
1980	12/31	99.15	01/16	72.90	99.15	1997	01/06	73.64	12/29	49.58	49.72
1981	01/12	105.75	06/08	89.90	96.70	1998	01/29	49.90	12/10	31.35	34.28
1982	10/18	104.49	03/08	70.20	84.31	1999	12/28	70.10	02/16	30.11	67.87
1983	08/15	87.47	02/22	68.70	82.65	2000	10/12	107.74	04/11	61.21	89.09
1984	02/01	90.09	07/30	72.30	73.32	2001	01/02	86.58	12/06	50.66	55.33
1985	11/22	89.86	06/11	67.04	78.35	2002	12/26	90.77	01/30	51.31	86.86
1986	01/06	76.73	07/14	31.71	49.95	2003	03/07	110.85	04/29	67.06	91.46
1987	10/16	57.92	03/02	43.30	49.99	2004	10/22	159.76	04/01	84.72	125.26
1988	01/07	53.79	10/06	37.24	52.29	2005	09/01	219.85	01/03	119.22	176.98
1989	12/29	75.25	06/13	45.10	75.25	2006	07/13	215.65	02/15	163.68	164.82
1990	10/09	106.15	06/07	46.90	79.20	2007	11/23	271.52	01/18	149.42	264.94
1991	01/16	84.67	12/30	50.16	51.10	2008	07/11	411.16	12/24	122.11	139.92
1992	10/15	66.30	01/08	49.36	57.21	2009	10/21	213.46	02/18	114.14	211.56
1993	03/04	59.81	12/28	43.97	44.52	2010	12/23	255.15	02/05	187.48	254.24
1994	08/01	54.26	03/28	41.21	51.23	2011	04/08	331.97	01/07	248.63	291.42
1995	12/27	60.61	03/14	44.98	58.62	2012*	02/24	331.30	05/31	270.32	AT PRESS TIME
1996	10/07	76.49	01/25	49.77	72.07						

*Through May 31, 2012

HEATING OIL NEAR-TERM CONTRACT MONTHLY CLOSING PRICES

	Jan	Feb	Mar	Apr	May	Jun	Jul	Aug	Sep	Oct	Nov	Dec
1980	81.75	75.25	75.80	78.05	79.35	76.84	77.37	76.00	80.80	86.86	95.62	99.15
1981	103.55	97.80	94.25	93.18	91.67	92.05	95.48	94.30	96.45	101.03	101.78	96.70
1982	86.26	78.00	78.55	88.84	92.46	89.19	88.62	94.39	99.68	99.15	86.52	84.31
1983	74.07	70.32	74.66	79.44	78.15	82.04	84.58	85.26	81.30	81.35	77.44	82.65
1984	86.78	77.85	78.11	77.75	81.96	77.95	72.43	79.23	83.12	79.01	76.61	73.32
1985	71.72	71.82	75.76	72.07	71.29	68.46	70.70	77.93	82.51	87.66	87.07	78.35
1986	55.28	45.66	35.16	39.88	38.91	37.30	33.37	44.59	42.16	41.92	42.89	49.95
1987	52.35	43.83	49.23	48.91	50.74	53.64	55.35	52.36	54.50	57.34	54.87	49.99
1988	47.19	44.51	46.15	48.37	47.18	41.08	45.10	43.32	38.73	42.75	48.24	52.29
1989	49.40	50.19	53.37	49.77	47.76	49.89	49.31	54.28	59.96	59.11	61.81	75.25
1990	57.56	56.56	54.34	51.45	49.35	48.62	58.35	76.56	105.92	91.13	88.42	79.20
1991	63.04	55.22	54.81	54.19	56.74	55.78	60.66	64.86	64.50	69.83	63.15	51.10
1992	53.81	51.58	52.97	56.90	60.31	60.41	61.22	60.90	63.62	59.97	56.67	57.21
1993	56.54	58.05	56.11	55.84	54.49	52.48	50.81	53.64	57.06	51.56	47.78	44.52
1994	49.55	44.89	44.07	47.09	49.53	50.52	53.25	49.24	51.24	49.40	49.55	51.23
1995	47.35	47.20	47.60	50.79	49.35	46.87	48.63	50.67	49.05	50.65	51.93	58.62
1996	52.01	54.39	56.75	55.09	51.07	53.90	56.71	63.12	70.75	66.85	71.68	72.07
1997	66.16	53.44	54.42	54.92	55.84	53.85	56.19	53.22	58.77	58.93	54.29	49.72
1998	48.11	43.46	43.42	44.21	40.37	39.15	36.73	35.69	43.40	39.86	32.13	34.28
1999	33.42	32.37	44.00	45.46	39.63	49.02	52.10	58.38	62.38	57.99	63.83	67.87
2000	74.34	76.45	68.65	67.19	72.33	83.28	75.65	98.70	92.56	93.58	102.25	89.09
2001	75.96	70.91	70.42	75.31	77.36	71.83	70.10	77.29	66.99	61.04	54.59	55.33
2002	53.16	57.15	67.33	69.19	64.11	68.03	68.62	76.35	80.77	74.90	75.98	86.86
2003	93.26	107.21	77.08	68.51	74.82	78.58	79.86	82.63	78.75	80.04	84.27	91.46
2004	91.56	94.19	89.56	94.49	100.29	102.08	116.93	112.30	138.61	146.41	141.83	125.26
2005	134.81	145.42	161.61	142.59	144.95	163.61	167.62	207.65	212.96	182.39	168.97	176.98
2006	184.79	172.24	186.33	201.29	199.53	202.86	203.76	201.11	175.35	166.70	185.00	164.82
2007	168.38	177.81	187.69	189.48	188.31	204.24	212.32	205.74	222.56	252.93	251.50	264.94
2008	252.91	280.69	290.61	315.80	366.67	391.00	345.93	319.19	289.47	208.42	172.71	139.92
2009	143.40	126.75	136.79	133.68	167.76	178.77	182.56	180.85	183.24	200.52	204.79	211.56
2010	191.30	203.53	217.90	231.57	200.45	201.43	208.81	199.17	226.78	223.77	232.44	254.24
2011	274.03	293.89	311.25	327.58	305.30	294.63	309.94	308.40	277.93	305.83	302.51	291.42
2012	305.09	320.59	317.01	318.42	270.32							

HEATING OIL NEAR-TERM CONTRACT MONTHLY PERCENT CHANGES

	Jan	Feb	Mar	Apr	May	Jun	Jul	Aug	Sep	Oct	Nov	Dec	Year's Change
1980	−6.0	−8.0	0.7	3.0	1.7	−3.2	0.7	−1.8	6.3	7.5	10.1	3.7	14.0
1981	4.4	−5.6	−3.6	−1.1	−1.6	0.4	3.7	−1.2	2.3	4.7	0.7	−5.0	−2.5
1982	−10.8	−9.6	0.7	13.1	4.1	−3.5	−0.6	6.5	5.6	−0.5	−12.7	−2.6	−12.8
1983	−12.1	−5.1	6.2	6.4	−1.6	5.0	3.1	0.8	−4.6	0.1	−4.8	6.7	−2.0
1984	5.0	−10.3	0.3	−0.5	5.4	−4.9	−7.1	9.4	4.9	−4.9	−3.0	−4.3	−11.3
1985	−2.2	0.1	5.5	−4.9	−1.1	−4.0	3.3	10.2	5.9	6.2	−0.7	−10.0	6.9
1986	−29.4	−17.4	−23.0	13.4	−2.4	−4.1	−10.5	33.6	−5.4	−0.6	2.3	16.5	−36.2
1987	4.8	−16.3	12.3	−0.7	3.7	5.7	3.2	−5.4	4.1	5.2	−4.3	−8.9	0.1
1988	−5.6	−5.7	3.7	4.8	−2.5	−12.9	9.8	−3.9	−10.6	10.4	12.8	8.4	4.6
1989	−5.5	1.6	6.3	−6.7	−4.0	4.5	−1.2	10.1	10.5	−1.4	4.6	21.7	43.9
1990	−23.5	−1.7	−3.9	−5.3	−4.1	−1.5	20.0	31.2	38.3	−14.0	−3.0	−10.4	5.2
1991	−20.4	−12.4	−0.7	−1.1	4.7	−1.7	8.7	6.9	−0.6	8.3	−9.6	−19.1	−35.5
1992	5.3	−4.1	2.7	7.4	6.0	0.2	1.3	−0.5	4.5	−5.7	−5.5	1.0	12.0
1993	−1.2	2.7	−3.3	−0.5	−2.4	−3.7	−3.2	5.6	6.4	−9.6	−7.3	−6.8	−22.2
1994	11.3	−9.4	−1.8	6.9	5.2	2.0	5.4	−7.5	4.1	−3.6	0.3	3.4	15.1
1995	−7.6	−0.3	0.8	6.7	−2.8	−5.0	3.8	4.2	−3.2	3.3	2.5	12.9	14.4
1996	−11.3	4.6	4.3	−2.9	−7.3	5.5	5.2	11.3	12.1	−5.5	7.2	0.5	22.9
1997	−8.2	−19.2	1.8	0.9	1.7	−3.6	4.3	−5.3	10.4	0.3	−7.9	−8.4	−31.0
1998	−3.2	−9.7	−0.1	1.8	−8.7	−3.0	−6.2	−2.8	21.6	−8.2	−19.4	6.7	−31.1
1999	−2.5	−3.1	35.9	3.3	−12.8	23.7	6.3	12.1	6.9	−7.0	10.1	6.3	98.0
2000	9.5	2.8	−10.2	−2.1	7.6	15.1	−9.2	30.5	−6.2	1.1	9.3	−12.9	31.3
2001	−14.7	−6.6	−0.7	6.9	2.7	−7.1	−2.4	10.3	−13.3	−8.9	−10.6	1.4	−37.9
2002	−3.9	7.5	17.8	2.8	−7.3	6.1	0.9	11.3	5.8	−7.3	1.4	14.3	57.0
2003	7.4	15.0	−28.1	−11.1	9.2	5.0	1.6	3.5	−4.7	1.6	5.3	8.5	5.3
2004	0.1	2.9	−4.9	5.5	6.1	1.8	14.5	−4.0	23.4	5.6	−3.1	−11.7	37.0
2005	7.6	7.9	11.1	−11.8	1.7	12.9	2.5	23.9	2.6	−14.4	−7.4	4.7	41.3
2006	4.4	−6.8	8.2	8.0	−0.9	1.7	0.4	−1.3	−12.8	−4.9	11.0	−10.9	−6.90
2007	2.2	5.6	5.6	1.0	−0.6	8.5	4.0	−3.1	8.2	13.6	−0.6	5.3	60.7
2008	−4.5	11.0	3.5	8.7	16.1	6.6	−11.5	−7.7	−9.3	−28.0	−17.1	−19.0	−47.2
2009	2.5	−11.6	7.9	−2.3	25.5	6.6	2.1	−0.9	1.3	9.4	2.1	3.3	51.2
2010	−9.6	6.4	7.1	6.3	−13.4	0.5	3.7	−4.6	13.9	−1.3	3.9	9.4	20.2
2011	7.8	7.2	5.9	5.2	−6.8	−3.5	5.2	−0.5	−9.9	10.0	−1.1	−3.7	14.6
2012	4.7	5.1	−1.1	0.4	−15.1								
TOTALS	−105.2	−82.5	66.9	61.5	6.0	50.1	61.8	170.9	118.5	−38.5	−34.5	1.0	
AVG.	−3.9	−2.5	2.0	1.9	0.2	1.6	1.9	5.3	3.7	−1.2	−1.1	0.03	
# Up	14	14	21	20	15	18	23	17	21	15	15	18	
# Down	19	19	12	13	18	14	9	15	11	17	17	14	

COPPER CYCLE, SEASONAL PATTERN, AND TRADING GUIDE

Copper was one of the first metal components mined by mankind. When mixed with tin over 5000 years ago, it helped create the Bronze Age. Since then, usage has flourished, as it is an excellent conductor of electricity. One of its largest industrial uses is for the production of electrical components and cable wire, followed closely by plumbing components and pipes. Copper is used extensively in electrical building wiring and in the manufacturing process for sheet metal facings. Copper is also used in automobiles for air conditioning; due to the fact that it is highly resistant to corrosion from salt water, it is also used to line interior hulls of cargo ships. Copper does have a tendency to make a major seasonal bottom in December and then has a tendency to post major seasonal peaks in May. This is perhaps due to the build up of inventories by miners and manufacturers, as we go into the construction building season in the late winter and early spring time, and ahead of the new car model year that begins in late summer.

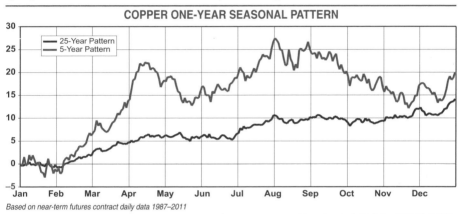

COPPER ONE-YEAR SEASONAL PATTERN

25-Year Pattern
5-Year Pattern

Based on near-term futures contract daily data 1987–2011

COPPER NEAR-TERM CONTRACT ANNUAL HIGHS, LOWS, AND CLOSES SINCE 1973

YEAR	HIGH DATE	HIGH CLOSE	LOW DATE	LOW CLOSE	YEAR CLOSE	YEAR	HIGH DATE	HIGH CLOSE	LOW DATE	LOW CLOSE	YEAR CLOSE
1973	11/20	105.85	01/02	50.20	84.80	1993	01/08	107.60	10/26	72.60	83.30
1974	05/03	136.10	12/31	53.60	53.60	1994	12/01	138.85	01/07	78.60	138.60
1975	08/25	63.30	06/11	51.70	55.30	1995	06/22	145.75	12/06	119.05	120.55
1976	07/06	78.30	01/26	53.80	63.20	1996	05/13	125.55	06/25	83.25	100.25
1977	03/18	72.40	08/12	52.60	60.30	1997	06/16	122.20	12/29	77.70	78.10
1978	12/27	71.15	02/23	56.10	71.05	1998	04/28	85.95	12/23	66.10	67.20
1979	10/01	113.00	01/02	70.05	105.20	1999	12/30	86.30	02/22	61.35	86.30
1980	02/12	145.20	12/11	81.10	86.55	2000	09/12	93.60	04/17	74.35	84.30
1981	01/05	90.90	12/10	72.55	75.70	2001	01/18	86.15	11/07	60.60	65.90
1982	01/04	75.90	06/18	54.40	69.65	2002	06/04	78.60	01/02	65.80	70.25
1983	05/10	81.50	11/07	61.10	67.00	2003	12/31	104.55	04/03	71.10	104.55
1984	03/30	71.75	10/17	55.50	57.20	2004	10/08	146.95	01/07	106.65	145.25
1985	04/12	65.90	01/02	56.40	64.15	2005	12/28	206.90	01/04	134.30	204.20
1986	03/21	68.60	08/18	56.95	61.15	2006	05/11	392.30	01/03	204.85	287.10
1987	12/31	127.40	01/20	60.20	127.40	2007	10/03	376.35	02/05	241.65	304.10
1988	11/28	154.80	02/26	84.70	135.50	2008	07/02	406.35	12/24	127.50	141.00
1989	01/23	149.55	07/06	98.80	106.40	2009	12/31	334.65	01/22	139.60	334.65
1990	08/15	133.55	01/30	95.65	116.85	2010	12/31	444.70	06/07	276.60	444.70
1991	01/02	119.30	12/10	96.60	97.55	2011	02/14	462.85	10/20	305.75	343.60
1992	07/16	116.35	01/09	94.35	103.60	2012*	02/09	397.85	05/31	336.55	*AT PRESS TIME*

Through May 31, 2012

COPPER NEAR-TERM CONTRACT MONTHLY CLOSING PRICES

	Jan	Feb	Mar	Apr	May	Jun	Jul	Aug	Sep	Oct	Nov	Dec
1973	54.50	64.20	67.35	67.50	71.45	78.30	87.60	81.40	80.90	92.50	86.70	84.80
1974	97.60	109.00	129.60	135.00	107.40	93.80	89.30	74.20	68.20	63.60	60.50	53.60
1975	52.40	59.50	62.90	56.70	54.70	56.50	57.90	60.00	56.50	56.90	54.30	55.30
1976	54.90	59.80	63.40	71.70	69.90	75.60	74.50	69.60	63.80	56.30	58.10	63.20
1977	64.70	68.90	70.60	64.10	60.40	60.80	56.30	55.40	56.40	55.00	57.90	60.30
1978	58.00	56.50	60.60	60.10	65.30	60.10	63.00	65.25	67.20	70.20	68.40	71.05
1979	78.90	92.70	94.60	93.60	79.50	81.30	81.30	92.10	107.00	90.90	102.70	105.20
1980	130.50	123.00	87.10	90.30	93.40	92.90	95.80	90.10	93.45	93.90	94.25	86.55
1981	84.20	82.55	86.40	83.55	81.45	77.85	83.75	81.30	76.70	77.05	75.65	75.70
1982	74.45	71.15	67.55	72.40	64.60	61.00	63.15	64.40	60.00	65.90	68.00	69.65
1983	75.25	75.20	75.15	78.75	78.35	76.30	76.95	73.85	66.95	62.95	67.80	67.00
1984	64.40	66.10	71.75	65.70	63.95	62.00	57.00	63.10	57.55	59.95	58.85	57.20
1985	62.60	59.60	62.60	61.90	60.65	59.55	61.10	61.85	59.35	60.25	61.85	64.15
1986	65.70	64.80	66.15	62.65	63.10	60.35	58.50	58.45	61.20	58.80	61.05	61.15
1987	60.40	63.40	62.45	62.15	65.90	71.45	78.15	75.10	79.75	82.15	102.20	127.40
1988	95.75	86.30	105.30	89.70	91.30	98.00	93.00	101.00	109.60	141.15	133.00	135.50
1989	142.90	131.20	132.60	138.70	114.35	103.90	111.50	128.95	122.90	114.00	109.15	106.40
1990	98.60	113.85	122.40	116.90	110.85	114.00	124.60	124.80	118.80	115.75	107.10	116.85
1991	106.40	111.50	106.20	105.10	96.85	101.00	101.30	103.15	104.80	106.60	101.00	97.55
1992	98.60	103.20	101.65	100.45	101.10	109.70	112.50	110.85	104.75	101.40	97.60	103.60
1993	98.95	95.95	96.20	84.50	79.85	86.50	88.30	86.00	74.90	73.15	75.00	83.30
1994	86.80	86.65	86.75	91.50	103.75	108.25	111.40	115.75	112.55	122.60	137.15	138.60
1995	136.30	130.10	136.70	127.10	131.00	136.70	135.30	131.95	131.65	124.75	132.25	120.55
1996	114.80	115.30	116.50	119.15	115.00	90.40	93.20	95.25	90.10	91.30	110.30	100.25
1997	103.75	110.90	113.00	111.35	119.10	112.15	108.90	99.30	97.00	90.75	84.05	78.10
1998	79.30	77.05	79.85	83.70	77.50	73.80	76.95	71.35	73.75	72.40	70.05	67.20
1999	64.50	63.25	62.75	72.75	62.80	76.65	76.25	79.20	82.65	80.55	81.80	86.30
2000	84.95	79.80	80.50	79.60	81.45	82.40	87.45	89.50	92.05	84.85	84.55	84.30
2001	84.55	81.60	76.40	77.70	75.75	71.35	68.25	68.70	65.20	62.50	73.20	65.90
2002	73.35	72.05	76.35	73.90	76.40	77.45	68.10	69.55	66.60	71.70	74.95	70.25
2003	79.45	78.10	71.45	73.10	78.25	75.30	82.05	81.05	81.85	93.85	91.40	104.55
2004	114.55	134.60	136.00	120.75	127.75	120.80	130.80	128.10	139.60	133.75	143.40	145.25
2005	143.50	149.85	150.25	146.40	145.65	151.00	164.45	161.95	172.75	181.10	192.60	204.20
2006	222.85	217.85	246.30	322.05	362.40	335.50	357.00	345.60	346.05	334.55	319.55	287.10
2007	259.45	275.20	314.60	355.65	339.55	345.05	364.85	339.70	364.00	347.30	318.45	304.10
2008	329.80	385.50	383.10	390.45	360.60	388.25	366.15	338.70	287.90	182.90	164.95	141.00
2009	146.85	153.85	184.45	204.75	219.75	227.20	262.35	282.65	281.90	295.55	317.70	334.65
2010	305.25	328.40	355.35	335.35	310.45	295.05	331.15	337.00	365.15	373.35	382.55	444.70
2011	445.85	449.65	430.75	417.90	417.75	428.25	447.95	420.45	315.20	363.20	357.55	343.60
2012	379.00	393.40	382.50	382.95	336.55							

COPPER NEAR-TERM CONTRACT MONTHLY PERCENT CHANGES

	Jan	Feb	Mar	Apr	May	Jun	Jul	Aug	Sep	Oct	Nov	Dec	Year's Change
1973	8.5	17.8	4.9	0.2	5.9	9.6	11.9	−7.1	−0.6	14.3	−6.3	−2.2	68.8
1974	15.1	11.7	18.9	4.2	−20.4	−12.7	−4.8	−16.9	−8.1	−6.7	−4.9	−11.4	−36.8
1975	−2.2	13.5	5.7	−9.9	−3.5	3.3	2.5	3.6	−5.8	0.7	−4.6	1.8	3.2
1976	−0.7	8.9	6.0	13.1	−2.5	8.2	−1.5	−6.6	−8.3	−11.8	3.2	8.8	14.3
1977	2.4	6.5	2.5	−9.2	−5.8	0.7	−7.4	−1.6	1.8	−2.5	5.3	4.1	−4.6
1978	−3.8	−2.6	7.3	−0.8	8.7	−8.0	4.8	3.6	3.0	4.5	−2.6	3.9	17.8
1979	11.0	17.5	2.0	−1.1	−15.1	2.3	N/C	13.3	16.2	−15.0	13.0	2.4	48.1
1980	24.0	−5.7	−29.2	3.7	3.4	−0.5	3.1	−5.9	3.7	0.5	0.4	−8.2	−17.7
1981	−2.7	−2.0	4.7	−3.3	−2.5	−4.4	7.6	−2.9	−5.7	0.5	−1.8	0.1	−12.5
1982	−1.7	−4.4	−5.1	7.2	−10.8	−5.6	3.5	2.0	−6.8	9.8	3.2	2.4	−8.0
1983	8.0	−0.1	−0.1	4.8	−0.5	−2.6	0.9	−4.0	−9.3	−6.0	7.7	−1.2	−3.8
1984	−3.9	2.6	8.5	−8.4	−2.7	−3.0	−8.1	10.7	−8.8	4.2	−1.8	−2.8	−14.6
1985	9.4	−4.8	5.0	−1.1	−2.0	−1.8	2.6	1.2	−4.0	1.5	2.7	3.7	12.2
1986	2.4	−1.4	2.1	−5.3	0.7	−4.4	−3.1	−0.1	4.7	−3.9	3.8	0.2	−4.7
1987	−1.2	5.0	−1.5	−0.5	6.0	8.4	9.4	−3.9	6.2	3.0	24.4	24.7	108.3
1988	−24.8	−9.9	22.0	−14.8	1.8	7.3	−5.1	8.6	8.5	28.8	−5.8	1.9	6.4
1989	5.5	−8.2	1.1	4.6	−17.6	−9.1	7.3	15.7	−4.7	−7.2	−4.3	−2.5	−21.5
1990	−7.3	15.5	7.5	−4.5	−5.2	2.8	9.3	0.2	−4.8	−2.6	−7.5	9.1	9.8
1991	−8.9	4.8	−4.8	−1.0	−7.8	4.3	0.3	1.8	1.6	1.7	−5.3	−3.4	−16.5
1992	1.1	4.7	−1.5	−1.2	0.6	8.5	2.6	−1.5	−5.5	−3.2	−3.7	6.1	6.2
1993	−4.5	−3.0	0.3	−12.2	−5.5	8.3	2.1	−2.6	−12.9	−2.3	2.5	11.1	−19.6
1994	4.2	−0.2	0.1	5.5	13.4	4.3	2.9	3.9	−2.8	8.9	11.9	1.1	66.4
1995	−1.7	−4.5	5.1	−7.0	3.1	4.4	−1.0	−2.5	−0.2	−5.2	6.0	−8.8	−13.0
1996	−4.8	0.4	1.0	2.3	−3.5	−21.4	3.1	2.2	−5.4	1.3	20.8	−9.1	−16.8
1997	3.5	6.9	1.9	−1.5	7.0	−5.8	−2.9	−8.8	−2.3	−6.4	−7.4	−7.1	−22.1
1998	1.5	−2.8	3.6	4.8	−7.4	−4.8	4.3	−7.3	3.4	−1.8	−3.2	−4.1	−14.0
1999	−4.0	−1.9	−0.8	15.9	−13.7	22.1	−0.5	3.9	4.4	−2.5	1.6	5.5	28.4
2000	−1.6	−6.1	0.9	−1.1	2.3	1.2	6.1	2.3	2.8	−7.8	−0.4	−0.3	−2.3
2001	0.3	−3.5	−6.4	1.7	−2.5	−5.8	−4.3	0.7	−5.1	−4.1	17.1	−10.0	−21.8
2002	11.3	−1.8	6.0	−3.2	3.4	1.4	−12.1	2.1	−4.2	7.7	4.5	−6.3	6.6
2003	13.1	−1.7	−8.5	2.3	7.0	−3.8	9.0	−1.2	1.0	14.7	−2.6	14.4	48.8
2004	9.6	17.5	1.0	−11.2	5.8	−5.4	8.3	−2.1	9.0	−4.2	7.2	1.3	38.9
2005	−1.2	4.4	0.3	−2.6	−0.5	3.7	8.9	−1.5	6.7	4.8	6.4	6.0	40.6
2006	9.1	−2.2	13.1	30.8	12.5	−7.4	6.4	−3.2	0.1	−3.3	−4.5	−10.2	40.6
2007	−9.6	6.1	14.3	13.0	−4.5	1.6	5.7	−6.9	7.2	−4.6	−8.3	−4.5	5.9
2008	8.5	16.9	−0.6	1.9	−7.6	7.7	−5.7	−7.5	−15.0	−36.5	−9.8	−14.5	−53.6
2009	4.1	4.8	19.9	11.0	7.3	3.4	15.5	7.7	−0.3	4.8	7.5	5.3	137.3
2010	−8.8	7.6	8.2	−5.6	−7.4	−5.0	12.2	1.8	8.4	2.2	2.5	16.2	32.9
2011	0.3	0.9	−4.2	−3.0	−0.04	2.5	4.6	−6.1	−25.0	15.2	−1.6	−3.9	−22.7
2012	10.3	3.8	−2.8	0.1	−12.1								
TOTALS	69.8	111.0	108.4	18.6	−72.2	4.5	98.4	−14.9	−56.9	−8.5	65.3	19.6	
AVG.	1.7	2.8	2.7	0.5	−1.8	0.1	2.5	−0.4	−1.5	−0.2	1.7	0.5	
# Up	22	21	28	18	16	21	26	18	17	19	20	21	
# Down	18	19	12	22	24	18	12	21	22	20	19	18	

151

GOLD CYCLE, SEASONAL PATTERN, AND TRADING GUIDE

Gold has a seasonal tendency to peak in late January after the holiday season, as jewelry demand starts to decline. Price increases can last into the first part of February, when inventories are being replenished by dealers preparing for retail sales for Valentine's Day gifts.

Gold tends to post seasonal bottoms in late July or early August, as demand increases when jewelers again stock up ahead of the wedding season in India and also, when investors return from summer vacations. Gold prices are also subject to spikes in demand from the investment community, which uses gold as a hedge or protection from concerns over inflation or times of economic instability and uncertainties. It is valued in terms of the U.S. dollar, so periods of dollar weakness help support gold's value. Longer-term cyclical forces can dramatically impact the seasonal price moves of this market.

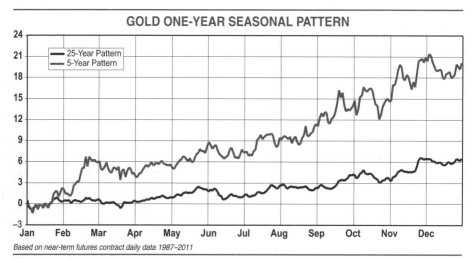

GOLD ONE-YEAR SEASONAL PATTERN

- 25-Year Pattern
- 5-Year Pattern

Based on near-term futures contract daily data 1987–2011

GOLD NEAR-TERM CONTRACT ANNUAL HIGHS, LOWS, AND CLOSES SINCE 1975

	HIGH		LOW		YEAR		HIGH		LOW		YEAR
YEAR	DATE	CLOSE	DATE	CLOSE	CLOSE	YEAR	DATE	CLOSE	DATE	CLOSE	CLOSE
1975	02/20	187.7	09/23	131.2	141.0	1994	09/27	401.4	04/22	372.1	384.4
1976	01/02	141.2	08/30	102.8	135.7	1995	04/18	397.8	01/06	372.2	388.1
1977	11/11	168.9	01/10	127.6	167.5	1996	02/02	417.7	12/31	369.2	369.2
1978	10/30	247.0	01/04	168.0	229.0	1997	01/02	366.6	12/12	284.8	289.9
1979	12/31	541.0	01/11	218.6	541.0	1998	04/23	315.8	08/28	277.9	289.2
1980	01/21	834.0	03/17	480.0	599.5	1999	10/05	326.0	07/19	253.9	289.6
1981	01/06	605.0	12/28	397.2	402.8	2000	02/10	318.7	11/13	265.3	273.6
1982	09/08	497.0	06/22	301.5	453.0	2001	09/26	294.8	04/02	256.6	279.0
1983	01/31	518.2	11/16	376.3	388.0	2002	12/27	349.7	01/03	278.5	348.2
1984	03/05	407.3	12/27	309.2	309.7	2003	12/30	417.2	04/07	322.2	416.1
1985	08/28	347.3	02/25	284.1	331.1	2004	12/03	457.8	05/13	374.9	438.4
1986	09/22	445.2	01/02	328.9	406.9	2005	12/12	531.5	02/08	414.3	518.9
1987	12/11	502.0	02/17	394.9	488.9	2006	05/11	721.5	01/05	527.8	638.0
1988	01/14	488.2	09/30	399.2	412.3	2007	12/28	842.7	01/05	606.9	838.0
1989	11/24	425.0	06/09	362.0	405.2	2008	03/18	1004.3	11/13	705.0	884.3
1990	02/05	427.5	06/14	349.8	396.2	2009	12/03	1218.3	01/15	807.3	1096.2
1991	01/16	404.5	09/12	348.2	355.2	2010	12/31	1421.4	02/05	1052.8	1421.4
1992	07/24	363.2	11/10	330.1	333.1	2011	08/22	1891.9	01/27	1319.8	1569.2
1993	07/30	411.3	03/10	326.9	391.9	2012*	02/28	1787.0	05/16	1536.6	AT PRESS TIME

*Through May 31, 2012

152

GOLD NEAR-TERM CONTRACT MONTHLY CLOSING PRICES

	Jan	Feb	Mar	Apr	May	Jun	Jul	Aug	Sep	Oct	Nov	Dec
1975	178.0	183.0	179.5	166.8	169.0	167.8	173.4	162.8	142.2	142.8	138.8	141.0
1976	129.0	132.6	129.7	128.9	127.3	123.9	114.2	103.2	116.1	123.8	132.6	135.7
1977	134.0	144.6	151.0	148.0	144.3	143.6	147.1	148.1	156.4	162.7	162.3	167.5
1978	178.9	184.4	186.2	170.6	187.0	183.7	209.8	210.6	220.9	240.7	196.4	229.0
1979	236.6	252.9	243.8	249.2	281.1	283.8	297.3	326.7	404.5	385.7	430.5	541.0
1980	704.0	640.0	519.0	507.0	555.0	654.0	642.0	656.0	688.5	642.0	644.5	599.5
1981	512.5	486.5	525.5	489.0	492.5	428.5	423.2	443.5	443.0	431.2	413.3	402.8
1982	391.8	364.5	334.2	346.5	329.0	317.8	355.5	418.5	404.8	423.0	449.0	453.0
1983	518.2	423.7	422.0	433.5	418.5	418.5	427.4	424.8	407.8	378.8	409.0	388.0
1984	379.2	398.9	394.3	379.6	393.6	376.1	350.3	358.0	351.3	336.0	333.5	309.7
1985	307.4	288.7	334.1	316.5	319.5	317.7	335.2	339.8	327.1	326.7	327.3	331.1
1986	352.9	341.0	334.8	348.1	347.1	347.7	369.7	393.3	429.8	405.5	394.8	406.9
1987	408.9	407.4	422.7	456.5	456.0	452.2	475.1	458.7	458.8	471.2	497.2	488.9
1988	458.5	431.9	457.9	452.6	459.8	437.7	447.3	439.9	399.2	415.1	429.6	412.3
1989	395.8	390.4	390.0	380.5	366.5	377.3	378.7	365.4	372.0	377.6	417.5	405.2
1990	417.8	408.9	375.0	371.4	368.6	359.9	379.2	389.2	408.1	381.3	385.7	396.2
1991	368.5	369.0	359.4	357.7	364.8	370.0	370.8	352.9	357.3	359.5	371.1	355.2
1992	358.9	354.1	345.5	337.9	338.4	344.4	361.4	345.3	349.4	340.1	335.5	333.1
1993	330.7	329.1	339.3	357.2	380.3	379.2	411.3	375.7	357.1	369.6	371.9	391.9
1994	383.6	382.5	394.3	377.8	390.0	387.3	389.2	390.8	397.6	384.9	384.5	384.4
1995	377.7	378.3	394.3	388.5	387.6	385.6	388.4	386.9	386.5	384.3	388.6	388.1
1996	408.5	401.2	398.4	393.5	394.4	381.6	393.1	391.3	380.5	379.1	375.0	369.2
1997	346.0	365.1	354.0	341.2	347.5	335.3	328.6	327.4	336.9	312.1	298.6	289.9
1998	304.6	300.1	303.3	307.9	295.1	298.1	290.5	278.9	299.0	293.7	295.1	289.2
1999	288.2	288.3	281.9	287.8	272.0	263.6	258.8	257.3	299.5	300.3	293.0	289.6
2000	286.2	294.2	281.4	274.7	274.8	291.5	283.2	282.1	276.9	266.4	273.3	273.6
2001	268.0	267.8	259.2	264.4	266.9	271.3	269.2	276.5	294.0	280.5	274.9	279.0
2002	282.9	297.1	303.7	309.2	327.5	313.9	305.2	313.9	325.2	318.4	317.8	348.2
2003	369.1	350.3	336.9	339.4	365.6	346.3	355.8	376.8	386.1	384.6	398.0	416.1
2004	402.9	396.8	428.3	387.5	394.9	393.0	393.7	412.4	420.4	429.4	453.2	438.4
2005	424.1	437.6	431.1	436.1	418.9	437.1	435.8	438.1	472.3	466.9	498.7	518.9
2006	575.5	563.9	586.7	654.5	649.0	616.0	646.8	634.2	604.2	606.8	652.9	638.0
2007	657.9	672.5	669.0	683.5	666.7	650.9	679.3	681.9	750.0	795.3	789.1	838.0
2008	928.0	975.0	921.5	865.1	891.5	928.3	922.7	835.2	880.8	718.2	819.0	884.3
2009	928.4	942.5	925.0	891.2	978.9	927.4	955.8	953.5	1009.3	1040.4	1182.3	1096.2
2010	1083.8	1118.9	1114.5	1180.7	1215.0	1245.9	1183.9	1250.3	1309.6	1357.6	1386.1	1421.4
2011	1334.5	1409.9	1439.9	1556.4	1536.8	1502.8	1631.2	1831.7	1622.3	1725.2	1750.3	1569.2
2012	1740.4	1711.3	1671.9	1662.5	1564.2							

GOLD NEAR-TERM CONTRACT MONTHLY PERCENT CHANGES

	Jan	Feb	Mar	Apr	May	Jun	Jul	Aug	Sep	Oct	Nov	Dec	Year's Change
1975	-3.2	2.8	-1.9	-7.1	1.3	-0.7	3.3	-6.1	-12.7	0.4	-2.8	1.6	-23.3
1976	-8.5	2.8	-2.2	-0.6	-1.2	-2.7	-7.8	-9.6	12.5	6.6	7.1	2.3	-3.8
1977	-1.3	7.9	4.4	-2.0	-2.5	-0.5	2.4	0.7	5.6	4.0	-0.2	3.2	23.4
1978	6.8	3.1	1.0	-8.4	9.6	-1.8	14.2	0.4	4.9	9.0	-18.4	16.6	36.7
1979	3.3	6.9	-3.6	2.2	12.8	1.0	4.8	9.9	23.8	-4.6	11.6	25.7	136.2
1980	30.1	-9.1	-18.9	-2.3	9.5	17.8	-1.8	2.2	5.0	-6.8	0.4	-7.0	10.8
1981	-14.5	-5.1	8.0	-6.9	0.7	-13.0	-1.2	4.8	-0.1	-2.7	-4.2	-2.5	-32.8
1982	-2.7	-7.0	-8.3	3.7	-5.1	-3.4	11.9	17.7	-3.3	4.5	6.1	0.9	12.5
1983	14.4	-18.2	-0.4	2.7	-3.5	N/C	2.1	-0.6	-4.0	-7.1	8.0	-5.1	-14.3
1984	-2.3	5.2	-1.2	-3.7	3.7	-4.4	-6.9	2.2	-1.9	-4.4	-0.7	-7.1	-20.2
1985	-0.7	-6.1	15.7	-5.3	0.9	-0.6	5.5	1.4	-3.7	-0.1	0.2	1.2	6.9
1986	6.6	-3.4	-1.8	4.0	-0.3	0.2	6.3	6.4	9.3	-5.7	-2.6	3.1	22.9
1987	0.5	-0.4	3.8	8.0	-0.1	-0.8	5.1	-3.5	0.0	2.7	5.5	-1.7	20.2
1988	-6.2	-5.8	6.0	-1.2	1.6	-4.8	2.2	-1.7	-9.3	4.0	3.5	-4.0	-15.7
1989	-4.0	-1.4	-0.1	-2.4	-3.7	2.9	0.4	-3.5	1.8	1.5	10.6	-2.9	-1.7
1990	3.1	-2.1	-8.3	-1.0	-0.8	-2.4	5.4	2.6	4.9	-6.6	1.2	2.7	-2.2
1991	-7.0	0.1	-2.6	-0.5	2.0	1.4	0.2	-4.8	1.2	0.6	3.2	-4.3	-10.3
1992	1.0	-1.3	-2.4	-2.2	0.1	1.8	4.9	-4.5	1.2	-2.7	-1.4	-0.7	-6.2
1993	-0.7	-0.5	3.1	5.3	6.5	-0.3	8.5	-8.7	-5.0	3.5	0.6	5.4	17.7
1994	-2.1	-0.3	3.1	-4.2	3.2	-0.7	0.5	0.4	1.7	-3.2	-0.1	0.0	-1.9
1995	-1.7	0.2	4.2	-1.5	-0.2	-0.5	0.7	-0.4	-0.1	-0.6	1.1	-0.1	1.0
1996	5.3	-1.8	-0.7	-1.2	0.2	-3.2	3.0	-0.5	-2.8	-0.4	-1.1	-1.5	-4.9
1997	-6.3	5.5	-3.0	-3.6	1.8	-3.5	-2.0	-0.4	2.9	-7.4	-4.3	-2.9	-21.5
1998	5.1	-1.5	1.1	1.5	-4.2	1.0	-2.5	-4.0	7.2	-1.8	0.5	-2.0	-0.2
1999	-0.3	0.0	-2.2	2.1	-5.5	-3.1	-1.8	-0.6	16.4	0.3	-2.4	-1.2	0.1
2000	-1.2	2.8	-4.4	-2.4	0.0	6.1	-2.8	-0.4	-1.8	-3.8	2.6	0.1	-5.5
2001	-2.0	-0.1	-3.2	2.0	0.9	1.6	-0.8	2.7	6.3	-4.6	-2.0	1.5	2.0
2002	1.4	5.0	2.2	1.8	5.9	-4.2	-2.8	2.9	3.6	-2.1	-0.2	9.6	24.8
2003	6.0	-5.1	-3.8	0.7	7.7	-5.3	2.7	5.9	2.5	-0.4	3.5	4.5	19.5
2004	-3.2	-1.5	7.9	-9.5	1.9	-0.5	0.2	4.7	1.9	2.1	5.5	-3.3	5.4
2005	-3.3	3.2	-1.5	1.2	-3.9	4.3	-0.3	0.5	7.8	-1.1	6.8	4.1	18.4
2006	10.9	-2.0	4.0	11.6	-0.8	-5.1	5.0	-1.9	-4.7	0.4	7.6	-2.3	23.0
2007	3.1	2.2	-0.5	2.2	-2.5	-2.4	4.4	0.4	10.0	6.0	-0.8	6.2	31.3
2008	10.7	5.1	-5.5	-6.1	3.1	4.1	-0.6	-9.5	5.5	-18.5	14.0	8.0	5.5
2009	5.0	1.5	-1.9	-3.7	9.8	-5.3	3.1	-0.2	5.9	3.1	13.6	-7.3	24.0
2010	-1.1	3.2	-0.4	5.9	2.9	2.5	-5.0	5.6	4.7	3.7	2.1	2.5	29.7
2011	-6.1	5.7	2.1	8.1	-1.3	-2.2	8.5	12.3	-11.4	6.3	1.5	-10.3	10.4
2012	10.9	-1.7	-2.3	-0.6	-5.9								
TOTALS	45.8	-11.2	-14.5	-13.4	44.6	-26.7	69.0	22.8	85.8	-25.9	75.6	33.0	
AVG.	1.2	-0.3	-0.4	-0.4	1.2	-0.7	1.9	0.6	2.3	-0.7	2.0	0.9	
# Up	17	18	14	16	22	12	24	19	24	17	23	18	
# Down	21	20	24	22	16	24	13	18	13	20	14	18	

SILVER CYCLE, SEASONAL PATTERN, AND TRADING GUIDE

Silver has a tendency to make a major seasonal bottom in September, and then has a tendency to post major seasonal peaks in April. It tracks the price moves of gold, but from a trader's or investor's perspective, it is considered the poor man's gold. Due to technology and the age of digital imaging, silver has lost a major portion of its industrial demand element because there is no longer a tremendous demand from the photo industry. It is still needed, however, for film and x-ray processing.

Silver prices are also subject to spikes in demand from the investment community, which uses silver as a hedge or protection from concerns over inflation or times of economic instability and uncertainties. Dollar weakness helps support silver's value. Longer-term cyclical forces can dramatically impact the seasonal price moves of this market.

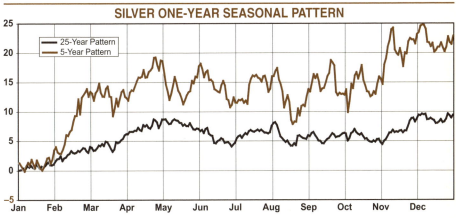

SILVER ONE-YEAR SEASONAL PATTERN

— 25-Year Pattern
— 5-Year Pattern

Based on near-term futures contract daily data 1987–2011

SILVER NEAR-TERM CONTRACT ANNUAL HIGHS, LOWS, AND CLOSES SINCE 1973

YEAR	HIGH DATE	HIGH CLOSE	LOW DATE	LOW CLOSE	YEAR CLOSE	YEAR	HIGH DATE	HIGH CLOSE	LOW DATE	LOW CLOSE	YEAR CLOSE
1973	12/31	329.7	01/22	196.1	329.7	1993	08/02	545.8	02/22	355.0	511.7
1974	02/26	624.2	01/04	329.0	447.0	1994	03/25	580.0	12/05	464.5	491.7
1975	08/07	528.5	01/21	398.5	423.6	1995	05/04	616.0	03/03	442.0	520.7
1976	07/06	518.8	01/26	385.3	439.0	1996	02/02	584.0	11/06	471.3	479.0
1977	03/21	500.8	08/15	432.6	484.9	1997	12/24	637.8	07/16	418.5	598.8
1978	10/30	636.5	02/08	484.8	613.7	1998	02/05	728.0	08/31	467.8	502.0
1979	12/31	2905.0	01/11	598.5	2905.0	1999	09/28	577.0	04/14	486.0	545.3
1980	01/21	4150.0	05/21	1140.0	1612.0	2000	02/04	557.2	11/21	463.0	463.5
1981	01/05	1670.0	11/19	816.0	829.0	2001	01/18	482.5	11/21	403.5	458.8
1982	12/29	1138.0	06/21	499.0	1110.0	2002	06/04	512.5	01/31	422.3	481.2
1983	02/16	1475.0	11/18	855.0	915.5	2003	12/30	599.3	03/21	435.3	596.5
1984	03/05	1021.0	12/31	638.0	638.0	2004	04/06	822.0	05/11	552.3	683.7
1985	04/08	673.5	03/11	558.5	590.5	2005	12/09	909.5	01/07	644.8	889.0
1986	01/24	633.5	05/19	489.5	546.0	2006	05/11	1493.5	01/05	887.2	1293.5
1987	05/15	950.0	02/17	540.5	677.0	2007	11/09	1554.5	08/16	1149.5	1492.0
1988	07/20	790.0	11/21	602.5	613.0	2008	03/05	2078.5	10/28	879.0	1129.5
1989	01/23	625.5	10/10	510.0	527.3	2009	12/02	1932.5	01/15	1044.0	1684.5
1990	01/12	538.8	12/14	400.5	424.7	2010	12/31	3093.7	02/05	1483.0	3093.7
1991	06/10	456.0	02/22	355.6	391.2	2011	04/29	4859.9	01/25	2680.5	2791.5
1992	01/16	433.8	11/10	364.5	369.0	2012*	02/28	3720.5	05/16	2719.6	AT PRESS TIME

*Through May 31, 2012

155

SILVER NEAR-TERM CONTRACT MONTHLY CLOSING PRICES

	Jan	Feb	Mar	Apr	May	Jun	Jul	Aug	Sep	Oct	Nov	Dec
1973	204.7	255.0	220.4	217.5	259.7	272.1	290.1	269.0	282.2	288.1	301.7	329.7
1974	406.0	587.0	536.9	574.0	493.5	480.0	500.2	429.5	442.5	484.5	474.0	447.0
1975	410.5	451.5	427.5	436.5	452.0	467.5	505.5	467.5	452.5	419.2	418.6	423.6
1976	397.0	424.5	405.3	450.0	471.0	489.0	451.2	414.2	437.2	433.2	433.6	439.0
1977	449.5	477.5	483.2	480.7	456.5	451.7	452.1	453.7	468.7	489.2	485.4	484.9
1978	499.8	502.8	549.0	503.0	543.0	528.5	569.2	559.7	571.5	621.5	609.0	613.7
1979	675.5	783.0	751.1	809.0	876.6.	878.0	906.5	1086.0	1680.0	1679.0	1927.0	2905.0
1980	3575.0	3634.0	1905.0	1300.0	1395.0	1690.0	1555.0	1684.0	2125.0	1910.0	1945.0	1612.0
1981	1345.0	1250.0	1203.0	1138.0	1088.0	880.0	864.0	972.0	938.0	925.0	844.0	829.0
1982	828.0	794.0	723.0	702.0	629.5	616.0	674.0	804.0	824.0	1009.0	1033.0	1110.0
1983	1421.0	1187.0	1075.0	1224.0	1310.0	1176.0	1191.0	1241.0	1107.0	863.0	985.0	915.5
1984	866.0	981.0	990.0	911.0	934.0	855.0	708.5	766.0	762.0	728.0	717.5	638.0
1985	639.0	570.0	672.5	624.0	619.0	619.0	633.0	637.0	609.5	612.5	621.0	590.5
1986	607.5	570.5	516.5	519.0	527.0	516.5	512.7	523.0	562.5	568.0	547.5	546.0
1987	552.5	549.3	622.0	808.0	767.0	741.0	835.0	753.0	761.0	699.0	719.0	677.0
1988	654.5	632.0	678.5	658.5	665.0	677.5	685.5	671.0	622.5	634.8	629.0	613.0
1989	583.5	593.5	582.3	570.5	520.5	524.3	531.3	516.5	531.0	521.8	579.5	527.3
1990	522.8	520.5	498.0	501.5	511.0	496.3	482.2	486.8	483.2	418.0	421.7	424.7
1991	385.1	377.3	386.8	401.5	411.7	447.5	407.8	387.0	417.3	410.8	411.3	391.2
1992	418.0	413.5	414.3	401.5	402.2	405.8	393.7	376.7	376.2	376.2	377.2	369.0
1993	366.0	359.7	389.2	441.7	462.2	458.7	540.8	488.5	408.2	436.7	446.5	511.7
1994	513.5	539.0	578.5	538.3	555.0	542.5	533.2	551.2	565.7	526.2	497.5	491.7
1995	466.3	456.5	531.0	578.3	531.0	506.5	505.2	539.0	548.5	536.0	526.7	520.7
1996	558.8	554.5	554.0	534.0	540.3	503.5	514.8	525.0	487.7	480.8	478.5	479.0
1997	492.0	536.0	507.5	469.3	467.5	464.8	449.0	468.5	523.2	473.7	529.8	598.8
1998	612.5	648.0	646.7	623.0	508.5	553.5	545.8	467.8	536.0	504.3	488.5	502.0
1999	523.5	563.0	497.0	543.0	489.5	528.7	546.5	522.0	561.5	518.0	524.0	545.3
2000	531.7	510.8	504.5	501.5	496.5	508.3	503.8	504.5	494.8	477.8	475.8	463.5
2001	481.5	451.5	429.5	435.8	441.0	432.7	422.8	421.0	467.5	422.5	415.7	458.8
2002	422.3	451.7	465.0	455.5	504.2	485.5	459.8	446.8	454.8	450.5	443.5	481.2
2003	486.0	460.0	446.5	465.2	453.3	456.8	512.0	513.2	514.2	506.5	538.2	596.5
2004	625.0	671.5	794.5	609.0	611.0	579.5	656.0	681.2	693.8	730.5	777.7	683.7
2005	674.7	739.5	718.0	694.0	745.2	707.5	726.2	685.5	751.2	758.0	838.5	889.0
2006	988.5	980.5	1152.0	1363.0	1245.5	1092.0	1137.0	1303.0	1154.0	1227.0	1411.5	1293.5
2007	1357.0	1423.5	1345.0	1357.5	1347.0	1247.3	1301.7	1223.0	1392.0	1443.8	1416.5	1492.0
2008	1699.5	1991.5	1731.0	1659.3	1686.5	1751.0	1779.0	1370.7	1227.5	973.0	1023.0	1129.5
2009	1256.5	1311.0	1298.5	1232.5	1561.0	1360.0	1394.0	1492.3	1665.8	1625.5	1852.5	1684.5
2010	1619.0	1652.1	1752.6	1863.9	1842.2	1870.8	1800.3	1943.2	2182.1	2456.4	2821.2	3093.7
2011	2816.9	3382.0	3788.8	4859.9	3830.5	3483.2	4010.6	4176.8	3008.3	3435.4	3280.4	2791.5
2012	3324.0	3472.0	3248.4	3101.0	2775.7							

SILVER NEAR-TERM CONTRACT MONTHLY PERCENT CHANGES

	Jan	Feb	Mar	Apr	May	Jun	Jul	Aug	Sep	Oct	Nov	Dec	Year's Change
1973	N/C	24.6	−13.6	−1.3	19.4	4.8	6.6	−7.3	4.9	2.1	4.7	9.3	61.1
1974	23.1	44.6	−8.5	6.9	−14.0	−2.7	4.2	−14.1	3.0	9.5	−2.2	−5.7	35.6
1975	−8.2	10.0	−5.3	2.1	3.6	3.4	8.1	−7.5	−3.2	−7.4	−0.1	1.2	−5.2
1976	−6.3	6.9	−4.5	11.0	4.7	3.8	−7.7	−8.2	5.6	−0.9	0.1	1.2	3.6
1977	2.4	6.2	1.2	−0.5	−5.0	−1.1	0.1	0.4	3.3	4.4	−0.8	−0.1	10.5
1978	3.1	0.6	9.2	−8.4	8.0	−2.7	7.7	−1.7	2.1	8.7	−2.0	0.8	26.6
1979	10.1	15.9	−4.1	7.7	8.4	0.2	3.2	19.8	54.7	−0.1	14.8	50.8	373.4
1980	23.1	1.7	−47.6	−31.8	7.3	21.1	−8.0	8.3	26.2	−10.1	1.8	−17.1	−44.5
1981	−16.6	−7.1	−3.8	−5.4	−4.4	−19.1	−1.8	12.5	−3.5	−1.4	−8.8	−1.8	−48.6
1982	−0.1	−4.1	−8.9	−2.9	−10.3	−2.1	9.4	19.3	2.5	22.5	2.4	7.5	33.9
1983	28.0	−16.5	−9.4	13.9	7.0	−10.2	1.3	4.2	−10.8	−22.0	14.1	−7.1	−17.5
1984	−5.4	13.3	0.9	−8.0	2.5	−8.5	−17.1	8.1	−0.5	−4.5	−1.4	−11.1	−30.3
1985	0.2	−10.8	18.0	−7.2	−0.8	N/C	2.3	0.6	−4.3	0.5	1.4	−4.9	−7.4
1986	2.9	−6.1	−9.5	0.5	1.5	−2.0	−0.7	2.0	7.6	1.0	−3.6	−0.3	−7.5
1987	1.2	−0.6	13.2	29.9	−5.1	−3.4	12.7	−9.8	1.1	−8.1	2.9	−5.8	24.0
1988	−3.3	−3.4	7.4	−2.9	1.0	1.9	1.2	−2.1	−7.2	2.0	−0.9	−2.5	−9.5
1989	−4.8	1.7	−1.9	−2.0	−8.8	0.7	1.3	−2.8	2.8	−1.7	11.1	−9.0	−14.0
1990	−0.9	−0.4	−4.3	0.7	1.9	−2.9	−2.8	1.0	−0.7	−13.5	0.9	0.7	−19.5
1991	−9.3	−2.0	2.5	3.8	2.5	8.7	−8.9	−5.1	7.8	−1.6	0.1	−4.9	−7.9
1992	6.9	−1.1	0.2	−3.1	0.2	0.9	−3.0	−4.3	−0.1	N/C	0.3	−2.2	−5.7
1993	−0.8	−1.7	8.2	13.5	4.6	−0.8	17.9	−9.7	−16.4	7.0	2.2	14.6	38.7
1994	0.4	5.0	7.3	−6.9	3.1	−2.3	−1.7	3.4	2.6	−7.0	−5.5	−1.2	−3.9
1995	−5.2	−2.1	16.3	8.9	−8.2	−4.6	−0.3	6.7	1.8	−2.3	−1.7	−1.1	5.9
1996	7.3	−0.8	−0.1	−3.6	1.2	−6.8	2.2	2.0	−7.1	−1.4	−0.5	0.1	−8.0
1997	2.7	8.9	−5.3	−7.5	−0.4	−0.6	−3.4	4.3	11.7	−9.5	11.8	13.0	25.0
1998	2.3	5.8	−0.2	−3.7	−18.4	8.8	−1.4	−14.3	14.6	−5.9	−3.1	2.8	−16.2
1999	4.3	7.5	−11.7	9.3	−9.9	8.0	3.4	−4.5	7.6	−7.7	1.2	4.1	8.6
2000	−2.5	−3.9	−1.2	−0.6	−1.0	2.4	−0.9	0.1	−1.9	−3.4	−0.4	−2.6	−15.0
2001	3.9	−6.2	−4.9	1.5	1.2	−1.9	−2.3	−0.4	11.0	−9.6	−1.6	10.4	−1.0
2002	−8.0	7.0	2.9	−2.0	10.7	−3.7	−5.3	−2.8	1.8	−0.9	−1.6	8.5	4.9
2003	1.0	−5.3	−2.9	4.2	−2.6	0.8	12.1	0.2	0.2	−1.5	6.3	10.8	24.0
2004	4.8	7.4	18.3	−23.3	0.3	−5.2	13.2	3.8	1.8	5.3	6.5	−12.1	14.6
2005	−1.3	9.6	−2.9	−3.3	7.4	−5.1	2.6	−5.6	9.6	0.9	10.6	6.0	30.0
2006	11.2	−0.8	17.5	18.3	−8.6	−12.3	4.1	14.6	−11.4	6.3	15.0	−8.4	45.5
2007	4.9	4.9	−5.5	0.9	−0.8	−7.4	4.4	−6.0	13.8	3.7	−1.9	5.3	15.3
2008	13.9	17.2	−13.1	−4.1	1.6	3.8	1.6	−23.0	−10.4	−20.7	5.1	10.4	−24.3
2009	11.2	4.3	−1.0	−5.1	26.7	−12.9	2.5	7.1	11.6	−2.4	14.0	−9.1	49.1
2010	−3.9	2.0	6.1	6.4	−1.2	1.6	−3.8	7.9	12.3	12.6	14.9	9.7	83.7
2011	−8.9	20.1	12.0	28.3	−21.2	−9.1	15.1	4.1	−28.0	14.2	−4.5	−14.9	−9.8
2012	19.1	4.5	−6.4	−4.5	−10.5								
TOTALS	102.5	156.8	−35.4	29.7	−6.4	−56.5	68.1	1.2	116.5	−42.9	101.6	45.3	
AVG.	2.6	3.9	−0.9	0.7	−0.2	−1.4	1.7	0.03	3.0	−1.1	2.6	1.2	
# Up	23	23	16	18	22	15	23	21	25	15	22	19	
# Down	16	17	24	22	18	23	16	18	14	23	17	20	

157

CORN CYCLE, SEASONAL PATTERN, AND TRADING GUIDE

Maize or corn, as it is more commonly called in the United States, is the world's most widely grown grain, with 844 million tonnes being produced worldwide in 2010, easily surpassing rice and wheat tonnage. The United States produces nearly half of the annual global harvest; China is a distant second, but rapidly gaining; and Brazil is third.

In the United States and many other parts of the world, one would find life without corn difficult, as it has an extremely diverse range of uses. Corn is used as a basic food staple, to manufacture plastic, and for nearly everything in between. Most recently, growing demand from ethanol production and animal feed has resulted in a tightening of supply and the growing concern for potential shortages.

Weather plays a significant role in corn production. Excess rain or cold weather can delay planting, and once the corn is in the ground, drought can be a threat to the harvest. The crop is most vulnerable to weather conditions in June and July in North America. Prices tend to make seasonal lows in the fall at harvest, when there is an abundance of supply, and then begin to rise steadily until spring planting begins.

CORN ONE-YEAR SEASONAL PATTERN

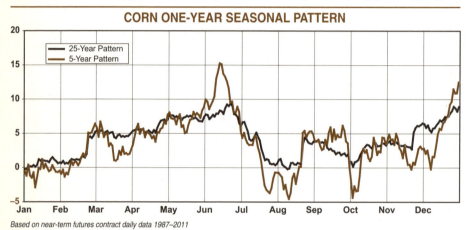

Based on near-term futures contract daily data 1987–2011

CORN NEAR-TERM CONTRACT ANNUAL HIGHS, LOWS, AND CLOSES SINCE 1970

YEAR	HIGH DATE	HIGH CLOSE	LOW DATE	LOW CLOSE	YEAR CLOSE	YEAR	HIGH DATE	HIGH CLOSE	LOW DATE	LOW CLOSE	YEAR CLOSE
1970	09/14	157 1/4	01/27	120 1/8	155 1/2	1992	03/09	278 3/4	10/28	205	216 1/2
1971	06/16	160 3/8	09/30	112 7/8	123 3/8	1993	12/30	306	02/08	211 3/4	306
1972	12/12	163 1/4	02/15	119 1/8	154 3/4	1994	01/13	310	10/10	213 3/4	231
1973	08/14	347 3/4	02/07	150 7/8	268 3/4	1995	12/29	369 1/4	01/03	228 1/2	369 1/4
1974	10/03	395	04/05	251 3/4	341 3/4	1996	05/17	504 1/2	12/30	258 1/4	258 1/4
1975	01/06	350 3/4	06/30	249	261 1/2	1997	04/01	313	07/07	229 1/4	265
1976	06/10	309	11/15	232	256 1/2	1998	03/11	282	08/31	199 1/2	213 1/2
1977	02/24	265 1/4	08/19	183 1/4	223 3/4	1999	03/22	232 1/4	07/13	186	204 1/2
1978	05/30	270	08/11	213 1/2	231 3/4	2000	05/03	250 3/4	08/11	174 3/4	231 3/4
1979	06/22	320 1/2	01/05	228 1/4	289 1/4	2001	07/12	234 1/4	06/21	188 1/4	209
1980	11/28	409	03/31	258 1/4	378	2002	09/11	292 1/2	04/15	196	235 3/4
1981	01/02	381 3/4	12/15	263	270 1/2	2003	05/15	255 3/4	07/23	205 1/2	246
1982	04/26	289	10/25	214	244 3/4	2004	04/02	330 1/2	11/11	197 1/4	204 3/4
1983	08/23	371	01/04	242 3/4	337 1/4	2005	07/18	260	11/18	191 1/4	215 3/4
1984	04/04	361 3/4	12/21	265 1/4	269 1/4	2006	11/30	390 1/2	01/19	205	390 1/4
1985	04/19	285 1/2	09/09	215 1/4	248 1/4	2007	12/31	455 1/2	07/23	310	455 1/2
1986	01/15	249 1/4	12/30	160	160	2008	06/26	768 1/4	12/05	309 1/4	407
1987	06/16	202 1/4	02/13	142 3/4	184 3/4	2009	06/02	449 1/2	09/04	306 1/4	414 1/2
1988	06/27	357 1/2	01/04	187 1/2	284 1/2	2010	12/31	629	06/29	333 1/4	629
1989	01/10	289 1/2	08/03	217 1/4	239 3/4	2011	06/10	787	12/15	579	646 1/2
1990	06/12	292 1/4	11/21	220 1/2	231 3/4	2012*	03/16	673	05/31	555 1/4	AT PRESS TIME
1991	04/23	263 1/4	07/08	219 1/2	251 1/2						

*Through May 31, 2012

CORN NEAR-TERM CONTRACT MONTHLY CLOSING PRICES

	Jan	Feb	Mar	Apr	May	Jun	Jul	Aug	Sep	Oct	Nov	Dec
1970	120 3/8	123 1/8	122 7/8	129 1/4	129 3/8	137 5/8	130 7/8	154 1/2	149 1/2	145 7/8	152 1/4	155 1/2
1971	153 7/8	152 1/2	146 1/8	144 1/2	149 7/8	150 1/4	132 1/2	118 5/8	112 7/8	115 3/4	119 3/4	123 3/8
1972	120 3/4	121 1/4	124 1/4	126 7/8	125 3/8	124 1/8	127 5/8	134 1/4	140 1/8	136 3/4	143 7/8	154 3/4
1973	161 1/2	158 5/8	155 1/2	164 7/8	218 3/8	199 3/4	288	250 1/2	252 1/4	238 1/2	265	268 3/4
1974	301 3/4	322 3/4	278	277 3/4	266	289 1/4	379 1/2	342 1/4	387 1/2	380 3/4	375 1/4	341 3/4
1975	311 1/4	262 1/4	298 3/4	285 1/4	270 1/2	249	287	302 3/4	303 1/4	277 3/4	279	261 1/2
1976	265	278	265 1/2	273 3/4	290 3/4	285 1/2	280 1/4	279 3/4	266 3/4	252 1/4	248 3/4	256 1/2
1977	253 1/2	262	251 3/4	252 1/2	249 1/2	225 3/4	194 1/4	191 3/4	203	214	228 3/4	223 3/4
1978	226 1/4	228 1/2	256 1/4	246 3/4	269 1/2	251 1/2	228	222 1/4	226 1/4	234 1/4	238 1/4	231 3/4
1979	234 1/4	246 3/4	251 1/2	265 3/4	268	299 1/2	281 1/2	286 3/4	282 1/2	264 1/2	291 1/4	289 1/4
1980	274 3/4	276 1/4	258 1/4	278 1/2	276 3/4	290 3/4	335 1/4	357 1/2	348 3/4	373 1/2	409	378
1981	355 1/2	369 3/4	364 3/4	367 1/2	351 3/4	334 1/2	338 1/2	306 1/4	288	287 1/2	280 1/4	270 1/2
1982	274	270	274 1/4	286 1/4	275	265 1/4	245 3/4	229 1/2	222	215 1/4	241	244 3/4
1983	267 3/4	281 1/2	312 3/4	318 1/4	304 1/2	297 1/4	320 1/4	359 1/2	354 3/4	344 3/4	340 3/4	337 1/4
1984	329 1/4	332 1/4	353 1/4	342 1/4	350 1/2	328 1/2	294 1/4	283 1/2	278 1/2	274 1/2	278 1/4	269 1/4
1985	272 1/2	271 1/4	281 1/4	279 3/4	274 1/2	255 1/2	231	218 3/4	224 3/4	232 3/4	243 3/4	248 1/4
1986	244	227	234 3/4	232 3/4	237	184	165 1/4	165 1/4	176 3/4	173 1/4	177 3/4	160
1987	157	153 3/4	162 1/2	184 1/4	188 3/4	186 1/2	163 1/2	166 1/2	179 3/4	179 1/2	196 1/2	184 3/4
1988	196 3/4	209 1/4	209 3/4	211 1/4	224 1/4	337 3/4	275	296 1/2	285 3/4	282 1/4	270 1/2	284 1/2
1989	274 3/4	278 1/2	268 1/2	270 1/2	260 3/4	255 1/2	222 1/2	236 3/4	233	237 1/2	241 3/4	239 3/4
1990	238 1/4	253 1/4	261 1/4	283	278	289 1/2	260 1/4	233 1/4	228	229 1/4	237 3/4	231 3/4
1991	244 1/4	251	252 3/4	254	245 3/4	224	258	254 3/4	249 1/4	251	247 1/2	251 1/2
1992	264 1/4	273 1/2	264 1/4	249 1/2	259 1/2	253 1/4	220 1/4	217 1/4	215 1/4	207 1/4	221 1/2	216 1/2
1993	214 1/2	219 1/4	230 1/4	232 1/2	224 1/2	229	235 3/4	237 1/2	244 3/4	257 3/4	285 1/2	306
1994	290 1/4	293 3/4	274 3/4	272	278 3/4	244 1/2	218 3/4	222 3/4	215 3/4	215 3/4	223	231
1995	229 1/2	242	250	255 1/4	266	278	281 3/4	293 3/4	311 3/4	332 1/2	337 3/4	369 1/4
1996	369	389 1/4	409	452	477 1/4	397 3/4	354 1/4	343 3/4	296 3/4	266	271	258 1/4
1997	270 1/4	295 1/4	310	293 1/4	270 3/4	238	265 1/2	269 1/4	257 3/4	279 3/4	280 3/4	265
1998	273	270 1/4	259	252 1/4	238 1/2	253 1/4	217 1/2	199 1/2	209	219	230	213 1/2
1999	214 1/2	210 1/4	225 1/2	218 3/4	219 1/2	216 1/4	203 1/4	219 1/4	208 1/4	199 1/2	200 1/2	204 1/2
2000	220	224	236	232	225	195 3/4	180 1/4	196 1/2	197 3/4	206	220 1/2	231 3/4
2001	209	222 1/2	203 1/4	207 1/2	192 3/4	197 1/4	218 3/4	232 1/4	214 1/2	205 1/2	220 1/2	209
2002	206	207 1/2	202 1/2	200 1/2	214	233	247 1/4	268	251 1/2	247 1/2	241 1/2	235 3/4
2003	238 1/4	233 1/4	236 1/2	231 1/4	244 1/4	223 3/4	206	241 3/4	220 1/4	247 1/4	248 3/4	246
2004	276 1/4	303	320	321 1/4	304	262 1/2	217 1/4	237 3/4	205 1/2	202 1/2	203 3/4	204 3/4
2005	197	222 3/4	213	213 1/2	222	222 1/4	236 1/2	216 1/2	205 1/2	196 1/4	201 3/4	215 3/4
2006	218 3/4	238 3/4	236	249	251 1/4	246	239	248	262 1/2	320 3/4	390 1/2	390 1/4
2007	404	435 1/2	374 1/2	367 1/2	390 1/4	340	325 3/4	340	373	375 1/2	401 1/2	455 1/2
2008	501 1/4	556 1/2	567 1/4	612 1/4	599 1/4	737 3/4	587 1/2	585	487 1/2	401 1/2	365 3/4	407
2009	379	359	404 3/4	403 1/2	436 1/4	354 1/2	339 1/2	329 3/4	344	366	417 1/2	414 1/2
2010	356 1/2	389	345	375 1/4	359	362 3/4	392 3/4	439 1/4	495 3/4	582	544	629
2011	659 1/2	731	693 1/4	756 1/2	747 1/2	648	665 1/2	767 1/2	592 1/2	647	608	646 1/2
2012	639	658	644	634 1/4	555 1/4							

CORN NEAR-TERM CONTRACT MONTHLY PERCENT CHANGES

	Jan	Feb	Mar	Apr	May	Jun	Jul	Aug	Sep	Oct	Nov	Dec	Year's Change
1970	−0.6	2.3	−0.2	5.2	0.1	6.4	−4.9	18.0	−3.2	−2.4	4.4	2.1	28.4
1971	−1.0	−0.9	−4.2	−1.1	3.7	0.2	−11.8	−10.5	−4.8	2.5	3.5	3.0	−20.7
1972	−2.1	0.4	2.5	2.1	−1.2	−1.0	2.8	5.2	4.4	−2.4	5.2	7.6	25.4
1973	4.4	−1.8	−2.0	6.0	32.4	−8.5	44.2	−13.0	0.7	−5.5	11.1	1.4	73.7
1974	12.3	7.0	−13.9	−0.1	−4.2	8.7	31.2	−9.8	13.2	−1.7	−1.4	−8.9	27.2
1975	−8.9	−15.7	13.9	−4.5	−5.2	−7.9	15.3	5.5	0.2	−8.4	0.5	−6.3	−23.5
1976	1.3	4.9	−4.5	3.1	6.2	−1.8	−1.8	−0.2	−4.6	−5.4	−1.4	3.1	−1.9
1977	−1.2	3.4	−3.9	0.3	−1.2	−9.5	−14.0	−1.3	5.9	5.4	6.9	−2.2	−12.8
1978	1.1	1.0	12.1	−3.7	9.2	−6.7	−9.3	−2.5	1.8	3.5	1.7	−2.7	3.6
1979	1.1	5.3	1.9	5.7	0.8	11.8	−6.0	1.9	−1.5	−6.4	10.1	−0.7	24.8
1980	−5.0	0.5	−6.5	7.8	−0.6	5.1	15.3	6.6	−2.4	7.1	9.5	−7.6	30.7
1981	−6.0	4.0	−1.4	0.8	−4.3	−4.9	1.2	−9.5	−6.0	−0.2	−2.5	−3.5	−28.4
1982	1.3	−1.5	1.6	4.4	−3.9	−3.5	−7.4	−6.6	−3.3	−3.0	12.0	1.6	−9.5
1983	9.4	5.1	11.1	1.8	−4.3	−2.4	7.7	12.3	−1.3	−2.8	−1.2	−1.0	37.8
1984	−2.4	0.9	6.3	−3.1	2.4	−6.3	−10.4	−3.7	−1.8	−1.4	1.4	−3.2	−20.2
1985	1.2	−0.5	3.7	−0.5	−1.9	−6.9	−9.6	−5.3	2.7	3.6	4.7	1.8	−7.8
1986	−1.7	−7.0	3.4	−0.9	1.8	−22.4	−10.2	N/C	7.0	−2.0	2.6	−10.0	−35.5
1987	−1.9	−2.1	5.7	13.4	2.4	−1.2	−12.3	1.8	8.0	−0.1	9.5	−6.0	15.5
1988	6.5	6.4	0.2	0.7	6.2	50.6	−18.6	7.8	−3.6	−1.2	−4.2	5.2	54.0
1989	−3.4	1.4	−3.6	0.7	−3.6	−2.0	−12.9	6.4	−1.6	1.9	1.8	−0.8	−15.7
1990	−0.6	6.3	3.2	8.3	−1.8	4.1	−10.1	−10.4	−2.3	0.5	3.7	−2.5	−3.3
1991	5.4	2.8	0.7	0.5	−3.2	−8.9	15.2	−1.3	−2.2	0.7	−1.4	1.6	8.5
1992	5.1	3.5	−3.4	−5.6	4.0	−2.4	−13.0	−1.4	−0.9	−3.7	6.9	−2.3	−13.9
1993	−0.9	2.2	5.0	1.0	−3.4	2.0	2.9	0.7	3.1	5.3	10.8	7.2	41.3
1994	−5.1	1.2	−6.5	−1.0	2.5	−12.3	−10.5	1.8	−3.1	N/C	3.4	3.6	−24.5
1995	−0.6	5.4	3.3	2.1	4.2	4.5	1.3	4.3	6.1	6.7	1.6	9.3	59.8
1996	−0.1	5.5	5.1	10.5	5.6	−16.7	−10.9	−3.0	−13.7	−10.4	1.9	−4.7	−30.1
1997	4.6	9.3	5.0	−5.4	−7.7	−12.1	11.6	1.4	−4.3	8.5	0.4	−5.6	2.6
1998	3.0	−1.0	−4.2	−2.6	−5.5	6.2	−14.1	−8.3	4.8	4.8	5.0	−7.2	−19.4
1999	0.5	−2.0	7.3	−3.0	0.3	−1.5	−6.0	7.9	−5.0	−4.2	0.5	2.0	−4.2
2000	7.6	1.8	5.4	−1.7	−3.0	−13.0	−7.9	9.0	0.6	4.2	7.0	5.1	13.3
2001	−9.8	6.5	−8.7	2.1	−7.1	2.3	10.9	6.2	−7.6	−4.2	7.3	−5.2	−9.8
2002	−1.4	0.7	−2.4	−1.0	6.7	8.9	6.1	8.4	−6.2	−1.6	−2.4	−2.4	12.8
2003	1.1	−2.1	1.4	−2.2	5.6	−8.4	−7.9	17.4	−8.9	12.3	0.6	−1.1	4.3
2004	12.3	9.7	5.6	0.5	−5.4	−13.7	−17.2	9.4	−13.6	−1.5	0.6	0.5	−16.8
2005	−3.8	13.1	−4.4	0.2	4.0	0.1	6.4	−8.5	−5.1	−4.5	2.8	6.9	5.4
2006	1.4	9.1	−1.2	5.5	0.9	−2.1	−2.8	3.8	5.8	22.2	21.7	−0.1	80.9
2007	3.5	7.8	−14.0	−1.9	6.2	−12.9	−4.2	4.4	9.7	0.7	6.9	13.4	16.7
2008	10.0	11.0	1.9	7.9	−2.1	23.1	−20.4	−0.4	−16.7	−17.6	−8.9	11.3	−10.6
2009	−6.9	−5.3	12.7	−0.3	8.1	−18.7	−4.2	−2.9	4.3	6.4	14.1	−0.7	1.8
2010	−14.0	9.1	−11.3	8.8	−4.3	1.0	8.3	11.8	12.9	17.4	−6.5	15.6	51.7
2011	4.8	10.8	−5.2	9.1	−1.2	−13.3	2.7	15.3	−22.8	9.2	−6.0	6.3	2.8
2012	−1.2	3.0	−2.1	−1.5	−12.5								
TOTALS	19.3	121.5	15.4	68.4	25.7	−86.0	−75.3	68.7	−55.3	32.3	144.2	23.9	
AVG.	0.4	2.8	0.4	1.6	0.6	−2.0	−1.8	1.6	−1.3	0.8	3.4	0.6	
# Up	21	32	23	25	21	15	16	23	17	19	32	20	
# Down	22	11	20	18	22	27	26	18	25	22	10	22	

SOYBEANS CYCLE, SEASONAL PATTERN, AND TRADING GUIDE

The United States is the leading producer of soybeans, followed by Brazil and Argentina. For the most part, this crop is grown in the Corn Belt, which consists of Illinois, Iowa, Indiana, Ohio, Missouri, and Minnesota. Generally, it is planted in April through June, but it can be delayed, if necessary. For this reason, soybeans can be used as an alternative crop for corn and cotton when weather affects the planting of other crops. Harvesting is generally complete by October.

There are three soybean-related futures contracts: soybeans, soybean meal, and bean oil. Soybeans are the cash crop and are grown to yield soybean meal and bean oil. Soybean meal is used to enrich the feed for hogs, cattle, and poultry. Bean oil is used in food-related products like shortening, salad dressings, and cooking oils. Of the two by-products, soybean meal is more valuable because there is little in the form of a competing product except for animal bone meal and fish meal, which are used as an animal feed.

Unfortunately, soybeans cannot be stored for extended periods, making their price more volatile. The seasonal price pattern shows a peak in May or June, as the U.S. crop is now in the ground and developing and the Southern Hemisphere crop is being marketed. Under normal growing conditions, with the exception of droughts, the July–August period is usually a bearish time for soybeans. The seasonal lows occur, in general, in the fall due to the harvest, which makes fresh supplies available. This also puts pressure on bean meal and bean oil.

SOYBEANS ONE-YEAR SEASONAL PATTERN

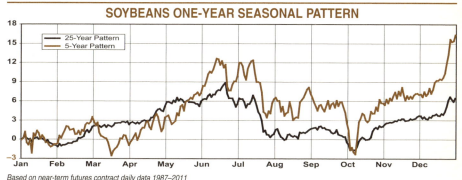

Based on near-term futures contract daily data 1987–2011

SOYBEANS NEAR-TERM CONTRACT ANNUAL HIGHS, LOWS, AND CLOSES SINCE 1969

YEAR	HIGH DATE	HIGH CLOSE	LOW DATE	LOW CLOSE	YEAR CLOSE	YEAR	HIGH DATE	HIGH CLOSE	LOW DATE	LOW CLOSE	YEAR CLOSE
1969	05/13	271 3/8	09/02	234 7/8	251 7/8	1991	08/02	642 3/4	07/08	515 3/4	557
1970	10/27	312	01/05	251 1/4	297 7/8	1992	06/02	630	10/02	527 1/4	574 1/4
1971	07/16	347 1/2	04/08	289 3/4	317	1993	07/19	737	02/08	564 3/4	712 1/2
1972	12/12	435 1/2	01/14	307	426 1/2	1994	05/23	732 1/4	10/07	527 1/4	561 1/2
1973	06/04	1211	01/08	422	586 1/4	1995	12/29	744 3/4	02/01	546 1/2	744 3/4
1974	10/04	949	05/06	523	715	1996	04/25	831	11/01	666 1/2	687 3/4
1975	01/02	723 1/2	12/15	445 1/4	459	1997	05/06	892	07/02	607 1/2	676 1/4
1976	07/09	750 1/4	01/26	456 3/4	711 1/4	1998	02/10	693	08/31	511 1/2	541 1/4
1977	04/21	1046 1/2	09/14	505 1/4	603 3/4	1999	01/08	555	07/08	410	469 3/4
1978	05/30	745 1/4	02/09	558 1/2	690 1/2	2000	05/04	572 1/4	08/07	446 3/4	509 3/4
1979	06/22	838 1/2	10/26	655 1/2	664 3/4	2001	07/17	528	12/31	422 1/4	422 1/4
1980	11/05	954 1/2	04/01	579 1/2	818 1/2	2002	09/11	588 3/4	01/02	418 1/4	565
1981	01/06	842 3/4	12/21	606 3/4	626 1/4	2003	10/29	803 1/2	07/31	509	794
1982	04/23	676	10/04	518 1/4	573 1/4	2004	03/22	1055 3/4	11/05	505 1/4	547 1/4
1983	09/09	948	01/04	571 1/2	832 3/4	2005	06/24	748 1/4	02/04	499 1/2	613 1/2
1984	05/21	893 1/4	12/12	584 3/4	585 1/4	2006	12/29	697 1/4	09/12	538 1/2	697 1/4
1985	03/19	609	11/25	484 3/4	542 3/4	2007	12/26	1239 1/2	01/09	664 1/2	1214 1/4
1986	01/08	554 1/2	08/25	468 1/4	494 3/4	2008	07/03	1649	12/05	783 1/2	980
1987	12/23	618 1/2	02/26	480 1/2	614 3/4	2009	06/11	1267	03/02	844	1048 1/2
1988	06/21	1046 1/2	02/02	597	819 1/4	2010	12/31	1403	02/03	908	1403
1989	01/06	829 1/2	10/13	544 1/4	582 1/4	2011	08/31	1457 1/2	12/14	1100	1207 3/4
1990	07/03	663 3/4	01/25	558 1/4	574 3/4	2012*	04/30	1505 1/2	01/13	1158 1/4	AT PRESS TIME

*Through May 31, 2012

SOYBEANS NEAR-TERM CONTRACT MONTHLY CLOSING PRICES

	Jan	Feb	Mar	Apr	May	Jun	Jul	Aug	Sep	Oct	Nov	Dec
1969	264 1/2	266 3/8	262 1/2	270	267 1/8	263 1/4	246 1/2	236 1/2	236 3/8	249 5/8	243 7/8	251 7/8
1970	254 1/8	261	259 1/4	268 5/8	271	290	283 3/4	279 1/4	286	308	299	297 7/8
1971	307 3/8	307 3/4	300 1/2	295 7/8	311	323	330 1/8	315	309 3/4	323 1/4	310 1/2	317
1972	314 3/8	335 1/8	343 1/2	350 1/2	350	338 3/4	334 1/2	336 5/8	347 5/8	354 7/8	379 1/2	426 1/2
1973	490 3/8	609 1/4	538 3/4	678 1/4	1058	860	910	701	645	540 1/2	602 1/2	586 1/4
1974	644	627 1/4	616 1/4	548 1/4	547	570 1/2	89	732 1/2	878	823 3/4	782 1/2	715
1975	602 3/4	507 1/4	610	533	502 3/4	496 3/4	582 1/2	569 1/2	568 3/4	503 1/2	485 1/2	459
1976	467 1/2	486 1/2	469 3/4	487 1/4	579	677 1/2	608 1/2	673	632	684	674 1/2	711 1/4
1977	723 1/2	782 1/4	893 1/2	983	960	713 1/2	566 1/2	516	534 1/4	559	585 3/4	603 3/4
1978	564 3/4	590 1/2	689 1/2	702 1/2	737	652 1/4	621 3/4	640 1/2	651	718	678	690 1/2
1979	706	766	771 1/4	735	739	741 1/2	715 1/2	721 3/4	712 1/4	667 3/4	681 3/4	664 3/4
1980	673	657 1/2	583	615 1/2	623 3/4	688	783 3/4	817	811	923	933	818 1/2
1981	725 1/2	761	783 1/2	801 1/4	764 3/4	710	739 1/4	671 1/2	648	671 1/2	646 1/2	626 1/4
1982	656 3/4	632 3/4	640	665 3/4	635 3/4	618	600 3/4	559 1/2	534 1/4	547	573 1/2	573 1/4
1983	604 1/2	575 1/2	637	657 1/4	607 1/2	619	708 1/2	911 1/2	866	830 1/2	796 1/2	832 3/4
1984	730 3/4	765	789	782 1/2	847	738 1/4	612 1/2	636 1/2	591 3/4	631	609	585 1/2
1985	601 1/4	573	605 1/2	594 1/2	567 1/2	551 3/4	521 3/4	511 3/4	512 3/4	527 1/2	499	542 3/4
1986	533	529 3/4	541 1/2	551	525 1/4	488 3/4	500 1/4	479 1/2	486 1/2	500	503 1/2	494 3/4
1987	500 1/4	483	496 1/2	537	548 3/4	543 1/2	524 1/2	504 1/4	532	541 1/2	605 1/4	614 3/4
1988	609 1/2	642 1/2	653 1/2	698 1/2	798	986	778 1/2	867 1/2	813	789 1/4	763 3/4	819 1/4
1989	772 3/4	773 1/2	738 1/4	729 1/2	714	670	588	587 1/2	568	572 1/4	582 3/4	582 1/4
1990	561	580 3/4	595	648 1/2	607 1/4	638 3/4	599 1/4	613 3/4	617 1/2	609 1/4	589 1/2	574 3/4
1991	566 3/4	588	574 3/4	589 1/2	581 3/4	531	590	590 1/2	587	567	557	557
1992	572	589 1/4	588 1/4	580 1/4	614	611	555 1/2	541	540 3/4	552 3/4	563 3/4	574 1/4
1993	574	580	588 1/4	591 1/4	608 1/2	656 1/4	686 1/2	663 1/2	629 3/4	629 1/2	671 1/2	712 1/2
1994	686 3/4	683 3/4	681 3/4	676 1/2	701	640 1/2	575 1/4	573 3/4	536	554	563 1/2	561 1/2
1995	547 1/2	564 3/4	574	580	580 3/4	588 1/4	606	623	646	684 1/2	686 1/4	744 3/4
1996	738 3/4	745	751	795	788 1/4	757 1/2	747	794 1/2	758	669	712 3/4	687 3/4
1997	738 1/4	793 1/4	855 3/4	887	880 1/2	644	685	625 1/2	621 1/2	696 1/4	718 1/4	676 1/4
1998	672 3/4	658 1/4	645	638 1/2	618 1/2	632	560 3/4	511 1/2	520 3/4	568 1/4	593 1/2	541 1/4
1999	506 3/4	458	483 3/4	486 1/2	461 3/4	450 1/2	433 1/4	483	491 1/4	482 3/4	476 1/4	469 3/4
2000	508	511	545 1/2	539 1/4	517 1/2	482 3/4	454	505	490 1/2	470 1/4	506	509 3/4
2001	459 1/2	455 3/4	428 1/2	438	451	474 1/4	512 1/2	486	451 1/4	436 3/4	444 1/2	422 1/4
2002	430 1/4	440 1/4	476 1/4	466 3/4	508 3/4	528 3/4	536 1/2	544 3/4	545 3/4	566 1/2	578 3/4	565
2003	564	575	574 1/2	627 1/4	624 1/2	614 1/4	509	589	677 1/4	797 3/4	756 1/4	794
2004	819 1/2	937 1/2	995	1013	814	782 1/2	569	627 1/4	527	533 1/2	534 3/4	547 1/4
2005	514 3/4	622	627 1/2	626 1/4	680 1/4	656	686 3/4	598 3/4	573 1/4	576	558	613 1/2
2006	594 1/4	594	571 1/2	601	579 1/2	600 1/2	599 3/4	555 3/4	547 1/2	644 1/4	685 1/2	697 1/4
2007	719 1/2	787 1/2	761 1/4	743	806 1/4	855 3/4	857 1/2	882 1/2	991 1/4	1025 3/4	1080	1214 1/4
2008	1274 1/2	1536 1/2	1197 1/4	1314	1363 1/2	1598	1404	1324	1045	933	883	980
2009	980	872	952	1055	1184	1119 1/4	982	979 1/2	927	976 1/2	1060 1/2	1048 1/2
2010	914	961	941	999	937 3/4	931	1005	1010	1106 3/4	1236	1243	1403
2011	1413	1364 3/4	1410 1/4	1394	1376	1299 1/2	1357 1/4	1457 1/2	1179	1217 1/4	1131 1/4	1207 3/4
2012	1199	1320	1403	1505 1/2	1340							

SOYBEANS NEAR-TERM CONTRACT MONTHLY PERCENT CHANGES

	Jan	Feb	Mar	Apr	May	Jun	Jul	Aug	Sep	Oct	Nov	Dec	Year's Change
1969	0.2	0.7	−1.5	2.9	−1.1	−1.5	−6.4	−4.1	−0.1	5.6	−2.3	3.3	−4.5
1970	0.9	2.7	−0.7	3.6	0.9	7.0	−2.2	−1.6	2.4	7.7	−2.9	−0.4	18.3
1971	3.2	0.1	−2.4	−1.5	5.1	3.9	2.2	−4.6	−1.7	4.4	−3.9	2.1	6.4
1972	−0.8	6.6	2.5	2.0	−0.1	−3.2	−1.3	0.6	3.3	2.1	6.9	12.4	34.5
1973	15.0	24.2	−11.6	25.9	56.0	−18.7	5.8	−23.0	−8.0	−16.2	11.5	−2.7	37.5
1974	9.9	−2.6	−1.8	−11.0	−0.2	4.3	56.9	−18.2	19.9	−6.2	−5.0	−8.6	22.0
1975	−15.7	−15.8	20.3	−12.6	−5.7	−1.2	17.3	−2.2	−0.1	−11.5	−3.6	−5.5	−35.8
1976	1.9	4.1	−3.4	3.7	18.8	17.0	−10.2	10.6	−6.1	8.2	−1.4	5.4	55.0
1977	1.7	8.1	14.2	10.0	−2.3	−25.7	−20.6	−8.9	3.5	4.6	4.8	3.1	−15.1
1978	−6.5	4.6	16.8	1.9	4.9	−11.5	−4.7	3.0	1.6	10.3	−5.6	1.8	14.4
1979	2.2	8.5	0.7	−4.7	0.5	0.3	−3.5	0.9	−1.3	−6.2	2.1	−2.5	−3.7
1980	1.2	−2.3	−11.3	5.6	1.3	10.3	13.9	4.2	−0.7	13.8	1.1	−12.3	23.1
1981	−11.4	4.9	3.0	2.3	−4.6	−7.2	4.1	−9.2	−3.5	3.6	−3.7	−3.1	−23.5
1982	4.9	−3.7	1.1	4.0	−4.5	−2.8	−2.8	−6.9	−4.5	2.4	4.8	−0.04	−8.5
1983	5.5	−4.8	10.7	3.2	−7.6	1.9	14.5	28.7	−5.0	−4.1	−4.1	4.6	45.3
1984	−12.2	4.7	3.1	−0.8	8.2	−12.8	−17.0	3.9	−7.0	6.6	−3.5	−3.9	−29.7
1985	2.7	−4.7	5.7	−1.8	−4.5	−2.8	−5.4	−1.9	0.2	2.9	−5.4	8.8	−7.3
1986	−1.8	−0.6	2.2	1.8	−4.7	−6.9	2.4	−4.1	1.5	2.8	0.7	−1.7	−8.8
1987	1.1	−3.4	2.8	8.2	2.2	−1.0	−3.5	−3.9	5.5	1.8	11.8	1.6	24.3
1988	−0.9	5.4	1.7	6.9	14.2	23.6	−21.0	11.4	−6.3	−2.9	−3.2	7.3	33.3
1989	−5.7	0.1	−4.6	−1.2	−2.1	−6.2	−12.2	−0.1	−3.3	0.7	1.8	−0.1	−28.9
1990	−3.6	3.5	2.5	9.0	−6.4	5.2	−6.2	2.4	0.6	−1.3	−3.2	−2.5	−1.3
1991	−1.4	3.7	−2.3	2.6	−1.3	−8.7	11.1	0.1	−0.6	−3.4	−1.8	N/C	−3.1
1992	2.7	3.0	−0.2	−1.4	5.8	−0.5	−9.1	−2.6	−0.1	2.2	2.0	1.9	3.1
1993	−0.04	1.0	1.4	0.5	2.9	7.8	4.6	−3.4	−5.1	−0.04	6.7	6.1	24.1
1994	−3.6	−0.4	−0.3	−0.8	3.6	−8.6	−10.2	−0.3	−6.6	3.4	1.7	−0.4	−21.2
1995	−2.5	3.2	1.6	1.0	0.1	1.3	3.0	2.8	3.7	6.0	0.3	8.5	32.6
1996	−0.8	0.8	0.8	5.9	−0.8	−3.9	−1.4	6.4	−4.6	−11.7	6.5	−3.5	−7.7
1997	7.3	7.5	7.9	3.7	−0.7	−26.9	6.4	−8.7	−0.6	12.0	3.2	−5.8	−1.7
1998	−0.5	−2.2	−2.0	−1.0	−3.1	2.2	−11.3	−8.8	1.8	9.1	4.4	−8.8	−20.0
1999	−6.4	−9.6	5.6	0.6	−5.1	−2.4	−3.8	11.5	1.7	−1.7	−1.3	−1.4	−13.2
2000	8.1	0.6	6.8	−1.1	−4.0	−6.7	−6.0	11.2	−2.9	−4.1	7.6	0.7	8.5
2001	−9.9	−0.8	−6.0	2.2	3.0	5.2	8.1	−5.2	−7.2	−3.2	1.8	−5.0	−17.2
2002	1.9	2.3	8.2	−2.0	9.0	3.9	1.5	1.5	0.2	3.8	2.2	−2.4	33.8
2003	−0.2	2.0	−0.1	9.2	−0.4	−1.6	−17.1	15.7	15.0	17.8	−5.2	5.0	40.5
2004	3.2	14.4	6.1	1.8	−19.6	−3.9	−27.3	10.2	−16.0	1.2	0.2	2.3	−31.1
2005	−5.9	20.8	0.9	−0.2	8.6	−3.6	4.7	−12.8	−4.3	0.5	−3.1	9.9	12.1
2006	−3.1	−0.04	−3.8	5.2	−3.6	3.6	−0.1	−7.3	−1.5	17.7	6.4	1.7	13.7
2007	3.2	9.5	−3.3	−2.4	8.5	6.1	0.2	2.9	12.3	3.5	5.3	12.4	74.1
2008	5.0	20.6	−22.1	9.8	3.8	17.2	−12.1	−5.7	−21.1	−10.7	−5.4	11.0	−19.3
2009	N/C	−11.0	9.2	10.8	12.2	−5.5	−12.3	−0.3	−5.4	5.3	8.6	−1.1	7.0
2010	−12.8	5.1	−2.1	6.2	−6.1	−0.7	7.9	0.5	9.6	11.7	0.6	12.9	33.8
2011	0.7	−3.4	3.3	−1.2	−1.3	−5.6	4.4	7.4	−19.1	3.2	−7.1	6.8	−13.9
2012	−0.7	10.1	6.3	7.3	−11.0								
TOTALS	−23.9	117.5	65.9	114.1	68.8	−59.3	−58.7	−7.9	−59.9	91.7	31.3	57.9	
AVG.	−0.5	2.7	1.5	2.6	1.6	−1.4	−1.4	−0.2	−1.4	2.1	0.7	1.3	
# Up	21	29	26	29	20	17	18	20	16	29	24	22	
# Down	22	15	18	15	24	26	25	23	27	14	19	20	

CBOT WHEAT CYCLE, SEASONAL PATTERN, AND TRADING GUIDE

This grade of wheat is called winter wheat, since it is planted in the fall and harvested in midsummer. CBOT wheat is a lower-end soft red wheat that is primarily used in pastries, cakes and cookies, and other related products.

Since harvest is typically around the June–July time period, this is when supplies are most abundant, even in years when crop yields are less than average. This is what we call the harvest lows, as we now begin to sell and export our inventories. After the new year, prices tend to continue to decline, as Southern Hemisphere supplies enter the world market. This may explain a well-known phenomenon called the "February Break," whereby wheat prices usually show some degree of decline during the month of February.

CBOT WHEAT ONE-YEAR SEASONAL PATTERN

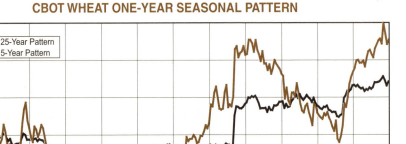

Based on near-term futures contract daily data 1987–2011

CBOT WHEAT NEAR-TERM CONTRACT ANNUAL HIGHS, LOWS, AND CLOSES SINCE 1969

YEAR	HIGH DATE	HIGH CLOSE	LOW DATE	LOW CLOSE	YEAR CLOSE	YEAR	HIGH DATE	HIGH CLOSE	LOW DATE	LOW CLOSE	YEAR CLOSE
1969	12/24	148	07/28	121 1/4	147 3/8	1991	12/26	405 3/4	01/15	246 1/4	404 3/4
1970	11/05	179	05/28	134 1/2	168 1/2	1992	02/10	459 1/2	08/13	305 3/4	353 3/4
1971	01/15	172 1/2	08/11	141 1/2	163 1/8	1993	01/19	392 1/2	06/17	277 1/2	378 1/4
1972	12/14	269 1/2	06/23	141 1/8	264	1994	10/11	416 1/4	07/06	313 1/2	401 1/4
1973	12/31	545	03/21	214 3/4	545	1995	12/29	512 1/4	03/10	341 1/2	512 1/4
1974	02/15	631 1/2	05/09	336	458 1/2	1996	04/25	628 1/2	11/05	368 3/4	381 1/4
1975	08/22	463	06/02	295 3/4	335 3/4	1997	04/22	447	07/07	321 3/4	325 3/4
1976	02/27	401 3/4	11/11	255 3/4	277 1/2	1998	03/11	348	08/05	246 3/4	276 1/4
1977	02/24	293 3/4	08/19	217 1/4	279 1/4	1999	03/29	294 1/4	12/13	237 3/4	248 1/2
1978	11/30	369	02/28	260 3/4	343 1/4	2000	06/22	289 3/4	08/07	233 1/2	279 1/2
1979	06/22	489 1/2	04/23	326 1/2	454 1/4	2001	11/23	296 1/4	06/28	254 1/2	289
1980	10/28	541 1/2	04/18	380 1/2	501	2002	09/09	422	04/29	265	325
1981	01/02	508 1/2	12/23	376 1/4	391 1/2	2003	12/03	414 3/4	03/28	279 1/4	377
1982	01/08	402	10/21	301 3/4	330 3/4	2004	03/22	422 3/4	12/02	296 1/4	307 1/2
1983	08/22	423 1/4	02/28	321 1/2	363 1/2	2005	03/15	368	02/04	287 3/4	339 1/4
1984	04/04	377 1/4	02/13	321 3/4	347 3/4	2006	10/16	542 1/2	01/18	322 1/2	501
1985	04/08	370 3/4	08/20	280 1/4	343 1/4	2007	12/14	979 1/2	04/03	419	885
1986	01/02	339 1/2	07/01	240 1/2	274 1/4	2008	03/12	1282 1/2	12/05	475 1/2	610 3/4
1987	12/18	321	07/21	256 3/4	310 3/4	2009	06/01	674 1/2	10/02	441 1/4	541 1/2
1988	12/23	440 1/2	03/10	297 3/4	440	2010	12/29	799 1/4	06/09	428	794 1/4
1989	01/06	448 3/4	06/08	381 3/4	409 1/4	2011	02/09	886	12/15	579 1/4	652 3/4
1990	01/03	410	11/20	245 1/4	260 1/2	2012*	05/21	704	01/18	592 1/4	AT PRESS TIME

*Through May 31, 2012

CBOT WHEAT NEAR-TERM CONTRACT MONTHLY CLOSING PRICES

	Jan	Feb	Mar	Apr	May	Jun	Jul	Aug	Sep	Oct	Nov	Dec
1969	134 3/8	131 5/8	125 7/8	130 1/8	128 1/8	127 3/4	123 3/4	133 5/8	134 7/8	135 1/4	143 5/8	147 3/8
1970	143 3/4	147 1/4	144 1/4	142 1/4	134 1/2	142	147 1/8	164 1/4	168 3/8	174 1/2	172 1/4	168 1/2
1971	166 1/2	162	158 1/8	151 3/4	157 1/2	156 1/2	147 5/8	149 3/4	146 7/8	161 3/8	155 1/2	163 1/8
1972	164 5/8	155	157 3/4	147 1/8	145 1/2	146	157 3/8	193 1/4	215 3/4	220 1/2	245 1/2	264
1973	247	235 3/4	222 3/4	233 3/8	281 1/4	268	364	497 1/2	491 1/2	430 1/2	472	545
1974	564 1/2	572	431 1/2	377	352 1/2	414	472	443 1/2	493	520 3/4	508 1/2	458 1/2
1975	379 1/2	349	387 1/4	328 3/4	305 1/2	307 1/2	366 3/4	425 1/2	429 1/2	386 1/4	355 1/2	335 3/4
1976	349 3/4	401 3/4	343 1/2	337 1/2	356 1/2	373 1/4	341	323 1/2	288 1/2	275	265 3/4	277 1/2
1977	274 1/4	275	272 3/4	265 1/2	246 1/4	251 1/2	225 1/2	230	252 1/4	259	275	279 1/4
1978	266 3/4	260 3/4	313 1/2	312	332	317 1/4	315 3/4	330 1/2	342 1/2	361 1/2	369	343 1/4
1979	351 1/2	353 1/4	339 3/4	347 1/2	366 3/4	433 1/2	410 1/2	456 1/2	450 3/4	421 1/4	456	454 1/4
1980	467 3/4	447 1/4	383 1/2	399 1/4	402 3/4	433 1/2	465	477	503 1/2	528 3/4	540 3/4	501
1981	465 3/4	457 1/2	433 3/4	443	412 1/4	389 3/4	407 1/2	417	424 3/4	439 1/4	439 1/2	391 1/2
1982	377	366 3/4	370 1/4	374 3/4	351 1/2	355 3/4	342 3/4	356 1/4	319 3/4	317 1/2	346	330 3/4
1983	343 1/2	321 1/2	360 1/4	361 1/2	343 1/4	356 3/4	372 3/4	410 1/4	370 3/4	354 1/2	355 3/4	363 1/2
1984	328 3/4	331 1/4	374	341 3/4	356	359 1/4	349 1/4	352	347	362 1/2	353 3/4	347 3/4
1985	350 3/4	336 1/4	356 1/2	327	315	321 1/4	295 1/4	287 3/4	297	323 3/4	334 3/4	343 1/4
1986	327 1/4	286 1/4	304 1/4	293 1/2	248 1/2	246	257 1/2	261 1/4	265 1/4	287	286 1/4	274 1/2
1987	288 1/4	280	284 1/2	274	274 1/4	263 1/4	261 1/4	286 3/4	289 1/4	296 1/2	318 1/4	310 3/4
1988	326	323 1/2	299 1/4	315 1/2	351 1/2	395 1/2	368 1/4	415 3/4	414 3/4	415 3/4	427 1/2	440
1989	440 1/2	434 3/4	403 3/4	405	387 1/2	404 3/4	384 1/2	399 1/4	407 1/4	394 1/4	407 3/4	409 1/4
1990	375 3/4	362 1/4	351 3/4	345 3/4	333 3/4	331	288 1/4	277 1/2	277 3/4	262	261 3/4	260 1/2
1991	263	269 1/2	286 3/4	283 1/4	287	275	294	321	332 1/2	363 1/2	366	404 3/4
1992	440 1/4	400	379	353 1/2	349 1/2	352 1/2	317 1/4	333	350 1/4	354 1/2	371	353 3/4
1993	380	333 1/4	347 1/4	301 1/4	288 1/4	287 1/4	304	315 1/2	318 3/4	335 1/2	350 1/2	378 1/4
1994	371 3/4	345 1/4	329 3/4	330 3/4	327 1/2	322 1/4	330 1/2	379 1/4	403 1/4	384 1/2	384 1/2	401 1/2
1995	373 1/2	347 1/4	343 1/4	351	373 1/4	446	464 1/4	462 3/4	492 1/4	497 3/4	495	512 1/4
1996	519 1/2	501 1/2	499 1/4	567	528 3/4	482 1/2	440	453 1/4	436	371 1/4	377 1/2	381 1/4
1997	359 3/4	375 1/4	397 1/2	433 1/2	360 1/4	332 1/4	362	394	354 1/4	360 1/2	357 3/4	325 3/4
1998	337 1/4	338 1/4	320 1/4	301 1/4	284 1/4	287 1/2	252 1/2	254	269 1/4	294 1/4	294 1/4	276 1/4
1999	275 1/2	248 1/2	280 1/4	268	252 1/4	264 1/4	263 3/4	282 1/4	275 3/4	255 3/4	249 1/2	248 1/2
2000	256 1/4	259	262 1/4	254 3/4	274 3/4	271 1/4	246 1/4	268 1/4	265	254 3/4	273 3/4	279 1/2
2001	273	276 3/4	255	283 1/4	267	258	278 1/2	289	270 3/4	293 1/4	289 1/2	289
2002	286	276	285	268 3/4	282 1/4	313	334	370	396 1/2	402 1/4	379 3/4	325
2003	320 1/2	310 1/4	286 3/4	282 3/4	324 1/4	310 1/2	348 1/2	381	360 1/4	369 1/2	406 3/4	377
2004	389	390 3/4	408	390	362	345 1/2	312 1/4	322 3/4	306 3/4	316 1/2	301 1/4	307 1/2
2005	291	345 1/4	331	326	331 3/4	331 1/2	327 3/4	317 1/2	346 1/4	317	320 3/4	339 1/4
2006	343 1/4	381	347 3/4	358 1/2	393 1/2	396	397 1/2	422 1/4	443	483	521 1/2	501
2007	467 1/2	488	438	495 1/2	517	597	630	775 1/2	939	808	885 1/2	885
2008	929 1/2	1086	929	801	761 1/2	858 3/4	783 3/4	801 1/4	680	536 1/4	561 1/4	610 3/4
2009	568	521 1/2	532 3/4	536 1/2	637 1/4	540 3/4	528 1/4	498 3/4	457 1/2	494 1/4	588 3/4	541 1/2
2010	474	519 1/4	450 1/2	503	457 3/4	480 1/4	661 1/2	685 3/4	674	717 1/4	690 3/4	794 1/4
2011	840 3/4	817	763 1/4	801 1/4	782 1/4	614 1/4	672 1/2	791 1/2	609 1/4	628 1/4	614	652 3/4
2012	666	668	660 3/4	654 1/2	643 3/4							

CBOT WHEAT NEAR-TERM CONTRACT MONTHLY PERCENT CHANGES

	Jan	Feb	Mar	Apr	May	Jun	Jul	Aug	Sep	Oct	Nov	Dec	Year's Change
1969	−0.8	−2.0	−4.4	3.4	−1.5	−0.3	−3.1	8.0	0.9	0.3	6.2	2.6	8.8
1970	−2.5	2.4	−2.0	−1.4	−5.4	5.6	3.6	11.6	2.5	3.6	−1.3	−2.2	14.3
1971	−1.2	−2.7	−2.4	−4.0	3.8	−0.6	−5.7	1.4	−1.9	9.9	−3.6	4.9	−3.2
1972	0.9	−5.8	1.8	−6.7	−1.1	0.3	7.8	22.8	11.6	2.2	11.3	7.5	61.8
1973	−6.4	−4.6	−5.5	4.8	20.5	−4.7	35.8	36.7	−1.2	−12.4	9.6	15.5	106.4
1974	3.6	1.3	−24.6	−12.6	−6.5	17.4	14.0	−6.0	11.2	5.6	−2.4	−9.8	−15.9
1975	−17.2	−8.0	11.0	−15.1	−7.1	0.7	19.3	16.0	0.9	−10.1	−8.0	−5.6	−26.8
1976	4.2	14.9	−14.5	−1.7	5.6	4.7	−8.6	−5.1	−10.8	−4.7	−3.4	4.4	−17.3
1977	−1.2	0.3	−0.8	−2.7	−7.3	2.1	−10.3	2.0	9.7	2.7	6.2	1.5	0.6
1978	−4.5	−2.2	20.2	−0.5	6.4	−4.4	−0.5	4.7	3.6	5.5	2.1	−7.0	22.9
1979	2.4	0.5	−3.8	2.3	5.5	18.2	−5.3	11.1	−1.2	−6.5	8.2	−0.4	32.3
1980	3.0	−4.4	−14.3	4.1	0.9	7.6	7.3	2.6	5.6	5.0	2.3	−7.4	10.3
1981	−7.0	−1.8	−5.2	2.1	−6.9	−5.5	4.6	2.3	1.9	3.4	0.1	−10.9	−21.9
1982	−3.7	−2.7	1.0	1.2	−6.2	1.2	−3.7	3.9	−10.2	−0.7	9.0	−4.4	−15.5
1983	3.9	−6.4	12.1	0.3	−5.0	3.9	4.5	10.1	−9.6	−4.4	0.4	2.2	9.9
1984	−9.6	0.8	12.9	−8.6	4.2	0.9	−2.8	0.8	−1.4	4.5	−2.4	−1.7	−4.3
1985	0.9	−4.1	6.0	−8.3	−3.7	2.0	−8.1	−2.5	3.2	9.0	3.4	2.5	−1.3
1986	−4.7	−12.5	6.3	−3.5	−15.3	−1.0	4.7	1.5	1.5	8.2	−0.3	−4.1	−20.0
1987	5.0	−2.9	1.6	−3.7	0.1	−4.0	−0.8	9.8	0.9	2.5	7.3	−2.4	13.2
1988	4.9	−0.8	−7.5	5.4	11.4	12.5	−6.9	12.9	−0.2	0.2	2.8	2.9	41.6
1989	0.1	−1.3	−7.1	0.3	−4.3	4.5	−5.0	3.8	2.0	−3.1	3.4	0.4	−7.0
1990	−8.2	−3.6	−2.9	−1.7	−3.5	−0.8	−12.9	−3.7	0.1	−5.7	−0.1	−0.5	−36.3
1991	1.0	2.5	6.4	−1.2	1.3	−4.2	6.9	9.2	3.6	9.3	0.7	10.6	55.4
1992	8.8	−9.1	−5.2	−6.7	−1.1	0.9	−10.0	5.0	5.2	1.2	4.7	−4.6	−12.6
1993	7.4	−12.3	4.2	−13.2	−4.3	−0.3	5.8	3.8	1.0	5.3	4.5	7.9	6.9
1994	−1.7	−7.1	−4.5	0.3	−1.0	−1.6	2.6	14.8	6.4	−4.7	N/C	4.4	6.1
1995	−7.0	−7.0	−1.2	2.3	6.3	19.5	4.1	−0.3	6.4	1.1	−0.6	3.5	27.6
1996	1.4	−3.5	−0.4	13.6	−6.7	−8.7	−8.8	3.0	−3.8	−14.9	1.7	1.0	−25.6
1997	−5.6	4.3	5.9	9.1	−16.8	−7.8	9.0	8.8	−10.1	1.8	−0.8	−8.9	−14.6
1998	3.5	0.3	−5.3	−5.9	−5.6	1.1	−12.2	0.6	6.0	9.3	N/C	−6.1	−15.2
1999	−0.3	−9.8	12.8	−4.4	−5.9	4.8	−0.2	7.0	−2.3	−7.3	−2.4	−0.4	−10.0
2000	3.1	1.1	1.3	−2.9	7.9	−1.3	−9.2	8.9	−1.2	−3.9	7.5	2.1	12.5
2001	−2.3	1.4	−7.9	11.1	−5.7	−3.4	7.9	3.8	−6.3	8.3	−1.3	−0.2	3.4
2002	−1.0	−3.5	3.3	−5.7	5.0	10.9	6.7	10.8	7.2	1.5	−5.6	−14.4	12.5
2003	−1.4	−3.2	−7.6	−1.4	14.7	−4.2	12.2	9.3	−5.4	2.6	10.1	−7.3	16.0
2004	3.2	0.4	4.4	−4.4	−7.2	−4.6	−9.6	3.4	−5.0	3.2	−4.8	2.1	−18.4
2005	−5.4	18.6	−4.1	−1.5	1.8	−0.1	−1.1	−3.1	9.1	−8.4	1.2	5.8	10.3
2006	1.2	11.0	−8.7	3.1	9.8	0.6	0.4	6.2	4.9	9.0	8.0	−3.9	47.7
2007	−6.7	4.4	−10.2	13.1	4.3	15.5	5.5	23.1	21.1	−14.0	9.6	−0.1	76.6
2008	5.0	16.8	−14.5	−13.8	−4.9	12.8	−8.7	2.2	−15.1	−21.1	4.7	8.8	−31.0
2009	−7.0	−8.2	2.2	0.7	18.8	−15.1	−2.3	−5.6	−8.3	8.0	19.1	−8.0	−11.3
2010	−12.5	9.5	−13.2	11.7	−9.0	4.9	37.7	3.7	−1.7	6.4	−3.7	15.0	46.7
2011	5.9	−2.8	−6.6	5.0	−2.4	−21.5	9.5	17.7	−23.0	3.1	−2.3	6.3	−17.8
2012	2.0	0.3	−1.1	−0.9	−1.6								
TOTALS	−46.5	−41.5	−72.1	−38.6	−17.7	58.5	74.1	277.0	7.8	10.8	101.1	1.6	
AVG.	−1.1	−0.9	−1.6	−0.9	−0.4	1.4	1.7	6.4	0.2	0.3	2.4	0.04	
# Up	21	18	17	19	18	23	21	36	24	28	25	21	
# Down	23	26	27	25	26	20	22	7	19	15	16	22	

COCOA CYCLE, SEASONAL PATTERN, AND TRADING GUIDE

The cocoa bean grows on a tropical plant, thriving only in hot, rainy climates with cultivation generally confined to areas not more than 20 degrees north or south of the equator. The tree takes four or five years after planting to yield cocoa beans and then takes anywhere from eight to ten years to achieve maximum production. That is why it is susceptible to frost scares. The fruit of the cocoa tree appears as pods, primarily on the trees trunk and lower main branches. When ripe, these pods are cut down and opened; and the beans are removed, fermented, and dried. The cocoa butter extracted from the bean is used in a number of products, ranging from cosmetics to pharmaceuticals, but its main use is in the manufacture of chocolate candy.

Currently, the Ivory Coast is the world's leading cocoa producing nation. Indonesia and Ghana rank next among major world producers, followed by Nigeria, Cameroon, Brazil, Ecuador, and Togo. Cocoa has two crop seasons due to the production areas of Ghana and South America. Cocoa has a strong seasonal tendency to bottom in June, due to the new crop harvest, and then peaks in March, when supplies have declined and confectioners and processors have accumulated inventories ahead of the high-consumption periods around Valentine's Day and Easter.

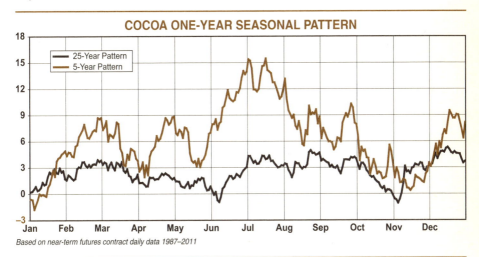

COCOA ONE-YEAR SEASONAL PATTERN

Legend:
- 25-Year Pattern
- 5-Year Pattern

Based on near-term futures contract daily data 1987–2011

COCOA NEAR-TERM CONTRACT ANNUAL HIGHS, LOWS, AND CLOSES SINCE 1981

YEAR	HIGH DATE	HIGH CLOSE	LOW DATE	LOW CLOSE	YEAR CLOSE	YEAR	HIGH DATE	HIGH CLOSE	LOW DATE	LOW CLOSE	YEAR CLOSE
1981	09/02	2272	06/05	1403	2054	1997	12/15	1762	01/23	1260	1630
1982	01/05	2159	07/19	1344	1603	1998	05/14	1748	12/30	1376	1379
1983	12/30	2755	01/04	1590	2755	1999	01/12	1392	11/08	806	836
1984	05/22	2730	08/01	1963	2052	2000	03/16	935	11/27	714	758
1985	03/29	2469	06/24	1968	2298	2001	11/29	1349	01/03	753	1310
1986	01/02	2307	06/02	1722	1935	2002	10/10	2374	01/18	1286	2021
1987	07/15	2125	12/08	1743	1814	2003	01/31	2409	10/17	1367	1515
1988	01/21	1942	09/29	1116	1500	2004	11/08	1792	05/17	1314	1547
1989	02/15	1566	12/14	898	925	2005	03/18	1844	11/07	1322	1504
1990	05/24	1493	01/03	912	1150	2006	07/10	1734	10/16	1406	1635
1991	12/16	1333	07/09	904	1245	2007	12/19	2132	01/26	1578	2035
1992	01/02	1253	06/24	831	936	2008	07/01	3275	11/06	1913	2665
1993	12/03	1316	06/07	849	1144	2009	12/16	3498	03/02	2213	3289
1994	07/15	1522	02/02	1051	1280	2010	01/19	3461	09/13	2610	3035
1995	02/24	1461	07/10	1216	1258	2011	03/03	3733	12/09	2067	2109
1996	06/12	1458	03/13	1211	1374	2012*	01/26	2452	01/05	2028	AT PRESS TIME

*Through May 31, 2012

COCOA NEAR-TERM CONTRACT MONTHLY CLOSING PRICES

	Jan	Feb	Mar	Apr	May	Jun	Jul	Aug	Sep	Oct	Nov	Dec
1981	1944	1992	2027	1944	1681	1554	2047	2178	2215	1931	1911	2054
1982	1942	1940	1638	1660	1488	1477	1395	1475	1529	1372	1465	1603
1983	1826	1740	1704	1935	2072	2143	2337	2093	2072	1963	2224	2755
1984	2521	2377	2562	2545	2616	2347	1981	2326	2174	2277	2117	2052
1985	2271	2163	2469	2093	2075	2031	2087	2222	2273	2103	2214	2298
1986	2146	2040	1862	1798	1759	1800	1942	2129	2011	1876	1886	1935
1987	1820	1888	1928	1977	1881	1997	1962	1988	1823	1807	1866	1814
1988	1760	1621	1570	1622	1619	1580	1468	1256	1132	1309	1476	1500
1989	1446	1485	1431	1211	1128	1229	1267	1149	1040	977	939	925
1990	962	1055	1183	1297	1415	1246	1248	1319	1281	1153	1283	1150
1991	1128	1138	1105	1035	1030	908	1036	1091	1220	1208	1231	1245
1992	1177	1116	986	933	864	954	1013	1092	1009	932	1008	936
1993	912	936	919	936	894	903	939	1079	1151	1120	1263	1144
1994	1088	1139	1148	1128	1388	1305	1490	1357	1320	1327	1228	1280
1995	1363	1427	1308	1408	1362	1289	1236	1336	1293	1311	1308	1258
1996	1242	1268	1306	1368	1376	1384	1333	1352	1377	1353	1416	1374
1997	1314	1286	1453	1400	1469	1713	1513	1717	1679	1603	1582	1630
1998	1556	1614	1652	1686	1673	1575	1552	1614	1512	1506	1441	1379
1999	1331	1278	1192	1019	874	1039	1001	951	1029	874	899	836
2000	795	778	800	774	842	835	825	795	797	755	729	758
2001	1020	1137	1073	987	936	964	957	949	1077	1017	1339	1310
2002	1344	1450	1494	1510	1598	1647	1787	2002	2191	1927	1703	2021
2003	2409	2034	1960	1991	1493	1651	1465	1761	1626	1440	1438	1515
2004	1520	1570	1549	1413	1465	1341	1645	1686	1453	1469	1651	1547
2005	1525	1730	1613	1492	1422	1452	1479	1404	1413	1351	1415	1504
2006	1484	1461	1489	1521	1473	1639	1486	1485	1472	1484	1557	1635
2007	1617	1732	1953	1798	1883	2062	1942	1824	2036	1945	1983	2035
2008	2326	2777	2321	2776	2723	3181	2858	2884	2558	2053	2294	2665
2009	2771	2413	2605	2375	2588	2510	2892	2794	3140	3297	3259	3289
2010	3184	2917	2969	3239	2965	2944	3091	2736	2814	2797	2807	3035
2011	3352	3695	2952	3340	2999	3151	2974	3113	2608	2696	2305	2109
2012	2291	2334	2219	2219	2083							

COCOA NEAR-TERM CONTRACT MONTHLY PERCENT CHANGES

	Jan	Feb	Mar	Apr	May	Jun	Jul	Aug	Sep	Oct	Nov	Dec	Year's Change
1981	−5.2	2.5	1.8	−4.1	−13.5	−7.6	31.7	6.4	1.7	−12.8	−1.0	7.5	0.2
1982	−5.5	−0.1	−15.6	1.3	−10.4	−0.7	−5.6	5.7	3.7	−10.3	6.8	9.4	−22.0
1983	13.9	−4.7	−2.1	13.6	7.1	3.4	9.1	−10.4	−1.0	−5.3	13.3	23.9	71.9
1984	−8.5	−5.7	7.8	−0.7	2.8	−10.3	−15.6	17.4	−6.5	4.7	−7.0	−3.1	−25.5
1985	10.7	−4.8	14.1	−15.2	−0.9	−2.1	2.8	6.5	2.3	−7.5	5.3	3.8	12.0
1986	−6.6	−4.9	−8.7	−3.4	−2.2	2.3	7.9	9.6	−5.5	−6.7	0.5	2.6	−15.8
1987	−5.9	3.7	2.1	2.5	−4.9	6.2	−1.8	1.3	−8.3	−0.9	3.3	−2.8	−6.3
1988	−3.0	−7.9	−3.1	3.3	−0.2	−2.4	−7.1	−14.4	−9.9	15.6	12.8	1.6	−17.3
1989	−3.6	2.7	−3.6	−15.4	−6.9	9.0	3.1	−9.3	−9.5	−6.1	−3.9	−1.5	−38.3
1990	4.0	9.7	12.1	9.6	9.1	−11.9	0.2	5.7	−2.9	−10.0	11.3	−10.4	24.3
1991	−1.9	0.9	−2.9	−6.3	−0.5	−11.8	14.1	5.3	11.8	−1.0	1.9	1.1	8.3
1992	−5.5	−5.2	−11.6	−5.4	−7.4	10.4	6.2	7.8	−7.6	−7.6	8.2	−7.1	−24.8
1993	−2.6	2.6	−1.8	1.8	−4.5	1.0	4.0	14.9	6.7	−2.7	12.8	−9.4	22.2
1994	−4.9	4.7	0.8	−1.7	23.0	−6.0	14.2	−8.9	−2.7	0.5	−7.5	4.2	11.9
1995	6.5	4.7	−8.3	7.6	−3.3	−5.4	−4.1	8.1	−3.2	1.4	−0.2	−3.8	−1.7
1996	−1.3	2.1	3.0	4.7	0.6	0.6	−3.7	1.4	1.8	−1.7	4.7	−3.0	9.2
1997	−4.4	−2.1	13.0	−3.6	4.9	16.6	−11.7	13.5	−2.2	−4.5	−1.3	3.0	18.6
1998	−4.5	3.7	2.4	2.1	−0.8	−5.9	−1.5	4.0	−6.3	−0.4	−4.3	−4.3	−15.4
1999	−3.5	−4.0	−6.7	−14.5	−14.2	18.9	−3.7	−5.0	8.2	−15.1	2.9	−7.0	−39.4
2000	−4.9	−2.1	2.8	−3.2	8.8	−0.8	−1.2	−3.6	0.3	−5.3	−3.4	4.0	−9.3
2001	34.6	11.5	−5.6	−8.0	−5.2	3.0	−0.7	−0.8	13.5	−5.6	31.7	−2.2	72.8
2002	2.6	7.9	3.0	1.1	5.8	3.1	8.5	12.0	9.4	−12.0	−11.6	18.7	54.3
2003	19.2	−15.6	−3.6	1.6	−25.0	10.6	−11.3	20.2	−7.7	−11.4	−0.1	5.4	−25.0
2004	0.3	3.3	−1.3	−8.8	3.7	−8.5	22.7	2.5	−13.8	1.1	12.4	−6.3	2.1
2005	−1.4	13.4	−6.8	−7.5	−4.7	2.1	1.9	−5.1	0.6	−4.4	4.7	6.3	−2.8
2006	−1.3	−1.5	1.9	2.1	−3.2	11.3	−9.3	−0.1	−0.9	0.8	4.9	5.0	8.7
2007	−1.1	7.1	12.8	−7.9	4.7	9.5	−5.8	−6.1	11.6	−4.5	2.0	2.6	24.5
2008	14.3	19.4	−16.4	19.6	−1.9	16.8	−10.2	0.9	−11.3	−19.7	11.7	16.2	31.0
2009	4.0	−12.9	8.0	−8.8	9.0	−3.0	15.2	−3.4	12.4	5.0	−1.2	0.9	23.4
2010	−3.2	−8.4	1.8	9.1	−8.5	−0.7	5.0	−11.5	2.9	−0.6	0.4	8.1	−7.7
2011	10.4	10.2	−20.1	13.1	−10.2	5.1	−5.6	4.7	−16.2	3.4	−14.5	−8.5	−30.5
2012	8.6	1.9	−4.9	N/C	−6.1								
TOTALS	50.3	32.1	−35.7	−21.4	−55.0	52.8	47.7	69.3	−28.6	−123.6	95.6	54.9	
AVG.	1.6	1.0	−1.1	−0.7	−1.7	1.7	1.5	2.2	−0.9	−4.0	3.1	1.8	
# Up	12	18	15	15	11	17	15	19	14	8	19	18	
# Down	20	14	17	16	21	14	16	12	17	23	12	13	

169

COFFEE CYCLE, SEASONAL PATTERN, AND TRADING GUIDE

Coffee is produced from trees or bushes that grow primarily in subtropical climates. Coffee beans are the seeds of cherry-sized berries, the fruit of the coffee tree. Coffee is primarily classified in two types—Arabica and Robusta. Arabian coffees, which make up the bulk of world production, are grown mainly in the tropical highlands of the Western Hemisphere. Robusta coffees are produced largely in the low, hot areas of Africa and Asia. Their flavors are less mild than the Arabica coffees. South and Central America produce the majority of the coffee trade in world commerce. Brazil and Vietnam, the largest growers of Arabica coffees, accounted for about 41% of the world green coffee production on average.

The demand for coffee is price inelastic. This means that when coffee prices rise, people do not reduce their coffee consumption proportionally; and when coffee prices fall, consumer demand for coffee does not proportionally increase to any great extent, unless it is met by a substantial price increase due to crop devastation from frost damage, as occured in the late 1970s. Coffee also has a strong seasonal tendency to peak in May, right before the Brazil harvest, as the market builds a price premium as a hedge against a potential frost scare. Then prices tend to decline through the summer months and bottom in August, as roasters build inventories ahead of the highest-consumption months in fall and winter.

COFFEE ONE-YEAR SEASONAL PATTERN

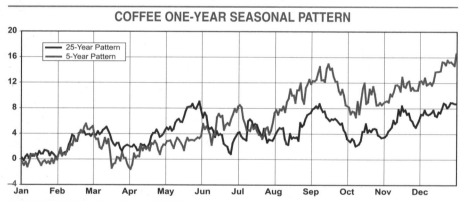

Based on near-term futures contract daily data 1987–2011

COFFEE NEAR-TERM CONTRACT ANNUAL HIGHS, LOWS, AND CLOSES SINCE 1974

YEAR	HIGH DATE	HIGH CLOSE	LOW DATE	LOW CLOSE	YEAR CLOSE	YEAR	HIGH DATE	HIGH CLOSE	LOW DATE	LOW CLOSE	YEAR CLOSE
1974	02/11	81.95	09/16	50.17	59.62	1994	07/12	246.80	01/05	71.55	168.85
1975	08/04	87.90	04/10	47.00	87.25	1995	03/10	187.75	12/28	93.90	94.90
1976	12/30	224.45	01/06	86.90	224.45	1996	04/22	130.95	01/02	91.25	116.90
1977	04/14	339.86	10/21	149.06	192.03	1997	05/29	314.80	01/06	114.05	162.45
1978	01/16	201.25	07/25	109.00	132.88	1998	02/05	181.95	09/18	101.10	117.75
1979	06/29	221.53	02/16	122.91	181.56	1999	12/03	144.05	10/01	81.35	125.90
1980	05/15	203.07	11/10	108.03	126.80	2000	07/18	119.05	12/19	65.05	65.55
1981	11/04	149.71	06/26	85.44	139.71	2001	01/22	71.25	10/22	42.50	46.20
1982	02/10	157.75	04/19	118.07	129.83	2002	12/02	72.85	02/08	44.55	60.20
1983	12/13	149.58	02/16	119.44	138.79	2003	09/11	72.05	03/27	57.15	64.95
1984	05/21	156.45	10/01	133.57	142.25	2004	12/29	107.95	08/05	65.90	103.75
1985	12/23	246.66	07/23	131.32	241.29	2005	03/10	138.10	09/19	86.45	107.10
1986	01/07	273.45	12/30	132.59	136.83	2006	12/14	128.90	07/24	94.05	126.20
1987	01/08	134.02	04/01	99.28	125.96	2007	10/12	139.30	05/03	104.35	136.20
1988	12/30	159.34	08/02	108.83	159.34	2008	02/28	167.50	12/05	103.20	112.05
1989	01/03	165.90	10/09	68.72	79.57	2009	12/16	148.30	03/02	105.70	135.95
1990	03/05	104.24	01/16	77.55	88.65	2010	12/31	240.50	02/05	128.80	240.50
1991	03/06	95.85	11/06	76.50	77.70	2011	05/03	306.15	12/16	215.10	226.85
1992	12/21	81.90	09/09	50.90	77.55	2012*	01/11	234.90	05/31	160.65	AT PRESS TIME
1993	09/10	83.15	04/08	53.50	71.55						

*Through May 31, 2012

COFFEE NEAR-TERM CONTRACT MONTHLY CLOSING PRICES

	Jan	Feb	Mar	Apr	May	Jun	Jul	Aug	Sep	Oct	Nov	Dec
1974	72.65	74.50	74.90	73.15	73.13	70.90	69.25	59.35	54.20	57.60	61.63	59.62
1975	54.75	51.75	51.90	48.95	54.11	55.25	84.05	83.70	80.93	80.10	79.90	87.25
1976	95.00	96.52	108.70	125.50	141.05	152.85	141.75	147.90	166.25	178.50	186.98	224.45
1977	222.93	267.49	308.75	301.99	273.12	235.92	222.00	180.50	165.50	184.50	170.33	192.03
1978	190.00	159.46	168.65	154.13	171.00	146.18	128.46	151.30	149.65	153.06	133.98	132.88
1979	127.76	127.47	137.49	156.04	155.82	221.53	198.00	207.46	213.81	212.30	205.85	181.56
1980	166.39	183.26	182.25	184.65	194.05	177.92	143.06	134.92	126.66	125.14	121.38	126.80
1981	122.36	123.09	128.66	126.84	113.78	92.02	123.13	98.08	129.15	141.12	129.68	139.71
1982	149.14	141.26	128.56	129.31	138.23	133.46	126.81	126.83	144.87	139.41	136.08	129.83
1983	122.81	120.12	123.23	124.35	131.75	125.19	126.07	129.90	136.48	141.54	144.01	138.79
1984	142.44	144.84	151.37	147.17	144.35	142.65	139.01	146.85	135.95	138.66	136.76	142.25
1985	150.05	139.96	144.43	145.67	144.10	143.56	133.49	138.63	138.00	161.55	168.56	241.29
1986	214.43	246.96	246.41	233.27	187.98	169.28	169.47	204.36	201.36	173.71	150.85	136.83
1987	123.98	129.31	100.04	120.56	119.46	105.75	101.54	118.52	112.77	122.52	129.70	125.96
1988	131.55	135.31	134.51	132.60	133.77	131.43	124.72	123.83	131.93	123.61	123.77	159.34
1989	132.64	127.32	128.13	127.45	130.68	108.06	78.99	85.76	80.60	74.85	77.70	79.57
1990	79.99	93.79	92.14	93.73	94.05	85.60	93.80	102.85	93.00	90.50	86.90	88.65
1991	83.00	92.75	94.70	89.35	86.70	85.90	81.40	89.00	82.90	80.55	83.80	77.70
1992	72.15	70.90	68.50	62.90	63.30	58.10	56.25	54.20	55.70	68.45	73.00	77.55
1993	58.30	64.85	58.60	64.20	63.55	61.35	76.55	77.90	74.50	79.30	77.60	71.55
1994	72.35	76.40	82.20	89.50	126.00	191.60	202.75	210.90	208.85	187.40	160.80	168.85
1995	155.50	181.25	166.30	174.15	153.85	130.30	145.70	147.50	117.25	121.55	104.85	94.90
1996	128.60	115.90	115.45	124.45	116.10	121.45	106.40	118.25	102.95	117.20	107.75	116.90
1997	139.40	176.85	191.15	210.40	276.40	172.40	184.50	179.90	162.50	148.65	155.05	162.45
1998	174.70	162.15	146.25	131.45	132.50	110.20	129.20	116.35	105.15	110.00	110.10	117.75
1999	103.90	102.90	109.70	104.00	121.60	101.40	91.10	89.85	82.45	100.20	134.60	125.90
2000	111.10	100.40	103.70	98.00	93.00	87.45	86.45	79.70	83.00	74.40	71.70	65.55
2001	63.75	65.90	60.30	64.45	57.15	58.50	51.95	54.35	48.30	43.90	46.20	46.20
2002	45.10	46.30	57.20	52.85	51.90	48.85	46.80	53.20	54.50	65.95	70.60	60.20
2003	65.30	59.15	58.65	69.25	58.35	61.10	63.45	63.40	62.90	58.65	60.65	64.95
2004	75.50	76.75	73.75	69.10	85.55	75.30	66.45	72.60	82.35	74.40	97.45	103.75
2005	105.35	121.55	126.40	127.95	118.35	108.05	103.15	101.05	93.45	96.65	97.00	107.10
2006	118.20	113.70	107.00	109.70	98.95	101.10	99.35	108.00	107.65	108.25	124.30	126.20
2007	117.65	118.50	109.25	106.15	111.90	112.80	114.30	115.85	128.65	121.35	129.20	136.20
2008	138.15	166.80	127.40	135.45	133.90	153.20	139.35	145.75	130.45	113.00	116.10	112.05
2009	118.90	111.90	115.75	115.90	137.40	119.90	127.85	122.30	127.80	135.50	142.00	135.95
2010	131.70	131.20	136.15	135.30	134.25	165.85	176.30	178.45	183.05	203.45	201.20	240.50
2011	244.80	271.70	264.15	299.85	264.60	265.60	239.55	288.25	228.90	226.95	236.90	226.85
2012	215.05	203.25	182.45	179.55	160.65							

COFFEE NEAR-TERM CONTRACT MONTHLY PERCENT CHANGES

	Jan	Feb	Mar	Apr	May	Jun	Jul	Aug	Sep	Oct	Nov	Dec	Year's Change
1974	7.8	2.5	0.5	−2.3	−0.0	−3.0	−2.3	−14.3	−8.7	6.3	7.0	−3.3	−11.5
1975	−8.2	−5.5	0.3	−5.7	10.5	2.1	52.1	−0.4	−3.3	−1.0	−0.2	9.2	46.3
1976	8.9	1.6	12.6	15.5	12.4	8.4	−7.3	4.3	12.4	7.4	4.8	20.0	157.2
1977	−0.7	20.0	15.4	−2.2	−9.6	−13.6	−5.9	−18.7	−8.3	11.5	−7.7	12.7	−14.4
1978	−1.1	−16.1	5.8	−8.6	10.9	−14.5	−12.1	17.8	−1.1	2.3	−12.5	−0.8	−30.8
1979	−3.9	−0.2	7.9	13.5	−0.1	42.2	−10.6	4.8	3.1	−0.7	−3.0	−11.8	36.6
1980	−8.4	10.1	−0.6	1.3	5.1	−8.3	−19.6	−5.7	−6.1	−1.2	−3.0	4.5	−30.2
1981	−3.5	0.6	4.5	−1.4	−10.3	−19.1	33.8	−20.3	31.7	9.3	−8.1	7.7	10.2
1982	6.7	−5.3	−9.0	0.6	6.9	−3.5	−5.0	0.0	14.2	−3.8	−2.4	−4.6	−7.1
1983	−5.4	−2.2	2.6	0.9	6.0	−5.0	0.7	3.0	5.1	3.7	1.7	−3.6	6.9
1984	2.6	1.7	4.5	−2.8	−1.9	−1.2	−2.6	5.6	−7.4	2.0	−1.4	4.0	2.5
1985	5.5	−6.7	3.2	0.9	−1.1	−0.4	−7.0	3.9	−0.5	17.1	4.3	43.1	69.6
1986	−11.1	15.2	−0.2	−5.3	−19.4	−9.9	0.1	20.6	−1.5	−13.7	−13.2	−9.3	−43.3
1987	−9.4	4.3	−22.6	20.5	−0.9	−11.5	−4.0	16.7	−4.9	8.6	5.9	−2.9	−7.9
1988	4.4	2.9	−0.6	−1.4	0.9	−1.7	−5.1	−0.7	6.5	−6.3	0.1	28.7	26.5
1989	−16.8	−4.0	0.6	−0.5	2.5	−17.3	−26.9	8.6	−6.0	−7.1	3.8	2.4	−50.1
1990	0.5	17.3	−1.8	1.7	0.3	−9.0	9.6	9.6	−9.6	−2.7	−4.0	2.0	11.4
1991	−6.4	11.7	2.1	−5.6	−3.0	−0.9	−5.2	9.3	−6.9	−2.8	4.0	−7.3	−12.4
1992	−7.1	−1.7	−3.4	−8.2	0.6	−8.2	−3.2	−3.6	2.8	22.9	6.6	6.2	−0.2
1993	−24.8	11.2	−9.6	9.6	−1.0	−3.5	24.8	1.8	−4.4	6.4	−2.1	−7.8	−7.7
1994	1.1	5.6	7.6	8.9	40.8	52.1	5.8	4.0	−1.0	−10.3	−14.2	5.0	136.0
1995	−7.9	16.6	−8.2	4.7	−11.7	−15.3	11.8	1.2	−20.5	3.7	−13.7	−9.5	−43.8
1996	35.5	−9.9	−0.4	7.8	−6.7	4.6	−12.4	11.1	−12.9	13.8	−8.1	8.5	23.2
1997	19.2	26.9	8.1	10.1	31.4	−37.6	7.0	−2.5	−9.7	−8.5	4.3	4.8	39.0
1998	7.5	−7.2	−9.8	−10.1	0.8	−16.8	17.2	−9.9	−9.6	4.6	0.1	6.9	−27.5
1999	−11.8	−1.0	6.6	−5.2	16.9	−16.6	−10.2	−1.4	−8.2	21.5	34.3	−6.5	6.9
2000	−11.8	−9.6	3.3	−5.5	−5.1	−6.0	−1.1	−7.8	4.1	−10.4	−3.6	−8.6	−47.9
2001	−2.7	3.4	−8.5	6.9	−11.3	2.4	−11.2	4.6	−11.1	−9.1	5.2	N/C	−29.5
2002	−2.4	2.7	23.5	−7.6	−1.8	−5.9	−4.2	13.7	2.4	21.0	7.1	−14.7	30.3
2003	8.5	−9.4	−0.8	18.1	−15.7	4.7	3.8	−0.1	−0.8	−6.8	3.4	7.1	7.9
2004	16.2	1.7	−3.9	−6.3	23.8	−12.0	−11.8	9.3	13.4	−9.7	31.0	6.5	59.7
2005	1.5	15.4	4.0	1.2	−7.5	−8.7	−4.5	−2.0	−7.5	3.4	0.4	10.4	3.2
2006	10.4	−3.8	−5.9	2.5	−9.8	2.2	−1.7	8.7	−0.3	0.6	14.8	1.5	17.8
2007	−6.8	0.7	−7.8	−2.8	5.4	0.8	1.3	1.4	11.0	−5.7	6.5	5.4	7.9
2008	1.4	20.7	−23.6	6.3	−1.1	14.4	−9.0	4.6	−10.5	−13.4	2.7	−3.5	−17.7
2009	6.1	−5.9	3.4	0.1	18.6	−12.7	6.6	−4.3	4.5	6.0	4.8	−4.3	21.3
2010	−3.1	−0.4	3.8	−0.6	−0.8	23.5	6.3	1.2	2.6	11.1	−1.1	19.5	76.9
2011	1.8	11.0	−2.8	13.5	−11.8	0.4	−9.8	20.3	−20.6	−0.9	4.4	−4.2	−5.7
2012	−5.2	−5.5	−10.2	−1.6	−10.5								
TOTALS	−12.9	109.4	−9.4	60.9	52.7	−104.4	−11.8	94.4	−67.6	69.1	58.9	113.4	
AVG.	−0.3	2.8	−0.2	1.6	1.4	−2.7	−0.3	2.5	−1.8	1.8	1.6	3.0	
# Up	18	22	20	20	17	12	14	24	13	20	22	21	
# Down	21	17	19	19	22	26	24	14	25	18	16	16	

SUGAR CYCLE, SEASONAL PATTERN, AND TRADING GUIDE

Sugar prices are not only affected by beet and cane supply, but also by domestic and international demand for its by-products, like molasses, methanol, and ethanol. It is a highly regulated industry; thus, many countries, such as the United States, that impose trade barriers, including production quotas, guaranteed prices, and import tariffs, impart a significant degree of distortion to international prices. The relatively longer plantation cycle, combined with restrictive trade practices, has in the past been the catalyst for the volatility in sugar prices.

In India, sugar production follows a three- to five-year cycle. Higher production leads to increased availability of sugar, thereby reducing the sugar prices. This leads to lower profitability for the companies and delayed payment to the farmers. As a result of higher sugarcane arrears, the farmers switch to other crops, thereby leading to a fall in the area under cultivation for sugar. This then leads to lower production and lower sugar availability, followed by higher sugar prices, higher profitability, and lower arrears; and thus, the cycle continues. Because of the many areas around the globe that produce sugar, it does have many seasonal price swings. Overall, it tends to bottom in late May through early September and peak in November prior to the Northern Hemisphere harvest of both sugarcane and sugar beets.

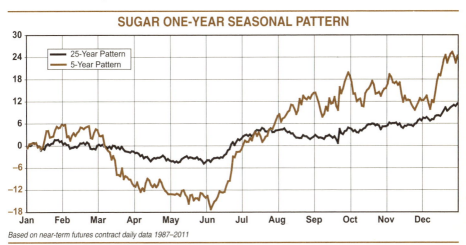

SUGAR ONE-YEAR SEASONAL PATTERN

Based on near-term futures contract daily data 1987–2011

SUGAR NEAR-TERM CONTRACT ANNUAL HIGHS, LOWS, AND CLOSES SINCE 1975

YEAR	HIGH DATE	HIGH CLOSE	LOW DATE	LOW CLOSE	YEAR CLOSE	YEAR	HIGH DATE	HIGH CLOSE	LOW DATE	LOW CLOSE	YEAR CLOSE
1975	01/03	45.60	06/25	11.54	14.40	1994	12/30	15.17	01/19	10.28	15.17
1976	05/07	15.74	12/27	7.65	8.04	1995	01/06	15.74	07/14	9.69	11.60
1977	04/22	10.95	07/12	7.12	9.40	1996	02/16	12.66	12/03	10.27	11.00
1978	10/30	9.75	07/25	6.01	8.43	1997	12/01	12.49	01/23	10.15	12.22
1979	12/26	16.98	04/20	7.64	16.31	1998	01/05	12.02	09/18	6.67	7.86
1980	11/05	45.64	01/03	15.37	30.58	1999	01/07	8.80	04/28	4.08	6.12
1981	01/06	33.78	09/17	10.76	13.18	2000	10/16	11.39	02/28	4.88	10.20
1982	01/27	13.99	09/15	5.99	6.85	2001	01/08	10.47	10/09	6.15	7.39
1983	05/31	13.36	01/12	6.10	8.18	2002	01/09	8.03	06/28	4.96	7.61
1984	01/12	8.15	09/17	3.80	4.16	2003	02/20	9.07	12/31	5.67	5.67
1985	12/05	6.51	06/20	2.70	5.62	2004	10/12	9.32	02/09	5.36	9.04
1986	04/07	9.39	09/19	4.81	6.16	2005	12/29	14.79	04/15	8.08	14.68
1987	12/31	9.49	08/28	5.60	9.49	2006	02/03	19.30	09/25	10.87	11.75
1988	07/19	15.30	02/26	7.74	11.15	2007	01/03	11.51	06/13	8.45	10.82
1989	11/17	15.36	01/24	9.40	13.16	2008	03/03	14.91	06/04	9.52	11.81
1990	03/16	16.13	10/15	9.13	9.37	2009	12/28	27.26	01/14	11.43	26.95
1991	06/19	9.97	05/10	7.63	9.00	2010	12/28	34.39	05/06	13.67	32.12
1992	06/17	11.05	02/11	7.88	8.41	2011	02/02	35.31	05/06	20.47	23.30
1993	05/14	13.19	02/02	8.04	10.77	2012*	03/22	25.91	05/31	19.42	AT PRESS TIME

*Through May 31, 2012

173

SUGAR NEAR-TERM CONTRACT MONTHLY CLOSING PRICES

	Jan	Feb	Mar	Apr	May	Jun	Jul	Aug	Sep	Oct	Nov	Dec
1975	35.65	28.40	25.40	18.90	15.20	13.65	17.09	17.05	13.75	14.22	13.13	14.40
1976	13.35	13.73	14.06	14.26	13.74	13.81	12.07	9.85	8.81	8.21	8.51	8.04
1977	8.89	8.75	9.37	10.23	8.63	8.30	7.98	7.72	8.33	8.63	9.27	9.40
1978	9.41	8.79	7.98	7.91	7.51	6.95	6.35	7.39	9.23	9.42	8.48	8.43
1979	8.22	8.88	8.51	8.20	7.88	8.75	8.47	9.69	11.56	14.08	16.86	16.31
1980	22.01	24.88	19.70	24.81	35.17	34.93	30.05	33.18	41.16	43.34	35.11	30.58
1981	26.79	24.03	21.12	16.78	17.99	15.40	16.70	12.42	13.11	12.52	13.01	13.18
1982	13.58	12.58	10.97	9.12	7.80	7.91	7.49	6.63	7.11	7.84	8.32	6.85
1983	6.20	6.32	7.09	7.98	13.36	11.55	11.68	10.39	10.94	9.36	9.57	8.18
1984	7.50	6.71	6.86	6.48	5.88	5.58	4.55	4.62	5.44	5.83	5.28	4.16
1985	4.32	4.12	3.85	3.55	3.14	2.95	4.50	4.75	5.65	6.14	6.13	5.62
1986	5.92	6.30	9.18	9.24	7.32	6.85	6.57	5.22	6.28	6.90	6.60	6.16
1987	7.74	8.24	6.72	7.31	6.72	6.97	5.94	5.63	6.96	7.59	8.01	9.49
1988	9.64	7.91	8.88	8.51	9.47	12.63	11.54	10.25	9.64	10.59	11.07	11.15
1989	10.49	11.63	12.62	11.54	10.86	14.43	14.65	13.39	14.16	13.97	14.15	13.16
1990	14.73	14.46	15.69	16.02	13.68	12.77	11.09	10.33	10.11	9.42	9.82	9.37
1991	8.79	8.78	8.90	7.73	8.05	8.52	9.68	8.83	9.01	8.98	8.92	9.00
1992	8.18	8.02	8.68	9.36	10.03	9.76	9.51	9.23	8.71	8.77	8.41	8.41
1993	8.30	9.96	11.89	12.82	10.76	10.45	9.36	9.07	10.45	10.62	10.36	10.77
1994	10.59	11.80	11.96	11.67	12.04	11.68	11.68	12.14	12.40	12.80	14.71	15.17
1995	14.12	14.42	14.28	11.56	11.72	10.79	10.50	10.86	10.18	10.56	10.97	11.60
1996	12.15	11.60	11.79	10.39	11.21	11.15	11.70	11.78	10.89	10.30	10.66	11.00
1997	10.45	10.97	10.79	10.96	11.17	11.19	11.68	11.60	11.56	12.39	12.24	12.22
1998	11.23	9.85	10.19	8.46	8.28	8.58	8.76	7.55	7.65	7.71	8.23	7.86
1999	7.11	6.26	5.91	4.33	5.00	6.22	5.98	6.82	6.93	6.88	5.78	6.12
2000	5.42	4.99	5.90	6.64	7.55	8.48	10.40	10.56	9.45	9.90	9.75	10.20
2001	9.95	8.99	7.75	8.50	8.55	9.36	7.93	7.91	6.63	6.74	7.68	7.39
2002	6.38	5.69	5.93	5.36	5.90	4.96	5.80	5.98	6.44	7.36	7.41	7.61
2003	8.64	8.45	7.68	7.20	7.08	6.22	7.21	6.29	6.44	5.93	6.25	5.67
2004	5.86	6.12	6.40	6.95	7.06	7.69	8.28	7.99	9.06	8.60	8.84	9.04
2005	9.22	9.17	8.70	8.66	8.76	9.33	9.83	10.07	11.23	11.33	12.43	14.68
2006	18.02	17.12	17.90	17.43	15.46	16.34	14.91	11.80	11.75	11.55	12.37	11.75
2007	10.60	10.56	9.88	9.10	9.34	9.52	10.33	9.48	10.15	9.98	9.75	10.82
2008	12.36	14.62	11.69	11.81	10.02	13.10	13.93	12.76	13.66	12.02	11.90	11.81
2009	12.67	13.73	12.67	14.36	15.58	17.85	18.61	24.39	25.39	22.81	22.64	26.95
2010	29.90	23.60	16.59	15.15	14.19	16.06	19.57	19.75	23.48	29.12	27.55	32.12
2011	33.97	29.45	27.11	22.25	23.18	26.34	29.81	29.68	25.29	25.77	23.69	23.30
2012	23.64	25.01	24.71	21.12	19.42							

SUGAR NEAR-TERM CONTRACT MONTHLY PERCENT CHANGES

	Jan	Feb	Mar	Apr	May	Jun	Jul	Aug	Sep	Oct	Nov	Dec	Year's Change
1975	−24.5	−20.3	−10.6	−25.6	−19.6	−10.2	25.2	−0.2	−19.4	3.4	−7.7	9.7	−69.5
1976	−7.3	2.8	2.4	1.4	−3.6	0.5	−12.6	−18.4	−10.6	−6.8	3.7	−5.5	−44.2
1977	10.6	−1.6	7.1	9.2	−15.6	−3.8	−3.9	−3.3	7.9	3.6	7.4	1.4	16.9
1978	0.1	−6.6	−9.2	−0.9	−5.1	−7.5	−8.6	16.4	24.9	2.1	−10.0	−0.6	−10.3
1979	−2.5	8.0	−4.2	−3.6	−3.9	11.0	−3.2	14.4	19.3	21.8	19.7	−3.3	93.5
1980	34.9	13.0	−20.8	25.9	41.8	−0.7	−14.0	10.4	24.1	5.3	−19.0	−12.9	87.5
1981	−12.4	−10.3	−12.1	−20.5	7.2	−14.4	8.4	−25.6	5.6	−4.5	3.9	1.3	−56.9
1982	3.0	−7.4	−12.8	−16.9	−14.5	1.4	−5.3	−11.5	7.2	10.3	6.1	−17.7	−48.0
1983	−9.5	1.9	12.2	12.6	67.4	−13.5	1.1	−11.0	5.3	−14.4	2.2	−14.5	19.4
1984	−8.3	−10.5	2.2	−5.5	−9.3	−5.1	−18.5	1.5	17.7	7.2	−9.4	−21.2	−49.1
1985	3.8	−4.6	−6.6	−7.8	−11.5	−6.1	52.5	5.6	18.9	8.7	−0.2	−8.3	35.1
1986	5.3	6.4	45.7	0.7	−20.8	−6.4	−4.1	−20.5	20.3	9.9	−4.3	−6.7	9.6
1987	25.6	6.5	−18.4	8.8	−8.1	3.7	−14.8	−5.2	23.6	9.1	5.5	18.5	54.1
1988	1.6	−17.9	12.3	−4.2	11.3	33.4	−8.6	−11.2	−6.0	9.9	4.5	0.7	17.5
1989	−5.9	10.9	8.5	−8.6	−5.9	32.9	1.5	−8.6	5.8	−1.3	1.3	−7.0	18.0
1990	11.9	−1.8	8.5	2.1	−14.6	−6.7	−13.2	−6.9	−2.1	−6.8	4.2	−4.6	−28.8
1991	−6.2	−0.1	1.4	−13.1	4.1	5.8	13.6	−8.8	2.0	−0.3	−0.7	0.9	−3.9
1992	−9.1	−2.0	8.2	7.8	7.2	−2.7	−2.6	−2.9	−5.6	0.7	−4.1	N/C	−6.6
1993	−1.3	20.0	19.4	7.8	−16.1	−2.9	−10.4	−3.1	15.2	1.6	−2.4	4.0	28.1
1994	−1.7	11.4	1.4	−2.4	3.2	−3.0	N/C	3.9	2.1	3.2	14.9	3.1	40.9
1995	−6.9	2.1	−1.0	−19.0	1.4	−7.9	−2.7	3.4	−6.3	3.7	3.9	5.7	−23.5
1996	4.7	−4.5	1.6	−11.9	7.9	−0.5	4.9	0.7	−7.6	−5.4	3.5	3.2	−5.2
1997	−5.0	5.0	−1.6	1.6	1.9	0.2	4.4	−0.7	−0.3	7.2	−1.2	−0.2	11.1
1998	−8.1	−12.3	3.5	−17.0	−2.1	3.6	2.1	−13.8	1.3	0.8	6.7	−4.5	−35.7
1999	−9.5	−12.0	−5.6	−26.7	15.5	24.4	−3.9	14.0	1.6	−0.7	−16.0	5.9	−22.1
2000	−11.4	−7.9	18.2	12.5	13.7	12.3	22.6	1.5	−10.5	4.8	−1.5	4.6	66.7
2001	−2.5	−9.6	−13.8	9.7	0.6	9.5	−15.3	−0.3	−16.2	1.7	13.9	−3.8	−27.5
2002	−13.7	−10.8	4.2	−9.6	10.1	−15.9	16.9	3.1	7.7	14.3	0.7	2.7	3.0
2003	13.5	−2.2	−9.1	−6.2	−1.7	−12.1	15.9	−12.8	2.4	−7.9	5.4	−9.3	−25.5
2004	3.4	4.4	4.6	8.6	1.6	8.9	7.7	−3.5	13.4	−5.1	2.8	2.3	59.4
2005	2.0	−0.5	−5.1	−0.5	1.2	6.5	5.4	2.4	11.5	0.9	9.7	18.1	62.4
2006	22.8	−5.0	4.6	−2.6	−11.3	5.7	−8.8	−20.9	−0.4	−1.7	7.1	−5.0	−20.0
2007	−9.8	−0.4	−6.4	−7.9	2.6	1.9	8.5	−8.2	7.1	−1.7	−2.3	11.0	−7.9
2008	14.2	18.3	−20.0	1.0	−15.2	30.7	6.3	−8.4	7.1	−12.0	−1.0	−0.8	9.1
2009	7.3	8.4	−7.7	13.3	8.5	14.6	4.3	31.1	4.1	−10.2	−0.7	19.0	128.2
2010	10.9	−21.1	−29.7	−8.7	−6.3	13.2	21.9	0.9	18.9	24.0	−5.4	16.6	19.2
2011	5.8	−13.3	−7.9	−17.9	4.2	13.6	13.2	−0.4	−14.8	1.9	−8.1	−1.6	−27.5
2012	1.5	5.8	−1.2	−14.5	−8.0								
TOTALS	27.3	−57.8	−37.8	−128.6	18.2	114.4	85.9	−96.9	175.2	77.3	33.1	1.2	
AVG.	0.7	−1.5	−1.0	−3.4	0.5	3.1	2.3	−2.6	4.7	2.1	0.9	0.03	
# Up	19	15	18	15	19	20	19	14	25	23	20	18	
# Down	19	23	20	23	19	17	17	23	12	14	17	18	

LIVE CATTLE CYCLE, SEASONAL PATTERN, AND TRADING GUIDE

Beef inventories here in the United States have declined in the last decade, as production costs have increased as a result of higher feed and transportation costs. Breeding is costly and requires a lengthy start-up time. For example, females can first be bred between 14 to 18 months of age, but gestation is approximately 9 months. Once the herd population is reduced, it may take up to 3 years to begin building up calf inventories.

Cattle prices are prone not only to seasonal tendencies but also to cyclical forces, as the country's herd population expands and contracts in response to production costs and farm operation profit margins. Typically, the seasonal low is in June, with a minor peak in November. Beef prices typically form a seasonal high in March, as packers have purchased inventory ahead of the summer grilling season.

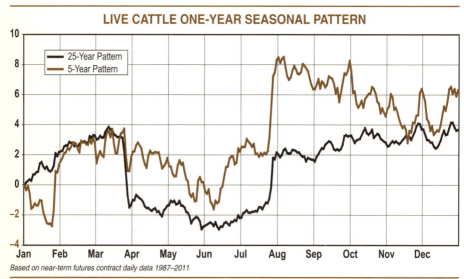

LIVE CATTLE ONE-YEAR SEASONAL PATTERN

Based on near-term futures contract daily data 1987–2011

LIVE CATTLE NEAR-TERM CONTRACT ANNUAL HIGHS, LOWS, AND CLOSES SINCE 1972

YEAR	HIGH DATE	HIGH CLOSE	LOW DATE	LOW CLOSE	YEAR CLOSE	YEAR	HIGH DATE	HIGH CLOSE	LOW DATE	LOW CLOSE	YEAR CLOSE
1972	12/29	40.825	08/22	32.800	40.825	1993	03/22	83.725	12/02	72.225	73.450
1973	08/13	60.775	09/25	38.550	48.650	1994	03/04	77.200	06/27	62.275	72.675
1974	01/28	53.825	06/11	33.825	39.575	1995	01/20	75.000	05/10	59.100	66.425
1975	06/18	52.075	03/03	34.300	42.925	1996	09/13	73.275	04/25	54.800	64.975
1976	04/20	49.550	01/26	36.275	40.400	1997	07/28	71.275	07/08	62.925	66.450
1977	05/02	46.250	01/14	36.375	42.375	1998	04/30	69.500	12/15	57.625	60.525
1978	05/26	61.975	01/10	41.175	58.925	1999	11/16	70.775	01/04	59.625	69.600
1979	04/26	78.825	08/07	56.525	70.675	2000	12/18	78.225	09/06	66.300	77.925
1980	07/25	73.950	04/02	60.600	68.075	2001	03/06	81.650	11/12	61.750	70.700
1981	04/27	72.150	12/31	54.650	54.650	2002	12/31	79.625	05/21	59.400	79.625
1982	05/17	73.125	12/06	55.150	58.325	2003	11/26	98.475	06/16	67.050	73.525
1983	04/13	70.750	09/02	55.550	67.850	2004	12/27	91.775	02/04	71.375	87.825
1984	03/23	72.125	09/26	60.725	66.675	2005	12/20	97.275	07/11	78.075	96.375
1985	02/04	68.800	07/26	51.675	61.150	2006	01/10	96.550	04/04	73.125	92.500
1986	01/27	63.300	06/03	50.125	55.525	2007	03/12	102.025	06/26	88.625	96.175
1987	05/11	70.125	01/02	55.975	63.125	2008	08/06	108.550	12/05	81.450	86.050
1988	10/12	75.250	06/23	62.225	73.950	2009	07/28	90.575	03/30	80.075	86.175
1989	03/21	78.675	05/30	66.650	77.375	2010	12/31	108.350	01/11	85.050	108.350
1990	11/26	79.750	04/26	72.600	77.200	2011	11/03	124.500	05/23	102.150	121.450
1991	03/08	81.900	08/08	68.650	72.400	2012*	02/22	131.150	04/24	111.575	AT PRESS TIME
1992	03/09	79.525	05/28	69.225	77.125						

*Through May 31, 2012

LIVE CATTLE NEAR-TERM CONTRACT MONTHLY CLOSING PRICES

	Jan	Feb	Mar	Apr	May	Jun	Jul	Aug	Sep	Oct	Nov	Dec
1972	34.725	34.675	33.775	35.375	36.225	38.075	33.800	33.850	37.150	35.750	38.000	40.825
1973	43.450	45.075	44.200	44.425	47.050	47.525	56.775	49.250	44.225	43.250	45.325	48.650
1974	53.175	44.600	45.400	43.700	37.275	42.575	50.725	40.650	43.400	41.075	41.300	39.575
1975	36.575	35.800	42.325	46.600	46.700	48.700	39.700	44.925	47.325	43.050	44.450	42.925
1976	37.600	37.800	44.150	47.075	47.225	42.000	41.125	40.750	37.250	39.550	40.800	40.400
1977	39.150	37.475	41.425	45.600	42.850	41.475	38.225	38.900	40.775	40.975	39.975	42.375
1978	43.700	46.100	50.475	53.675	58.925	51.525	52.650	53.175	56.175	53.550	57.725	58.925
1979	66.700	71.100	71.350	78.350	69.650	66.725	59.400	68.450	73.000	67.325	72.600	70.675
1980	69.300	68.575	63.600	64.825	65.375	68.700	70.575	68.725	68.925	69.225	71.175	68.075
1981	66.025	65.050	68.550	70.175	67.100	66.325	64.975	66.925	65.825	63.800	62.350	54.650
1982	61.700	64.225	66.425	69.575	68.075	63.250	62.425	61.650	59.025	59.525	58.250	58.325
1983	60.400	64.575	69.625	66.125	62.525	61.425	60.475	55.975	60.750	59.425	62.750	67.850
1984	66.125	70.400	68.700	66.175	62.600	64.725	61.600	63.600	63.550	63.975	66.525	66.675
1985	68.050	65.025	67.200	62.650	62.875	58.350	55.925	56.100	61.825	66.250	65.075	61.150
1986	61.900	61.375	58.250	57.200	51.400	56.700	59.050	61.775	56.200	59.575	59.175	55.525
1987	62.875	64.975	63.425	67.200	62.400	63.300	62.775	66.050	66.600	62.400	61.725	63.125
1988	67.800	71.500	70.875	70.900	67.825	64.600	69.100	71.775	73.775	74.175	72.625	73.950
1989	76.425	78.050	73.025	71.450	66.950	70.150	75.525	73.750	74.325	74.450	74.100	77.375
1990	76.025	75.450	72.925	72.975	73.100	73.075	78.975	76.325	76.450	77.450	75.150	77.200
1991	77.525	80.225	77.125	76.100	73.725	72.225	73.200	70.050	76.775	73.500	74.725	72.400
1992	77.150	77.400	74.775	73.100	69.475	72.425	73.625	73.750	73.650	73.775	74.150	77.125
1993	76.850	80.225	76.250	76.775	73.375	75.050	75.200	75.150	74.125	74.050	72.500	73.450
1994	76.450	77.100	74.275	71.300	65.750	64.150	71.725	70.850	68.500	70.000	67.250	72.675
1995	74.150	74.275	61.700	62.950	59.700	62.800	65.875	63.325	66.650	68.350	67.625	66.425
1996	63.850	63.925	62.475	57.350	64.525	65.825	68.550	72.225	68.150	66.675	63.675	64.975
1997	66.825	69.625	65.075	64.750	64.925	64.450	70.625	67.200	67.100	67.525	68.625	66.450
1998	67.475	64.375	65.775	69.500	66.300	65.025	59.925	59.000	61.750	65.000	62.775	60.525
1999	65.075	68.025	63.600	62.825	62.800	62.625	64.375	66.550	69.300	68.650	70.050	69.600
2000	72.050	71.175	68.975	69.275	67.250	66.725	68.800	66.975	70.675	72.675	74.050	77.925
2001	76.825	81.375	72.675	71.650	74.475	74.000	73.900	73.150	67.325	68.075	70.175	70.700
2002	75.525	74.200	65.800	63.625	60.950	63.550	67.750	67.200	70.625	73.200	78.475	79.625
2003	79.975	75.825	70.375	71.925	69.750	69.875	77.700	82.850	84.950	90.900	93.175	73.525
2004	73.425	76.850	76.225	80.400	88.625	85.750	88.750	84.650	87.275	84.475	89.550	87.825
2005	88.325	86.050	85.250	85.625	84.700	79.300	83.400	82.250	90.000	90.925	95.725	96.375
2006	91.575	87.225	74.350	73.500	80.075	85.675	88.700	93.125	89.850	87.825	89.100	92.500
2007	93.175	97.050	94.875	94.125	91.475	90.275	99.950	96.900	99.800	94.925	95.775	96.175
2008	94.275	94.325	87.750	93.475	101.850	103.425	106.300	104.050	100.375	92.700	87.650	86.050
2009	85.100	85.925	81.700	82.500	81.825	85.250	90.200	86.675	86.125	85.675	85.725	86.175
2010	89.375	91.925	93.550	94.225	89.250	90.025	94.600	97.275	99.600	98.825	106.375	108.350
2011	114.050	112.900	120.975	113.350	105.375	110.875	117.325	114.025	122.650	118.600	123.600	121.450
2012	128.575	129.750	116.150	114.150	118.900							

LIVE CATTLE NEAR-TERM CONTRACT MONTHLY PERCENT CHANGES

	Jan	Feb	Mar	Apr	May	Jun	Jul	Aug	Sep	Oct	Nov	Dec	Year's Change
1972	1.5	−0.1	−2.6	4.7	2.4	5.1	−11.2	0.1	9.7	−3.8	6.3	7.4	19.4
1973	6.4	3.7	−1.9	0.5	5.9	1.0	19.5	−13.3	−10.2	−2.2	4.8	7.3	19.2
1974	9.3	−16.1	1.8	−3.7	−14.7	14.2	19.1	−19.9	6.8	−5.4	0.5	−4.2	−18.7
1975	−7.6	−2.1	18.2	10.1	0.2	4.3	−18.5	13.2	5.3	−9.0	3.3	−3.4	8.5
1976	−12.4	0.5	16.8	6.6	0.3	−11.1	−2.1	−0.9	−8.6	6.2	3.2	−1.0	−5.9
1977	−3.1	−4.3	10.5	10.1	−6.0	−3.2	−7.8	1.8	4.8	0.5	−2.4	6.0	4.9
1978	3.1	5.5	9.5	6.3	9.8	−12.6	2.2	1.0	5.6	−4.7	7.8	2.1	39.1
1979	13.2	6.6	0.4	9.8	−11.1	−4.2	−11.0	15.2	6.6	−7.8	7.8	−2.7	19.9
1980	−1.9	−1.0	−7.3	1.9	0.8	5.1	2.7	−2.6	0.3	0.4	2.8	−4.4	−3.7
1981	−3.0	−1.5	5.4	2.4	−4.4	−1.2	−2.0	3.0	−1.6	−3.1	−2.3	−12.3	−19.7
1982	12.9	4.1	3.4	4.7	−2.2	−7.1	−1.3	−1.2	−4.3	0.8	−2.1	0.1	6.7
1983	3.6	6.9	7.8	−5.0	−5.4	−1.8	−1.5	−7.4	8.5	−2.2	5.6	8.1	16.3
1984	−2.5	6.5	−2.4	−3.7	−5.4	3.4	−4.8	3.2	−0.1	0.7	4.0	0.2	−1.7
1985	2.1	−4.4	3.3	−6.8	0.4	−7.2	−4.2	0.3	10.2	7.2	−1.8	−6.0	−8.3
1986	1.2	−0.8	−5.1	−1.8	−10.1	10.3	4.1	4.6	−9.0	6.0	−0.7	−6.2	−9.2
1987	13.2	3.3	−2.4	6.0	−7.1	1.4	−0.8	5.2	0.8	−6.3	−1.1	2.3	13.7
1988	7.4	5.5	−0.9	0.04	−4.3	−4.8	7.0	3.9	2.8	0.5	−2.1	1.8	17.1
1989	3.3	2.1	−6.4	−2.2	−6.3	4.8	7.7	−2.4	0.8	0.2	−0.5	4.4	4.6
1990	−1.7	−0.8	−3.3	0.1	0.2	−0.03	8.1	−3.4	0.2	1.3	−3.0	2.7	−0.2
1991	0.4	3.5	−3.9	−1.3	−3.1	−2.0	1.3	−4.3	9.6	−4.3	1.7	−3.1	−6.2
1992	6.6	0.3	−3.4	−2.2	−5.0	4.2	1.7	0.2	−0.1	0.2	0.5	4.0	6.5
1993	−0.4	4.4	−5.0	0.7	−4.4	2.3	0.2	−0.1	−1.4	−0.1	−2.1	1.3	−4.8
1994	4.1	0.9	−3.7	−4.0	−7.8	−2.4	11.8	−1.2	−3.3	2.2	−3.9	8.1	−1.1
1995	2.0	0.2	−16.9	2.0	−5.2	5.2	4.9	−3.9	5.3	2.6	−1.1	−1.8	−8.6
1996	−3.9	0.1	−2.3	−8.2	12.5	2.0	4.1	5.4	−5.6	−2.2	−4.5	2.0	−2.2
1997	2.8	4.2	−6.5	−0.5	0.3	−0.7	9.6	−4.8	−0.1	0.6	1.6	−3.2	2.3
1998	1.5	−4.6	2.2	5.7	−4.6	−1.9	−7.8	−1.5	4.7	5.3	−3.4	−3.6	−8.9
1999	7.5	4.5	−6.5	−1.2	−0.04	−0.3	2.8	3.4	4.1	−0.9	2.0	−0.6	15.0
2000	3.5	−1.2	−3.1	0.4	−2.9	−0.8	3.1	−2.7	5.5	2.8	1.9	5.2	12.0
2001	−1.4	5.9	−10.7	−1.4	3.9	−0.6	−0.1	−1.0	−8.0	1.1	3.1	0.7	−9.3
2002	6.8	−1.8	−11.3	−3.3	−4.2	4.3	6.6	−0.8	5.1	3.6	7.2	1.5	12.6
2003	0.4	−5.2	−7.2	2.2	−3.0	0.2	11.2	6.6	2.5	7.0	2.5	−21.1	−7.7
2004	−0.1	4.7	−0.8	5.5	10.2	−3.2	3.5	−4.6	3.1	−3.2	6.0	−1.9	19.4
2005	0.6	−2.6	−0.9	0.4	−1.1	−6.4	5.2	−1.4	9.4	1.0	5.3	0.7	9.7
2006	−5.0	−4.8	−14.8	−1.1	8.9	7.0	3.5	5.0	−3.5	−2.3	1.5	3.8	−4.0
2007	0.7	4.2	−2.2	−0.8	−2.8	−1.3	10.7	−3.1	3.0	−4.9	0.9	0.4	4.0
2008	−2.0	0.1	−7.0	6.5	9.0	1.5	2.8	−2.1	−3.5	−7.6	−5.4	−1.8	−10.5
2009	−1.1	1.0	−4.9	1.0	−0.8	4.2	5.8	−3.9	−0.6	−0.5	0.1	0.5	0.1
2010	3.7	2.9	1.8	0.7	−5.3	0.9	5.1	2.8	2.4	−0.8	7.6	1.9	25.7
2011	5.3	−1.0	7.2	−6.3	−7.0	5.2	5.8	−2.8	7.6	−3.3	4.2	−1.7	12.1
2012	5.9	0.9	−10.5	−1.7	4.2								
TOTALS	82.9	30.2	−65.6	33.1	−65.2	13.8	97.0	−14.4	64.8	−24.4	55.8	−6.5	
AVG.	2.0	0.7	−1.6	0.8	−1.6	0.3	2.4	−0.4	1.6	−0.6	1.4	−0.2	
# Up	27	25	13	23	15	20	27	17	25	20	25	23	
# Down	14	16	28	18	26	20	13	23	15	20	15	17	

LEAN HOGS CYCLE, SEASONAL PATTERN, AND TRADING GUIDE

Demand for pork has increased in recent years, building a solid base, as consumers are switching to lower cholesterol and leaner protein meat sources. This in turn has helped to increase the overall demand for pork, which has been named "the other white meat." However, unlike beef, the breeding cycle is significantly shorter for pork. Female pigs can start breeding at an average of seven months of age, and the gestation period is less than four months. Thus, production can better maintain pace with demand.

Price action of the hog market has a reasonably defined seasonal price pattern. Pork is heaviest, both in supply and in weight, at the end of October into November, when feed grain is more abundant and less expensive due to harvest pressure. From March through May, we typically see packers buy, preparing for summer grilling season demand. As hog inventories start to decline, we see a typical peak in May. During summer months, demand and prices tend to decline, as inventories are used up on grills and fewer people cook indoors.

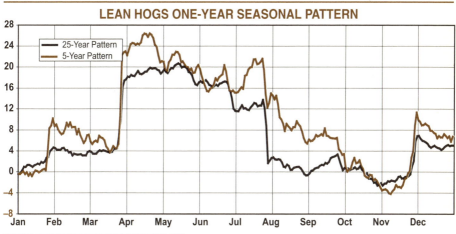

LEAN HOGS ONE-YEAR SEASONAL PATTERN

Based on near-term futures contract daily data 1987–2011

LEAN HOGS NEAR-TERM CONTRACT ANNUAL HIGHS, LOWS, AND CLOSES SINCE 1970

YEAR	HIGH DATE	HIGH CLOSE	LOW DATE	LOW CLOSE	YEAR CLOSE	YEAR	HIGH DATE	HIGH CLOSE	LOW DATE	LOW CLOSE	YEAR CLOSE
1970	01/06	28.450	10/28	16.150	16.350	1992	05/08	48.950	07/28	37.725	43.625
1971	12/30	25.050	01/08	16.050	25.050	1993	03/31	56.225	01/06	42.450	45.350
1972	12/27	32.975	02/28	23.350	32.550	1994	03/28	53.425	11/23	31.650	39.350
1973	08/13	57.050	02/07	30.075	44.300	1995	12/13	50.725	01/06	37.100	48.575
1974	01/07	48.100	06/11	24.025	41.900	1996	12/30	79.500	01/31	44.350	79.225
1975	10/02	65.050	01/17	36.975	48.475	1997	04/17	85.450	12/31	57.700	57.700
1976	06/14	53.275	11/03	29.825	37.625	1998	06/16	62.800	12/16	27.950	32.650
1977	06/03	47.700	08/01	33.850	43.325	1999	05/10	60.700	01/04	30.725	54.500
1978	05/16	56.050	01/30	41.325	49.100	2000	04/24	77.475	10/30	50.750	56.825
1979	01/19	54.125	08/01	31.425	41.675	2001	04/16	73.175	10/25	47.575	57.050
1980	11/28	57.450	04/02	32.050	47.750	2002	02/05	62.725	09/03	30.050	51.600
1981	06/08	56.850	03/20	38.825	43.350	2003	06/09	68.450	11/26	48.450	53.425
1982	09/08	64.750	01/04	43.825	56.750	2004	06/23	78.125	01/12	51.775	76.400
1983	01/14	59.700	10/10	40.200	51.250	2005	04/01	80.800	07/27	56.625	65.275
1984	04/03	57.750	02/23	44.225	53.325	2006	06/19	76.925	01/26	57.175	61.700
1985	01/02	53.750	09/09	34.800	46.625	2007	04/16	77.850	11/06	51.125	57.875
1986	07/25	59.600	02/28	38.075	47.250	2008	07/24	79.725	01/11	54.000	60.875
1987	06/15	59.275	12/22	40.650	41.075	2009	04/09	74.275	08/12	43.975	65.600
1988	05/31	54.725	09/06	37.550	46.525	2010	04/21	87.075	11/01	65.200	79.750
1989	11/24	51.125	09/11	38.750	48.700	2011	03/31	103.875	01/04	77.300	84.300
1990	05/21	67.000	02/02	46.550	48.875	2012*	03/27	93.725	01/11	82.900	AT PRESS TIME
1991	04/30	58.925	12/30	39.125	39.300						

*Through May 31, 2012

179

LEAN HOGS NEAR-TERM CONTRACT MONTHLY CLOSING PRICES

	Jan	Feb	Mar	Apr	May	Jun	Jul	Aug	Sep	Oct	Nov	Dec
1970	27.500	27.900	27.250	27.100	25.875	24.550	20.675	19.675	19.400	16.150	16.950	16.350
1971	17.675	17.600	19.875	20.575	22.900	21.275	19.125	18.125	20.800	21.250	23.575	25.050
1972	25.975	23.875	27.200	27.825	28.750	29.150	26.300	27.900	29.325	29.100	29.600	32.550
1973	31.125	35.875	36.275	37.175	40.450	43.050	55.575	46.775	43.450	43.850	44.975	44.300
1974	45.050	38.250	36.750	33.300	28.500	35.325	41.325	34.275	43.500	41.575	44.300	41.900
1975	40.175	38.600	45.250	46.800	49.875	52.725	48.700	55.525	63.675	51.100	50.200	48.475
1976	40.550	43.825	47.700	51.050	50.475	47.375	38.075	38.425	32.950	30.100	31.700	37.625
1977	34.925	34.700	38.425	43.650	46.550	45.250	34.500	37.825	36.950	39.125	39.350	43.325
1978	42.750	44.075	50.850	51.850	54.525	44.500	45.850	46.475	52.250	50.400	52.200	49.100
1979	51.125	52.300	48.000	50.250	43.850	35.550	32.400	36.875	37.200	37.725	42.325	41.675
1980	38.950	36.850	34.300	34.475	34.775	40.250	43.700	42.250	50.750	49.925	57.450	47.750
1981	47.350	43.600	49.825	49.000	56.075	51.275	49.350	49.450	50.250	48.700	45.525	43.350
1982	49.450	45.825	55.475	59.925	62.650	57.800	59.525	61.750	59.550	54.475	58.125	56.750
1983	54.200	51.350	52.100	49.300	47.075	45.125	40.325	43.050	40.950	43.325	47.525	51.250
1984	46.800	45.650	56.125	54.425	56.075	55.775	47.425	47.550	45.950	48.450	53.925	53.325
1985	48.750	46.625	49.575	46.300	51.100	48.350	40.000	36.300	43.200	46.725	47.650	46.625
1986	42.000	38.075	43.825	46.600	48.125	56.075	54.700	57.725	51.600	51.600	52.450	47.250
1987	45.975	43.275	47.825	53.475	54.800	53.100	48.800	50.375	45.275	42.975	42.625	41.075
1988	44.150	43.250	49.300	48.800	54.725	45.275	39.325	38.550	43.025	41.150	43.775	46.525
1989	43.475	43.725	46.475	46.625	46.975	47.425	39.825	40.475	44.375	46.575	49.800	48.700
1990	46.875	50.350	57.025	63.125	62.400	58.300	54.825	48.300	52.700	51.775	48.200	48.875
1991	50.500	51.875	58.425	58.925	54.800	50.575	45.250	44.175	44.725	41.725	42.475	39.300
1992	40.025	39.725	45.675	48.100	45.000	44.700	37.850	40.050	42.875	42.425	43.375	43.625
1993	43.800	45.525	56.225	51.350	49.650	44.900	45.725	47.175	47.400	49.050	46.475	45.350
1994	51.700	49.500	52.850	51.225	47.225	45.350	42.325	38.575	36.400	35.275	34.400	39.350
1995	39.650	39.750	42.950	42.350	44.325	46.625	44.225	44.650	46.600	43.700	48.275	48.575
1996	44.350	48.550	54.850	59.750	58.225	51.525	53.625	52.425	57.300	54.400	78.350	79.225
1997	74.750	74.475	81.875	83.550	80.650	81.950	75.150	70.450	63.425	62.225	60.475	57.700
1998	57.625	49.025	59.975	59.925	59.800	54.925	42.450	37.275	40.400	37.400	36.575	32.650
1999	43.025	43.000	52.350	59.075	55.500	44.575	43.350	45.800	46.625	46.525	56.175	54.500
2000	60.250	58.075	73.150	76.650	68.600	69.025	57.450	52.925	54.200	51.175	56.675	56.825
2001	57.150	62.800	69.000	67.575	66.600	69.050	60.175	58.250	54.825	51.650	55.250	57.050
2002	60.900	60.350	60.500	52.050	47.775	46.725	41.700	30.875	40.550	43.125	54.200	51.600
2003	56.850	54.550	58.350	62.775	67.525	63.975	51.300	54.775	53.600	53.325	55.200	53.425
2004	59.200	62.025	74.650	74.075	75.275	76.700	69.225	65.975	69.125	67.450	77.150	76.400
2005	75.550	74.225	79.275	77.450	71.400	65.025	57.525	63.700	63.350	61.675	67.350	65.275
2006	61.825	61.475	65.275	67.000	66.425	70.375	61.750	66.900	60.850	64.950	65.175	61.700
2007	68.225	67.750	75.400	75.100	74.525	70.675	75.200	66.825	62.250	53.875	62.300	57.875
2008	66.450	59.950	67.950	73.475	78.100	70.900	74.350	68.425	64.200	54.800	67.025	60.875
2009	62.975	60.900	72.400	64.525	65.625	60.650	53.900	48.150	49.600	56.700	66.875	65.600
2010	68.600	72.800	82.900	86.325	82.600	81.650	79.025	75.150	74.875	66.200	75.775	79.750
2011	94.000	88.800	103.875	95.225	89.925	91.675	92.400	85.500	87.800	87.475	91.575	84.300
2012	88.875	89.425	90.400	85.925	91.000							

LEAN HOGS NEAR-TERM CONTRACT MONTHLY PERCENT CHANGES

	Jan	Feb	Mar	Apr	May	Jun	Jul	Aug	Sep	Oct	Nov	Dec	Year's Change
1970	0.9	1.5	−2.3	−0.6	−4.5	−5.1	−15.8	−4.8	−1.4	−16.8	5.0	−3.5	−40.0
1971	8.1	−0.4	12.9	3.5	11.3	−7.1	−10.1	−5.2	14.8	2.2	10.9	6.3	53.2
1973	3.7	−8.1	13.9	2.3	3.3	1.4	−9.8	6.1	5.1	−0.8	1.7	10.0	29.9
1973	−4.4	15.3	1.1	2.5	8.8	6.4	29.1	−15.8	−7.1	0.9	2.6	−1.5	36.1
1974	1.7	−15.1	−3.9	−9.4	−14.4	23.9	17.0	−17.1	26.9	−4.4	6.6	−5.4	−5.4
1975	−4.1	−3.9	17.2	3.4	6.6	5.7	−7.6	14.0	14.7	−19.7	−1.8	−3.4	15.7
1976	−16.3	8.1	8.8	7.0	−1.1	−6.1	−19.6	0.9	−14.2	−8.6	5.3	18.7	−22.4
1977	−7.2	−0.6	10.7	13.6	6.6	−2.8	−23.8	9.6	−2.3	5.9	0.6	10.1	15.1
1978	−1.3	3.1	15.4	2.0	5.2	−18.4	3.0	1.4	12.4	−3.5	3.6	−5.9	13.3
1979	4.1	2.3	−8.2	4.7	−12.7	−18.9	−8.9	13.8	0.9	1.4	12.2	−1.5	−15.1
1980	−6.5	−5.4	−6.9	0.5	0.9	15.7	8.6	−3.3	20.1	−1.6	15.1	−16.9	14.6
1981	−0.8	−7.9	14.3	−1.7	14.4	−8.6	−3.8	0.2	1.6	−3.1	−6.5	−4.8	−9.2
1982	14.1	−7.3	21.1	8.0	4.5	−7.7	3.0	3.7	−3.6	−8.5	6.7	−2.4	30.9
1983	−4.5	−5.3	1.5	−5.4	−4.5	−4.1	−10.6	6.8	−4.9	5.8	9.7	7.8	−9.7
1984	−8.7	−2.5	22.9	−3.0	3.0	−0.5	−15.0	0.3	−3.4	5.4	11.3	−1.1	4.0
1985	−8.6	−4.4	6.3	−6.6	10.4	−5.4	−17.3	−9.3	19.0	8.2	2.0	−2.2	−12.6
1986	−9.9	−9.3	15.1	6.3	3.3	16.5	−2.5	5.5	−10.6	N/C	1.6	−9.9	1.3
1987	−2.7	−5.9	10.5	11.8	2.5	−3.1	−8.1	3.2	−10.1	−5.1	−0.8	−3.6	−13.1
1988	7.5	−2.0	14.0	−1.0	12.1	−17.3	−13.1	−2.0	11.6	−4.4	6.4	6.3	13.3
1989	−6.6	0.6	6.3	0.3	0.8	1.0	−16.0	1.6	9.6	5.0	6.9	−2.2	4.7
1990	−3.7	7.4	13.3	10.7	−1.1	−6.6	−6.0	−11.9	9.1	−1.8	−6.9	1.4	0.4
1991	3.3	2.7	12.6	0.9	−7.0	−7.7	−10.5	−2.4	1.2	−6.7	1.8	−7.5	−19.6
1992	1.8	−0.7	15.0	5.3	−6.4	−0.7	−15.3	5.8	7.1	−1.0	2.2	0.6	11.0
1993	0.4	3.9	23.5	−8.7	−3.3	−9.6	1.8	3.2	0.5	3.5	−5.2	−2.4	4.0
1994	14.0	−4.3	6.8	−3.1	−7.8	−4.0	−6.7	−8.9	−5.6	−3.1	−2.5	14.4	−13.2
1995	0.8	0.3	8.1	−1.4	4.7	5.2	−5.1	1.0	4.4	−6.2	10.5	0.6	23.4
1996	−8.7	9.5	13.0	8.9	−2.6	−11.5	4.1	−2.2	9.3	−5.1	44.0	1.1	63.1
1997	−5.6	−0.4	9.9	2.0	−3.5	1.6	−8.3	−6.3	−10.0	−1.9	−2.8	−4.6	−27.2
1998	−0.1	−14.9	22.3	−0.1	−0.2	−8.2	−22.7	−12.2	8.4	−7.4	−2.2	−10.7	−43.4
1999	31.8	−0.1	21.7	12.8	−6.1	−19.7	−2.7	5.7	1.8	−0.2	20.7	−3.0	66.9
2000	10.6	−3.6	26.0	4.8	−10.5	0.6	−16.8	−7.9	2.4	−5.6	10.7	0.3	4.3
2001	0.6	9.9	9.9	−2.1	−1.4	3.7	−12.9	−3.2	−5.9	−5.8	7.0	3.3	0.4
2002	6.7	−0.9	0.2	−14.0	−8.2	−2.2	−10.8	−26.0	31.3	6.4	25.7	−4.8	−9.6
2003	10.2	−4.0	7.0	7.6	7.6	−5.3	−19.8	6.8	−2.1	−0.5	3.5	−3.2	3.5
2004	10.8	4.8	20.4	−0.8	1.6	1.9	−9.7	−4.7	4.8	−2.4	14.4	−1.0	43.0
2005	−1.1	−1.8	6.8	−2.3	−7.8	−8.9	−11.5	10.7	−0.5	−2.6	9.2	−3.1	−14.6
2006	−5.3	−0.6	6.2	2.6	−0.9	5.9	−12.3	8.3	−9.0	6.7	0.3	−5.3	−5.5
2007	10.6	−0.7	11.3	−0.4	−0.8	−5.2	6.4	−11.1	−6.8	−13.5	15.6	−7.1	−6.2
2008	14.8	−9.8	13.3	8.1	6.3	−9.2	4.9	−8.0	−6.2	−14.6	22.3	−9.2	5.2
2009	3.4	−3.3	18.9	−10.9	1.7	−7.6	−11.1	−10.7	3.0	14.3	17.9	−1.9	7.8
2010	4.6	6.1	13.9	4.1	−4.3	−1.2	−3.2	−4.9	−0.4	−11.6	14.5	5.2	21.6
2011	17.9	−5.5	17.0	−8.3	−5.6	1.9	0.8	−7.5	2.7	−0.4	4.7	−7.9	5.7
2012	5.4	0.6	1.1	−5.0	5.9								
TOTALS	81.7	−52.6	468.9	48.9	6.8	−121.3	−288.7	−76.8	118.6	−101.2	304.5	−49.9	
AVG.	1.9	−1.2	10.9	1.1	0.2	−2.9	−6.9	−1.8	2.8	−2.4	7.3	−1.2	
# Up	24	15	39	24	21	14	10	20	24	12	34	14	
# Down	19	28	4	19	22	28	32	22	18	29	8	28	

BRITISH POUND CYCLE, SEASONAL PATTERN, AND TRADING GUIDE

The British economy is driven by manufacturing, agricultural production, and energy production from oil, coal, and natural gas, which is considered to account for as much as 10% of Britain's gross domestic production. In addition, London is considered the world's leading international financial service center.

Their economy runs on a fiscal year that begins in April. Since the pound is valued against the U.S. dollar, we have a tendency to see bottoms in March, as multi-conglomerate international companies make their fiscal year-end adjustments. We see a major peak in December against the U.S. dollar, as money flows back into the United States for year-end tax adjustment purposes, also referred to as repatriation of funds.

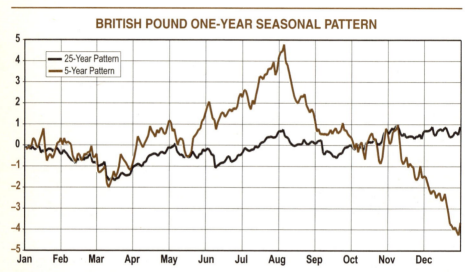

BRITISH POUND ONE-YEAR SEASONAL PATTERN

Based on near-term futures contract daily data 1987–2011

BRITISH POUND NEAR-TERM CONTRACT ANNUAL HIGHS, LOWS, AND CLOSES SINCE 1976

YEAR	HIGH DATE	HIGH CLOSE	LOW DATE	LOW CLOSE	YEAR CLOSE	YEAR	HIGH DATE	HIGH CLOSE	LOW DATE	LOW CLOSE	YEAR CLOSE
1976	02/26	202.40	10/28	154.05	166.40	1995	03/07	164.42	12/12	152.88	155.14
1977	12/30	191.95	01/03	166.95	191.95	1996	12/31	171.24	05/01	149.02	171.24
1978	10/30	209.75	05/19	180.05	204.10	1997	11/12	170.32	08/12	157.54	164.66
1979	07/24	231.75	02/02	197.20	220.15	1998	10/08	170.52	01/09	160.68	165.68
1980	10/23	244.55	04/03	213.55	241.85	1999	10/21	167.70	07/09	154.86	161.90
1981	01/20	244.40	09/25	177.35	190.40	2000	01/20	165.38	11/24	140.06	149.48
1982	01/04	193.20	11/24	158.65	162.95	2001	01/05	150.30	06/12	136.84	144.86
1983	02/28	162.80	12/13	141.95	146.25	2002	12/31	160.22	01/28	140.38	160.22
1984	02/28	148.85	12/31	115.40	115.40	2003	12/31	177.39	04/07	154.48	177.39
1985	11/29	148.85	02/25	105.00	143.90	2004	12/07	194.53	05/11	175.12	190.71
1986	04/28	154.90	02/04	136.65	147.20	2005	03/04	192.30	11/25	171.28	171.87
1987	12/31	188.25	01/07	145.75	188.25	2006	12/01	198.06	03/10	172.82	195.72
1988	04/18	189.65	09/22	165.38	179.92	2007	11/08	210.64	03/05	192.23	197.85
1989	01/03	180.98	06/14	149.26	158.88	2008	03/07	201.37	12/30	143.82	147.57
1990	11/27	197.30	03/21	156.88	190.94	2009	08/05	170.19	03/10	137.30	161.71
1991	02/06	198.90	07/02	158.58	184.48	2010	01/19	163.55	05/18	143.21	155.81
1992	09/02	199.96	12/28	147.96	149.86	2011	04/29	167.01	09/22	153.42	155.00
1993	04/26	158.02	02/12	141.18	146.84	2012*	04/27	162.64	01/13	152.93	*AT PRESS TIME*
1994	10/25	163.74	02/09	145.78	156.70						

*Through May 31, 2012

BRITISH POUND NEAR-TERM CONTRACT MONTHLY CLOSING PRICES

	Jan	Feb	Mar	Apr	May	Jun	Jul	Aug	Sep	Oct	Nov	Dec
1976	201.80	202.30	189.90	182.80	175.60	175.70	176.70	177.25	162.55	156.15	164.90	166.40
1977	169.70	171.10	170.70	171.45	171.30	171.05	173.40	174.20	175.25	183.50	181.70	191.95
1978	195.30	193.95	186.00	181.45	183.85	184.00	192.70	193.80	195.75	206.45	194.05	204.10
1979	197.75	202.40	206.45	206.65	206.85	216.10	223.50	226.00	219.20	207.70	219.20	220.15
1980	225.65	225.45	216.15	225.45	234.30	232.25	230.40	240.10	237.25	242.30	236.00	241.85
1981	236.60	220.00	224.80	214.90	207.75	194.55	184.45	183.95	180.90	187.75	195.85	190.40
1982	187.90	181.60	179.20	182.50	178.10	174.60	174.10	172.15	169.80	167.70	163.15	162.95
1983	151.80	150.65	148.25	156.15	160.20	152.80	151.45	149.65	149.45	149.30	146.40	146.25
1984	140.40	148.85	144.65	140.40	138.75	136.55	130.25	130.85	123.80	122.50	119.30	115.40
1985	111.95	107.30	123.20	122.45	129.00	129.60	140.75	138.75	138.50	143.65	148.85	143.90
1986	140.55	143.80	145.75	153.50	147.20	153.15	148.65	149.05	142.95	139.80	143.15	147.20
1987	150.50	154.35	159.55	166.15	162.85	161.00	158.65	162.95	161.75	171.90	182.95	188.25
1988	176.10	177.15	188.10	187.20	183.55	170.44	170.24	168.22	168.14	175.64	184.80	179.92
1989	174.52	174.14	167.84	167.96	156.90	154.22	165.40	156.54	160.12	156.86	156.72	158.88
1990	166.60	167.52	162.62	162.80	167.24	172.56	184.82	188.58	184.86	193.20	193.76	190.94
1991	195.16	190.52	171.90	171.82	169.30	160.42	167.62	167.70	173.38	172.86	176.38	184.48
1992	177.08	175.18	171.38	176.24	182.38	188.02	191.24	198.32	175.56	154.86	151.34	149.86
1993	148.00	142.54	150.44	156.74	155.98	148.30	147.76	148.88	148.82	147.66	148.54	146.84
1994	150.26	148.56	148.26	151.80	150.98	154.24	153.88	153.46	157.46	163.46	156.56	156.70
1995	157.96	158.42	162.00	161.04	158.96	159.04	159.66	155.12	157.82	157.94	153.08	155.14
1996	151.12	153.18	152.56	150.68	155.02	155.16	155.46	156.18	156.46	162.60	168.12	171.24
1997	159.78	162.92	163.86	162.26	164.04	166.06	163.72	161.94	161.14	167.18	168.68	164.66
1998	162.88	164.38	166.56	166.88	163.02	166.08	162.80	167.78	169.24	167.02	164.68	165.68
1999	164.50	160.12	161.08	160.86	160.10	157.92	162.26	160.68	164.64	164.48	159.90	161.90
2000	161.56	157.94	159.40	155.28	149.82	151.86	150.08	145.10	147.70	145.04	142.54	149.48
2001	146.24	144.56	141.58	142.90	141.58	140.94	142.28	145.38	146.68	145.16	142.28	144.86
2002	140.66	141.58	141.90	145.34	145.48	152.44	155.82	154.68	156.26	156.00	155.40	160.22
2003	164.20	157.26	157.24	159.44	163.76	164.68	160.46	157.40	165.36	168.94	172.03	177.39
2004	181.79	186.46	183.16	177.24	183.04	180.57	181.24	179.83	180.23	183.12	190.90	190.71
2005	187.78	192.18	188.26	190.30	181.66	178.63	175.49	180.18	176.03	176.93	172.89	171.87
2006	178.02	175.45	173.80	182.28	186.97	185.08	187.00	190.52	187.30	190.82	196.62	195.72
2007	196.38	196.37	196.69	199.86	197.94	200.55	203.33	201.61	204.19	207.85	205.58	197.85
2008	198.48	198.63	197.12	198.29	197.88	198.19	197.63	181.56	178.40	161.06	153.71	145.57
2009	144.43	143.23	143.48	148.20	161.38	164.63	166.87	162.66	160.00	164.42	164.22	161.71
2010	159.86	152.45	151.74	152.73	145.64	149.56	156.93	153.72	157.20	160.13	155.69	155.81
2011	160.20	162.68	160.52	167.01	164.50	160.51	164.23	162.38	156.09	161.26	156.97	155.00
2012	157.49	159.19	159.88	162.29	154.11							

BRITISH POUND NEAR-TERM CONTRACT MONTHLY PERCENT CHANGES

	Jan	Feb	Mar	Apr	May	Jun	Jul	Aug	Sep	Oct	Nov	Dec	Year's Change
1976	0.7	0.2	−6.1	−3.7	−3.9	0.1	0.6	0.3	−8.3	−3.9	5.6	0.9	−17.0
1977	2.0	0.8	−0.2	0.4	−0.1	−0.1	1.4	0.5	0.6	4.7	−1.0	5.6	15.4
1978	1.7	−0.7	−4.1	−2.4	1.3	0.1	4.7	0.6	1.0	5.5	−6.0	5.2	6.3
1979	−3.1	2.4	2.0	0.1	0.1	4.5	3.4	1.1	−3.0	−5.2	5.5	0.4	7.9
1980	2.5	−0.1	−4.1	4.3	3.9	−0.9	−0.8	4.2	−1.2	2.1	−2.6	2.5	9.9
1981	−2.2	−7.0	2.2	−4.4	−3.3	−6.4	−5.2	−0.3	−1.7	3.8	4.3	−2.8	−21.3
1982	−1.3	−3.4	−1.3	1.8	−2.4	−2.0	−0.3	−1.1	−1.4	−1.2	−2.7	−0.1	−14.4
1983	−6.8	−0.8	−1.6	5.3	2.6	−4.6	−0.9	−1.2	−0.1	−0.1	−1.9	−0.1	−10.2
1984	−4.0	6.0	−2.8	−2.9	−1.2	−1.6	−4.6	0.5	−5.4	−1.1	−2.6	−3.3	−21.1
1985	−3.0	−4.2	14.8	−0.6	5.3	0.5	8.6	−1.4	−0.2	3.7	3.6	−3.3	24.7
1986	−2.3	2.3	1.4	5.3	−4.1	4.0	−2.9	0.3	−4.1	−2.2	2.4	2.8	2.3
1987	2.2	2.6	3.4	4.1	−2.0	−1.1	−1.5	2.7	−0.7	6.3	6.4	2.9	27.9
1988	−6.5	0.6	6.2	−0.5	−1.9	−7.1	−0.1	−1.2	−0.1	4.5	5.2	−2.6	−4.4
1989	−3.0	−0.2	−3.6	0.1	−6.6	−1.7	7.2	−5.4	2.3	−2.0	−0.1	1.4	−11.7
1990	4.9	0.6	−2.9	0.1	2.7	3.2	7.1	2.0	−2.0	4.5	0.3	−1.5	20.2
1991	2.2	−2.4	−9.8	−0.1	−1.5	−5.2	4.5	0.1	3.4	−0.3	2.0	4.6	−3.4
1992	−4.0	−1.1	−2.2	2.8	3.5	3.1	1.7	3.7	−11.5	−11.8	−2.3	−1.0	−18.8
1993	−1.2	−3.7	5.5	4.2	−0.5	−4.9	−0.4	0.8	−0.04	−0.8	0.6	−1.1	−2.0
1994	2.3	−1.1	−0.2	2.4	−0.5	2.2	−0.2	−0.3	2.6	3.8	−4.2	0.1	6.7
1995	0.8	0.3	2.3	−0.6	−1.3	0.1	0.4	−2.8	1.7	0.1	−3.1	1.3	−1.0
1996	−2.6	1.4	−0.4	−1.2	2.9	0.1	0.2	0.5	0.2	3.9	3.4	1.9	10.4
1997	−6.7	2.0	0.6	−1.0	1.1	1.2	−1.4	−1.1	−0.5	3.7	0.9	−2.4	−3.8
1998	−1.1	0.9	1.3	0.2	−2.3	1.9	−2.0	3.1	0.9	−1.3	−1.4	0.6	0.6
1999	−0.7	−2.7	0.6	−0.1	−0.5	−1.4	2.7	−1.0	2.5	−0.1	−2.8	1.3	−2.3
2000	−0.2	−2.2	0.9	−2.6	−3.5	1.4	−1.2	−3.3	1.8	−1.8	−1.7	4.9	−7.7
2001	−2.2	−1.1	−2.1	0.9	−0.9	−0.5	1.0	2.2	0.9	−1.0	−2.0	1.8	−3.1
2002	−2.9	0.7	0.2	2.4	0.1	4.8	2.2	−0.7	1.0	−0.2	−0.4	3.1	10.6
2003	2.5	−4.2	−0.01	1.4	2.7	0.6	−2.6	−1.9	5.1	2.2	1.8	3.1	10.7
2004	2.5	2.6	−1.8	−3.2	3.3	−1.3	0.4	−0.8	0.2	1.6	4.2	−0.1	7.5
2005	−1.5	2.3	−2.0	1.1	−4.5	−1.7	−1.8	2.7	−2.3	0.5	−2.3	−0.6	−9.9
2006	3.6	−1.4	−0.9	4.9	2.6	−1.0	1.0	1.9	−1.7	1.9	3.0	−0.5	13.9
2007	0.3	−0.01	0.2	1.6	−1.0	1.3	1.4	−0.8	1.3	1.8	−1.1	−3.8	1.1
2008	0.3	0.1	−0.8	0.6	−0.2	0.2	−0.3	−8.1	−1.7	−9.7	−4.6	−5.3	−26.4
2009	−0.8	−0.8	0.2	3.3	8.9	2.0	1.4	−2.5	−1.6	2.8	−0.1	−1.5	11.1
2010	−1.1	−4.6	−0.5	0.7	−4.6	2.7	4.9	−2.0	2.3	1.9	−2.8	0.1	−3.6
2011	2.8	1.5	−1.3	4.0	−1.5	−2.4	2.3	−1.1	−3.9	3.3	−2.7	−1.3	−0.5
2012	1.6	1.1	0.4	1.5	−5.0								
TOTALS	−24.3	−13.3	−6.5	30.2	−12.3	−9.9	30.9	−9.8	−23.6	19.9	0.8	13.2	
AVG.	−0.7	−0.4	−0.2	0.8	−0.3	−0.3	0.9	−0.3	−0.7	0.6	0.2	0.4	
# Up	16	18	16	24	14	19	20	17	16	20	15	19	
# Down	21	19	21	13	23	17	16	19	20	16	21	17	

EURO CYCLE, SEASONAL PATTERN, AND TRADING GUIDE

The euro is quoted in terms of the U.S. dollar, which is considered the world's reserve currency in which most internationally traded goods are priced. This contract from a historic perspective is relatively new. One can adjust the value to reflect the more historic theoretical value by combining the prices of the German Deutsche mark, the French franc, and the Italian lira.

The market has seen a tendency of bottoms in September, as multi-conglomerate international companies make their fiscal year-end adjustments; and we see peaks in December against the U.S. dollar, as money flows back into the United States for year-end tax adjustment purposes. We are keeping a close eye on the euro's seasonal trends. They are still evolving due to its relatively short 13-year history. In addition, the European bank crisis has been muting and magnifying the euro's value and seasonal pattern, especially as the Greek, Spanish, Italian and other euro zone nation's economies recover.

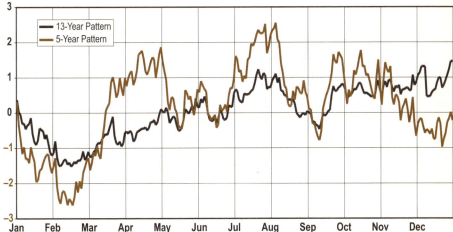

EURO ONE-YEAR SEASONAL PATTERN

— 13-Year Pattern
— 5-Year Pattern

Based on near-term futures contract daily data 1999–2011

EURO NEAR-TERM CONTRACT ANNUAL HIGHS, LOWS, AND CLOSES SINCE 1999

YEAR	HIGH DATE	HIGH CLOSE	LOW DATE	LOW CLOSE	YEAR CLOSE	YEAR	HIGH DATE	HIGH CLOSE	LOW DATE	LOW CLOSE	YEAR CLOSE
1999	01/04	116.09	12/03	106.68	107.35	2006	12/01	133.43	02/27	118.64	132.36
2000	01/11	108.44	10/25	97.82	103.60	2007	11/26	148.72	01/11	129.28	145.90
2001	01/05	104.45	12/24	87.35	88.78	2008	04/22	159.64	11/12	124.89	139.21
2002	12/31	104.71	01/31	85.68	104.71	2009	11/25	151.37	03/05	125.43	143.34
2003	12/31	125.34	01/02	103.30	125.34	2010	01/11	145.19	06/07	119.36	133.64
2004	12/30	136.59	05/13	118.11	135.58	2011	05/04	148.33	01/07	129.29	129.68
2005	01/03	134.90	11/16	117.06	118.80	2012*	02/24	134.60	05/31	123.68	AT PRESS TIME

*Through May 31, 2012

EURO NEAR-TERM CONTRACT MONTHLY CLOSING PRICES

	Jan	Feb	Mar	Apr	May	Jun	Jul	Aug	Sep	Oct	Nov	Dec
1999	113.64	111.78	110.63	109.66	108.63	108.58	110.31	109.54	110.26	109.46	107.01	107.35
2000	105.12	104.85	104.52	102.04	103.31	104.39	102.93	100.83	100.67	98.90	100.02	103.60
2001	103.17	102.61	100.37	100.79	98.65	98.77	100.10	101.91	101.85	101.33	101.18	88.78
2002	85.68	86.82	86.82	89.90	93.17	98.85	97.49	98.02	98.34	98.71	99.35	104.71
2003	107.36	107.95	108.68	111.59	117.83	114.69	112.26	109.66	116.20	115.59	119.84	125.34
2004	124.48	124.89	122.80	119.69	122.10	121.78	120.07	121.69	124.32	127.87	132.92	135.58
2005	130.35	132.43	129.82	128.79	123.06	121.37	121.51	123.44	120.59	120.23	118.04	118.80
2006	121.78	119.29	121.79	126.52	128.24	128.50	128.13	128.23	127.39	127.96	132.60	132.36
2007	130.57	132.42	133.94	136.76	134.63	135.68	137.11	136.47	142.93	145.10	146.43	145.90
2008	148.59	151.85	157.29	156.09	155.46	156.90	155.57	146.31	141.34	127.41	127.00	139.21
2009	127.85	126.96	132.83	132.61	141.31	140.40	142.54	143.30	146.45	147.26	149.91	143.34
2010	138.65	136.21	135.36	133.08	123.24	122.55	130.45	126.65	136.25	138.88	130.09	133.64
2011	136.88	138.01	141.81	148.20	143.79	144.88	143.48	143.77	134.15	139.20	134.36	129.68
2012	130.86	133.39	133.39	132.42	123.68							

EURO NEAR-TERM CONTRACT MONTHLY PERCENT CHANGES

	Jan	Feb	Mar	Apr	May	Jun	Jul	Aug	Sep	Oct	Nov	Dec	Year's Change
1999	−1.7	−1.6	−1.0	−0.9	−0.9	−0.1	1.6	−0.7	0.7	−0.7	−2.2	0.3	−7.1
2000	−2.1	−0.3	−0.3	−2.4	1.2	1.0	−1.4	−2.0	−0.2	−1.8	1.1	3.6	−3.5
2001	−0.4	−0.5	−2.2	0.4	−2.1	0.1	1.3	1.8	−0.1	−0.5	−0.1	−12.3	−14.3
2002	−3.5	1.3	N/C	3.5	3.6	6.1	−1.4	0.5	0.3	0.4	0.6	5.4	17.9
2003	2.5	0.5	0.7	2.7	5.6	−2.7	−2.1	−2.3	6.0	−0.5	3.7	4.6	19.7
2004	−0.7	0.3	−1.7	−2.5	2.0	−0.3	−1.4	1.3	2.2	2.9	3.9	2.0	8.2
2005	−3.9	1.6	−2.0	−0.8	−4.4	−1.4	0.1	1.6	−2.3	−0.3	−1.8	0.6	−12.4
2006	2.5	−2.0	2.1	3.9	1.4	0.2	−0.3	0.1	−0.7	0.4	3.6	−0.2	11.4
2007	−1.4	1.4	1.1	2.1	−1.6	0.8	1.1	−0.5	4.7	1.5	0.9	−0.4	10.2
2008	1.8	2.2	3.6	−0.8	−0.4	0.9	−0.8	−6.0	−3.4	−9.9	−0.3	9.6	−4.6
2009	−8.2	−0.7	4.6	−0.2	6.6	−0.6	1.5	0.5	2.2	0.6	1.8	−4.4	3.0
2010	−3.3	−1.8	−0.6	−1.7	−7.4	−0.6	6.4	−2.9	7.6	1.9	−6.3	2.7	−6.8
2011	2.4	0.8	2.8	4.5	−3.0	0.8	−1.0	0.2	−6.7	3.8	−3.5	−3.5	−3.0
2012	0.9	1.9	N/C	−0.7	−6.6								
TOTALS	−15.1	3.1	7.1	7.1	−6.0	4.2	3.6	−8.4	10.3	−2.2	1.4	8.0	
AVG.	−1.1	0.2	0.5	0.5	−0.4	0.3	0.3	−0.6	0.8	−0.2	0.1	0.6	
# Up	5	8	6	6	6	7	6	7	7	7	7	8	
# Down	9	6	6	8	8	6	7	6	6	6	6	5	

SWISS FRANC CYCLE, SEASONAL PATTERN, AND TRADING GUIDE

The Swiss economy is driven by exporting technologically advanced machinery, agricultural products, and some chemical production. However, it is a major player in the banking community as a safe haven for international investors and a store house for gold bullion. Many times we see the value of the franc rise, as gold prices move up and the value of the U.S. dollar declines. In time of political and economic uncertainties, we also see the value of the franc rise against the U.S. dollar.

Their economy runs on a fiscal year that begins in January and ends in December. Since the franc is valued against the U.S. dollar, we have a tendency to see bottoms in June–August, when, coincidently, gold prices have a tendency to bottom. And we see a major peak in December against the U.S. dollar, as multi-conglomerate international companies make their fiscal year-end adjustments and as money flows back into the United States for year-end tax adjustment purposes, also referred to as repatriation of funds.

SWISS FRANC ONE-YEAR SEASONAL PATTERN

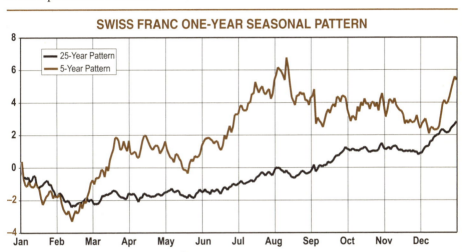

Based on near-term futures contract daily data 1987–2011

SWISS FRANC NEAR-TERM CONTRACT ANNUAL HIGHS, LOWS, AND CLOSES SINCE 1976

YEAR	HIGH DATE	HIGH CLOSE	LOW DATE	LOW CLOSE	YEAR CLOSE	YEAR	HIGH DATE	HIGH CLOSE	LOW DATE	LOW CLOSE	YEAR CLOSE
1976	06/02	41.70	01/02	38.44	41.24	1995	04/18	90.03	01/03	76.44	87.31
1977	12/30	50.79	03/09	39.15	50.79	1996	01/02	87.02	12/27	74.65	75.20
1978	10/30	69.22	01/18	50.14	63.47	1997	01/02	74.88	08/05	65.52	68.97
1979	10/01	66.26	05/29	57.72	63.94	1998	10/07	77.28	07/09	65.28	73.31
1980	01/07	64.91	04/07	54.42	56.97	1999	01/14	74.11	12/02	62.75	63.47
1981	01/06	58.34	08/10	45.86	56.68	2000	01/05	64.82	10/26	55.19	62.17
1982	01/04	56.48	11/11	44.90	50.70	2001	09/21	63.29	07/05	55.04	60.20
1983	01/10	52.65	09/01	45.68	46.58	2002	12/31	72.49	01/31	58.11	72.49
1984	03/08	48.04	12/31	38.79	38.79	2003	12/31	80.66	09/02	70.57	80.66
1985	12/31	49.08	03/05	34.27	49.08	2004	12/30	88.76	04/23	76.08	87.96
1986	09/19	62.52	01/14	48.02	62.47	2005	01/03	87.52	11/16	75.77	76.56
1987	12/31	79.50	01/05	61.71	79.50	2006	12/12	84.06	02/27	75.74	82.54
1988	01/04	78.44	08/23	62.41	67.28	2007	11/26	91.11	02/12	80.05	88.38
1989	01/03	67.16	05/22	55.87	64.74	2008	03/17	101.23	11/21	81.75	93.64
1990	11/20	80.29	01/02	62.98	78.75	2009	11/25	100.39	03/13	84.33	96.89
1991	02/06	81.06	07/11	62.66	73.00	2010	12/31	107.14	06/04	86.10	107.14
1992	09/01	80.77	04/21	64.21	67.81	2011	08/09	139.96	02/11	102.70	106.70
1993	09/10	71.64	03/09	64.55	67.02	2012*	02/24	111.77	05/31	103.00	AT PRESS TIME
1994	10/20	80.91	01/03	66.86	76.73						

*Through May 31, 2012

SWISS FRANC NEAR-TERM CONTRACT MONTHLY CLOSING PRICES

	Jan	Feb	Mar	Apr	May	Jun	Jul	Aug	Sep	Oct	Nov	Dec
1976	38.61	39.04	39.74	40.03	40.83	40.92	40.71	40.40	41.26	41.29	40.94	41.24
1977	40.10	39.21	39.48	39.80	40.00	40.75	41.79	41.83	43.00	45.17	46.40	50.79
1978	50.87	55.17	54.66	51.81	52.89	54.81	57.90	61.02	66.45	68.22	58.01	63.47
1979	59.44	60.22	60.26	58.87	58.05	61.58	60.72	60.74	65.85	61.62	63.07	63.94
1980	61.69	58.60	55.33	60.62	60.51	61.89	60.59	60.91	61.47	58.88	57.61	56.97
1981	52.41	51.17	52.70	49.87	48.38	49.50	47.00	46.61	51.29	55.55	56.57	56.68
1982	54.66	52.66	52.83	51.79	50.24	48.60	48.05	47.24	46.68	45.55	47.40	50.70
1983	49.95	48.38	48.56	48.71	47.59	48.03	46.87	46.04	47.74	46.70	46.55	46.58
1984	44.94	46.20	47.37	44.95	44.46	43.52	40.88	41.63	40.02	40.58	39.15	38.79
1985	37.43	34.93	38.87	38.38	39.12	39.67	44.01	43.29	45.80	46.80	48.19	49.08
1986	49.64	53.16	51.75	54.93	51.74	56.45	59.98	61.19	61.12	58.63	60.99	62.47
1987	64.94	65.19	66.77	68.54	66.40	66.58	65.21	66.92	65.58	70.26	74.73	79.50
1988	73.46	71.93	74.01	71.94	69.26	67.08	64.32	63.26	63.83	66.69	69.14	67.28
1989	62.74	64.42	60.72	59.89	58.48	60.07	62.42	58.94	61.79	61.95	62.84	64.74
1990	66.55	66.69	66.76	68.86	69.85	70.45	74.23	76.24	77.04	77.75	78.29	78.75
1991	79.44	75.34	68.41	69.07	67.31	64.23	65.52	65.43	68.57	67.86	69.65	73.00
1992	69.42	67.17	66.04	65.76	68.53	72.02	75.32	79.90	80.23	72.47	69.62	67.81
1993	67.03	65.38	66.83	69.70	70.52	65.79	65.49	67.62	69.97	66.91	66.71	67.02
1994	68.61	70.12	70.91	71.38	71.23	75.06	74.60	75.08	77.83	79.71	75.39	76.73
1995	77.98	80.96	88.88	87.73	85.87	87.51	87.35	83.25	87.16	88.51	85.02	87.31
1996	82.77	83.44	84.64	80.72	80.12	80.30	83.88	83.37	80.39	79.14	76.83	75.20
1997	70.56	67.83	69.56	68.29	70.93	69.08	66.38	67.12	69.56	71.85	70.24	68.97
1998	68.09	68.43	66.18	66.94	67.54	66.28	67.39	69.41	73.08	74.36	71.74	73.31
1999	71.03	69.22	67.92	65.99	65.46	65.10	67.46	66.20	67.33	66.04	63.04	63.47
2000	60.56	60.27	60.55	58.27	59.50	61.62	60.17	57.48	58.28	55.87	57.89	62.17
2001	61.11	59.94	57.62	57.82	55.70	55.80	57.90	60.01	61.78	61.22	60.90	60.20
2002	58.11	58.91	59.43	61.98	63.73	67.56	67.31	66.70	67.91	67.68	67.39	72.49
2003	73.34	73.97	74.04	73.90	77.10	74.06	73.02	71.25	75.89	74.59	77.40	80.66
2004	79.55	79.28	79.08	77.29	79.92	80.17	78.10	78.91	80.54	83.86	87.82	87.96
2005	84.23	86.15	83.95	83.85	80.14	78.50	77.93	79.84	77.72	77.96	76.20	76.56
2006	78.54	76.32	77.35	80.97	82.21	82.41	81.73	81.40	80.60	80.81	83.60	82.54
2007	80.73	82.25	82.83	83.14	81.73	82.32	83.46	82.97	86.45	86.71	88.52	88.38
2008	92.56	95.90	100.66	96.76	95.93	98.10	95.46	90.63	89.63	86.64	82.41	93.64
2009	86.07	85.60	87.89	87.83	93.65	92.20	93.62	94.39	96.60	97.58	99.39	96.89
2010	94.35	93.08	95.13	92.90	86.82	92.90	96.20	98.41	101.95	101.51	99.68	107.14
2011	106.04	107.68	109.18	115.81	117.20	119.07	126.82	124.30	110.61	114.60	109.56	106.70
2012	108.76	110.69	110.86	110.27	103.00							

SWISS FRANC NEAR-TERM CONTRACT MONTHLY PERCENT CHANGES

	Jan	Feb	Mar	Apr	May	Jun	Jul	Aug	Sep	Oct	Nov	Dec	Year's Change
1976	0.6	1.1	1.8	0.7	2.0	0.2	−0.5	−0.8	2.1	0.1	−0.8	0.7	7.5
1977	−2.8	−2.2	0.7	0.8	0.5	1.9	2.6	0.1	2.8	5.0	2.7	9.5	23.2
1978	0.2	8.5	−0.9	−5.2	2.1	3.6	5.6	5.4	8.9	2.7	−15.0	9.4	25.0
1979	−6.3	1.3	0.1	−2.3	−1.4	6.1	−1.4	0.03	8.4	−6.4	2.4	1.4	0.7
1980	−3.5	−5.0	−5.6	9.6	−0.2	2.3	−2.1	0.5	0.9	−4.2	−2.2	−1.1	−10.9
1981	−8.0	−2.4	3.0	−5.4	−3.0	2.3	−5.1	−0.8	10.0	8.3	1.8	0.2	−0.5
1982	−3.6	−3.7	0.3	−2.0	−3.0	−3.3	−1.1	−1.7	−1.2	−2.4	4.1	7.0	−10.6
1983	−1.5	−3.1	0.4	0.3	−2.3	0.9	−2.4	−1.8	3.7	−2.2	−0.3	0.1	−8.1
1984	−3.5	2.8	2.5	−5.1	−1.1	−2.1	−6.1	1.8	−3.9	1.4	−3.5	−0.9	−16.7
1985	−3.5	−6.7	11.3	−1.3	1.9	1.4	10.9	−1.6	5.8	2.2	3.0	1.8	26.5
1986	1.1	7.1	−2.7	6.1	−5.8	9.1	6.3	2.0	−0.1	−4.1	4.0	2.4	27.3
1987	4.0	0.4	2.4	2.7	−3.1	0.3	−2.1	2.6	−2.0	7.1	6.4	6.4	27.3
1988	−7.6	−2.1	2.9	−2.8	−3.7	−3.1	−4.1	−1.6	0.9	4.5	3.7	−2.7	−15.4
1989	−6.7	2.7	−5.7	−1.4	−2.4	2.7	3.9	−5.6	4.8	0.3	1.4	3.0	−3.8
1990	2.8	0.2	0.1	3.1	1.4	0.9	5.4	2.7	1.0	0.9	0.7	0.6	21.6
1991	0.9	−5.2	−9.2	1.0	−2.5	−4.6	2.0	−0.1	4.8	−1.0	2.6	4.8	−7.3
1992	−4.9	−3.2	−1.7	−0.4	4.2	5.1	4.6	6.1	0.4	−9.7	−3.9	−2.6	−7.1
1993	−1.2	−2.5	2.2	4.3	1.2	−6.7	−0.5	3.3	3.5	−4.4	−0.3	0.5	−1.2
1994	2.4	2.2	1.1	0.7	−0.2	5.4	−0.6	0.6	3.7	2.4	−5.4	1.8	14.5
1995	1.6	3.8	9.8	−1.3	−2.1	1.9	−0.2	−4.7	4.7	1.5	−3.9	2.7	13.8
1996	−5.2	0.8	1.4	−4.6	−0.7	0.2	4.5	−0.6	−3.6	−1.6	−2.9	−2.1	−13.9
1997	−6.2	−3.9	2.6	−1.8	3.9	−2.6	−3.9	1.1	3.6	3.3	−2.2	−1.8	−8.3
1998	−1.3	0.5	−3.3	1.1	0.9	−1.9	1.7	3.0	5.3	1.8	−3.5	2.2	6.3
1999	−3.1	−2.5	−1.9	−2.8	−0.8	−0.5	3.6	−1.9	1.7	−1.9	−4.5	0.7	−13.4
2000	−4.6	−0.5	0.5	−3.8	2.1	3.6	−2.4	−4.5	1.4	−4.1	3.6	7.4	−2.0
2001	−1.7	−1.9	−3.9	0.3	−3.7	0.2	3.8	3.6	2.9	−0.9	−0.5	−1.1	−3.2
2002	−3.5	1.4	0.9	4.3	2.8	6.0	−0.4	−0.9	1.8	−0.3	−0.4	7.6	20.4
2003	1.2	0.9	0.1	−0.2	4.3	−3.9	−1.4	−2.4	6.5	−1.7	3.8	4.2	11.3
2004	−1.4	−0.3	−0.3	−2.3	3.4	0.3	−2.6	1.0	2.1	4.1	4.7	0.2	9.1
2005	−4.2	2.3	−2.6	−0.1	−4.4	−2.0	−0.7	2.5	−2.7	0.3	−2.3	0.5	−13.0
2006	2.6	−2.8	1.3	4.7	1.5	0.2	−0.8	−0.4	−1.0	0.3	3.5	−1.3	7.8
2007	−2.2	1.9	0.7	0.4	−1.7	0.7	1.4	−0.6	4.2	0.3	2.1	−0.2	7.1
2008	4.7	3.6	5.0	−3.9	−0.9	2.3	−2.7	−5.1	−1.1	−3.3	−4.9	13.6	6.0
2009	−8.1	−0.5	2.7	−0.1	6.6	−1.5	1.5	0.8	2.3	1.0	1.9	−2.5	3.5
2010	−2.6	−1.3	2.2	−2.3	−6.5	7.0	3.6	2.3	3.6	−0.4	−1.8	7.5	10.6
2011	−1.0	1.5	1.4	6.1	1.2	1.6	6.5	−2.0	−11.0	3.6	−4.4	−2.6	−0.4
2012	1.9	1.8	0.2	−0.5	−6.6								
TOTALS	−74.2	−5.0	19.8	−3.4	−16.1	34.0	26.8	2.3	75.2	2.5	−10.3	77.3	
AVG.	−2.0	−0.1	0.5	−0.1	−0.4	0.9	0.7	0.1	2.1	0.1	−0.3	2.1	
# Up	12	19	26	16	16	25	16	18	27	20	17	25	
# Down	25	18	11	21	21	11	20	18	9	16	19	11	

JAPANESE YEN CYCLE, SEASONAL PATTERN, AND TRADING GUIDE

The Japanese economy has been considered the second most technologically advanced economy in the world, but the gap is closing with China and the combined eurozone nations. This market and economy are driven by finished goods production, as Japan is a net importer of raw materials. The Japanese economy is heavily dependent on crude oil imports.

Their economy runs on a fiscal year from April through March, but since the yen contract is valued against the U.S. dollar, we have a tendency to see bottoms in late August, as multi-conglomerate international companies make their fiscal year-end adjustments. We see peaks in October against the U.S. dollar, as money flows back into the United States for year-end tax adjustment purposes, also referred to as repatriation of funds.

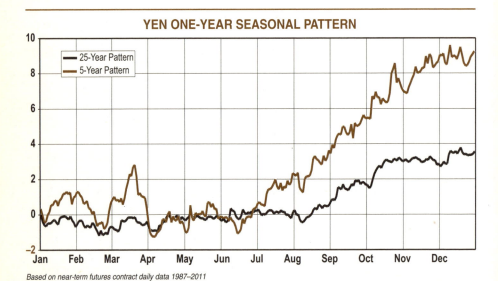

YEN ONE-YEAR SEASONAL PATTERN

Based on near-term futures contract daily data 1987–2011

YEN NEAR-TERM CONTRACT ANNUAL HIGHS, LOWS, AND CLOSES SINCE 1978

YEAR	HIGH DATE	HIGH CLOSE	LOW DATE	LOW CLOSE	YEAR CLOSE	YEAR	HIGH DATE	HIGH CLOSE	LOW DATE	LOW CLOSE	YEAR CLOSE
1978	10/30	57.23	02/03	41.45	52.70	1996	01/02	97.21	12/30	87.00	87.13
1979	01/02	52.72	11/26	39.99	41.97	1997	06/11	91.29	12/05	76.89	77.36
1980	12/30	50.33	04/07	38.48	50.25	1998	12/31	88.84	08/11	68.19	88.84
1981	01/05	51.13	08/04	41.21	46.24	1999	12/22	99.56	05/20	80.65	98.92
1982	01/04	46.43	11/03	36.10	43.15	2000	01/03	99.64	12/29	88.27	88.27
1983	01/10	44.26	09/01	40.51	43.71	2001	01/03	88.99	12/27	76.22	76.29
1984	03/08	45.48	12/31	39.87	39.87	2002	07/19	86.66	02/26	74.34	84.47
1985	12/31	50.04	02/22	38.07	50.04	2003	12/29	93.72	03/21	82.51	93.18
1986	09/19	65.97	01/03	49.30	63.54	2004	12/31	97.97	05/13	87.40	97.97
1987	12/31	83.16	01/05	62.99	83.16	2005	01/14	98.38	12/07	82.76	85.51
1988	12/08	82.87	09/01	73.41	80.69	2006	05/16	91.54	10/10	84.30	84.84
1989	01/03	81.49	06/14	67.65	69.68	2007	11/26	92.94	06/22	81.62	90.13
1990	10/18	80.30	04/17	62.73	73.84	2008	12/17	113.79	08/15	90.62	110.29
1991	12/31	79.91	06/10	70.30	79.91	2009	11/30	115.91	04/06	99.17	107.40
1992	09/29	83.68	04/23	74.13	80.04	2010	10/29	124.29	04/02	105.66	123.28
1993	08/17	98.93	01/15	79.25	89.59	2011	10/28	132.10	04/06	117.13	130.10
1994	10/25	103.87	01/05	88.78	101.08	2012*	01/31	131.34	03/14	119.57	AT PRESS TIME
1995	04/18	124.91	11/02	96.75	97.73						

*Through May 31, 2012

JAPANESE YEN NEAR-TERM CONTRACT MONTHLY CLOSING PRICES

	Jan	Feb	Mar	Apr	May	Jun	Jul	Aug	Sep	Oct	Nov	Dec
1978	41.60	42.17	46.16	44.67	45.60	49.88	53.16	52.25	53.61	56.29	50.50	52.70
1979	49.95	49.69	48.13	45.40	45.39	46.27	46.34	45.70	44.99	42.77	40.17	41.97
1980	42.17	39.80	40.37	41.83	44.74	45.18	43.76	45.75	47.68	47.66	46.21	50.25
1981	48.98	47.83	47.94	46.76	44.95	44.83	42.16	43.24	43.75	43.44	46.86	46.24
1982	44.31	42.21	41.06	42.76	41.14	39.73	38.98	38.51	37.53	36.25	40.18	43.15
1983	41.77	41.78	42.06	42.17	41.77	42.06	41.23	40.73	42.71	42.75	43.12	43.71
1984	42.80	42.92	44.98	44.40	43.28	42.65	40.92	41.43	40.96	41.00	40.43	39.87
1985	39.28	38.53	40.14	39.72	39.94	40.39	42.46	41.84	46.40	47.38	49.42	50.04
1986	52.17	55.51	56.56	59.24	57.37	61.60	65.22	64.99	64.91	61.34	61.82	63.54
1987	65.16	65.31	68.93	71.56	69.62	68.63	66.93	70.33	68.74	72.54	75.82	83.16
1988	78.38	78.02	80.87	80.22	79.98	75.65	75.45	73.45	75.38	79.92	82.49	80.69
1989	77.14	78.97	76.32	75.75	70.06	70.07	73.48	68.98	72.43	70.24	70.12	69.68
1990	69.39	67.20	63.42	63.07	65.73	65.86	68.59	69.58	72.18	76.92	75.38	73.84
1991	76.14	75.10	70.55	73.22	72.27	72.47	72.66	73.05	75.10	76.38	76.95	79.91
1992	79.32	77.14	75.30	74.98	78.32	79.46	78.60	81.22	83.22	81.00	80.21	80.04
1993	80.11	84.56	87.04	90.10	93.17	93.49	95.51	95.47	94.30	92.27	91.66	89.59
1994	92.16	95.65	98.21	98.70	95.49	102.11	100.15	99.99	101.48	103.58	101.23	101.08
1995	100.75	103.55	116.57	119.54	118.74	119.21	114.00	102.94	101.26	98.60	98.15	97.73
1996	94.02	95.25	94.26	95.83	92.66	92.21	94.37	92.00	90.76	88.22	88.02	87.13
1997	82.81	83.43	81.78	79.25	86.22	88.26	84.81	82.81	83.92	83.59	78.42	77.36
1998	79.15	79.48	75.87	75.67	72.22	72.66	69.54	71.07	73.90	86.71	81.34	88.84
1999	86.37	84.16	84.86	84.20	82.50	83.48	87.87	91.47	95.00	96.59	98.33	98.92
2000	93.68	91.00	99.08	93.18	93.15	95.77	92.24	93.96	93.73	92.47	90.85	88.27
2001	86.47	85.36	80.08	81.32	84.07	80.79	80.32	84.32	84.15	81.98	81.03	76.29
2002	74.36	74.89	75.67	78.02	80.54	84.03	83.68	84.33	82.43	81.68	81.59	84.47
2003	83.52	84.74	84.82	84.24	83.87	83.69	83.04	85.80	89.96	90.99	91.34	93.18
2004	94.68	91.62	96.04	90.73	90.61	92.20	89.92	91.56	91.27	94.66	97.21	97.97
2005	96.75	95.77	93.83	95.69	92.27	90.92	89.40	90.54	88.77	86.42	83.65	85.51
2006	85.63	86.55	85.85	88.52	88.98	88.32	87.84	85.39	85.59	86.08	86.56	84.84
2007	83.36	84.73	85.75	84.17	82.34	82.01	84.69	86.45	87.97	87.16	90.12	90.13
2008	94.25	96.29	100.71	96.50	94.91	94.71	92.92	92.02	94.98	101.40	104.65	110.29
2009	111.38	102.19	101.04	101.37	105.11	103.89	105.50	107.56	111.62	111.13	115.91	107.40
2010	110.25	112.53	107.03	106.51	109.69	113.15	115.85	118.96	120.01	124.29	119.59	123.28
2011	121.96	122.34	120.40	123.30	122.73	124.33	129.82	130.60	129.87	128.21	128.99	130.10
2012	131.34	123.21	120.78	125.36	127.67							

JAPANESE YEN NEAR-TERM CONTRACT MONTHLY PERCENT CHANGES

	Jan	Feb	Mar	Apr	May	Jun	Jul	Aug	Sep	Oct	Nov	Dec	Year's Change
1978	−1.3	1.4	9.5	−3.2	2.1	9.4	6.6	−1.7	2.6	5.0	−10.3	4.4	25.0
1979	−5.2	−0.5	−3.1	−5.7	−0.02	1.9	0.2	−1.4	−1.6	−4.9	−6.1	4.5	−20.4
1980	0.5	−5.6	1.4	3.6	7.0	1.0	−3.1	4.5	4.2	−0.04	−3.0	8.7	19.7
1981	−2.5	−2.3	0.2	−2.5	−3.9	−0.3	−6.0	2.6	1.2	−0.7	7.9	−1.3	−8.0
1982	−4.2	−4.7	−2.7	4.1	−3.8	−3.4	−1.9	−1.2	−2.5	−3.4	10.8	7.4	−6.7
1983	−3.2	0.02	0.7	0.3	−0.9	0.7	−2.0	−1.2	4.9	0.1	0.9	1.4	1.3
1984	−2.1	0.3	4.8	−1.3	−2.5	−1.5	−4.1	1.2	−1.1	0.1	−1.4	−1.4	−8.8
1985	−1.5	−1.9	4.2	−1.0	0.6	1.1	5.1	−1.5	10.9	2.1	4.3	1.3	25.5
1986	4.3	6.4	1.9	4.7	−3.2	7.4	5.9	−0.4	−0.1	−5.5	0.8	2.8	27.0
1987	2.5	0.2	5.5	3.8	−2.7	−1.4	−2.5	5.1	−2.3	5.5	4.5	9.7	30.9
1988	−5.7	−0.5	3.7	−0.8	−0.3	−5.4	−0.3	−2.7	2.6	6.0	3.2	−2.2	−3.0
1989	−4.4	2.4	−3.4	−0.7	−7.5	0.01	4.9	−6.1	5.0	−3.0	−0.2	−0.6	−13.6
1990	−0.4	−3.2	−5.6	−0.6	4.2	0.2	4.1	1.4	3.7	6.6	−2.0	−2.0	6.0
1991	3.1	−1.4	−6.1	3.8	−1.3	0.3	0.3	0.5	2.8	1.7	0.7	3.8	8.2
1992	−0.7	−2.7	−2.4	−0.4	4.5	1.5	−1.1	3.3	2.5	−2.7	−1.0	−0.2	0.2
1993	0.1	5.6	2.9	3.5	3.4	0.3	2.2	−0.04	−1.2	−2.2	−0.7	−2.3	11.9
1994	2.9	3.8	2.7	0.5	−3.3	6.9	−1.9	−0.2	1.5	2.1	−2.3	−0.1	12.8
1995	−0.3	2.8	12.6	2.5	−0.7	0.4	−4.4	−9.7	−1.6	−2.6	−0.5	−0.4	−3.3
1996	−3.8	1.3	−1.0	1.7	−3.3	−0.5	2.3	−2.5	−1.3	−2.8	−0.2	−1.0	−10.8
1997	−5.0	0.7	−2.0	−3.1	8.8	2.4	−3.9	−2.4	1.3	−0.4	−6.2	−1.4	−11.2
1998	2.3	0.4	−4.5	−0.3	−4.6	0.6	−4.3	2.2	4.0	17.3	−6.2	9.2	14.8
1999	−2.8	−2.6	0.8	−0.8	−2.0	1.2	5.3	4.1	3.9	1.7	1.8	0.6	11.3
2000	−5.3	−2.9	8.9	−6.0	−0.03	2.8	−3.7	1.9	−0.2	−1.3	−1.8	−2.8	−10.8
2001	−2.0	−1.3	−6.2	1.5	3.4	−3.9	−0.6	5.0	−0.2	−2.6	−1.2	−5.8	−13.6
2002	−2.5	0.7	1.0	3.1	3.2	4.3	−0.4	0.8	−2.3	−0.9	−0.1	3.5	10.7
2003	−1.1	1.5	0.1	−0.7	−0.4	−0.2	−0.8	3.3	4.8	1.1	0.4	2.0	10.3
2004	1.6	−3.2	4.8	−5.5	−0.1	1.8	−2.5	1.8	−0.3	3.7	2.7	0.8	5.1
2005	−1.2	−1.0	−2.0	2.0	−3.6	−1.5	−1.7	1.3	−2.0	−2.6	−3.2	2.2	−12.7
2006	0.1	1.1	−0.8	3.1	0.5	−0.7	−0.5	−2.8	0.2	0.6	0.6	−2.0	−0.8
2007	−1.7	1.6	1.2	−1.8	−2.2	−0.4	3.3	2.1	1.8	−0.9	3.4	0.01	6.2
2008	4.6	2.2	4.6	−4.2	−1.6	−0.2	−1.9	−1.0	3.2	6.8	3.2	5.4	22.4
2009	1.0	−8.3	−1.1	0.3	3.7	−1.2	1.5	2.0	3.8	−0.4	4.3	−7.3	−2.6
2010	2.7	2.1	−4.9	−0.5	3.0	3.2	2.4	2.7	0.9	3.6	−3.8	3.1	14.8
2011	−1.1	0.3	−1.6	2.4	−0.5	1.3	4.4	0.6	−0.6	−1.3	0.6	0.9	5.5
2012	1.0	−6.2	−2.0	3.8	1.8								
TOTALS	−31.3	−13.5	22.1	5.6	−2.3	28.1	0.9	11.6	48.5	25.8	−0.1	40.9	
AVG.	−0.9	−0.4	0.6	0.2	−0.1	0.8	0.03	0.3	1.4	0.8	−0.003	1.2	
# Up	13	19	19	17	13	21	14	19	20	16	16	19	
# Down	22	16	16	18	22	13	20	15	14	18	18	15	